The
Writings
of
T. Austin-Sparks

Volume V

A limited edition

Spiritual Foundations

Spiritual Foundations
All *new* material in this edition
Copyrighted by SeedSowers Publishing House
Printed in the United States of America
All rights reserved

Published by   The SeedSowers
              P.O. Box 3317
              Jacksonville, FL 32206

Library of Congress Cataloging-in-Publication Data

Sparks, T. Austin
        Spiritual Foundations / T. Austin-Sparks
        ISBN 0-940232-80-4
        1. Spiritual Life 1. Title

Times New Roman 12 pt

Spiritual Foundations

by
T. Austin-Sparks

This volume contains
six of T. Austin-Sparks' books,
all on the subject of
Spiritual Foundations.

Preface

T. Austin-Sparks is one of the great figures of the twentieth century who ministered outside of the organized church. For over forty years he held forth at Honor Oak in London, England. The conferences he spoke at, both in Europe and America, have had a profound influence on our time.

Brother Sparks published over one hundred books and pamphlets. The majority of them have ceased to be available to the Christian family. This has been a great loss, as the content of his message has placed him in the category of only a few men of the last one hundred years.

T. Austin-Sparks and Watchman Nee, more than any other men, have influenced the lives of believers who are outside traditional churches. We have felt very strongly that all of brother Sparks' books and pamphlets should be brought back into print if at all possible.

Read T. Austin-Sparks. It is our hope that in republishing his works, his ministry will take wings again, and the influence of his word will spread across the English-speaking world. Hopefully this will give his message a greater influence than ever before.

We send these volumes forth with a prayer that what he ministered will become realties in the 21st century.

The SeedSowers

GOD'S REACTIONS
TO
MAN'S DEFECTIONS

GOD'S REACTIONS
TO MAN'S DEFECTIONS

T. AUSTIN-SPARKS

CONTENTS

PART ONE
THE NEW THING WHICH IS OLD

PART TWO

GOD'S METHODS AND MEANS OF RECOVERY

FOREWORD

THE substance of Part I consists of a slightly revised version of a book which has for some time been out of print. There has been an increasing urge to renew this message, and not a small factor in this urge has been the very definite movement, observable all over the world, toward a reconsideration of the whole testimony of the Church. There is a deep and growing dissatisfaction and disappointment with the spiritual state and impact of the Church. The rumblings of this are heard everywhere, and many conferences are being held and books written in relation to this matter. There is a strong feeling in many quarters that God must act again and do " a new thing ". The tremendous emphasis upon ' Revival ' is only one aspect of this.

But it is a big and open question whether God *can* send the kind of revival that is sought, without involving the whole possibility of supporting a false position. So long as suspicion, rivalry, contention, adverse propaganda, and all such things continue between Christians, and *things* are put in the place of the Lord Himself, how can He bless? There have always been steps that the people of God were called upon to take before God would bless them, and there never was a time when the Church needed more to look to its own house than it does at present. It might be that the Lord would do His new thing quite apart from the established Christian system. This book shows that this is what He has done on many occasions.

Part II is the substance of a more recent conference ministry and concerns the inner spiritual life which is the nature and object of all God's reactions.

The book is intended to be, neither critical nor censorious, but, if at all possible, a contribution to the " building up of the body of Christ, till we all attain unto . . . the measure of . . . the fulness of Christ ".

I am only too conscious of the many imperfections in the manner of presentation, but I trust that the Lord may be able to use these messages to provoke to a greater utterness for Himself on the part of some, at least, who read.

T. AUSTIN-SPARKS.

13 Honor Oak Road,
   London, SE 23.
      JUNE, 1956.

PART ONE

THE NEW THING
WHICH IS OLD

CHAPTER ONE

THE NEW THING WHICH IS OLD

NOTE.—The term 'reaction', as employed in these chapters, means that acting-again on the part of God when that which ostensibly represents Him no longer truly represents Him, either vitally or adequately. He reacts *against* what is merely ostensible and *for* what is living and wholly according to His mind.

THERE ARE TWO THINGS which we need to keep very clearly before us. These two things, as we put them, may seem to contradict one another or be paradoxical.

I. All the way through the ages, God has constantly done a new thing.

II. That which, from man's standpoint, has always been God's new thing, from His own standpoint has not been new at all.

"Known unto God are all his works from the beginning of the world" (Acts xv. 18, A.V.*)*

"The works were finished from the foundation of the world" (Hebrews iv. 3).

In all His fresh activities and revelations, God is working backward to an original position and design. God never leaves His original premise.

This is a far more important truth and law than may at first be recognised. It carries with it these three things : —

1. God has before Him all the time the finished and completed thing, and He knows exactly, to a detail, what He wants.

11

2.   He must and will have that. He cannot be denied it, and He will never give it up or take less.

3.   Whenever there is a deviation from or a falling short of it there will be a Divine reaction, and God will begin again, somewhere, somehow. A hurried survey of these reactions through history will both establish the fact and bring out the nature and features of that upon which He has set His heart and which He is determined to have. The earlier instances and forms are very simple, but the greater truths and principles are there, either patent or latent.

When the first deviation—that of Adam and Eve—has taken place, the reaction of God is through Abel and his altar. That altar stands for the securing for God of His rights in creation—in man and the earth. While Cain offers the fruit of the earth and of his own effort, he ignores the curse resting upon all such, and he with his offering is rejected. God's seal is upon Abel's way. The elements are these : —

1.   God has a right to all.

2.   God can and will only have that without the trace of the curse in it.

3.   In order to remove the curse, the cursed thing must be destroyed in death, in either an actual or a representative living form ; and a new life must emerge over which death has no power.

4.   Fellowship with God is thus, and only thus, possible.

From Abel to Noah the deviation becomes more intense and deliberate. The earth—which is the Lord's—is taken possession of by man for his own ends. God reacts to this in the deluge. Emerging from the judgment, Noah builds an altar and offers sacrifice, and in so doing declares, in intent and effect: " The earth " (the renewed earth) " is the Lord's, and the fulness thereof " (Ps. xxiv. 1). Again God gets His rights—*prophetically*—through death and resurrection. But all too soon deviation sets in again. Even Noah is a part of it and fails.

Babel is built and cursed, and under that curse men are scattered to the four corners of the earth. Enoch breaks a long line of death and darkness, as God's reaction. Then, when it would appear that the testimony has disappeared from the earth, there is another Divine reaction and Abraham is apprehended. With Abraham, while the old elements reappear, new ones appear. The features of his life are : —

1. Revelation.—Vision.
2. A walk of faith.—Relationship.
3. A country.—The Instrument.
4. An altar.—The Basis.
5. Conflict.—The Challenge.
6. A covenant.—The Assurance.
7. A city.—The ultimate Object.
8. Death and Resurrection.—The Method.

These factors are elemental and eternal, and behind all historical, typical, symbolic, or earthly presentations, spiritual realities persist unto a universal realisation. Isaac comes in, not as a separate breaking in of God, but to give special prominence to the method by which everything has its fulfilment. In his very being he is death and resurrection, and, as such, the way by which human limitation is changed for universal expansion and realisation (Genesis xxii. 16, 17). There are other elements in his life which foreshadow the intentions of God—such as his marriage with Rebekah.

The next reaction of God comes with the growing up

of Jacob and Esau. These were twin brothers, and represent two halves of a whole ; two developments from a spiritual origin ; two histories from a holy beginning. Esau takes the earth course, the course of the world and the flesh. Heavenly callings and inheritances are obscured by temporal interests, pursuits, and fancies. The gratifying of the soul life in its earthward relationship is the limit of his horizon. Jacob becomes the type of that which receives the heavenly calling and vision, and passes through the experience of the withering of the flesh to be a spiritual instrument in relation to a heavenly purpose. With Jacob there is a still further introduction of Divine elements. Up to this point the altar has fixed the bounds of advance. That factor remains basic, but Jacob goes a further step. At Luz he has an open Heaven ; a revelation of God ; a connecting link between Heaven and earth ; a voice from God heard ; and certain truths from God deposited with him. On the strength of all this he erects a pillar, anoints it with oil, and calls that place " Bethel ", " the house of God ".

Thus, the House of God, an abiding heavenly object, comes into view, and is defined by all those elements which we have mentioned. A " pillar " in Scripture always stands for a witness or a testimony (Genesis xxxi. 51 ; Isaiah xix. 19, 20 ; I Timothy iii. 15 ; and many others). All this has to be seen more fully ; we are only seeking in this chapter to indicate the truth and establish our fact, or rather to point out an established fact.

We make a long leap and come to Israel in Egypt. Here in this mighty reaction or intervention of God all the elements so far mentioned are gathered up. God is working back to His original purpose. The elements are clearly seen : —

The Altar ; the heavenly people for a House of God ; a revelation ; a testimony ; a conflict ; a country and city in view, and so on. This God secures, even if it means hurling a mighty empire to judgment.

Thus commences the long and chequered history of that which was intended to be in itself a revelation of the mind of God. But again and again they departed and deviated and the Lord had to take up things from the inside. Thus we have those movements back to God's original thought under Hezekiah (II Chron. xxix. 1—9), under Josiah (II Chron. xxxv. 17 – 19), and others. But in none of these was the heart of the entire people restored. It was a partial thing. No sooner had the leader gone than the apostasy and declension set in and deepened. It was not the common inclination of the whole people to return, but the strong lead of a few which influenced them for a time— and then they declined or reverted to their worldliness and idolatry. These were beautiful breaks of sunshine in days of deepening spiritual darkness and departure. At length, even these ceased ; there was hardly a residue of faithfulness found amongst the people, and they were all sent into captivity. Babylon is the synonym for confusion, lost distinctiveness, lost testimony, spiritual paralysis, and a false life. Yet, even here God does not abandon His intention, and in Babylon He reacts to things in and by a small group of men : Daniel, Shadrach, Meshach, Abed-nego. They are faithful to all the elements of the Divine purpose and have their prayer-gaze fixed upon Jerusalem.

At length the Lord breaks in and reacts again. It is by but a remnant, but this weak and chastened remnant is His instrument for reviving and perpetuating His testimony in the earth. There follow the heart-warming events as recorded in Ezra, Nehemiah,

Haggai and Zechariah. It is a great epoch, but, alas—

> ' The radiant morn hath passed away,
> And spent *too soon* her golden store.'

More apostasy, declension, until we get the terrible conditions recorded in Malachi, leading up to the awful announcement: " Ye are cursed with a curse." How black and dark things are! Were they ever worse? And yet—and yet—God is not defeated; for, in the midst of and over against the blackness, there is that which—because of the darkness—represents the most blessed triumph.

" Then THEY that feared the Lord spake often one with another: and the Lord hearkened (bent down), and heard, and a book of remembrance was written before him, for them that feared the Lord, and that thought upon his name. And they shall be mine, saith the Lord of hosts, in the day wherein I do make A PECULIAR TREASURE " (Mal. iii. 16, 17).

Malachi closes, and for three or four hundred years there is chaos. Surely now the testimony has ceased and faithfulness has disappeared? Surely now the Lord has lost everything?

Take up the New Testament record, as Luke essays to give a certain history to his friend Theophilus. He does not travel far before he lights upon certain people of whom he says very significant things from our present point of view. He speaks of one Zacharias and his wife Elisabeth, " both righteous before God, walking in all the commandments and ordinances of the Lord blameless" (Luke i. 5, 6).

Then he speaks of Mary, to whom the angel Gabriel said: " Thou that are endued with grace, the Lord is with thee " (i. 28).

A little later he refers to another thus: " And behold,

there was a man in Jerusalem, whose name was Simeon ; and this man was righteous and devout, *looking for the consolation of Israel*: and the Holy Spirit was upon him. And it had been revealed unto him by the Holy Spirit . . ." (ii. 25, 26).

And yet a little further on this: " And there was one Anna, a prophetess . . . she . . . spake of him to ALL THEM THAT WERE LOOKING for the redemption of Jerusalem " (ii. 36, 38).

Thus we see that there is still left a remnant of the faithful after hundreds of years of seeming death. God maintains a representative company.

Then comes the revival of Pentecost—surely a new beginning of God. They are wonderful days ; but again, all too soon, we come upon signs of declension. In not a few places in the New Testament Scriptures do we find expressions indicating that the general condition is marked by sad contradiction of and inconsistency with the testimony. Jude, for instance, has a sorry business in his letter ; but even there we find the thing which is true, indicated by the discriminating words: "*But ye,* beloved, building up yourselves on your most holy faith . . ." (Jude 20). This is the offset to the declension to which he refers.

At length we come to the Revelation, where parts of the Church are well-nigh completely decadent. Grievous things have to be laid to its charge. What will the Lord do? He may have to set the main thing aside, but He will not abandon His purpose. There are those in every place who are true, hungry, dissatisfied with things as they are, wanting to go on with the Lord. These are the Lord's reactionary instrument. These are the ' overcomers ' who hear what the Spirit is saying. These are God's new beginning by which He comes back to His first purpose.

B

We have thus hurriedly ranged the whole Scriptures to reveal the method of God. We should like to pursue it through the ages since New Testament times, but that must wait. We close this introductory consideration by saying that what God has always done He will do again, and when that which is ostensibly His representative instrument on the earth ceases to be actually and vitally such, although He may have raised it up Himself and used and blessed it, He may have to look within the general condition for those who will pay the price and give to Him that fuller measure for which He ever seeks.

CHAPTER TWO

THE NEW CRUSE

Reading : II Kings ii. 19 — 22 ; Acts i, ii ; Mark ix. 50.

WHEN THE ABOVE PASSAGES are read together it will be seen that they are bound by a common tie ; namely, salt, and what it signifies. Throughout the Scriptures salt stands for recovery, preservation, and permanence.

In the first passage mentioned, we have the waters of Jericho lacking in some constituent, which resulted in the miscarriage of the trees ; the fruit falling ere it ripened. Nothing reached its intended end ; nothing fulfilled its promise. All fell short of its design. Thus the labour proved in vain, and all the toil ended in heart-breaking disappointment. There was the field, there were the trees, there was water, there were labourers, there was much energy, there were good motives. Withal nothing got fully and finally through ; it all stopped short somewhere. There was no maturity, satisfaction, and full justification of all the expenditure and effort. Some essential property was absent, and this absence made all else futile as to the ultimate issue. How different from the " tree planted by the streams of water, that bringeth forth its fruit in its season ", mentioned in Psalm i. 3 !

Now, while it is the " salt " that is the vital and most important thing, it is rather of the cruse that we shall speak for the moment. Acts ii undoubtedly brings the salt into view, but Acts i precedes that. Our attention is first drawn to Elisha's request for a new cruse. (In this passage, the " cruse " probably meant a small pan or dish ; the word is related to the " pans " of II Chron. xxxv. 13. In other O. T. passages, a flask is probably intended.) Why use a vessel at all? Why not take a handful? And then, why a NEW cruse? Why will not any cruse do? Well, that is just the point. For work like this a vessel must be specially prepared and set apart. What is the nature of the work to be done? What is the condition needing to be dealt with? At rock bottom it is the loss and absence of a distinctive *something*. It is deficiency in respect of a certain distinctiveness. Everything is there but *that*.

The modern spiritual counterpart of this is that things have degenerated into indefiniteness, vagueness, uncertainty, ambiguity, as to real meaning, life, and purpose spiritually. The original meaning of things is no longer there. Things said and done do not mean what they did at first. Terms have come to be applied to, and be used of, that which is not permissible in the realm of their original Divine employment. There is a difference of meaning, and the tragedy is that so many have gone on with the form and fail to see that the power is not there.

If we take the book of Acts as the model, and the epistles as revealing the truth intended by the Lord to be the abiding basis of that which sprang into being in Acts, we cannot fail to be impressed with the presence of a certain something which made everything at that time very much alive and superlative. Whether in respect of what was individual and personal, in salvation, service, and suffering, or of what was corporate, in fellowship and practice, there is only one phrase that expresses the effect of that great something: it is *Resurrection Life.* There is hardly a chapter in this book but—when you have read it —provokes the spontaneous ejaculation: ' That is life!'

Now, without further delay, what was it that produced this atmosphere and spirit of life? What was it that made everything so wonderful to those concerned? There is only one answer. It was—

THE LORD JESUS HIMSELF.

The Lord Jesus had been glorified, and the Holy Spirit had come as the Spirit of the glorified Lord to glorify Him on the earth (John xvi).

Was it the matter of salvation? Well, it was not salvation as such. It was not just *being saved,* either from something or unto something, but it was the *Saviour.* The message of salvation was all focused in who the Lord Jesus was. Look at the preaching. " They ceased not . . . to preach Jesus as the Christ " (Acts v. 42). Find a discourse anywhere in the Acts which ' got through ', and you will see that it is—not a treatise on Evangelical Theology—but a presentation of the glorified Lord Jesus. If it was Christ crucified, it was Christ not dead but risen and glorified. Look at the address at Pentecost (Acts ii. 32, 33, 36). See the words to the lame man and the subsequent address in the Temple (ch. iii). Listen to the words addressed to the Council in chapter iv. Whether it be to individuals or to companies, it is always the Lord Jesus who is in full view.

It is the same in the matter of service. In the Acts service is never something appended to salvation as a further consideration. One of the striking omissions in this record is that of exhortations and urgings to propagate the Gospel. Service here is never the result of organization or special pleading and appeals. It is free, spontaneous, eager, ' natural '. It is not of constraint from without. It is not by an appeal to a sense of duty or obligation. It was not something which was special in its connection and time. It was at all times, in every place, under all circumstances: irrepressible testimony, proclamation, in direct, public manner and in ordinary conversation. " There arose . . . a great persecution . . . and they were all scattered abroad . . . They therefore that were scattered abroad went about preaching . . . " (Acts viii. 1); " travelled . . . speaking the word . . . preaching the Lord Jesus " (xi. 19, 20).

What was it that created and produced this? It was the Holy Spirit's glorifying of the Lord Jesus in their hearts! He—the glorified One—was so real to them, and the wonder of who He—" Jesus of Nazareth ", the Crucified One—really was, as now revealed and manifested to them and in them, was so great, that even these " new bottles " were finding that unless they let it out this new wine would burst them.

And what was true in the matters of salvation and service, was also the secret of their ability to suffer. There is no doubt that it cost dearly in those days to take sides with ' The Nazarene '—this as amongst men ; but to take sides with " The Son of God " was something which provoked Hell. Put together, there is not a little in the record which indicates this suffering ; but it was accepted in a spirit of " rejoicing " (Acts v. 41). It all seemed in the spirit of Hebrews x. 34: " Took joyfully the spoiling of your possessions ", or : " Received the word in much affliction, with joy " (I Thess. i. 6). This cannot be attributed to optimism, sanguineness, or merely human good temper. It was not a ' make-the-best-of-it ' resolve. *It was the reality of the Lord Jesus as Sovereign and reigning.*

As it was in these matters which came so directly home
to the individual, and which were always individual tests,
so it was in the matters which were more of a corporate
nature. A 'BAPTISMAL SERVICE' in the Acts was a wonderful time, always accompanied by great rejoicing and a
living witness of the Holy Spirit. There was nothing formal
about it. It was not just a bit of ' Church ' order or teaching.
It was not just a command obeyed, or something just for
personal blessing. It certainly was not a matter of compulsion, persuasion, or argument. It took place as in full view
of the Lord Jesus, as the One who died in the stead of all ;
whose death was the death of all ; and in whose resurrection " they which live should no longer live unto themselves, but *unto him* who for their sakes died and rose
again " (II Cor. v. 15).

It was *Unto Him*. It was a testimony to a living reality,
and a mighty spiritual fact, namely, that the one supreme
object of life and all living was the Lord Jesus. All other
objects, interests, concerns and visions had gone in their
union with Him in His death, and all and only that which
was of Him had come for them in union with His resurrection. This matter was lifted out of the realm of ordinances
(such as the Jewish) and into the realm of testimonies.
Jewish ordinances were looking on to something to come,
and they never made anything complete (Heb. vii. 19 ; ix.
9 ; x. 1). These *testimonies* looked back to something consummated, into which there was experimental entry.

Just the same atmosphere of glory surrounded the
' LORD'S TABLE '—the " breaking of bread " (Acts ii. 42,
46). There was nothing of ' Church ' duty or rule or regula-
tion in this. This was not something apart and separate
from the other life of the Church. This was not a ' service ',
as something by itself. At the beginning it suffered nothing

by frequency—though, alas, it all too soon dropped from this plane. It was the centre and spring of all else. Worship, praise, prayer, the ministry of the Word spontaneously sprang out of this. It was living, and fraught with " great joy " (Acts viii. 8 ; xv. 3). It was to those who thus gathered and worshipped that " the Lord added . . . day by day those that were being saved " (Acts ii. 47).

What, again, was the secret? It was the appreciation of the Lord Jesus. That table gathered all other testimonies into itself and became an all-inclusive testimony. There was the Offering wholly given to God without a reservation, and the will of God utterly done. There was union with that offered One in His death, burial, and resurrection. There was the one life shared by all, as represented in the Blood. There was the one loaf, which is the one Body, the corporate oneness of all believers. There was the " one hope " (Eph. iv. 4), " that blessed hope " (Tit. ii. 13), His coming again—' till He come '. So, then, ought not there to be a wonderful attestation of the Holy Spirit in the hearts of all? Yes, it was a time of great glorying in the Lord—the Lord was there !

THE LORD'S PRESENT NEED

Each of the matters mentioned really needs a book to itself, but we merely touch them to lead on to our further point and object. Referring back to what we said in connection with the waters of Jericho, is it not true that in all these matters at the present day, in a very widespread way, the constituent of wonder and glory and life—that spontaneity and overflow in all matters which relate to the Lord Jesus—is lacking? What is needed? Our conviction is that, whatever may or may not be recognised as needed by that which ostensibly stands to represent God in the world to-day, His own need in the earth is that which will lift all the phases and aspects of the Church's life and work into the realm where this glorying in and glorifying of the Lord Jesus is the dominant characteristic ; where formalism yields to life ; where all is aglow with His wonderfulness ; where His train *fills* the temple ; where ' ordinances ' are living testimonies ; and where all is vital, dynamic and effectual.

No one will disagree with this, but they may with the next. What is necessary to the Lord to bring this about? It is a new cruse, a new vessel. There is so much mixture in the constitution of the vessels to-day. The world has got in, on the one hand, and the natural man has so much taken hold, on the other. Tradition, formalism, ecclesiasticism and ' mechanicalism ' are like chains and fetters upon the Lord. Moreover, as we have already said, things are given different meanings to-day from what they had at first under the sanction of the Holy Spirit.

A new cruse is needed, and it must be that which has been made like unto the Lord's vessel at the first. It must be :

(1)   That which stands upon an absolutely New Testament basis.

(2)   That which marks the point where God has a clear way because the Cross has brought to zero all the personal interests and resources and confidence of such as form that vessel.

(3)   That which recognises, yields fully to, and glories in, the absolute government of the Holy Spirit in every detail of life and service.

(4)   That which recognises the utter Lordship of the Lord Jesus.

(5)   That which sees in Him all the fulness of wisdom, power, knowledge, grace and everything needed, and draws only upon Him.

(6)   That which is completely selfless and has only one object in view, and that passionately the glory of the Lord Jesus.

We leave till later the matter of securing the vessel, but here emphasize the necessity for it. When the Lord gets it —and He is getting it—He will make it the instrument for the restoration and preservation of His testimony in the earth. This newness may be costly, but then, special usefulness to the Lord is always costly.

No, this is not an appeal for a new sect! It is an appeal for a people embodying the principle and power of " newness of life ".

CHAPTER THREE

THE NEW CRUSE (continued)

W<small>E</small> EXPRESSED THE FEELING THAT, while many would agree with the statement that a general renewal of spiritual life is very much needed at this time, there might not be such agreement that what is needed specifically is a " new cruse ", an instrument conformed to the mind of God, solely upon the basis of sympathy with the Holy Spirit's order and requirements. If there were pictured some new exclusive body ; some select company ; some iconoclastic movement ; some spiritually superior class—such reservations would be justified, and might lead to suspicion, fear, apprehension. Such an attitude, though quite unjustified, and betokening the "flesh" and the activity of the Spoiler—the Adversary—might lead to much unnecessary loss, and make things more difficult for the Lord than they need have been.

Now, we need to recognise the fact that in the history of the Divine reactions the instrument has always been a definitely related or relative one, not exclusive and isolated. Although it may have been comparatively small in itself, it was representative and linked with the whole company of the elect.

27

RELATIVE AND REPRESENTATIVE MINISTRY

Did Esther represent an instrument brought to the throne " for such a time as this "—the occasion of a Satanic plot for the death of God's people and the wiping out of His testimony from the earth? Then her life and the life of the whole company—although they were in captivity and ' out of the way '—were one, however privileged and exalted may have been her calling. She was involved in the testimony, and this brought her into a travail concerning the whole chosen race. We shall have more to say about Esther.

This same relative and representative function characterized Daniel and his brethren. They took the condition of the whole captive nation upon their hearts, and entered into what we might call a vicarious repentance for the sins of all their brethren. They themselves were the ' overcomers ' of that time, but all their experience, revelation, and victory was in a deep relationship to the people of God, though apostate.

When Hezekiah was instrumental in turning back the awful idolatry and wickedness made so complete by Ahaz, he first of all instituted a sin-offering " for ALL Israel " (II Chron. xxix. 24), and then sent letters throughout all Israel to call them to the Passover at Jerusalem (xxx. 1 – 10). This is striking when we remember that Hezekiah was king over Judah, not Israel ; the kingdom being rent, and entirely schismatic, with Israel much more idolatrous even than Judah. Hezekiah's heart went out to all, and did not allow the grossest idolatry to create a *spiritual* abandonment of his so greatly erring and sinning brethren.

This principle of relationship and representation can be traced throughout the Word, and it is a most important

one. There is no such thing as a ' section ' of the Body
of Christ. " The body is one ", but there are " bands "
and " joints of supply ", fulfilling special related and
representative functions or ministries. All the " members " may not be in equally good health, development,
life, fellowship, but they are not thereby cut off. *Christ will
never have a mutilated Body.*

We are not unaware of the greatness of the difficulty
and problem with which we are here confronted. At the
same time we make bold to tackle it for the Lord's glory.
If only certain principles are recognised and established,
there is hope of improvement, at least to some extent. We
must, therefore, in the first place keep clearly before us
that it is only the really born-anew children of God, in
whom there is something of the Spirit, who are in view—
not the vast accretions to ' Christendom ', or ' organized '
and traditional Christianity, of ' mixed multitudes '. However bad may be the spiritual condition of the former, they
are not to be excluded from the *spirit* of fellowship. That
does not mean fellowship in works or that which is wrong,
but it does mean earnest and loving solicitude for recovery
therefrom. How patiently and diligently and ingeniously
has many a surgeon or doctor worked to find some point of
contact with life in a patient whose hold and interest was
practically imperceptible ! Should it be less so with us in
this so much greater battle with spiritual death?

But the main point is this. *The Lord must have an instrument which He has formed in the fire and to which He has
given peculiar knowledge of Himself.* This instrument will
have to stand upon a peculiarly pure basis of life in God.
Whatever the rest may do, it dare not take its lead from
them. Its methods, means, and standards must be those
which have shed the less mature elements. Of some it

would stand as God's plummet to reveal that which is ' out of the straight '; that which is short of God's best—or God's better ; for who would claim to have reached God's best? A much greater cost will have to be met by such an instrument ; and there will be little place left, if it is spiritually constituted as against mentally apprehended, for spiritual pride.

Now the chief difficulty, as history has shown, is how to realise such a ministry, constituted by knowledge of the Lord through suffering, and how to hold it in relation to ALL the Lord's people, avoiding separation in spirit, schism in the Body, exclusiveness and ' watertightness '. It is the easiest thing to withdraw to some given point and look down on all others, as though to say : ' We are *the* people —you must come to us.' The Lord will lose much this way. No ; while in *practical* matters, for consistency's sake, there may *have* to be withdrawal, as also where error predominates, yet the preservation of what there is of God must be diligently sought in spirit. While there can be no official link with what is wrong, there can and must be a reaching out in spirit to keep the door open for the " more excellent way ".

The next thing is to apprehend the Divine meaning behind the creating of this instrument. Surely it is twofold.

Firstly, to have for Himself in the earth that which is as close an approximation to His own mind as possible ; that it should not be true that there is nothing which is in any real way an expression of the Lord's mind. Thus, further, He would have that which cleaves a way through for others. So it ever was in battles of old. The specially trained and disciplined troops broke through for others.

Secondly, that there may be that which gives the Lord His point toward which to work. As He creates a sense of need in His people, and leads them on thereby, He would have that which can be His means of meeting that need in spiritual knowledge. That the Lord directs hungry ones to those who know Him through special dealings is a principle not far to seek in the Divine record. We remember how Cornelius was brought into touch with Peter (Acts x), Apollos with Aquila and Priscilla (Acts xviii), and so on. There is such a thing as *election to special service*, and there ought to be mutual recognition of this. When the Lord Jesus took Peter and James and John into the more inward activities and revelations of His life, especially up to the Mount of Transfiguration, He was not guilty, in principle, of an act of schism in the Body. What the others thought or felt we do not know, but in the long run we know that ministry was in view, not personal preference. He was not making of them a specially privileged and separate company. A great need was coming, and this was His method of providing for the need which would one day be created.

The appreciation of what He did and what they knew had to tarry until that need arose. There will never be an appreciation of special resource without conscious need, but such need will justify God's methods, and prove His wisdom sound. God has from the beginning of the world always had His escape ready before the fire broke out—His lifeboat before the wreck—His store before the famine—His Cross before the curse. His peculiar ways with some are in view of a coming need which will give them a peculiar ministry. There are those who are out on a general basis of activity with the Lord, going all the time in a continuous stream of good works. There are also those who are cut off from anything great as to measure, and are reserved for what the others cannot do ; less in bulk, but perhaps of indispensable worth and service in emergency, and beyond a certain general point of attainment. The latter have to bide their time in patience, but when their time does come it is *their* time in the Lord, and no one else can do the work.

Let us return to our main principle, namely that *remnants are relative.* The remnants of which we spoke in our first chapter were not something conclusive in themselves. Sometimes a remnant of only a couple of tribes is referred to as " all Israel ", showing their representative character. While in the first instance the movement was on the part of a few, comparatively, there was from time to time a trickling after them, as there was that to which such tricklings could come. The remnant was not conclusive.

We must keep clearly and strongly before us the fact that, while the Lord must have His testimony maintained in the earth, and while He desires all His people to enter into the fulness of light and truth, and while there are clearly seen to be different companies of His people in Heaven, both as to time and as to position, the main characteristic of any company which may be termed ' a remnant ', or ' overcomers ', is that of vocation : that is, they stand in a vocational relationship to all other really born-anew children of God. It is something which they are called to be and to do which is preparatory for the rest. They have, amongst other things, to ' pass over armed before their brethren ' (Deut. iii. 18), to cleave a way and take the first shock of spiritual antagonism.

Now, before defining the nature of this instrument, we will say just a little more on this matter of fellowship. We have recognised two things, namely, that fellowship is limited to the measure of life and of the Spirit, and that for fuller fellowship there must be progress in the life of the Spirit; and then that, inasmuch as every true child of God has *something* of Himself in them, there should be care and diligence in discovering, unearthing, and fostering that. We have now to see that, no matter how we may seek to go on with the Lord, there can only be *true building up* of the Body on the ground of fellowship and love.

A SATANIC MASTER-STROKE

Perhaps one of the most *significant* things to any who are " not ignorant of his (Satan's) devices " is that there never has been a specially spiritual movement of God in the earth, calculated to serve Him in a particularly useful way, but what Satan's animosity thereto has been manifested along the line of division, schism, discord, separation, and a breaking down of fellowship. And how often has the real sting and stigma been modified by a feigning of love unbroken and preserved, when the divided parties would have no association with each other in the things of God. Love, let us again say emphatically, is incumbent upon the Lord's people toward " all men ", whether of the " household " or otherwise (Gal. vi. 10), but fellowship is something more. It is the most spiritual things which suffer the greatest shocks in this matter, and again we say this carries its own Satanic significance.

The methods of the enemy are numberless, the " wiles " unfathomable by human wit. A suggestion of suspicion, if it finds lodgment, is enough to completely paralyse the work of God and spiritual progress. Have a doubt and you are done. There never was a time when positive spiritual work was more jeopardised by suspicion than now. It would seem that hell is largely employed in issuing forth smoke, clouds, vapours, mists of suspicion, question, re-

C

servation, in order to infect with uncertainty, mystification, prejudice, fear, discrediting, distrust, aloofness. It is in the "heavenlies" that this is most registered; that is, the higher ranges of spiritual things. It is an *atmosphere,* and it is everywhere. You sense it wherever you go. In some places it is stifling—there is no clear breath of the Spirit, and a word of life is almost choked back.

Of course, this is no new thing, although now so intensified. The New Testament is full of it. The Lord Jesus met it—not in spiritual people, only in religious people. John met it. Paul met it in every direction. It was made to circle round his person, his methods, his character, and his message. Even some members of the mother assembly at Jerusalem showed suspicion and lack of cordiality toward him. Paul's setting aside of the Law, for instance, seemed to them to go beyond even the Lord Himself, who had not openly abrogated it. Then Paul appealed to "visions and revelations" (II Cor. xii. 1), but they asserted that these were dubious, or at best they could only serve to ratify his own personal convictions. Again, both Paul and his opponents appealed to the Old Testament, but the letter of the Old Testament seemed undoubtedly to favour the literalists, and his 'attempt to read new meanings' into the old revelation seemed to them mere cleverness. They looked on it as barefaced denial of the Divine Word. To them it looked as though he did not believe the Bible. They regarded his innovations as morally dangerous.

Of course, this in *substance* ought to have no parallel to-day, but it has in spirit. *There is nothing added by revelation to the Scriptures since the New Testament was closed, but there is much to be* RECOGNISED *in them by the enlightenment of the Spirit. There is no new meaning, but there is much new* RECOGNITION *of the meaning.*

CAUSES AND PRECAUTIONS

The point is, not that there never was or never will be an absence of this Satanic enterprise of smoke to prevent or destroy fellowship, but—what is to be our attitude in such circumstances?

It would be vain to try to deal with all the secondary causes. Sometimes the ground of the adversary's success, either in ourselves or in " them that oppose themselves ", is that we may be living in certain respects in some proximity to the " flesh " and the " natural man ". Some secret pride may make possible jealousy, criticism, envy, ' hurtness ', fear of loss, self-pity, comparison, or a wish to be out of the place of difficulty. Sometimes it may be immaturity ; sometimes imperfect knowledge or understanding—' seeing through a glass darkly '. There are worse things than these, too ; but there are also such things as are either utterly imaginary, or real only because they seem real to those who register them. That is, the enemy can set up situations which are utterly false in themselves —they have no foundation in *fact*. They are phantoms— but how terribly real phantoms can be !

How shall we meet all this? It seems so hopeless, and would almost drive us to ultra-individualism. Let us not abandon hope until we have been faithful to the exhortations, ' Give diligence to keep the unity of the Spirit ' (Eph. iv. 3), and " Prove all things " (I Thess. v. 21). The final test will, of course, be—Is the Lord present in blessing? If so—and we ought to have spiritual discernment— then up to that point we ought neither to oppose nor to refuse all fellowship.

But before we are so general, perhaps we have a duty which costs a little more.

Seeing how great was the matter involved—no less than the Holy Spirit's presence and ministry—Aquila and Priscilla might easily have labelled Apollos as in error, altogether wrong and wanting, and left him and the assembly of which he was 'pastor'. But they saw the lack and lovingly took him and in a humble spirit helped him to see it (Acts xviii. 24 – 28). There is a fine record of the man after this. It could so easily have been a breach and a loss.

We must always be sure that those who seem to us to be wrong are not capable of being helped on those matters which are absolutely vital to fellowship. What have we done and what do we do in the matter? To come to a conclusion and forthwith to abandon those from whom we differ is a positive violation of scriptural method and instruction. This is often great loss to the Lord when there might have been gain. It would seem from the Word that the grounds of separation, *when established,* are brought within a small range as to number, though of course outweighing all others in importance. They are : the denial of the person of Christ, that He is truly God come in the flesh (II John 7, 10) ; the denial of the necessity for and sufficiency of His death for reconciling men to God (Gal. i. 6 – 9) ; the practice of moral evil (I Cor. v. 9) ; the defying of the united judgment of the whole assembly in a matter of wrong doing (Matt. xviii. 17) ; and, finally, the refusal to accept the authority, in the house of God, of the Apostles and their writings (II Thess. iii. 14, 15). All else is gathered up in these.

It would seem necessary to say again here what we have said earlier, that we are not dealing with the matter of co-operation in doubtful methods and on an unspiritual basis, or of a compromise on truth. There will ever have to be separation in these matters. Our point is the *spirit* of

fellowship—that we should not close ourselves up, as
though we were apart from and superior to all others.
Many of us have to confess to a time when our lives were
by no means conspicuous for their spirituality, and we owe
much to the spirit of fellowship on the part of others. If
so be we feel that, in the mercy of God, we have been
given something more than some, we must be out to help,
to win, to cherish. Above all, we must keep our hearts
open and our spirit pure. It is terribly possible to get to a
SET place where no one can teach us, but we can teach
others—they are the ones who are not going on with the
Lord. This is entirely fatal to fellowship.

Now we must close this chapter, but with one important reminder. A great safeguard and security to that fellowship without which there is no building and progress in
the House of God is to *recognise,* and bear continually in
mind, that the master tactic of the enemy is somehow, by
hook or by crook, to get in between the Lord's people and
cause strain and break. Our ' diligence ' must be along the
lines of ' proving all things ' ; refusing the opinions and
judgments of others—even the most spiritual ; not listen-
ing to gossip or criticism ; not going by appearances ; and
always keeping a very close walk with the Spirit and listen-
ing to Him on all matters.

When the Scripture says that we are to " prove all
things ", we should apply that especially to the " things "
which could serve the evil powers in their propaganda of
suspicions, leading to divisions.

We should " prove " whether our judgment of persons
and things is absolutely right. We should prove whether
the things said by a person, by word or writing, are what
we have taken them to mean, or whether they might not
mean something that we have not recognised.

We should prove whether a person about whom we have a question is not open to being helped from the Word of God to see differently or better than he now sees.

We should prove whether love has no influence with such, and whether he is ' *proved* ' to be bigoted, proud, and unapproachable.

Have we adopted such lines, or hurried to destroy by open attack or by the spread of suspicion?

CHAPTER FOUR

THE OVERCOMER

BEFORE WE PROCEED to consider more definitely the nature of that ' new cruse' of which we have been speaking, a few further words on the relative aspect of this vessel are needed. In the Scriptures, as we have pointed out, it is clearly seen that all the reactionary instruments of God are of a relative character ; that is, that they are related to and on behalf of a body larger than themselves. This is an underlying principle in the progressive activities of God. The point which needs to have extra emphasis is that, in *securing* all the elect territory, habitation and inheritance, whether as His first choice or as of necessity by reason of so general an apathy and worldliness on the part of His people, the Lord uses what might be termed ' advance parties'. It is not necessary in this connection to present or argue for any theory or ' teaching' concerning ' selectiveness ', or ' partial' or ' first-fruits ' in the matter of ' rapture '. The historical, literal and time aspect is of secondary importance. What is of primary account is the *spiritual* fact, and this, we believe, is incontrovertible. It is a principle in every realm of creation and Divine method. There are—

HARBINGERS IN EVERY SPHERE.

Originally a harbinger was one who went before to provide lodgings, but the term has now come to be applied to any forerunner. An adequate recognition of the *spiritual* element in this universal fact, and especially in relation to " the eternal purpose ", would correct and adjust much on both sides—acceptance and rejection—of a set teaching of ' partial rapture '. That is, if the vocational factor were kept in view it would supply the motive and stimulus so commonly lacking amongst many who reject that teaching ; which lack has very largely become the strength of the teaching and its propagation. And, on the other hand, it would both obviate the difficulty concerning ' all being of Grace ' and not of works, and remove any ' selectiveness ' of spirit and temper—as ' the elect of the elect '. Let us repeat with strength : There is undoubtedly an advance party in every movement of God. This is spiritual before anything else, and it is vocational rather than meritorious. That there will be special rewards for such seems quite clear and beyond doubt, but rewards do not contradict grace.

When we contemplate the churches in Asia as presented in the Revelation, and admit the respective age application, it is difficult, if not impossible, in respect of at least five, to conclude that we are dealing with the unsaved and ungodly—with assemblies of religious people without any true spiritual history. It is undoubtedly a case of declension, of failure to go on with the Lord. Are all these to be eternally lost? And yet they represent the majority in every age.

We know that one answer to this is that all will be adjusted at the Judgment Seat of Christ ; but what concerns us is—what about the others, the 'overcomers'? Surely more is involved than being different from the rest and getting a better reward. Yes: the point is that the Lord must and will have His testimony in the earth according to His own mind, and those who provide Him with the instrument for this fulfil a special mission, not only in the earth, but in the heavenlies—both now, and then.

Really, the focal point of this whole matter is not the two or more raptures. The fact is that the Lord has shown unmistakably that He has made no provision for a 'second-best' in the life of a believer or of the Church, but has called all His people to the fullest degree of faithfulness and devotion. There *is* a second-best, as see I Corinthians iii. 15, etc. Let us not fasten upon unscriptural labels, such as 'partial rapture' or 'selective rapture', but upon the facts—that there *are* such people as 'overcomers', and also, evidently, those who are *not*, and that there is a difference of no mean importance between the two.

It is all just an appeal to take no chances—" make no provision for the flesh "—but to be utter for God, whatever it costs.

We are now able to come to the more definite consideration of the nature and function of this peculiar vessel for God.

There is a great difference between a people moved by mere disaffection, discontent, 'disgruntledness', difference of opinion, personal dislike or preference, and one moved by the constraint of a great Divine vision—by the inwrought reaction of God, registered with pain in the heart.

This inward heart-longing found expression long ago in classic words : —

" *By the rivers of Babylon,*
There we sat down, yea, we wept,

When we remembered Zion.
Upon the willows in the midst thereof
We hanged up our harps . . .
How can we sing Jehovah's song
In a strange land ?
If I forget thee, O Jerusalem,
Let my right hand forget her skill.
Let my tongue cleave to the roof of my mouth,
If I remember not thee ;
If I prefer not Jerusalem above my chiefest joy."
                    (Psalm cxxxvii. 1, 2, 4 — 6, A.R.V.*)*

The implications of these great heart-yearnings represent the crystallizing of the Divine purpose from before times eternal. The ultimate thing in the heart of God, and that into which all the interests of those in real oneness of spirit with Him will be gathered, is presented in what is known as—

THE HOUSE OF GOD AND THE CITY OF GOD.

When we speak of the ' *ultimate* ' thing, we mean that which is to be the eternal consummation of all the Divine method and means. The thing which is primary and final is the place, worship and glory of God in the universe. This factor will be implicit in all that we have to say. Were we asked what are the major lines and subjects of Divine revelation throughout the whole Scriptures, we should say with considerable conviction that they are : —

1. The Person of the Lord Jesus Christ.
2. His Cross—death, burial and resurrection.
3. The Church or House of God.
4. The Coming again of Christ.
5. The City of God.

There are other phases, but these *taken relatively* are the primary themes, or aspects of one theme.

While the Person of the Lord Jesus as God manifest in the flesh is the sum of all revelations, it requires the Cross to give the full *meaning* and reveal the full *value* of that manifestation; it demands the Church to display the full *content* of that manifestation ultimately; and it calls for the City to define the *nature* of that manifestation. In leading men on to the appreciation of the Person, God begins with the Cross. If the House is the House of the Divine Son, and if the City is the City of the great King, then the House and the City are based upon the Cross. Moreover, if the House and the City are for the glory of God in Christ and His universal worship, then the Cross represents the nature of worship and the way of glory.

To put this more precisely: If the Lord has in view a people for His glory, by whom the content of the Son of Man is ultimately displayed to the universe, then this people will be fundamentally *a people of the Altar*. This we believe to be the all-inclusive theme of Scripture. *The Cross is the central recognition of the eternal rights of God.* At the Cross and in the Cross all the rights of God from eternity to eternity are recognised and acknowledged. That is central to Calvary. God has rights. God's rights are that the whole universe should render Him undivided, unrivalled, unreserved worship, acknowledging that all things are His by right, and that no one else in the universe has a right before Him. That great fact is here gathered up in the Person of the Lord Jesus Christ, and He brings to God in His own Person His rights, offering Himself in the greatness of who He is and what He is—the rights of God.

God, by His Son, created the world for His Glory. The Holy Spirit was agent in the creation of the world for the Glory of God, in order that the whole earth should be full of His Glory. The Holy Spirit is likewise agent in the redemption of the world for the Glory of God. It is of per· haps deeper significance than we have recognised that the great song of the redeemed at the end, when the work of Calvary is consummated, is gathered up into one sentence: *" Hast redeemed . . . to God " (Rev. v. 9).* Redemption is unto God: it is bringing back to God His rights, and the Holy Spirit is the agent in this redemptive work which has the Glory of God as its objective, just as the Holy Spirit was the agent in creation for the same end.

Worship, then, with all its depth and fulness, is the key word. In the great consummation when God is to be worshipped in the whole universe, and the different songs of worship break forth—the song of one company, " a hundred and forty and four thousand ", worshipping God and the Lamb (Rev. vii. 4), and then the song of the ' great multitude which no man can number ' worshipping God and the Lamb (vii. 9)—there is the unveiling of the worship of the beast, and that is another consummation. The two consummations of worship are there unveiled.

The worship of the beast is one which has been going on ever since Lucifer secured a following, a reverence from angels in high estate in heaven. When he found it in his own heart to make a bid for the place of the Almighty —to exalt his throne above the clouds, to ascend into the heavens, to be equal with the Most High (Is. xiv. 13, 14) —he managed to gather to himself a company, all with the intent of drawing heaven's worship away from God to himself ; and ever since that lifting up of his heart in that infamous ambition another worship has been going on.

He drew that company with him, the company of angels
" who kept not their own principality ", and are " kept in
everlasting bonds under darkness " (Jude 6). Then he appeared on the earth, and sought again to usurp the place
of God in the worship of His Creation here ; and in this
he succeeded, and became, by reason of a conquest and the
consent of man, " the god of this age ", " the prince of this
world ".

THE TWO WORSHIPS

From that moment he set up a spiritual system of worship which is perceivable behind the whole record of
history. We have the breaking in of this evil element all
along the line of worship, wherever and whenever the
rights of God are recognised by sacrifice. Immediately Abel
recognised the rights of God and erected his altar, slaying
his sacrifice and shedding sacrificial blood, in the simplicity
of the testimony of faith that here on the earth God has
sole rights, there broke in this very thing against that
testimony. The murderer came in to withstand and destroy
the testimony, with Cain as his instrument, who also set
up an altar and made a pretence in his darkened understanding to worship God. But he never got through to
God, and that was the very ground upon which the Satanic
element of jealousy and pride was churned up within him,
and he became, because the Devil had got a purchase upon
him, the instrument against the worship of God. The
enemy's scheme is deep laid ; he knows what he is doing.
Through the other worship he breaks in against the recognition of the Divine Rights, the worship of God ; and from
Abel onward it is always so.

Noah set up his altar upon the renewed earth, and in

so doing declared that "the earth is the Lord's and the fulness thereof". But very quickly there broke in the other thing again. Even in that representative one the element of evil rises up to contradict the testimony, and before long the worship of God becomes associated with shame, and the glory is hidden again. We see the testimony on the one hand and the breaking in to contradict on the other.

Abram's life-story heads up to the incident in Genesis xv, where that altar is finally set and the sacrifice is offered —and then the battle begins. While Abram holds on to God and waits and stands, the vultures descend, and a mighty conflict ensues for the preservation of that testimony to the rights of God, the worship of God; and then comes the horror of great darkness. When Israel, in the fulfilment of the vision which was then given to Abram in that very hour of conflict, came out into the wilderness and the worship of God was set up, there broke in this very same element, and you find the golden calf.

And so the story goes on. You come to Balaam seeking to curse Israel, but not permitted, and then setting up by insinuation the evil thing, fornication—a form of idolatry —and the Lord's glory obscured once more. It was a beautiful picture that Balaam gave in his prophecy, perhaps one of the most beautiful things in the Old Testament. As Balaam stands, desiring for gain to curse, but constrained by the Spirit of God to bless, and as he speaks concerning this people dwelling alone, wonderful things are said and the glory of the Lord is presented concerning Israel; and then, as round by a back door, for that gain he teaches Israel to commit fornication. The glorious picture fades, and the glory of God is again obscured in Israel, because of this other worship. The rights of God are all the time disputed.

Then we have the wonderful story of Solomon. On the one hand, his building of the House, his setting up of the altar, and the glory of God descending. Here you have the Cross and the Church and the Spirit. On the other hand, the after-story of Solomon. What a tragedy—what a ghastly tragedy! the glory of God contradicted again by the very man who had so beautifully set up the testimony in Israel. The Devil is breaking in all the time to take God's rights from Him, to rob Him of His glory.

It is the story of Elijah, fighting for the testimony in Israel in a day when the glory of God was hidden. On Carmel the great issue is the altar—the Cross, and the fire—the Spirit. The testimony is once more established in Israel; but the reaction of the powers of darkness is then through Jezebel to destroy the man who has restored the testimony. The issue in the word of Elijah is: "How long halt ye between two opinions? if the Lord be God, follow Him: but if Baal, then follow him" (I Kings xviii. 21). You cannot divide the issue—it is one thing or the other. That is the testimony of God having His rights utterly and no one else getting a look in. And let the critics say what they like about Elijah destroying the prophets of Baal, four hundred on the spot—there is a very deep principle involved, a deep principle. The destroying of the prophets of Baal is the outward demonstration of the spiritual principle that there can be no quarter given to that which is set against the Throne of God. Whether it be Agag (I Sam. xv.) or the prophets of Baal, the point at issue is God's rights. Is *He* having the worship and the honour and the glory in this universe?

That is a very brief survey, through the Old Testament, of the constant breaking in of this evil element along the line of worship.

THE DEPTH OF CALVARY

Now, the Cross of the Lord Jesus gathered all this up, and " through the eternal Spirit " Christ secured the rights of God in His own Risen Person : so that " through the eternal Spirit " Christ met the whole of this thing in the universe at Calvary—He met it all.

Let us get behind Calvary, ever more and more behind, until we get to the ultimate. The Lord has led us by degrees deeper and deeper into the meaning of the Cross. There was a time when we thought that we had fathomed the Cross, when we saw the " old man " being dealt with, but we find that there are still ranges that we have not before seen. It was the Throne of God that Christ was standing for at Calvary ; it was the ultimate and universal glory of God that He was fighting for in Calvary ; and He met all this that was set against the Throne, and met it victoriously, and secured those eternal universal rights of God in His own risen Person : which means that Christ risen and ascended has secured in His own Person all the rights of God for the glory of God for evermore. In the Lord Jesus God has His rights secured.

I hope the Lord enables you to enter into that. Jesus Christ, " who through the eternal Spirit offered himself " (Heb. ix. 14), now standing in the Presence of God, has secured in His own Person all God's rights for ever, and the ultimate filling of the universe with the glory of God is secured in the Risen Person of Christ. There is no longer any doubt about the issue. God is going, without any question, to be universally worshipped, and the glory of God is going to fill the whole universe without any rival, because THE LORD JESUS is in the presence of God, victorious over every other thing that was against the Throne of God. This is something immense. He said: " Lo, I am come . . . to do thy will " (Heb. x. 7), and the will of God done utterly is the recognition of the utter rights of God, and God becoming possessed of them.

When we talk about doing the will of God and wanting to know the will of God, oh, let us get the immense range of such words. The will of God means nothing else than that God shall be universally glorified and that He shall be the central object of worship in the universe. Read the Revelation again with that thought, and the book will become new. You will find then that the book of the Revelation is the book of worship, and you will see that that worship, which is there in ever widening circles to the ultimate bounds of the universe—that worship is brought about by the Lamb, " through the eternal Spirit ": the Lamb in the midst of the Throne.

The Holy Spirit is thus the minister of the glorified Christ, as He was the agent and the dynamic for the accomplishment of this great end in the Cross, and the securing of it in the Person of Christ in the glory. He is now the minister of the glorified Christ to work this out in the earth, and in doing so He will bring us to certain very important issues.

He will bring us first of all to this : *that those who enter most fully into the meaning of the Cross—which is the will of God wholly done—will encounter the supreme assault of Satan.*

Do you wonder that Satan hates the Cross? Do you wonder that he by any means will get the Cross set on one side? Do you wonder that those who go into the meaning of the Cross spiritually find that they have immediately come up against the whole system of antagonism from the Devil? It is so, inevitably. We have seen Abel in the very

D

earliest and simplest form of the presentation of the meaning of the Cross. When he enters into relationship with
that blood, that sacrifice, that altar, he immediately and
automatically comes up against the adversary. The Holy
Spirit, through John, says of Cain that he " was of the evil
one " (I John iii. 12).

So with Abraham, so with Joseph, so with Moses ; so
even in what might be thought to be the simple case of
Esther. Let us pause with Esther for a moment. The book
of Esther has been thought to be a commentary upon, an
exposition of, the providence and sovereignty of God.
Well! it is that, but there is a bigger background to the
book. Here is one who is " come to the kingdom for such
a time . . . " (Esth. iv. 14). What time? A time when the
testimony of God in His people was so set against by the
enemy that he wanted the last Jew exterminated. You
know the story of Haman—" Haman the Agagite "—a
remnant of that Amalakite seed which had always been
against God. Haman the Agagite had become inspired
with the further purpose, utterly and finally to exterminate
the Jews. Esther came to the kingdom for such a time as
that, and put her life in the balances—" if I perish, I
perish "—and met that awful deep-laid scheme of Satan.
It is ever an illustration of the ultimate controversy of the
Cross. You meet with that when you stand for the testimony of God in the earth. We will come back to Esther
presently.

The story of Daniel is the same thing. Two gods : the
god set up by Nebuchadnezzar, and THE God. Who is
going to be worshipped? Daniel does not need to deliberate over his decision that Jehovah alone, and no other god,
is to be worshipped in this universe ; His rights alone are
to be recognised. He meets the power behind that world-

system and is called upon to pay the price. It is the same issue with Daniel's three friends, Shadrach, Meshach and Abed-nego.

THE SUPREME EFFORT OF SATAN

From the very birth of the Lord Jesus, it is known to Satan who He is ; and the scheme is put into operation to engulf Him in the massacre of a whole multitude of infants. The cruelty of the evil one to murder a mass to get *one*! He is after One, he is not after the crowd.

We have no record of any efforts of the enemy from that time until the Lord steps across the line which runs between His private life and His public life—and then He meets the enemy immediately. And what is the question? " If Thou wilt . . . worship me " (Matt. iv. 9). That is what he is after. It is right out—he is betrayed at once ; and it is that issue right up to the Cross. " If Thou wilt worship me." It comes in a multitude of different ways. Satan ' only ' wants an acknowledgment, the ascribing to him of some rights in the universe.

But, ah, the Lord never recognised those rights—just as Mordecai refused to recognise the right of Haman. This is one of the most beautiful things in the book of Esther. Here is Haman claiming to be somebody : he has gained eminence, and everybody is bowing to him. But Mordecai refuses to recognise any of his glory, and ignores it all. And you remember Haman's story to his family. ' I am a great man ; I have much goods, many children : but what is the good of it all if this one man will not recognise me?' (Esther v. 9 — 13). It is a foreshadowing. There is One who counts more than all the rest, and until He can be captured or got out of the way the enemy's fulness is divided. That One will not recognise Satan's ' rights ' and that One is destined to bring about his doom.

The Lord Jesus met that all the way through, refusing to attribute to Satan one atom of right in this universe. He was out to challenge that, to secure all the rights for God in His own Person, and to come to the Throne Himself with those rights. And when He has done it we see the same thing going on with the Church. It is still the Church's great issue : the worshippers and the worshipped, and the place or the no-place of the enemy. We shall deal with that when we come to speak of the Church.

Now, only the Holy Spirit, in the power of the victorious Christ and by virtue of His shed Blood, can meet that challenge. We do not talk glibly, lightly, frivolously, about this thing. We view the ultimate issue with joy and exultation, but we recognise that it is "not by might, nor by power, but by my Spirit, saith the Lord of Hosts" (Zechariah iv. 6). And if the Lord Jesus Himself needed that it should be through the Eternal Spirit that this thing was wrought out, oh, how much more we! How much more we to-day! We should not rush into this battle ; we recognise that nothing but the mighty energizing of the Holy Spirit could meet this great issue and challenge. But we recognise also with confidence that the Holy Spirit is the minister of the victorious Christ, and that His very advent is on the ground of that victory, to work that victory out in the universe ; and we thank God for it. Why has the Holy Spirit come? Oh! not that we might have blessings and what we call power and influence and opportunity and service. No, He has come as Representative and Agent of the Christ, who has secured the rights of God in His own Person. To bring about the recognition and realisation of those rights in this earth—that is the work of the Holy Spirit.

The second thing that comes out of this is that *the Holy Spirit always demands the ground of the Cross for His activity, if the glory of God is in view*. But then, the Cross registers the removal of all that serves Satan. Now, it would take a long time to cover that ground again to see the things that served Satan. What was it that served Satan in Cain? Covetousness, personal ambition, jealousy, pride! That worked itself out in the murder of Abel— but the murder of Abel as an expression of hatred for God (although Cain may have been blind to the deeper nature of the thing). What was it that served Satan in Balaam? Greed, covetousness, world-gain. The Cross registers the removal by destruction of all that served Satan, and for us it is gathered up in one word: SELF.

What a wide word that is—what a comprehensive word! The stronger term is " the flesh ". Some people do not know what you mean when you talk about the "flesh". They begin to think of positive vices and iniquities of deep dye. But the " flesh " is only another term for " self ". Self is a very subtle thing, a many-sided thing. It includes self-interest, self-glory, self-preservation, self-realisation, self-advancement—all those considerations of influence and good-standing and prestige and following, and being understood and spoken well of. The phases of " self " are legion, and they, every one of them, serve Satan.

Moreover, they serve him in this other sense, that they divide the rights of God and usurp the place of God : and therefore, wherever there is the slightest suggestion or in-sinuation of self, the Glory of God is obscured and the Cross has got to be applied there. The Cross is not applied in the work of God just because God wants us out of it for the sake of having us out of it, to humble, to crush, to break us ; no, it has this great end in view—HIS GLORY.

And our glory depends upon His glory. We cannot come to glory until He receives His rights in the universe; and the Cross is the way there. The Holy Spirit demands the ground of the Cross in us, because the glory of God is in view. The Cross, dear friend, means utter devotion to God's glory. The Holy Spirit only works on that ground— He has only ever worked on that ground. A pure work of the Holy Spirit, completely immune from Satan's touch, requires the Cross, which means complete separation from all of the old ground.

Perhaps you have read the wonderful record of what God did in China through His servant, Dr. Jonathan Goforth—a work of the Spirit in mighty revival. I think I have read few things which are more literal fulfilments of words which are often mentioned amongst us: "Call unto me, and I will answer thee, and will shew thee great things, and difficult, which thou knowest not" (Jeremiah xxxiii. 3). When this true man of God arrived at a certain place, he was told immediately that he must not expect anything there such as he had had elsewhere, for there were difficulties. But there the Holy Spirit came in, and under His constraint different people got up and confessed such things as were never suspected—confessed them in public—in a mighty movement of God. But the Spirit of the Lord kept very short accounts with His servant, and every suggestion and insinuation of the Devil through his "flesh" had to be met.

CHAPTER FIVE

THE ALTAR, THE HOUSE, THE NAME

Let us now gather up in a positive presentation—even at the risk of some repetition—what we believe to be the essence and substance of that testimony for which the Lord has ever reacted, and would now react, in a day of declension. There are three words which represent this testimony, and these three words may be clearly seen to govern and interpret the whole of the Scriptures. There is no part of the Scriptures which does not relate in some way to one or more of the objects which these words denote. They are, in the Old Testament: THE ALTAR, THE HOUSE, THE NAME ; or, in the New Testament: THE BLOOD, THE CHURCH, THE SOVEREIGNTY.

THE ALTAR AND THE BLOOD

Every reaction and new beginning that has come from God has been by an altar. The first of these was that of Abel, although there must have been an earlier shedding of blood, when the consciousness of being uncovered led to God's clothing or covering the expelled two with skins of animals. Then, when that world was wiped out in judgment by the flood, a new beginning was made with Noah's altar. When there was nothing of a distinctive character speaking for God in the days of Abram, the Lord laid His hand upon him, called him out as an elect instrument, and brought him to an elect land; and there, with the man and the place of His new beginning brought together, an altar was erected. There was a brief lapse when Abram went down to Egypt, but on his return the original ground was re-taken with a reconstructed altar.

Thus a distinctive seed was marked out; and some four hundred years later, that seed being constituted a corporate testimony against world-wide misrepresentation of God, an altar was the conspicuous factor, initially and continuously. It is significant that, although many thousands of lambs were slain on the night of the separation of that people from Egypt, the record always speaks in the singular, never in the plural. It was always " the lamb " or " a lamb ". In God's sight there was only One Lamb, and although every threshold was an altar, there was only one Altar in Heaven's view. (The word in Exodus xii. 22, translated " bason ", is in the Hebrew " threshold ".)

This truth of new beginnings with the altar can be clearly seen afterward in the case of the receiving of the Law and the pattern of the heavenly things by Moses. The great altar of the Tabernacle and Temple governed the life of Israel for many years, until the times of declension set in, and then each movement back toward God was marked by the altar coming again into its place. It was so in Elijah's stand, in I Kings xviii; and it was so with the revival under Hezekiah, in II Chronicles xxx. It was so again with Josiah—II Chronicles xxxv. But hardly had Josiah passed off the scene than his work fell in ruins. Judgment fell, Jerusalem was destroyed, the Temple burnt, and the people went into captivity. After seventy years a remnant returned, and we read in Ezra iii. 3 that the first thing that the remnant did was to " set the altar in its place ".

This is God's new work in reaction. We have not gathered in every instance, but only enough to indicate, and perhaps establish a recognition of, the principle. We leave the matter of the altar there for the time being, while we consider the essential element in the altar, which is the *Blood.*

The testimony of the altar is the testimony of the Blood. As we approach this sacred thing, may we urge our readers to give it the most careful heed? Here we touch the heart of everything. There has been nothing so assailed as the testimony of the Blood: by ridicule, by a sneer, by intellectual superiority, from one direction ; by an ignorant and false refinement which pretends to be shocked, from another ; by a merely rationalistic and philosophical interpretation, which sees no more than a crude system of ritual and rite by which a universal religious instinct expresses itself—a form and idea which belongs to times of immaturity and unenlightenment—from yet a third; these and many other modes of assault from its opponents. Then from its would-be friends it suffers in numerous ways, ranging from the ritualistic and sacerdotal debasement, which has names and forms without life and power, to the other swing of the pendulum, marked by a superficial, cheap, frivolous, noisy, jazz-chorus singing about this most holy and sacred thing—" the precious Blood ".

There is nothing in the universe more bitterly hated and more terribly feared by the adversary than the Blood of the Lord Jesus Christ. But if it is to be a mighty operative factor in life and service, faith must have as intelligent a basis concerning it as possible ; and we are especially concerned with the vocation of the people of God here! Let us then see what the Blood stands for.

THE MEANING OF THE BLOOD

There are two aspects of this whole matter of the Blood.

One (concerning which we have already said something) is that a death has taken place, and in that death one whole kind of humanity has, in the mind of God, been set aside. This relates to " Him who knew no sin . . . made . . . sin on our behalf " (" in our stead ") (II Cor. v. 21).

The other, about which we shall now speak more particularly, is that which sets forth the inherently incorruptible life of God's Son made flesh. If all that is said about the Blood relates only to death, then its sacredness cannot be understood, but becomes a supreme problem. We have dealt with this aspect in the book entitled " The Centrality and Universality of the Cross ", but we will point out the essential elements here:

Firstly, let us note the sacredness of life as in the blood. We are now familiar with the scriptural teaching that " the life . . . is in the blood " (Lev. xvii. 11), and " the blood is the life " (Deut. xii. 23). There is a tremendous emphasis in Scripture upon the sacredness of blood. Indeed the word ' soul ' is often used interchangeably with both ' blood ' and ' life ', and all the characteristics and values of the soul are associated in the same way with the ' blood ' and the ' life '. But the blood as the life is related in a peculiar way to God, as representing His specific prerogatives. Thus the whole matter is gathered up in a reservation and a provision as laid down in Leviticus and in John's Gospel.

In Leviticus the Lord repeatedly stresses that blood is

not to be drunk. This rule would be broken under a penalty of death (Lev. vii. 26, 27 ; xvii. 10 – 12). The law concerning blood and its sacredness was carried so far that if a man went hunting and killed a quarry, he was to pour out the blood on the ground and cover it over with dust (Lev. xvii. 13). He was not to leave the blood exposed, but honour it, show it the same reverence, as he would the body of a fallen man.

Now does it not strike you with a great force of significance that, when we have repeatedly read : " Ye shall eat no manner of blood . . . Whosoever eateth any blood . . . shall be cut off ", then we turn and read in John vi. 53 : ' *Except* ye drink the blood of the Son of Man, ye have no life '? Surely the very first thing which this implies is that the whole question of life has been shut up by God to the Person and Cross of the Lord Jesus Christ. It is the life of the Person, and gives to the Person a uniqueness and distinctiveness which no other in history has ever had. Then it gives to the Cross of the Lord Jesus a unique and supreme meaning and value, in that it was there that He shed His Blood and poured forth His life ; releasing that life to be received by all who believed on the Person and accepted the meaning of His Cross.

The spiritually blind Jewish religious leaders of John vi would naturally be very scandalized at His words about drinking blood, and would revert to the tradition of the letter of Leviticus. This would be because on the one hand they did not realise the meaning of that reservation, and on the other hand they did not recognise who Jesus was. To recognise the Lord Jesus is to be lifted above law into life.

The thought of the sacredness of the Blood as the life is that of the Divine relationship of it : that is, that it is bound up with the Lord and no man can touch it. All of a piece with this is—

THE HOLINESS OF THE BLOOD

We are familiar with the injunctions concerning the spotlessness of the offerings of old—" without spot, or blemish ". There was a sense in which the priests were expert fault-finders! Their business was to find fault if they could. The discovery of a blemish in a proffered sacrifice meant its immediate rejection. Their eyes were as the eyes of God in this matter. A beast was passed only after the most scrupulous investigation, when the formula ' It is perfect ' was pronounced over it.

Such, likewise, then, was the blood, and this is the testimony of the holiness of the life of the Lord Jesus, and consequently of the nature of that Divine deposit within the born-anew child of God. We are not perfect or spotless, but the life from Him in us is, and by its vital activity through faith and obedience we are to be conformed to His image, and are assured that one day we shall be like Him. Blessed be God, we have the earnest of perfection. This precious Blood does cleanse.

This leads us at this point to say a brief word on—

THE SHEDDING AND SPRINKLING OF THE BLOOD.

If we are not mistaken, the shedding relates to the whole question of sin, guilt, death, judgment ; and by the shedding there is remission, and the whole ground of salvation is secured.

The sprinkling is that by which we are brought into living vocational fellowship with God. The Tabernacle and Priesthood of old represented, not only Israel's salvation, but Israel's priestly ministry in the nations. They were meant to be "a kingdom of priests", and God's ministering instrument among and to all nations.

Hence there was a special significance given to the sprinkling of the blood. Although the Tabernacle was perfect as a structure; although the "pattern" was carried out to the last detail; although the priesthood was complete in number and adornment: nothing and no one could function until every part—altar, laver, table, curtains, candlestick, golden altar, mercy-seat, vessels, instruments, ear, thumb, toe, etc.—had been sprinkled with the blood. It was regarded as a higher function to catch the blood for sprinkling even than to slay the sacrifice and thus shed the blood.

Nothing lives in the service and ministry of God, save in virtue of sprinkled blood. Oh that men would see this to-day! The most perfect structure, the most complete outfit, the most ornate edifice, the most extensive organization, the most fastidious order, and the most devout purpose will all fail to function in the eternal interests of God, apart from the virtue of the precious Blood of the Lord Jesus. The Holy Spirit—the Fire of God—is indispensable to spiritual life and energy, and He only comes where that Blood has been sprinkled. The Blood and the Spirit are one, and always go together—one as the preparation, the other as the attestation. Calvary precedes Pentecost. The Cross is the way to the glorifying. To be crucified with Christ is to have put away that "flesh" upon which the Holy Oil may not come. God is never going to quicken and vitalise what He has for ever put away; neither will He glorify and use in His service that which is of man.

Whatever the means and methods or necessities which

come in their course, *the one all-inclusive object of the Divine reactions is to have that in the earth which is wholly and undividedly of God.* To this end it is essential that the Cross be wrought so deeply into the experience of the Lord's servants that they shall come to utter despair as to themselves and all else, and send up a full heart-cry for the fulness of the Holy Spirit. To such a crisis the Lord will work by all manner of means, slowly breaking down all other ground of confidence, and writing ' failure ' on all other resource.

The testimony of the Blood, the Cross, then, is the testimony of that which is uniquely, wholly, sacredly of God in absolute holiness.

THE INCORRUPTIBILITY OF THE BLOOD

The next related factor in the Blood as the Life is its incorruptibility and indestructibility. These elements go together and are one. What is incorruptible is indestructible.

This is a life over which death has no power. Death has been met in the power of this life. Hades has been entered and plundered in the power of this life. Satan and his entire kingdom have had their might exhausted by the power of this life. He who was and is this Life, now lives for evermore, as the Testimony to the universal triumph of His own Blood over every force that has stood in the way of God's end.

By this imperishable life He has perfected salvation. Nothing of old was ever perfect, because the mediators constantly changed by death ; death breaking in all the time meant no completeness. But this High Priest perfects for ever, because He lives after the power of an *endless*, " indissoluble ", life. Therefore He is able to save to the uttermost, *i.e.*, the ultimate and final end (Heb. vii. 16, 23 — 25).

By this imperishable life He has bound His own to Himself. They share this life by new birth, and they will never die. Death is not cessation of being ; it is something spiritual. Life triumphant over death is spiritual, and means ascendency over sin, self, Satan, death. In other words, it is power and victory.

By this indestructible life the Lord Jesus has inaugurated a ministry and a work which will persist to its ultimate consummation, in spite of every force of earth and hell which may be hurled against it. Mighty empires and powerful hierarchies have been brought to ruins in setting themselves against that which He said He would build. " The gates [*i.e.*, counsels] of Hades " have *not* prevailed, intensely as they have striven.

It is a blessed thing to be in and a part of that work which shall abide for ever. For a man's work to go to pieces when he is withdrawn is no compliment to him. It only means that it was *man's* work, not God's. Like kingdoms, men rise and wane. Are we seeking to make a name for *ourselves*? This is very short-sighted, at best. The testimony to which God is reacting relates to a work which stands and persists when every destructive force has spent itself. This testimony, and such a work, are in virtue of the Blood of the Lord Jesus.

There are all kinds of alarms to-day because of rapid and drastic changes. Historic creeds are being treated as mere scraps of paper, and that by leading ecclesiastical representatives. Hoary institutions and traditions are rapidly losing their hold and influence. Organized Christianity is markedly on the wane. The maintenance of the religious system is demanding all the resource, acumen, wit, ingenuity and even cunning of men. There never were so many ' attractions ', schemes, popularising methods, etc., to keep up the ' church ' (?). Even in fairly evangelical quarters the appeals for help are so numerous that it is becoming— as someone has said—a matter of not being able to afford to go to church.

All this and much more speaks of failure and defeat, but the Lord will have that in the earth which is His triumph. To " contend earnestly for the faith which was once for all delivered unto the saints " (Jude 3) is something more than to contend for orthodoxy of doctrine ; to champion an evangelical creed ; to be a ' fundamentalist '. It is to recognise and fervently seek to secure for God that upon which His own heart is set : namely, a people of the Altar, the Cross, the Blood. A people who have been crucified with Christ in spiritual reality and apprehension, and whose life is an abiding testimony to Calvary's victory over all Christ's foes, within and without, and from whom there flows to the ends of the earth the stream of Divine, holy, mighty, energizing and indestructible life.

CHAPTER SIX

THE TESTIMONY OF THE BLOOD (continued)

There is nothing which Satan fears so terribly and contests so fiercely as a true and living testimony concerning the Blood of the Lord Jesus : not a teaching, doctrine, creed or phraseology, but that which is wrought out in the power of the Holy Spirit. It is therefore necessary for us to seek to recognise this fact, to understand, as far as we can, why it is so, and to know our position of victory because of the Blood. Unto this threefold apprehension we shall begin at the ultimate issue of the testimony, which is—

THE DIVINE SEED IN PROSPERITY AND SOVEREIGNTY.

It is this that Satan cannot bear to contemplate, and against which he is bitterly set, because it represents a menace to his kingdom at every point.

There is a very great significance attached to the introduction of the book of Exodus with " the names of the sons of Israel, who came into Egypt ". The title " sons of Israel" represents their dignity as sons of " a prince of God ". They came into Egypt and were in great prosperity and strength, while yet a separate and unabsorbed people. This dignity, prosperity and power came to be regarded as a distinct peril to the king of Egypt, and he projected a plan for humbling them, bringing them into bondage, and making them rather to contribute to his own prosperity and power.

Thus Exodus presents, firstly, God's mind concerning the princely dignity and spiritual prosperity and ascendency of the " sons " ; then the activity and object of the adversary concerning them ; and finally the Divine thought and intention established in the realm of " far above all rule and authority " in virtue of the shed blood of chapter xii. So then, sonship and sovereignty are the two factors present throughout. Sonship is the basic principle. Sovereignty is the issue involved in the conflict. The Blood is the instrument by which both are established. " These are the names of the sons of ' the Prince of God ' . . . " is the introduction. " Let my son go, that he may serve me ", is the challenge to Pharaoh ; and " Thou hast refused . . . behold, I will slay thy son ", is the sovereign factor at issue (Ex. iv. 23).

Now these elements are carried forward throughout all the Scriptures. It does not matter where you look : that which lies behind all the conflicts in the history of the people of God concerns the existence of a Divine seed in prosperity and power—spiritually—and the factor which is mainly involved is that of the altar and the blood. Everything hangs on that. This all heads up and finds its supreme expression in the Person and work of the Lord Jesus. As with Moses typically, so with Him anti-typically, there was the recognition of the one through whom this Divine seed would be constituted in its " authority . . . over all the power of the enemy " (Luke x. 19). So from birth a ' dead set ' was made for His destruction—not only by direct onslaught, but by subtle subterfuge to get Him to act upon a level of self by which the Divine protection would be forfeited.

The point at which we meet this whole matter of the testimony of the Blood is with—

AN ELECT IN BONDAGE.

There is abundant Scripture to show what was the original thought and intention of God for His spiritual seed, and this is a very important matter for the apprehension of the Lord's people. But what particularly concerns us now is its realisation. It is not a little impressive that of the twenty-seven 'books' of the New Testament at least twenty-one have to do with the bringing of the Lord's children into their right spiritual place. And how many of them are directly concerned with the matter of the actual or threatening loss of spiritual prosperity and ascendency through some form of bondage. There is the bondage of iniquity, of sin and sins, of the Law, of tradition, of fear, of the flesh, of the carnal mind, of reason, of the righteousness of the flesh, the wisdom of the flesh, the ' spirituality ' of the flesh, and many other forms of bondage. The bonds of Satan are very numerous, and he suits the kind to the case. A prince in chains, a member of the seed royal in servile oppression, is a pitiable sight, and this is what the Devil delights in. The " man-child ", whether individual as in Moses and Christ (Exodus i and Matthew ii), or corporate as in Revelation xii, is the object of the Dragon's venom. This is the Divine seed.

Think of the sons of the ' Prince of God ' engaged in building store-cities for Pharaoh, and thus adding wealth and glory to his world-system instead of serving the Lord in freedom and victory ! Such is the state of the elect, more or less. From the position of servitude to sin, self, the world and the Devil before salvation, through all the stages and phases of spiritual weakness and defeat to paralysing introspection and spiritual self-analysis, the true dignity of princeliness, of sonship, is assailed.

Now, if we did but know it, there is always some ground
for the bondage. Satan must have ground. His power cannot function without ground. He was utterly impotent in
the case of the Lord Jesus because there was no ground.
" The prince of the world cometh : and he hath nothing
in me " (John xiv. 30). The ground which issues in defeat
and bondage at the hands of the adversary is as varied as
the bondage itself.

Is it the natural condition of the sinfulness of human
nature, that what is in man is quite unfit and unsuitable
for the presence of God? Is it that the Divine will represents a standard of perfection in moral excellence which
sets back from God even the very best among men? Is it a
secret thing, hidden in the inward parts, which in itself becomes a weapon in the enemy's hand to knock us down?
Is it sin done in ignorance, where the intention was good,
but where fuller light reveals that it was wrong after all?
Is it sin unconsciously committed, in the sense that we did
not even know that we did the thing?

Yes, all these, and many more, are grounds that Satan
uses—and rightly so, if we fail in one all-embracing respect. This failure is in the matter of recognising the virtue
of the precious Blood, and the worth of Him who shed it.

In saying this we are but bringing into view the offerings of Exodus, Leviticus, and Numbers. A close study of
these offerings will reveal two things. One is that *God has
searched out sin and tracked it to its most hidden and
secret lair, even to the place of unconsciousness.* The acci-
dental, unwitting, and unsuspected is all taken into His
consideration. He regards sin now as a state, not merely as
a matter of a deliberate act. It is here, universal, operating
in innumerable ways and finding common ground of affection in the whole race. This all comes out so clearly

in a careful reading of Exodus, Leviticus, and Numbers.

But, having tracked sin to its remotest haunt, God has made provision for dealing with it to the very last suggestion.

(1) A *whole Burnt offering,* that the believer may stand accepted and perfect in relation to all the will of God (Col. iv. 12). (Lev. i. ; Heb. x.).

(2) A *Meal offering,* that he may be able to come into possession of moral perfection, not his own, but presented by faith. (Lev. ii. ; Rom. xii. 1, 2 ; Heb. x. 10 ; xiii. 21, etc.).

(3) A *Peace offering,* that there may be not only access and standing, but fellowship and oneness with God. (Lev. iii. ; Col. i. 20 ; Rom. v. 10, etc.).

(4) A *Sin offering,* that sin in its more positive aspects, and sin in ignorance and without consciousness, may not interfere with living fellowship by bringing in spiritual death, either through our own failure or through the contamination of contact. (Lev. iv, v, etc.).

And not only in the matter of our relationship with God does the Blood make an all-sufficient provision, but in co-operation with God by priestly ministry, in effective spiritual service in its many-sidedness.

So, then, the first and primary thing in a living testimony to the complete overthrow of the dominion of Satan and the destruction (bringing to nought) of his works is *a due and adequate apprehension and appreciation of the Lord Jesus in the value of His Blood.*

There is something almighty in the death of Jesus Christ. Many of God's people have failed to recognise the important distinction between His crucifixion and His death. The crucifixion is man's side. The death is His own.

All the crosses ever made, and all the men who ever conceived them, could never have brought about the death of the Lord Jesus, apart from His own voluntary act of laying down His life. " I lay down my life . . . No man taketh it from me . . . I lay it down of myself. I have power (jurisdiction) to lay it down, and I have power (jurisdiction) to take it again. This commandment have I received of my Father " (John x. 17, 18).

The preaching of Christ crucified is not the preaching merely of what men did to Him, but of what He *allowed* men to do, and, in and through *what they did, what He did*. The *death* of Christ, in its real meaning, is not man's act, nor is it the Devil's act. Satan and men had made many unsuccessful attempts to kill Him, but *His* hour had not come. *He* fixes the time for what *He* will do. The rulers said, " Not during the feast " (Mark xiv. 2), but the Lord Jesus took it out of their hands, and out of the hands of Judas, and precipitated it on that day in the Upper Room ; so deftly heading it up that Judas was as one under authority : " That thou doest, do quickly " (John xiii. 27).

When He ' lays down ' His life that He may ' take it again ', there is infinitude in the deliberate act, and it relates to universal sovereignty. Sin, as the principle ; the old creation, as the sphere ; Satan, as the ruler in that realm ; death, as the consequence ; and judgment, as the inevitable prospect and reality : all are involved in the death of Christ. That entire ground was dealt with, and that régime brought to an end, in that death. The whole thing centres in the Person of the Lord Jesus. The same person must be able both to act as representative of man rejected of God because of sin, and, as representative, receive all the judgment of God upon man and sin, and yet at the same time, because sin is not inherent in Him, but in Himself He is utterly sinless, render death and hell incapable of holding Him. There never was such an one, other than Jesus Christ: Son of man—Son of God.

The pouring out of His Blood was, on the one side, His voluntary yielding to wrath and destruction from the face of God, as Man for man; and, on the other side, a saying in effect to death, the Devil and the grave, ' I concede you all your claims unto the last atom, and exhaust all your demands, in being made sin and a curse. But you have another in Me also, over whom you have no power or rights, because you have no ground in him. You cannot hold Me—I defy you; and, what is more, I now take you as My prisoners. Henceforth I am your Lord, and I will plunder your domain and rob you of your spoil.'

" O death, where is thy victory? O death, where is thy sting?" (I Cor. xv. 55).

> ' Up from the grave He arose,
> With a mighty triumph o'er His foes ".

> ' . . . He invaded death's abode
> And robbed him of his sting '.

> ' . . . He hath crushed beneath His rod
> The world's proud rebel king.
> He plunged in His imperial strength
> To gulfs of darkness down,
> He brought His trophy up at length,
> The foiled usurper's crown '.

So He, because of His sinless perfection, can stand in complete acceptance with God, suitable to God, and this representatively as man (though more than man). His Blood, therefore, representing His sinless and victorious life, is given to us, and in virtue of it there is constituted that princely seed in all the good of His triumph. This does not make us sinlessly perfect, but He who is in us is so.

What remains to bring us into that good is a spiritual appreciation and apprehension of the transcendent greatness of the Lord Jesus, the Holy Spirit revealing Him in us; and then the link of faith unto obedience between what we are not and what He is. The bridge is faith. Some act as though it were struggle or puzzle, or any one of a number of things which are in the nature of self-effort. It will be found, indeed, that faith is no mere passive acquiescence. But it is not the *degree* of faith only, but the *object* of faith. It is, after all, the place which *Christ* has in the apprehension of His people which makes for the prosperity and ascendency which should characterize them. The supreme days of Israel's history were those when Christ in type was largest and most dominating. The Feast of the Passover was the focal point and the pivot. There never was such rejoicing as then; and, in later times, when idolatry had gained a strong footing, it was after the restoration of this feast that the people instinctively returned to destroy the false system.

Thus the testimony of the Blood is basic to victory, ascendency, and spiritual prosperity, and is the most deadly force against all the works of the adversary.

CHAPTER SEVEN

"A CANDLESTICK ALL OF GOLD"

W̲E̲ ̲A̲R̲E̲ ̲N̲O̲W̲ ̲G̲O̲I̲N̲G̲ ̲T̲O̲ ̲L̲O̲O̲K̲ at the fourth chapter of
Zechariah, which features in a remarkable way conditions
and Divine aims in the 'end times'. There are striking
similarities in it, as we shall see, to certain things mentioned in the first chapters of the Revelation. Its great
value lies in its concentrated presentation of essentials.
When you have these you have everything vital.

What first comes into view is—

AN ANGEL TALKING.

"The angel that talked with me" *(vv. 1, 4).* The
parallel to this in the Revelation is the phrase, seven times
repeated (note: seven = spiritual perfection, completeness):
"what the Spirit saith to the churches".

The Lord has something to say at the end. The book of
the Revelation is full of voices. It begins with: "I turned
to see the voice" (i. 12). A strange way of putting things!
Did anyone ever see a voice? There is, however, no mistake made. A vital reality is in this seeming error, as we
shall see. We have known much to be made of this

"voice" factor in the Bible. True as it is that God can make Himself vocal and audible, taking up men and articulating His thoughts through them, as He has ever done, we would point out that in this case it is not the voice of man; indeed, it is not primarily the voice at all. It is that God has something to say, and a very important something.

The most pertinent question that can possibly be asked at this time is—

WHAT IS GOD SAYING TO-DAY ?

A striking feature of our time is that so few of the voices have a distinctive message. There is a painful lack of a clear word of authority for the times. While there are many good preachers of the Gospel, and while we are not without champions of the vital verities of the Faith, we are sadly in need of the Prophet with his "Thus saith the Lord", which he has received in a commission born of a peculiarly chastened fellowship with God.

Why is it so? May it not be that so many who might have this ministry have become so much a part of a system: a system which puts preachers so largely upon a professional basis, the effect of which is to make preaching a matter of demand and supply; of providing for the established religious order and programme? And not only in the matter of preaching, but in the whole organization and activity of 'Christianity' as we have it in the systematized form to-day. There is not the freedom and detachment for speaking ONLY when "the burden of the word of the Lord" is upon the prophet, or when he could say: "The hand of the Lord was upon me". The present order requires a man to speak every so often:

hence he *must* get something, and this necessity means either that God must be offered our programme and asked to meet it (which He will not do), or that the preacher must *make* something for the constantly recurring occasion.

This is a pernicious system, and it opens the door to many dangerous and baneful intrusions of what is of man and not of God. The most serious aspect of this way of things is that it results in voices, voices, voices—a *confusion* of voices—but not the specific voice with the specific utterance of God for the time. Too often it has the effect of causing men to hear and read just with a view to getting preaching matter, subjects for sermons ; the value of things is judged by their suggestiveness of themes. The man may be a godly man and the message may be the truth, but there is something more than this—is it *the* message which relates to the immediate time-appointed purpose of God? There are many good men who are giving out what they know and believe of the truth, but at the same time there are many of the Lord's children who are hungry and not being fed.

The food question amongst the Lord's people to-day is a very acute one, and a more or less good ministry is not going to meet the need. There is a growing concern to know, as distinct from the generalisations of truth and service, what is the Lord's word for now, where we are, and what in the Divine purpose belongs to this present hour.

This brings us back to the first thing in our chapter : God has something to say ; but it also leads us to the next thing : "The Angel that talked with me came again, and *waked me, as a man that is wakened out of his sleep*". Here we have the necessity for—

AN AWAKENING TO WHAT GOD HAS TO SAY.

In the Revelation this is : " He that hath an ear, let him hear ", and in the case of Laodicea—which represents the end—it is : " I counsel thee to buy of me . . . eyesalve . . . that thou mayest see " (Rev. iii. 18). " I turned to *see* the voice which spake with me ", said John. God is speaking ; He has something to say ; but there must be " a spirit of wisdom and revelation in the knowledge of him ; having the eyes of your heart enlightened " (Eph. i. 17, 18).

Spiritual discernment, perception, understanding and intelligence are all too rare. The causes are many. The engrossment with the work and its multifarious concerns ; the rush and hurry of life ; the restless spirit of the age : these, with an exhaustive provision of external religious facilities, all tend to render the inner place of Divine speaking inoperative or impossible of functioning. Perhaps we have forgotten that the Bible not only *is* a revelation, but also *contains* a revelation, and that that deeper spiritual content is only possible of recognition and realisation by such as have had their eyes and ears opened ; in other words, by those who have been awakened. Some of the Lord's most faithful servants are still only occupied with the letter of the Word, the contents of books, topics, themes, subjects, outlines, analyses, etc., and are not, *in the deepest sense*, in spiritual understanding. (This is not meant as a criticism.) The difference too often is that between a ministry to the mind or head, and one to the heart or spirit. The former will sooner or later tire and weary both the minister and those ministered to. The latter is a ministry of life to both, and is inexhaustible in freshness.

Whether it comes at the beginning or later, it is the greatest day in our history of which we can say : " It pleased God . . . to reveal his Son IN me ". ' I received it, not from man . . . but by revelation of Jesus Christ ' (Gal. i. 15, 16 ; 12). That is the beginning of an inwardness of things which may have many critical issues. One of these is that of which we are particularly thinking now, namely, the awakening to see what is the thought and desire of God at given and specific times. Such a revelation—through the Scriptures—is nothing less than revolutionary, and usually costly.

Would to God that there was an adequate number at this time who, like the men of Issachar, " had understanding of the times " (I Chron. xii. 32).

We now proceed to see what comes into view when God's instrument is awakened, and is able to answer the heavenly interrogation : *" What seest thou ?"*

" BEHOLD, A CANDLESTICK ALL OF GOLD "

Every ministry in the Scriptures appointed by God was constituted upon something having been *seen*. The test of a Divine commission may be found in this question, " What seest thou ?", and the answer, upon the basis of God having shown something very concrete, may well provide the credentials. It is not the matter of winning the sermon or winning the audience, but declaring the truth for the time as it has been made a fire in the bones. It would be pertinent, rather than impertinent, to challenge the servants of God with this question, relative to the time in which they live, and relative to the immediate concern of God—" What seest thou ?"

There is no doubt that what God has seen at all times as His objective is " a candlestick all of gold ", but from time to time there has been a special necessity for Him to bring it into the view of the people, and especially of His prophets. It is for this that He reacts, and the end-time must see a renewal of His reaction.

Now, ignoring the fact that there is a difference between the seven-branched candlestick or lampstand of the Old Testament, and the seven lampstands of the Apocalypse, there is a relationship of the two in a common principle. That common principle is that they both represent—

THE INSTRUMENT OF THE TESTIMONY IN THE HOUSE OF GOD.

While that innermost light of the Most Holy Place—the light of Christ in the presence of God—remains undimmed and inviolate, there is that which is midway between Heaven and earth—the Holy Place—where the testimony has to be kept clear both Godward and manward. Concerning this—as differing from the other—God has given very careful and explicit instructions and injunctions for its perpetual maintenance. He is peculiarly jealous over this testimony. Thus, we find that it is here, in the sphere of this, that the prayer-life (Altar of incense) and the feeding-fellowship (Table of shewbread) of the Lord's people have their true value and vitality.

The instructions for the making of the Candlestick in Exodus xxv and xxxvii are full of the richest significance. First in these is the material—" pure gold ". If it is to have a *sevenfold* fulness, intensity and expression, which refers to spiritual completeness, then it must be pre-eminently suitable to the Divine purpose. The meaning of the " all of gold ", then, is that it is—

ABSOLUTELY ACCORDING TO GOD.

Be sure to get the force of this : an instrument of the testimony wholly according to God! There is only One who is thus wholly according to God's mind and heart—the Lord Jesus, and if the whole Tabernacle in every part came firstly from God and then was Christ in type throughout, then this lampstand speaks of a vessel of the testimony of God in which the Lord Jesus is absolute and complete. God would have everything according to Christ. This fact governs the whole revelation in the Scriptures, from Genesis to Revelation. It is typified and prophesied in the Old Testament. It is presented in the Gospels ; demonstrated in the Acts ; defined in the Epistles ; and consummated in the Revelation. But, alas, what a tragic and heart-breaking history is associated with this fact, and how difficult has it ever been to get anything wholly according to Christ.

In an earlier chapter we saw God's reactions to this in Bible times, and suggested that since then He has again and again so reacted.

The Reformation was such a reaction, and by it He recovered the great foundational truth of Justification by Faith ; which puts Christ into His absolute place as the Chief Corner-stone of the House of God. It was a grand thing, though very costly. But all too soon men pulled it down to the earth, and the ' Protestant Church ' as such issued ; a tree in the branches of which almost every kind of credal bird can lodge. Protestantism, as such, is by no means a synonym for what is wholly according to Christ.

Since then the reactions of the Lord have been seen in many other instances.

The Moravian Brethren, through a great fight and affliction, were used to recover the great truth of the Church's responsibility for the testimony of Jesus in all the nations. Not the responsibility of a missionary society or adjunct to the Church, but of the Church itself directly. This was, and is, wholly according to Christ. But again, human hands mould this movement into a ' church ', with all the outward elements of a religious order. There is no question but that there has been considerable spiritual loss.

A further reaction of God was seen in the Wesleys and Whitfield. Here, in addition to a mighty recovering of soul-saving evangelism, there was the recovery of the doctrine of practical holiness. This was grand while the instrument remained ; but, alas, there came those human hands again, and an earthly organizing into a system—' the Wesleyan Church '. We are perfectly sure that Wesley would not have wished this.

Then about a hundred years ago, there was what all ought to recognise as a movement of God in the shape of the ' Plymouth Brethren '. There were several most precious recoveries made in this instance. The Lord Jesus was given an exclusive place which was not common in those days, nor is it common now. The great truth concerning the Body of Christ—the One Church—was brought again into view, after perhaps centuries of obscurity. God was in this, and is still in it, but the most ardent devotee to this community is both grieved and ashamed to contemplate its divisions to-day. Is it that men have again been insinuated or have insinuated themselves? Has this, like so much more, been taken into the governing hands of men? Has that subjective work of the Cross, by which in a very deep way man is cut off and the Holy Spirit governs, failed of adequate application or acceptance here? These are questions, not charges ; we are seeking to speak, not destructively, but constructively.

Many more are the reactions of God through the past nineteen centuries ; we only use these by way of illustration. It will be seen that each fresh movement was an advance upon those that preceded it in the matter of truth recovered : from the Divine standpoint it was a movement nearer to the original position. The big question which at once arises is : Will the Lord do a new thing yet? Are we to know of a fresh reaction to His first position? The only answer we can give to this question is that, whether or not there should be anything in the nature of a ' movement ', as open to general recognition, we are certain that there is a more or less hidden movement on the part of the Spirit of God, working through deepening dissatisfaction with things as they are toward that which is nearer the original thought than has been since the beginning. It will be such a thing as cannot be ' joined ' by men, but in which only those will share who are moved by deep inward exercise, so that it becomes a matter of a common spiritual travail.

What next comes before us in Zechariah's vision, which is more than Jewish, but has that invariable double application of Old Testament revelation, is—

THE TWO OLIVE TREES AND THE TWO ANOINTED ONES.

The symbolism here is familiar. Two is the number of testimony or witness. Trees are very often symbolic of man as witness, or men as witnesses. The olive, as is apparent in this chapter, especially relates to the oil. The position of these two trees is on either side of the candlestick. From verse 14 we learn that *"These are the two anointed ones (sons of oil), that stand by the Lord of the whole earth"*.

F

There is no doubt that the two olive trees bring into view, firstly and historically, Joshua the High Priest and Zerubbabel the Governor. Chapter iii deals with the one and chapter iv with the other. The first discourse concerned the High Priesthood and its ministry; the second (iv. 1) concerns the Government or sovereignty. This, interpreted prophetically, relates to the Lord Jesus. His High Priestly work and position come first into view, and are established in glory; then He is established by God as Lord and Sovereign Head. On these two sides of His one Person He ever gives the meaning of the candlestick: that is, He defines the nature of its vocation, and supplies the unfailing resource for that testimony. It is, as we have said, constituted according to Christ, and maintained by Him in all the fulness of His anointing.

The Divine explanation of this is: *"This is the word of Jehovah unto Zerubbabel, saying, Not by might, nor by power, but by my Spirit, saith the Lord of Hosts"* *(verse 6)*. Here we reach the central meaning of the vision as to the execution of the purpose of God. It speaks for itself. Its clear affirmation is that this instrument and this testimony must be utterly in the hands of the Holy Spirit. Not might, nor power, of brain, will, emotion, organization, machinery, committee, influence, reputation, numbers, name, personality, outfit, enthusiasm, etc., but solely the Holy Spirit! The accounting for this will never be, *in truth*—whatever superficial observers may say—attributable to any human force or resource, but all who have any spiritual intelligence will have to recognise that its energy and power is Divine. This will also be proved by its endurance and persistence through the intense fires of opposition and antagonism.

Here the Holy Spirit is allowed to govern and dictate,

to direct and choose or reject, just as in the " Acts " at the beginning. To have such an instrument and such a testimony there will need to be a very revolutionary re-shaping of ideas. It will be necessary to realise that all those things, upon which men have come to count as most important factors in the Lord's work, are really not necessary factors at all. It will have to be recognised that education, personal ability, business ability, worldly wisdom, money, etc., *as such* have nothing to do with the work of the Holy Spirit or with Christianity. The Lord may use these, call them in, and if they are kept in their right place they may serve Him greatly ; but they are secondary, and He can easily dispense with them. It is of infinitely greater importance and value that men should be filled with the Holy Spirit, and if a choice is to be made, this should ever be the very first consideration. There is a wisdom, judgment, discernment, knowledge, understanding by the Holy Spirit which alone is equal to the demands of that which is to be wholly according to God.

Thus the Lord Jesus, as the Great Mediator and Sovereign Head, would maintain His testimony wholly in accordance with His own nature and mind in the fulness of the Spirit of His own anointing. When things are thus there is no need to be unduly oppressed by—

THE GREAT MOUNTAIN.

" Who art thou, O great mountain? before Zerubbabel thou shalt become a plain " (verse 7). The mountain is a figure of the accumulation of difficulties. The completing of the House of God will be no less fraught with difficulty and obstruction than the commencement ; but, as then, so at the end, where the Holy Spirit is absolute Lord, these

difficulties will be proved rather complementary than otherwise. The " many adversaries " will only be sovereignly used to further, rather than arrest, the consummation of " the eternal purpose ".

" *The hands of Zerubbabel have laid the foundation of this house ; his hands shall also finish it* " *(verse 9)*. The Greater Zerubbabel laid those foundations at Pentecost. The finishing will be by His hands alone. The same glorious Lord Jesus will " bring forth the topstone with shoutings of Grace, grace, unto it ".

Then there is presented for our contemplation, by way of an interrogation, a matter which is indeed very challenging—

THE DAY OF SMALL THINGS.

" *Who hath despised the day of small things?* " *(verse 10)*. There is amongst the Lord's people in these days an unhealthy lust for big things. Something to attract attention ; a demonstration to capture, an appearance to impress. Big names, big places, big titles, big sounds, big movements, big sweeps ! If the dimensions are big according to men's standards, the success is judged accordingly.

In order to obtain and maintain that which will preserve the recognition of wholly Divine factors, God has ever found it necessary to reduce. End-times are always days of small things : see the testimony in the Revelation —it is only represented by the few who ' overcome '. Bigness is material or temporal. Greatness is spiritual and eternal. Too often men—even Christians—despise that in which God delights. The significance of things according to God is so often seen in an " upper room ", as over against the whole city, but the city succumbs to the upper room. When dealing with the "world rulers of this darkness" the Lord has frequently made an upper room His Throne-room.

"*These seven eyes of Jehovah shall rejoice when they see the plummet in the hand of Zerubbabel*" *(verse 10).* What is this? The seven eyes symbolize the perfection of spiritual vision, which takes in everything as it is. The plummet is that by which crookedness is brought to light and made manifest. When Jehovah sees the Lord Jesus with that instrument in His hand, which so represents His own standard that by it He can correct all that deviates, and expose all the unsuspected leanings, bulgings, angles, and dangers of that which is related to His House ; when He has that instrument by which He can make manifest how His House should be built according to Christ—then His perfect spiritual vision will rejoice and be satisfied. This is what He needs. O, that we might be to Him such an instrument ! It will not be a popular ministry ; it will cost ; but it will be precious to the Lord.

As we close, let us just note the names of the Lord in this chapter. The purpose as in view is related to *Jehovah* —the Almighty, Eternally Self-Sufficient One (verses 6, 10). The executing and sufficiency of the purpose is related to *Jehovah-Sabaoth*—the Lord of Hosts (verse 6). The place of the testimony is related to *Adon*—Master, or Lord (verse 14) ; that is, He who owns and has the rights of proprietorship.

CHAPTER EIGHT

"GATHER MY SAINTS TOGETHER"

" *Gather my saints together unto me ; those that have made a covenant with me by sacrifice* " *(Psalm i. 4).*

" *Now we beseech you, brethren, touching the coming of our Lord Jesus Christ, and our gathering together unto him . . .*" *(II Thess. ii. 1).*

" *Not forsaking our own assembling together, as the custom of some is, but exhorting one another ; and so much the more, as ye see the day drawing nigh* " *(Hebrews x. 25).*

IN ALL OF THE ABOVE PASSAGES there is one common factor : namely, that an end-time movement and feature is dominant. It must be remembered that the Psalms themselves represent what remains when a history of outward things, as to the general instrumentality, has ended in failure. The history of Israel in its first great phase closed with the book of Kings in a calamitous and shameful way. Weakness, paralysis, declension, reproach, characterized the instrument in general. But out of that history now so concluded the Psalms are carried forward, as that which represents permanent spiritual gain.

This is pre-eminently a personal, inward spiritual knowledge of the Lord, gained through experience. That is why they always reach the heart and never fail to touch experience at every point. To them the saints have turned in times of deep experience. They are the ministry of experience to experience—the only ministry which is permanent. The end-time instrument will always be that which knows the Lord in a deep, inward, living way, through a history fraught with much experience of the heights and depths.

What David gave to the Chief Musician for the wind instruments and the stringed instruments touches the highest and deepest notes of a mortal's knowledge of God. Worship, Salvation, Sorrow, Appeal, Victory, Battle, Faith, Hope, Glory, Instruction, are great themes interwoven with the mass of matters touched ; but the point is that all came in *real life*—he passed through it all. It is this, and this alone, which can serve the Lord when what He first raised up has failed Him as a public instrument. So the Lord would take pains to secure this, and this may explain much of the suffering and sorrow through which He takes His chosen vessels.

The Psalms form only one of the four books born of the history of Israel, each of which has its own feature to contribute to that which represents the permanent work of God, but especially as relating to an instrument of Divine reaction. But the Psalms show clearly where God begins and what in principle is basic to the first and most abiding work of God.

It does not need pointing out that, in the other two passages with which we commenced, the end-time is in view ; they definitely state it. There is a further common feature of the three, however, which is more particularly the subject before us. They all definitely refer to *gathering together* as something related to the end-time.

A history of a religious system, born out of something

which the Lord raised up in the first place, has ended in weakness, chaos and shame. Therefore, there is to be a re-gathering to the Lord of His saints.

The Lord is coming, and there is a gathering to Him.

The Day is drawing nigh: therefore there is to be a " so much the more " assembling together.

THE PARTICIPANTS IN THE GATHERING

Before we deal with the nature of this end-time gathering, we must have clearly in view those that are concerned in it. The passage in the Psalm would embrace and include those referred to in the other two passages.

" My saints . . . those that have made a covenant with me by sacrifice."

It need hardly be remarked that, when all has been said and done through type, symbol and figure, the covenant means an entering into what the Lord Jesus has done by His shed Blood. It is an appreciation and apprehension of Him in His great work by the Cross. But we need to be reminded of what that involves as a covenant of God into which we enter. It is a theme which demands a book to itself. In order to reduce it to a few lines, let us consider a concrete instance. We find a conspicuous illustration of this matter in the life of Abram, as recorded in Genesis, chapters xv and xxii.

In chapter xv we have the basis of a covenant concerning Abram's seed. Firstly, there is the comprehensive inclusion of the offerings which came in later in Leviticus: a heifer, a goat, a ram, a turtle-dove and a pigeon. These—with the exception of the birds—were divided in the midst, and laid one half on this side and the other half on that side. These were the two sides of the covenant, God's and

Abram's. Later we see a flaming torch passing between the two halves (verse 17).

Now, it is clear that Abram knew what this all meant. He realised that it involved him in something. God was saying quite clearly that He was wholly for Abram, that all that He was and had was being committed to this covenant. He would keep nothing back from him, but would, so to speak, place His very life, honour, name, glory, to the good of His word to Abram. This was adequately proved in the long run when He became incarnate in the seed of Abraham for universal blessing. But there were two sides to the covenant, and Abram understood this. He also was handing himself over to God with all that he was and had, to the very dearest possession, and if need be, to death. That burning torch—that Fire of the Spirit—sealed the oneness of the consecration or devotion of each to the other.

Now this explains chapter xxii. By that time Isaac was born and had grown out of childhood. He had taken his place, and was to Abraham what a first-born son is to his father in the East. But he was more, because of the miracle of his birth and the long-deferred hope. He was everything to Abraham—more than life itself. All his father's hopes, expectations, vindications, promises and Divine assurances were bound up with him. Accordingly—

" *It came to pass after these things, that God did* PROVE *Abraham, and said unto him, Abraham ; and he said, Here am I. And he said, Take now thy son, thine only son, whom thou lovest, even Isaac . . . and offer him . . . for a burnt offering . . .* "

This 'proving' was concerning the covenant. Did Abram mean his part of it? Would he stand to it? Did he so utterly believe that God would be faithful to His part that, no matter what happened to Isaac, God could be trusted and His promise would be fulfilled? What a test! But "Abraham believed God" (Rom. iv. 3). His faith in God enabled him to stand by his part of the covenant, and "he wavered not" (iv. 20).

The issue was that, when Isaac had *virtually* been offered, the Lord said to him: *"Now I know that thou fearest God, seeing thou hast not withheld thy son, thine only son, from me"* (Gen. xxii. 12).

And then the Lord came in with His oath: *"By myself have I sworn . . . because thou hast done this thing, and hast not withheld thy son, thine only son: that in blessing I will bless thee, and in multiplying I will multiply thy seed as the stars of the heaven . . ." (verses 16 — 18).*

Do we now see the meaning of 'a covenant by sacrifice'? Then we shall see who it is that will be in this 'gathering together'. It will certainly be only those to whom the Lord is everything, to whom He is all and in all; those who are all for the Lord without reservation, without personal interest, without anything less or other than Himself. Spiritual oneness is only possible on this basis.

The Lord's word at the end to Abraham was: "Now I know that thou fearest God". Malachi's end-time word was: "Then they that feared the Lord . . ." (iii. 16). The fear of the Lord is an utter abandonment to Him, at any cost. It is His will being supreme, claiming and obtaining the measure of a whole burnt-offering.

THE NATURE OF THE GATHERING

Being, then, clear as to *who* are concerned—and that constitutes a test, even as they constitute a testimony—we are able to look at the nature of the 'gathering together'.

We are well aware that there is a widespread doubt as to whether we are to expect anything in the way of a corporate movement or testimony at the end. Indeed, it is strongly held by some that everything at the end is individual—a conviction that rests, for the most part, upon the use of the phrase, " If any man . . .", in the message to Laodicea (Rev. iii. 20).

Let us hasten to say, then, that we have nothing in mind in the nature of an organized movement, a sect, a society, or a fraternity.

Having said this, however, there are some things which need saying quite definitely on the other side.

The Church of the New Testament never was an organized movement. Neither was there any organized affiliation of the companies of believers in various places with one another. It was a purely spiritual thing, spontaneous in life, united only by the Holy Spirit in mutual love and spiritual solicitude. There were other factors that acted as spiritual links, which we will mention presently. Further, and still more important, there was the abiding fact that a ' Body ' had been brought into being. This is called ' The Body of Christ '. You can divide a society and still it remains, but you cannot divide a body without destroying the entity.

Are we to understand from the exponents of the individualistic interpretation that all the teaching of the Lord, in nearly all the Scriptures concerning the House of God, and concerning the Body of Christ in nearly all the letters of Paul, is now set aside or is only an idea without any expression on the earth? Are we to blot out the mass of the New Testament and live our own individual Christian lives with no emphasis upon working fellowship with other believers? Surely not. This would be contrary to all the ways of God in history, and would certainly spell defeat, for if there is one thing against which the adversary has set himself it is the fellowship of God's people. Ultra-individualism is impossible if the truth of the ' One Body ' still stands. What is more, the Lord's people are becoming more and more conscious of their absolute need of fellowship, especially in prayer. The difficulty of ' getting through ' alone in prayer is becoming greater as we approach the end.

What, then, is the nature of this ' gathering together '?

(1)   " UNTO HIM "

It is a gathering to the Lord Himself.

" Gather my saints together *unto me . . .* "

" Our gathering *unto Him . . .* "

In times past there have been gatherings to men, great preachers, great teachers, great leaders ; or to great institutions and movements, centres and teachings. This is not now the Lord's way. Not that men sought to draw to themselves, or that the Lord was not reached through them, but people have a way of making a greatly used servant of God the object of attraction.

God's End is Christ, and as we get nearer the end He must take the place even of instrumentalities and become almost immediately the only object of appreciation. Our oneness and fellowship is not in a teaching, a ' testimony ', a community or a place, but in a Person, and in Him not merely doctrinally, but livingly and experimentally. Any movement truly of God must, as its supreme and all-inclusive feature, confess that it is the Lord Jesus alone who is the object of heart adoration and worship: not things, themes, experiences, but the Lord Jesus Himself.

(2) PRAYER-FELLOWSHIP

This gathering is a gathering together in prayer-fellowship. One of the last things said in the Epistle which presents for all time and eternity the true nature of the Church as the Body of Christ—the Epistle to the Ephesians—is :
" Praying at all seasons in the Spirit . . . *for all the saints*" (Eph. vi. 18).

If the first thing in spiritual gathering together is " holding fast the Head " (Col. ii. 19), or having the Lord Jesus as the centre, the second thing is prayer-fellowship with and for all the saints. " Gather my *saints* together." This is geographically impossible of full realisation, but it is spiritually possible by prayer. There is no space or time in the realm of prayer. A deep and travailing concern in prayer for the spiritual well-being of all the saints has ever marked an end-time movement of God ; not alone for those who were true and faithful, and had gone all the way with God ; but for *all* the people of God—although such as were more immediately the objects of Satanic malice, by reason of their faithfulness, might provoke a special cry to the Throne.

What we see is the Lord having a prayer-instrument in every end-time, when total destruction threatens that which represents Him. And the very burden of prayer which He lays upon His own in every part of the world is His way of uniting. If we prayed more for all saints we should find many of the things which divide—and wrongly divide—falling away and ceasing to do so. Prayer is a wonderfully ' gathering ' factor.

(3) SPIRITUAL FOOD

Another great factor in gathering spiritually is food. The Old Testament brings before us many an instance of fellowship by feasting. Indeed, feasts were the nature of the fellowship, although not the occasion of it.

The New Testament takes up the spiritual principle, and the Lord Jesus makes the ' breaking of bread ' not only the remembering and proclaiming of His death and Himself, but the testimony of the ' one Loaf—one Body '. The Lord's Supper is represented as food and fellowship.

In the first years of the Church, Christ was ministered to the saints by the Holy Spirit through ministering servants who moved from place to place. It was thus that the saints were brought into fellowship with one another. Not—let us say again—by an organized affiliation, but by a ministration of Christ through His Word in the Spirit. The ministers were " joints of supply " (Eph. iv. 16).

It is all too obvious a thing to say that to-day there is a very real hunger amongst the Lord's people. They are not being fed. What so many of them are getting is not ' bread '. In every part of the world there are such hungry ones ; one here, another there ; a little company in one place, another in another, and often unknown to each other. The persistent and perplexing question asked almost everywhere is : ' What are we to do? There is no spiritual food where we are.'

(4) MINISTRY

Will not the Lord raise up a ministry to these? We are persuaded that He will, and that He is now seeking to do so. A method of gathering together according to Christ will be that a ministration of Christ is sent forth and the hungry will be found gathered in spite of everything. For as there is a dissatisfaction with the religious systems of the day on the part of so many who want to go on with the Lord, so there is springing up in the hearts of many of

God's servants a longing to be free to minister to the saints irrespective of traditional ties and distinctions.

There is no mistaking the fact that this matter of food as a uniting factor was ministered to the churches through anointed ministries. In the book of the Acts we see how the scattered churches were held together largely through the ministries of servants of God who were qualified to ' build ' the body corporate. They were everywhere recognised, accepted and honoured, and they were in a very large way a substitute for organized affiliation, government and centralisation. As the individual members of Christ form one corporate Body, so the individual churches were like corporate members of the whole corporate Body, and there was great gain to all by corporate ministries passing between them.

This all has its own perils, but we cannot fail to see the movement of God at the present day, and it is a gathering movement—to Himself.

The passage in Hebrews (x. 25) specifically has the local assembling in view. No one can deny that this is the Divine order. The Lord desires to have in every place a representation of and a testimony to His House. His will is to have all such constituted according to Christ. But only the Holy Spirit can do this constituting. We cannot take a new Testament mould and pour people and places into it. We must come into it by the Spirit. This necessitates that the Holy Spirit have absolute sovereignty, clearness and right-of-way ; and this, in turn, requires that the flesh be crucified and man be absolutely subject to Christ.

We see nothing in Scripture to lead us to conclude that this can never again be. It may be a " day of small things ", but in the hands of God such days are mightier than all the great movements of men.

PART TWO

GOD'S METHODS AND
MEANS OF RECOVERY

CHAPTER ONE

THE REINFORCEMENT OF SPIRITUALITY

In the life of the people of god, whether
individually or corporately, there constantly occur times of
crisis, or turning-points. The Old Testament describes
many such times of particular and peculiar peril in the life
of the Lord's people, and shows how God has moved to
meet the situation at such times. This has been true also in
the history of the Church, again and again, ever since New
Testament times ; and it is true in the life of any local
company of the Lord's people. When, for some reason,
conditions are critical, and a turning-point has been
reached, at such a time it is very important to know how
the Lord would meet the situation and the need.

THE CORNER BOARDS OF THE TABERNACLE

May I remind you of a provision which the Lord made
in the construction of the Tabernacle in the wilderness?
The Lord gave instructions that, in the erection of the
boards of the Tabernacle, at the corners there should be an
extra board, reinforcing the turning-points. Of course,
corners are always delicate things, perilous things ; turning-
points are always fraught with great possibilities. You come
up to a point where a turn is going to made, a new course
is going to be followed, and that turning-point needs to be
negotiated with much wisdom and care. Something extra
must come in there to cover it. And in that infinite wisdom

99

of God—the recognition not only of the weakness of a corner in natural things, but of the perils connected with turning-points in spiritual life—the Lord made and makes a provision ; He covers it, prescribes for it. As in the boards of the Tabernacle, there must be some real reinforcement at that delicate and dangerous point of crisis.

Let us just dwell for a moment or two upon the Tabernacle ; we shall come back to it again presently. You know that it was, in type, the shrine of God's testimony. It is called the " Tabernacle of testimony ", or " The Testimony ". In type it was what Paul, in his letter to the Colossians, calls " the mystery of Christ "—the shrine of the mystery of Christ into which no natural eyes may peer. And in this shrine of the testimony of God concerning His Son, Jesus Christ, there are these turning-points ; and because this testimony is involved, they are, as we have said, always precarious places and times. If something goes wrong here, if something goes wrong at this juncture, it is going to have very serious effects in the future. The next phase of things is going to be affected by what happens as we turn this corner, by just how far we negotiate this present difficult situation—whether in our lives, or in the work of God, or in the history of the Lord's people, locally or generally. The future is involved.

We have come up to this point : here are the boards all leading up to it, and from this point onwards a new course has to be taken ; but oh, this new course has got to be very, very carefully safeguarded. All that has been in the past, all the labour, the work, the suffering and the cost, may be hazarded at a point of crisis by any weakness or lack of care, when we come to this issue. All the future may be made unsafe, weak, clouded by regrets, if this turning-point is unguarded.

PAUL'S LETTERS TO TIMOTHY: A CRITICAL POINT

Now it is with such a turning-point in the Church's history, and with the Lord's way of handling it, that we are confronted when we take up Paul's two letters to Timothy. We find ourselves at one of the major turning-points in the history of the Church—a turning-point fraught with momentous issues ; and those issues have thrown their shadows right down the centuries to the present day. We need to know what was God's provision—which remains as His provision—to meet that which came in at the turn of the road then. For the values that we have given us here in these two letters—and you will never call them ' little ' letters again, if ever you have—were meant to cover this whole age, because the Holy Spirit, who gave these letters through Paul, foresaw the far-reaching effects of what was happening. And what is of general and comprehensive importance here has its own application to all those minor crises that occur in our own personal lives, or in our life together as God's people.

Such a crisis, then, was the occasion of Paul writing these two letters to Timothy. And may I say again, for I do want to make clear this very, very important thing : this is an inclusive and comprehensive example of all crises in the spiritual life, an example in principle and in nature : that is, it has all the features of any spiritual crisis, and it there- fore contains all God's method and means of meeting any spiritual crisis. We are not just dealing with Church history—we are dealing with our own history. We need to be met at that very point in our own spiritual lives.

Inclusively, then, the Divine method of meeting any critical situation is—what? It is *the reinforcement of fundamental and essential realities*. That is what these two letters contain. The reinforcement of the boards at the corner, in the re-*in*forcement—and *en*forcement, if you like, for Paul commands here, as well as exhorts—of fundamental and essential realities, is God's inclusive method of dealing with any threat, or any possibility, or any actual change in the course of things. And there is one all-comprehending fundamental of true Christianity, and that is spirituality—its essentially spiritual nature. So that God's method in meeting any critical situation in the Christian life is to reinforce, or to recover, spirituality.

CHRISTIANITY WHOLLY SPIRITUAL

For true Christianity, from its very beginning, through all its growth, to its final perfecting, is wholly spiritual. A true Christian is fundamentally and essentially, by his very being and existence, a spiritual person. All our growth in grace is not the growth of time, of years, or of the acquiring of knowledge about the things of God. True growth is just our own spiritual growth, and before God there is no other stature, no other growth. God takes infinite pains to see that our growth is spiritual growth. And the consummation and the perfecting of the life of the Christian is a wholly spiritual thing. For the consummation is a spiritual body. " If there is a natural body, there is also a spiritual body . . . that is not first which is spiritual, but that which is natural " (I Cor. xv. 44, 45). Those words, as you know, apply to the resurrection body. " It is sown a natural body ; it is raised a spiritual body " (vs. 44). So it needs a spiritual person to occupy a spiritual body ; and if the spiritual body is the consummation of the Christian life, then the Lord would have, not a poor, little spiritual person occupying a consummate body ; He would have us full-grown, so that the perfecting of the Christian life is in keeping with its consummation : it must be spiritual.

Everything else in the Christian life is spiritual. As the people are spiritual people by their very birth by the Spirit, so their work and service are spiritual. It is not a matter only of how many things we do, but of the spiritual quality of what we do. There can be tremendous spiritual value intrinsically in a ' small ' thing done in the Holy Spirit, while very little may come of a vast amount of feverish activity in what is called Christian work. Everything is judged in Heaven by its spiritual value. The warfare is spiritual ; you have no need to be reminded of that. " Our wrestling is not against flesh and blood, but . . . against the spiritual hosts of wickedness . . . " (Eph. vi. 12). Our knowledge and our understanding as Christians are spiritual. Our fellowship is spiritual—our relationship with one another is a spiritual relationship, in the unity of the Spirit.

All government amongst Christians is spiritual. It is not autocratic, it is not official—it is spiritual. Very, very few Christians to-day are able to discern and discriminate between human government and spiritual government in the House of God. They confuse the two, and thereby bring in many, many complications. Government in the Christian realm is spiritual government. Guidance is spiritual guidance—" led by the Spirit " (Rom. viii. 14). The methods and resources of the Church, of Christians, are spiritual methods and resources. All this makes up the comprehensive truth that the fundamental reality of the true Christian life is spirituality: that is, that it is all of the Holy Spirit.

In one of the closing chapters of the prophecies of Ezekiel (xlvii. 1 — 12), there is brought into view the river —the river rising in the sanctuary, broadening and deepening on its way—and on its banks trees, bearing fruit every season, and the leaf unfading. I believe that to be a fore-shadowing, a pre-figuring, of what we have in the book of the Acts. The trees are men, planted by God, drawing their life from the river of God. How that river broke out in the sanctuary in the days of the ' Acts ' ! And how we see the men planted then by God on the banks of that river ; and the fruit—how abundant was the fruit ! Trees, sustained by heavenly life, carrying on a heavenly testimony : in a word, spiritual people, men and women whose life and resource and everything was the Spirit of God—for it was the Spirit of God who broke out in the sanctuary on the day of Pentecost. God's testimony down the whole course of the river requires spiritual people, drawing upon spiritual resources, and that is what we have there.

SPIRITUALITY MUST BE RECOVERED OR REINFORCED

Now, all the troubles inside of Christianity—and ' Christianity ' is a big term, it comprehends a very great deal ; you can localise it and personalise it, if you like—all the troubles in Christianity are due to loss or lack of spirituality. God's method, ever and always, in getting over some trouble in us, whether personally or together, locally or in His Church, is always a reinforcement of the spiritual life. We never get over any trouble without some strengthening of our spiritual life. Is that not true? When we are faced with some crisis, we are just not going to be able to patch it up, put it right, do something about it outwardly —we have got to come into a new spiritual position about this. We shall never get through until we have got a new spiritual position, or until our spiritual measure has been increased.

It is futile to try to get rid of any troubles in Christianity at large, or locally, or in ourselves, along any other line but God's line: recognising, ' This is a crisis—everything in the future depends upon how we get round this awkward corner, this difficult situation—all the past is going to be jeopardised if we do not negotiate this spiritual situation triumphantly.' How will it be done? By an extra board—by the reinforcement of what has been in the past against the future, holding everything intact by a strengthening of our spiritual life. So the Divine safeguard, or remedy, for every trouble is the reinforcement, or recovery, of spirituality.

Just look again at those boards of the Tabernacle. Firstly, they were made of acacia wood, which is known for its great strength and power of endurance. Secondly, they were of considerable height—ten cubits—which is higher than any man naturally: this is something of greater stature than you or I are naturally—we who comprise the House of God. Thirdly, they were upright, standing on their feet. Those three things are very significant. Here is something that needs strength that is more than ordinary strength, for endurance. Here is something that means stature that is more than ordinary human stature, to rise above. And here is something that must really be on its feet, established.

SPIRITUAL STRENGTH OF CHRISTIANITY AT THE BEGINNING

Now you have the New Testament crowded into those few things. And these letters to Timothy, from which we have momentarily digressed, are just full of those very things. How wonderful these things are seen to be in the beginnings, are they not? For, you know, even at the beginning of the Church's history, it was a tremendous corner that was being turned. The coming of Christ Himself represented the biggest crisis in all history. It was a universal turning-point; from that time onward, things were going to change. And into that tremendous crisis right at the beginning the Church was thrown; it was a delicate, dangerous, perilous time. All the succeeding generations would be coloured by how the Church behaved and got through those critical days.

Look at the strength of the human ' boards '! Was it just human strength? Think of Peter only a very little while before: how much could he take, by that fire in the courtyard, with the finger of the maid pointing at him? He just crumpled under it! But look at him—and the others—now! Are these men on their feet? are they standing upright? They are not only standing on their feet in the Lord—they are putting other people on their feet! Look at that poor fellow who has been lying there at the gate all those years, unable to use his feet (Acts iii). Peter takes him by the right hand, and up he comes—he is on his feet right enough! The same thing happens again later (Acts xiv. 8): they are putting people on their feet.

And out of that grew the rich ministry that we have in the New Testament about being "established". Being established just means ' standing up '. You and I will be no good to the testimony of the Lord unless we are spiritually on our feet, standing up. When we lose our feet, when we break down, when we let go, it means that the testimony is let down. If you have lost your feet, been knocked off your feet, or if you have not been on your feet for a long time, or if you have been up and down over a long period, you will have to have a crisis over this. You have got to get round that corner. All that has been is in the balances with this present issue ; all that the Lord would have in the future is made possible, or will be all wrong, unless you get round this corner quickly, and get your feet in the Lord.

You know what I mean by ' getting your feet in the Lord ': it is having what Paul calls " full assurance "—assurance, that is, about your salvation. For these boards, as you know, were founded in two basic things—two sockets—made of silver. Now silver signifies redemption, and the double testimony under their feet emphasized or reinforced this twice over. Two is always sufficiency of testimony, is it not?—and they were in that. We need to have assurance of our salvation, certainty about this matter. Until that is so, there is no strength and there is no uprightness ; there is no endurance, no stature, no measure. And that applies to many other things besides our foundation, our confidence, our faith, our certainty with the Lord. These are things which must really characterize the true Christian. These are the constituents of a spiritual man, or a spiritual Church.

A DISPENSATIONAL CRISIS

Now, if you have been thinking in Timothy's letters, if you know those letters at all, does it not all come back to you? Paul's Lord was making him write those letters on these very things at a time of tremendous crisis. The whole crisis in Christianity, at this turning-point in its history, was focused in this young man himself. These letters to Timothy are nothing less than dispensational in their significance. They contain far more than those favourite texts: " Take thy part in suffering hardship, as a good

soldier of Christ Jesus" (II Tim. ii. 3); or, "Fight the
good fight of the faith" (I Tim. vi. 12); or, "That the
man of God may be complete, furnished completely unto
every good work" (II Tim. iii. 17); or, "A vessel unto
honour . . . prepared unto every good work" (II Tim. ii.
21).

How we love these fragments! Yes, but do remember
that every one of them is set in the background of a crisis
for the dispensation, for, until you recognise that, you
have not really got the value of the fragments. Why
'take your share of hardship as a good soldier of Christ
Jesus'? Because the dispensation hangs upon it, Timothy!
This is not only for you, but for the future. Why be
"a vessel unto honour", why "lay hold on eternal life",
why "fight the good fight"? There are far, far-reaching
issues at stake, right on to the end of Christianity's history
—that is why! These letters were not written to
Timothy just for Timothy's sake, for the time being,
to help this young fellow along in his own Christian
life. And they were certainly not written just to give
us nice fragments for our own Christian life. These
letters were written at a most critical time in Christianity's
history, and all their fragments relate to that.

IMMINENT DEPARTURE OF PAUL

Now take the fragments in their setting, and they acquire new meaning, new significance. You will understand
why Paul is so serious—his appeals, his exhortations; his
repeated "O man of God", "O man of God" (I Tim. vi.
11; II Tim. iii. 17). Was there a crisis on? Well, there
are plenty of proofs in the letters themselves of that fact.
You can pick out some of the indications. First of all, be

reminded that these were the last writings of the Apostle. The second letter was probably the last thing that Paul ever wrote, and he wrote it within perhaps hours of his execution. Paul is going, Paul is passing from this scene ; Paul's personal ministry, in word and in writing, is coming to a close. There is going to be a real loss and a real gap, tremendous loss to the Church. It is a crisis. If God takes away any servant of His through whom He has met His people in some rich, full way, there is always a great gap, and that gap does not become smaller as time goes on. You are always wishing that that servant of God were back to help ; you are always saying, ' Now what would he say, what would he do?' I do not exaggerate the point. This letter contains this. Paul says : " I am already being offered up " (II Tim. iv. 6). Is that a crisis? Well, if it is—and it is —we need something, Paul, from the Lord to meet this situation. The Lord must reinforce us at this turn in the road.

SECESSION FROM PAUL

And these letters do that ! You see that, as we go on. Ah, but not only so—the letters reveal a secession from Paul. He cries : " all that are in Asia turned away from me " (I Tim. i. 15). And, although we know that some did leave him because it was too costly to stay with him, and that the peril of his death was overshadowing any association, it is difficult, in looking into this matter, not to conclude that the turning from Paul by those in Asia was *on doctrinal grounds.* You say, ' Where have you the evidence for that?' The evidence is abundant, and will be brought forward presently. There is a secession from Paul because of his teachings, his line of things ; because of the standard that he has raised, because of the level that he has insisted upon. They cannot go on with Paul, and that is a crisis. Anticipating somewhat, we may go further, and say that the outcome of that secession from Paul may be seen in the first chapters of the book of the Revelation. The condition of the very churches in Asia that Paul had been used to bring into being, beginning with Ephesus, of which Timothy was the overseer—the condition of those churches in the first chapters of the Revelation is seen to be resultant upon their turning from the man whom God had used to bring them into being. It is a very critical thing to let go something that God has done, to lower your standard. We shall come back later to consider how terribly the standard was lowered. It is most dangerous, it represents a tremendous crisis, to weaken on anything that the Lord has shown to be His will. So, they were leaving Paul.

SPIRITUAL DECLINE

And then, look at the change in the nature of things indicated by these letters. They are just full of a lowering level of spiritual life, in every way, a loss of spirituality, a decline. It is a crisis. Without going into details, all I will say at this point is this: that, where God has given richly, where God has given in any fulness, where God has called to anything more than the nominal and shown His mind to be spiritual fulness, the peril is always present of losing, letting go, declining, dropping away to some lower level, perhaps because of the cost of going on, or for some other reason. This peril is always present.

Now I come back for a moment to where we started: reinforcement. The Lord is always seeking to strengthen our spirituality in order to guard against these threats and perils which are ever imminent, never far away. And is it not impressive that, when there is a time of danger, of peril, of a threat, of a crisis in the spiritual life, the Lord puts us into such a state of agony and suffering and distress that we have got to get a new position with Him altogether, or we shall not get through? How faithful He is! Because of a threat, because of a danger, He may plunge us right into a sea of difficulty and trial, in order to strengthen our swimming powers, to get us into some fuller measure, so that we shall not so easily be caught there again. When anything like that reappears, we shall recognise it for what it is, and know that we have got to keep our feet, keep our balance, keep steady.

So these letters are just full of exhortations to Timothy —" Be strong ", in other words ' Be steady ' ; " Take your share of hardship " ; " Lay hold on eternal life "—all because of what Timothy signifies in the whole dispensation.

CHAPTER TWO

THE DIVINE REACTION

LET US CONSIDER A LITTLE FURTHER some of the indications of the existence of a real crisis at the time when Paul wrote these letters to Timothy. We have noted the first feature of that crisis in the imminent departure and withdrawal of Paul himself from the scene. Undoubtedly the Apostle was writing largely for that very reason. The things he was saying to Timothy were said largely because he was going. These things needed saying, because the responsibility was going to be left to others, and to Timothy in a particular way. It constituted a very big change that Timothy and the faithful men mentioned by the Apostle (II Tim. ii. 2) were to take up the work and the responsibility, to stand in the place that Paul had occupied. And so the Apostle was laying the burden very heavily upon Timothy and these others, because of his near-at-hand departure.

Then we took note of that secession from himself, to which he refers. All those who were in Asia had turned from him; they were no longer prepared to follow Paul, no longer standing with him in the truth and purpose for which he had given his life, no longer faithful to the great revelation which God had given him. Perhaps they did not have an adequate apprehension of how great a thing it was that had come through Paul. For it is difficult to believe

that anyone who had a real apprehension of the greatness
of those things could turn away like this. However, be that
as it may, they were leaving Paul, which meant that they
were leaving what Paul had sought to realise.

PERIL OF MORAL LAXITY

Furthermore, we began to note the change toward a real
state of spiritual depreciation, indicated by the content of
these two letters. I will not turn you to every fragment and
every passage indicative of these things, but it does not
take very long to read these letters, and I would suggest
that, after having had it pointed out, you take them up
anew and read them carefully. Read them again and again.
The Apostle refers to some things that are worse than sad
or grievous—they are quite evil. There are things creeping
in and having a place amongst Christians, such as moral
laxity—carelessness in moral conduct and relationships ;
truly a sign of a lowering of spiritual temper, temperature,
standard. The beginnings of it, so far as the Church, so far
as Christianity was concerned, are traceable in these letters.
The Apostle is saying, in effect : ' These two things cannot
go together : spirituality—a real, true spiritual life—and
moral laxity.'

Perhaps you think that that is a terrible subject even to
mention. I do not know whether that is so, but the world
is a terrible place, a terrible place, morally, and we all
have to live here. The atmosphere is full of it, the papers
are full of it, and it is not always easy to keep that atmosphere, if not that kind of life, altogether at bay. It
insinuates itself, and it is a very, very persistent means
employed by the Devil to ruin the spiritual life. The enemy
will not scruple to catch the people of God on the line of

H

moral laxity, and if he can do that, he has ruined their testimony.

You remember that we began our last chapter by referring to the Tabernacle as the shrine of the testimony of God, and to God's recognition of the need to reinforce the corners, the turning-points—that is, to reinforce spirituality against the perils and dangers of a corner, a change-round from one line to another. You see, it is the *testimony* that is involved. And let me say this : that, far from being the least involved, or the most immune, Christian people are more in danger of this very thing than anyone else. If the enemy can get a Christian on that low level of life, at that point, he has struck a master-blow. If he can get a servant of God overcome there, he has surely consolidated his ground against the testimony of Jesus. Therein is a long and terrible history ; it explains much. Hence— ' Timothy, Timothy, " flee youthful lusts " (II Tim. ii. 22) : beware of the encroachment and inroads of this moral laxity that is in the world—flee from it.' Is that an unnecessary word? Forgive me, if you think so. But we have got to reinforce against anything like that for the testimony's sake.

BECOMING BEHAVIOUR AND APPAREL
IN THE HOUSE OF GOD

But that is not the whole of it. I must say here some things that I would rather not say, and if they do not apply to you personally, your enlightenment and being made aware may be helpful to some others in danger. For another feature of the change and the lowering level of spirituality marked in this letter is unbecoming behaviour in the House of God. The House of God is mentioned, as you notice here, and one of Paul's emphatic words here is "how men ought to behave themselves in the house of God" (I Tim. iii. 15); that is why he wrote this. There is such a thing as unbecoming behaviour. And he touches upon the women —the women with unbecoming dress, or lack of becoming dress. Now that is not something that we like to mention; but should it not be mentioned? It is a mark of poor spiritual life, of a low spiritual level, when that happens; these things are a barometer of spiritual life. For spirituality is pre-eminently practical. When we speak of 'spiritual' things and 'spirituality', people sometimes make a joke of it and say, 'Oh, they are so spiritual!' Well, if you can think or talk like that, you have not any idea of what spirituality is. Spirituality is tremendously practical: it touches your dress, it touches your behaviour, it touches your conduct as a Christian! Spirituality says, 'You will not overdo it and you will not underdo it; you will have a proper, dignified behaviour'. That is what is here.

But is it not a pity that these things which Paul wrote, concerning women, sisters, for instance, have been taken out and made subjects in themselves, so that Paul has been reproached that he ever said such things? That is complete mishandling. Why not recognise that this is set in a decline of Christianity, and that these things are marks of spiritual decline? That is why they have to be spoken about; they are not things in themselves. Naturally, you may have your feelings about them. You might, for instance, be called old-fashioned, not up-to-date; you have not moved with the times. But if you are spiritual, you will have another kind of argument. You will not be behind the times, and you will not be moving with the times: you will be moving with Heaven, and that is a different standard altogether.

BEGINNINGS OF FORMALISM,
INSTITUTIONALISM, ECCLESIASTICISM, IN THE CHURCH

Let us note other indications in these letters. On the outside there was the beginning of an altogether new situation with Christianity itself. We here have quite clearly indicated the beginning of ecclesiasticism, clericalism, formalism, officialdom in Christian orders. It is all here, it has started. Paul died, Paul was executed, and there was a period of some twenty-five years without any historical record of what was happening. Then we come to the writings of John, followed by silence again. And then men began to write, and we have the writings of men called the Fathers. What do we find? Immediately they begin to write, at the end of the first Christian century, we find that clericalism is in full force and so is ecclesiasticism. The whole principle of spiritual men as overseers has been resolved into a system of prelates, bishops, and what not— a non-New Testament system. This is officialdom : men in high position ecclesiastically, governing in an official way. It has come ; here are the beginnings. That which was spiritual—spiritual men, men of God, functioning as overseers of the Church and of the churches, because they were spiritual men—has now given place to men who are officials, ecclesiastics, clerics, and so on. A tremendous change has taken place, and it has come right down through all the Church's history.

The Christian ordinances were changed and the Christian doctrines were changed. The ordinance of baptism, for instance, was changed at the end of the first century. I am not going to enlarge upon these things ; I am taking them as indications of a change—the turning of a corner—the coming in now of something organized in the place of that which was organic, of something institutional in the place of that which was spiritual. It is the movement away from what was spontaneous. And how spontaneous it was ! In the early days the Church was just springing up and pressing on and expanding and growing by the sheer life that was in it ; now it is organized, now it is a self-conscious entity, making its own appointments, and so on. The change led to infinite loss of power, and all the unhappy conditions that we have to-day.

RESPONSIBLE MEN IN THE CHURCH
MUST BE SPIRITUAL MEN

Now, the point is that the Holy Spirit saw this encroachment, saw this thing beginning, and sought to react to it. Through Paul He wrote these letters, pointing out that elders and overseers in the Church must be essentially spiritual men : they must be known for their spiritual life and measure, as well as for their moral character ; and everything in the House of God must be spiritual in its nature and value, not official. The Lord's word, then, now and ever, is : If you want to recover the power of testimony in this world, recover spirituality ! If you want to have that impact and registration which was known at the beginning you must recover the spiritual state which existed at the beginning. Everything must be like *that*, not like this. A man's position in the House of God depends, where God is concerned, on his spiritual value and nothing more. You may dress him up and decorate him and ' lord ' him, and call him by this name or that, but with God it is no more than that man's spiritual value that counts.

And what is true in the realm of those in positions of responsibility is true of everyone. Paul calls Timothy a

" man of God "; indeed, he makes it personal, and says,
" O man of God . . ." That is because of Timothy's particular position of responsibility ; but, mark you, Paul uses
that phrase of all others too, in the same writing. Why are
the Scriptures given and to whom are they given? Are
they only given to Timothy and to overseers and to men
in particular responsibility? Not at all. " Every scripture
inspired of God is . . . profitable for " this and that, " that
the man of God . . ." (II Tim. iii. 16, 17). Who is that?
Every one to whom the Scripture is given is called a " man
of God ". So, if you have the Scriptures, you come into that
category, under that designation ; you are supposed to be
a man of God, a woman of God. We are all supposed to be
' God's men '. What are God's men, the men of God?
Again, that title belongs only to those who are in a spiritual position, not in any formal, official position. They are
where they are because of their spiritual life, measure and
value. We cannot underline that too strongly.

We thus see something of the crisis involved in this
change from what was inward to everything being outward
—offices and functions and positions and titles—the introduction of formalism. Paul is bringing it back to where it
ought to be—to the person himself, the person herself.
That is where he fastens it. In order to recover, and to
safeguard, and to protect, responsibility must be in the
hands of spiritual men and women.

JOHN'S WRITINGS : A RENEWED
RECALL TO SPIRITUALITY

These are indications of the course of things, of the
change that was coming over Christianity, and, as I said
earlier, there is so much proof of this. Paul went, but some-

where John was going on. You know that Paul went in the terrific holocaust of persecution that led to John's exile. John is somewhere—and then he writes his Gospel, the Gospel of pre-eminent spirituality. You do not need that I should stay to show that the Gospel written by John was written with the object of bringing things back to spiritual principles. And then he wrote his letters: and John's letters are just full, from beginning to end, of spiritual essentials—life, light, love, and so on. And when you come to his Revelation, and read those chapters containing the Lord's challenge to the churches in Asia—Paul's churches —what do you find? Full development of those things of which we have been speaking! Moral laxity: "thou sufferest the woman Jezebel"; formalism, empty show: "thou hast a name that thou livest, and thou art dead"; and so on. The thing has come about.

But, again, what is the Lord's reaction? It is a reaction to a spiritual position. What are 'overcomers'? Overcomers are simply those who have maintained or recovered spiritual ground. It is not easy, in a world like this, in the present course of things, in Christianity as it has become, to recover or to maintain purely spiritual ground. You will suffer for it, so the Lord said. I venture to say that it is far more difficult to keep a clear, straight spiritual course in the Christian life, than it is to live just as a Christian in this world. To live as a Christian in the world may be difficult, but you will find that there are difficulties in Christianity which you will never encounter from the world. Am I right? Yes, "a man's foes shall be they of his own household" has a very much larger meaning. A spiritual course in Christianity is exceedingly difficult—because of Christians. Christianity has become very largely the enemy of spirituality.

These are strong things to say, but, you see, it is a matter
of the effectiveness of testimony, the purity of testimony.
I am not at the moment touching upon the doctrinal side
of things. A large part of these letters is given up to departure from former doctrine, and I may come to that in
some measure later on. What I am concerned with just
now is to demonstrate two things: firstly, that this kind of
crisis happens, it is the kind of thing that happens again
and again, it is a besetting peril all along the line, to drop
from the full, high, spiritual level to which the Lord has
called, away to something lower and something less; and
then, secondly, that God has ever and always reacted, and
still does react, by trying to get His people on to a more
spiritual level of things, to increase their spiritual measure,
their spiritual life. It is the only way to overcome, it is the
only way to get through and (to come to the letters again)
to be able at the end to hand back the deposit to the Lord
unspoilt. " O Timothy, guard that which is committed
unto thee " (I Tim. vi. 20). ' Guard the deposit! Hand it
back at the end, unsullied, unspoilt, undiminished, intact!'
Paul, on that very matter, says: " I have finished the
course, I have kept the faith " (II Tim. iv. 7)—' Timothy,
take it up and do the same.' That is the effect of it. " Guard
that which is committed unto thee "—the deposit of
God.

TIMOTHY AN INSTRUMENT OF THE DIVINE REACTION

Now let us come to the Divine reaction more particularly and specifically. I would ask you to take note of this.
Timothy himself is at this point being marked out as the
instrument of the Divine reaction to the existing trend of
things. And Timothy therefore assumes the rôle of a *sign*.

Now, that is not a new idea in the Bible, is it? Ezekiel was told by the Lord that He had made him a sign for the house of Israel (Ezek. xii. 6, 11 ; xxiv. 24, 27). And Timothy comes into that position or function, as a sign : he must himself be indicative of what spiritual features are, what spirituality is. Let us then look at Timothy—first of all, shall we say, negatively—remembering that he is himself a symbol of things essential to recovery. We are going to find much comfort and help here, all of us. What are these things?

First of all, weakness. You can despise Timothy, if you like ; they did that when he was alive. Paul said to him : " Let no man despise thy youth " (I Tim. iv. 12). Naturally, he was despised, and in weakness. Then, dependence. It looked as though Paul was providing him with a set of crutches to help him to keep on his feet ! So much of what Paul wrote to Timothy indicated these things about him. Speaking of Timothy naturally, you might say that he was evidently a very timid, nervous sort of young man, who needed all the time to be bucked up. Surely, Timothy must have been very weak, seeing all these things were necessary !

WEAKNESS AND DEPENDENCE
THE GROUND FOR SPIRITUALITY

Look at it that way, if you like ; but there are other ways of looking at it. This is the most suitable and promising ground for spirituality—indeed, it is absolutely essential to the thing that God is after and Paul was after ! What shall we say about Timothy? Paul thought a very great deal of him ; Paul, who did not usually err in the matter of wisdom and discretion, put Timothy into a very, very important place. Timothy was an apostle, although he was never called that. Timothy was an elder, although he was never called that. But Timothy was more. There was in Timothy a combination of all the functions from an evangelist to a church-builder. "Do the work of an evangelist". He was *the* elder amongst the elders of the church at Ephesus—no small responsibility! Think of Ephesus. What was Paul thinking of, sending someone like Timothy to put things right at Ephesus, to take charge in Ephesus, to correct and to build in Ephesus? Preposterous to send a young fellow like that, of this kind!

Well, spiritual and natural abilities are in altogether different worlds! And when God reacts to recover, or acts to provide against a threat, a peril, a danger that has the characteristics we have noted, He brings His instrument down to nothingness—He empties it out and makes it more conscious of its weakness and of its dependence than of anything else. In this greatest of all works of God—the maintaining of His testimony in absolute purity and truth —there is no place whatever, amongst those who are involved, for assumption: for assuming that they are something, or assuming that they can do something, or assuming that they are called to this or that. There is no place, either, for presumption—that is, running ahead of God, running ahead of the Spirit. There is no place for self-importance, for self-sufficiency, for self-assertiveness—no place for any of these things. If you and I are going to be used for spiritual purposes, God will take us in hand to drain us of the last drop of anything like that, until we know that of all men we are the most unfit and unsuited to the thing to which God has called us ; that from all natural standpoints we have no right to be in that position at all. That is God's way of making spiritual men and women.

STRENGTH THROUGH GRACE

Now, if you are acute in your mental activity, you may have thought you are catching me out on this, because in these letters Paul is telling Timothy he must be strong, and I have just said he must be weak! Paul is as good as telling him he must be full, and I have said he must be empty! Ah, yes, but if Timothy was to be all that Paul said he must be, then it would all be spiritual and not natural. Is that borne out by the context? Of course it is! " Be strong "— but it does not stop there. " Be strong *in the grace that is in Christ Jesus* " (II Tim. ii. 1). That is not self-strength, that is not natural strength of any kind. " The grace that is in Christ Jesus "—be strong in that. So we see what is the strength in the case of Timothy, as the symbol of God's reactionary method and means in a day of declension. The strength is to be spiritual strength.

That works both ways. It is a word of encouragement to those who are conscious of no strength, who only feel their weakness ; as though to say : ' Look here, that is not the criterion, how weak you feel, at all : the criterion is " the grace that is in Christ Jesus ".' And it works the other way. If any of us should feel that we can do it, and press into the situation or into the position, and take it on, assuming or presuming, then we are in for a bad time under the hand of God—that is, if we are going to be of any use to the Lord. Any such attitude is going to be emptied out.

ALL FUNCTIONS TO BE SPIRITUAL, NOT NATURAL OR OFFICIAL

" Let no man despise thy youth ". Well, then, what is to be the reaction of Timothy when he finds men despising him? Suppose you are a young man : how would you react if you were in his place, and I said: 'Don't you let them despise you! Don't you let them have that attitude toward you!'? What would you do? You could act very much in the flesh, couldn't you? You could begin, as they say in America, to be 'chesty'—peacockish, they mean—and spoil it all by a false dignity, by an artificial personality that is not yourself. Authority in the House of God is spiritual. There is authority about a man or woman who has real spiritual measure, that weighs, that counts, and has influence. They may naturally be despised, but let spiritual measure be found with them, and you will find that in times of difficulty they are the ones to whom people turn. We may touch again upon spiritual authority later.

The knowledge and the understanding are to be spiritual. The office, if you like to use that word, whether it be of elder, overseer, teacher, evangelist, or whatever it is, is to be spiritual, not official. You do that because you *are* that. It simply comes out because that is how you are spiritually constituted—it is how the Holy Spirit has constituted you. And it is a poor thing to try to be an evangelist, or a teacher, if the Holy Spirit has not constituted you one. Oh, what tragedies we have seen, through people trying to be teachers, or whatever it may be, because they like it, it appeals to them, and the Holy Ghost has not qualified them for it. It is just like the peacock's tail—when it has gone! Still strutting about, but there is nothing behind it! Is there anything more pathetic? What is the good of it all, if it is not of the Holy Ghost?

ENDURANCE ONLY POSSIBLE
THROUGH SPIRITUAL MEASURE

"Endure hardness"—hardship—"as a good soldier" (II Tim. ii. 3, A.V.). Endure. Just think for a moment what

Timothy was called upon to endure at that time. You perhaps have not any idea of the situation. I have re-read lately the account of those persecutions of the Christians which came about through Nero, and through the Jews—the unspeakable horrors of cruelty to men, to women, to children, to families. I should shock you if I mentioned the inhuman, indescribable atrocities that literally hundreds of thousands of Christians suffered at the hands of those Roman Emperors. When Nero commanded the burning of Rome, a scapegoat had to be found upon whom the blame could be laid, and it was laid upon the Jews: and the Jews said No, it was the Christians; and so the Christians were taken. You are not surprised at the sufferings of the Jews, are you? Not only Christ, but hundreds of thousands of His precious children were tortured in unspeakable agony, for many decades.

Timothy was in the presence of that growing shadow. He knew that his father in Christ was in prison and shortly to suffer death. He knew that those who had been near Paul in Rome had left him. And Paul said: " At my first defence no one took my part, but all forsook me " (II Tim. iv. 16). Timothy was in the presence of that! Endurance! Who *could* endure but by the mighty power of the Spirit? You want spiritual measure for that, you need the enduring power of Christ for that; that is spiritual endurance, not just natural courage.

We see, then, that, at all times of peril to His Church, at all times of danger, when things are threatening, and a change seems to be coming about, the Lord, in the first place, always tries to get His people on to higher spiritual ground: He always seeks to increase spiritual measure, to bring things over from the merely professional and formal on to the ground of spiritual life and spiritual character.

And, secondly, He seeks to remind us that we are ' *God's men* ' : we are not the men of a system, not men of the world, not men of our own natural ambitions—we are God's men. It is significant, is it not, that Timothy's name (*Timo-theos*) means ' honouring God '. That is the key to everything, as with him, so with us ; that is spirituality.

CHAPTER THREE

THE DIVINE RESOURCE

In THINKING ABOUT TIMOTHY as himself a symbol of the need, and of God's method of meeting it, we noted, on the one side, the neediness of Timothy—how he is presented in these letters as one in need in every way—and, on the other side, the urge that the Apostle brought to bear upon him, the tremendous responsibility which the Apostle indicated as resting upon him. We noted all the words of exhortation and command, which seemed to make such great demands upon this young man. " O Timothy . . .", says the Apostle, " I charge thee in the sight of God . . . "; and he appeals to him more than once to " Be strong ", " Endure hardship as a good soldier ", " Give diligence to show thyself approved unto God ", and so on. And all this, as we saw, was in the light of the situation which was developing at that time—the terrible, terrible persecution of Christians that was coming about, to which Paul, so soon after writing this last letter, fell a victim—and Timothy knew all about it. It was indeed putting much upon a weak vessel. It was making tremendous demands upon one who, in himself, speaking quite naturally, was not of great account. Even physically he was apparently at a discount, for the Apostle refers to " thine oft infirmities." Evidently Timothy went down under some malady, repeatedly and often.

Well, what did it all amount to? This is the point; we only need to re-emphasize it. Paul was not calling upon Timothy to be more of a man than he was; he was not calling upon him to be a kind of super-man. If we talked to one another like that when we were a bit down under, it would not get us very far. If in our human language we used such expressions as: 'Well now, buck up!' or: 'Now then, none of that, no giving way!' or: 'Remember you are a man, remember you are a responsible person! You ought to behave better than that!'—I do not know how far that would get us. It might make us feel all the worse, thoroughly ashamed of ourselves; such utterly worthless creatures that we wanted to get out of it altogether. And so might Timothy have felt, if this had been what Paul was doing. He might have said, ' Well, Paul evidently does not think much of me; he has got a very poor opinion of me. I am good for nothing—I had better just give it all up.'

But that was not what Paul was doing. It is important to notice this great feature about his letters; we shall probably enlarge upon it in other connections later. Paul was not telling Timothy to be a super-man—for it wanted a super-man to stand up to this situation, to carry this load, to meet these emergencies—or to be more of a man than he was, *in himself*. Paul was indicating to Timothy all the way through that Timothy's very life and work, his ministry and his position of responsibility, rested upon a Divine and super-natural basis. " The gift of God which is in thee . . . " Paul refers to that more than once in his letters (I Tim. iv. 14; II Tim. i. 6). " God gave us not a spirit of fearfulness " (II Tim. i. 7). Read them through again and note this. The strength that Timothy was to have, the ability that was to be his for doing and for enduring, was a strength and an ability which would not come from any spring in himself. He could be, and Paul was calling upon him to be, a super-man—but not in himself. " Be strengthened *in the grace that is in Christ Jesus*" (II Tim. ii. 1). He was really being called upon to be and to do far more than any human person could measure up to ; far more than was possible even for the best of men, the strongest and the wisest of men—let alone a Timothy! But the Lord never lays upon us an impossibility. If He charges, if He calls or demands, He provides : His is the strength, His is the wisdom.

CHRISTIANS ARE SUPER-MEN IN CHRIST

Now, without taking that any further, I bring it to this focal point. Difficult as it may be for you and for me to believe it, especially at times, it is true that in a sense, and a very real sense, every Christian is a super-man or a super-woman. Every Christian is supposed to be something that no other person in this world, even at their best, can be. Every Christian is supposed to have knowledge and understanding of that which no other person at their wisest can know. Every Christian is supposed to do what no one outside of Christ can possibly do ; and every Christian is supposed to go through what no one else can go through, in the way in which a Christian is supposed to go through it. There are imposed upon Christians demands which are super-human. There are given to Christians resources which are super-natural. The Christian life is super-natural, from start to finish.

It is very important for young Christians to recognise this, and for all of us to call it to mind. When the whole story is told, when we know as we are known, when we see all things clearly and no longer through the glass darkly.

I

the one thought that will, I am sure, overwhelm us will be this : ' It took the infinite power of Almighty God to do that, and I didn't know it ! ' Our salvation demanded that. Salvation is not the simple little thing that I am afraid many people think it is, or make it out to be. However simple may be the turning-point, there are vast immensities of Divine power lying behind the rebirth of any one soul. And to get that soul right through and bring it at last into His presence, glorified, calls for the " exceeding greatness of his power to us-ward ". Thank God, that power is available !

Now is that not true, dear Christian? You have been on the way long enough. You know quite well that you could not have got through ; you may have said, ' It is no good, I give it all up ', and contemplated another course, looked for a way out—the situation was so difficult, so trying. Indeed, it may even have been worse : perhaps you actually broke down, and went all to pieces. Yet, in spite of everything, in spite of yourself, in spite of the Devil and all his forces, you are here ! How do you account for it? Well, there is something to account for it that is not in us, and in that sense we have surmounted a tremendous force of opposition and antagonism to our getting through to a glorious end. I have often said that, when we are there, we shall look at one another and say : ' Well, brother, we are here ! You did not expect to be, did you?—but you are here !' Yes, even Timothy will be there. With all that he had to face, and all that was put upon him, he could yet " be strengthened in the grace that is in Christ Jesus." That lifts us above the level of any human possibility.

Let us remember that we are, as Christians, supposed to be something other than, and more wonderful than, any other people in this world, in every way. That wonder may be secret and hidden, not manifest to the world, but it is there. May the Lord help us to lay hold upon that which He has presented to us—for it is miraculous. " Lay hold " says Paul, " on eternal life ".

CHAPTER FOUR

THE RETROSPECTIVE FEATURE

I WANT AT THIS POINT TO RETURN for a few moments to the matter of the boards of the Tabernacle, referred to in our first chapter, when we saw God's provision for reinforcing the corners, the turning-points, with an extra board. Turning-points or angles are always danger spots, and the Lord has always made special provision for such points in the course of His people's history. It is something to be taken up, if ever you are disposed to do so, in the Bible, and you will see how true it is. I have only to remind you, by way of instance, of the first chapter of the book of Joshua. You could not have any chapter in the Bible which represents a greater reinforcement of everything, taking up the past to carry it on to the future. That was a big turning-point, from the wilderness into the Land, and it certainly needed strength to turn that corner and negotiate that crisis safely.

In using again this illustration of the Tabernacle, the point that I want afresh to indicate is this : that the corners of the Tabernacle may be taken as setting forth an arrival at a certain point. That point had, so to speak, a past. Things had moved up to that point, and from that point there was a future, a new phase, a new course in the road. And the reinforcement at the corner was a taking up of what had been up to that point, and saying, ' Now, we must safeguard that, we must conserve that, we must ratify that ; we must be quite sure that that does not suffer loss or is allowed any weakness, in order that everything that is yet to be shall take up those values and continue them in strength.' For God does not intend a fundamental change in things, a change in character, a change of nature, at any point: He just means that all that He has done and given shall be carried on safely and in strength up to and through the next phase.

Now, when we come to these letters of Paul to Timothy, we have to recognise that they are the last writings of the Apostle—a fact which in itself represents a corner being turned, one phase closing and another phase coming. It was like that; things changed when Paul went. And it was because Paul himself was conscious of this that he wrote to Timothy as he did. These letters are therefore by way of reinforcing the things of God, taking up what has been in the past and confirming and consolidating for the future. That is what God meant by these letters. And so we find in them first of all what we may call a retrospective feature, a look-back to the past. Timothy is taken back, right back to the beginning: to the beginning of Christianity, and to the beginning of his own work and ministry.

"REMEMBER JESUS CHRIST"

Let us consider the retrospect as to the beginning of Christianity, which is Christ. Paul makes here a very strong and a very comprehensive throw-back to Christ, in two passages—one just a recall, the other a very inclusive statement. The first comes in the second letter, chapter two, verse eight: "Remember Jesus Christ, risen from the dead, of the seed of David, according to my gospel". "*Remember Jesus Christ*". We have come to a crisis, we have come to a turn, we have come to a point where things are chang-

ing. What is our safeguard at this point? "Remember
Jesus Christ". It is only a way of saying: 'Bring *Him* into
view again.' That is always God's method at any crisis—
bring Jesus Christ into view again. Whether it be a crisis
in a church, or a personal crisis in our own spiritual lives
—"Remember Jesus Christ". How often the Apostle resorted to that method of dealing with difficult situations!
At Philippi, for instance, where there was some trouble,
some disagreement, some lack of singlemindedness, Paul
resorted to this method: "Have this mind in you, which
was . . . in Christ Jesus" (Phil. ii. 5).

I will not stay to gather up all the material on this point.
Let me just remind you of the big turning-point which we
find at the beginning of the book of the Revelation. What
a turning-point in the Church's history was there! Remember that the beginning of that book is a re-presentation of
Jesus Christ, comprehensively and matchlessly. "Remember Jesus Christ". It is always like that. Suppose you are
having a bad time—so bad that it is creating a real crisis
for you. "Remember Jesus Christ". It is the greatest help
in every such time. Is there some trouble between you and
another Christian? "Remember Jesus Christ". Is there
trouble in the assembly? "Remember Jesus Christ". The
greatest corrective is to *remember Jesus Christ.*

CHRIST THE EMBODIMENT OF GODLINESS

But here is this other great statement, in the first letter,
chapter three, verse sixteen: "And without controversy
great is the mystery of godliness" (or 'God-likeness');
"He who was manifested in the flesh, justified in the Spirit,
seen of angels, preached among the nations, believed on in
the world, received up in glory." That is Christianity in a

nutshell, a comprehensive and inclusive representation of everything upon which Christianity rests. There are other fragmentary retrospective features in these letters, but that is enough. The first great throw-back of the Apostle at this point of crisis and danger is to Christ, back to Christ; for Christ is ever the standard, not only backward but forward. At any given point where there are dangers, where changes are threatened, we must refer back to Christ, and from that point we have to carry on what has been of Christ from the beginning.

Here it says that Christ is the embodiment of godliness, or God-likeness. It is a mystery: ' great is the mystery of God-likeness '. The Greek word (*eusebeia*) combines the thoughts of worship, devotion, and piety. Here Christ is said to be the inclusive, comprehensive embodiment of all this—God's likeness indeed. Now that has a very practical application in this letter, for the real purpose of God in the Church is God-likeness, or conformity to the likeness of God's Son. It is the great dominating purpose and objective of God in our very lives as His people. How shall we explain or define godliness? It is Christ—the reproduction of Christ, the expression of Christ. It is the bringing of Christ into the present situation. He is the embodiment of godliness.

INCORRUPTIBLE LIFE IN CHRIST

Just consider for a moment who Christ is. I am sure that many of us Christians have not really understood Christ— and we do need to understand Him. You see, Christ was more than one man among many, albeit better than the rest, a real improvement on all other men. You might find somewhere a man of very high moral character, of unim-

peachable integrity, and you might say, ' A splendid specimen of moral uprightness and goodness—and Jesus goes
one better.' No, He is not just one better than the best. He
is not one man amongst many, although better than all.

Let me put it another way. The goodness of Jesus was
Divine goodness, and not human goodness. It was by Him,
Jesus, that life and incorruption were brought to light,
through the Gospel (II Tim. i. 10). The very best specimen
of mankind, morally, that you can find is still corruptible :
he can still be corrupted—he has the seeds of corruption
in his nature. But not so Jesus Christ. There is no corruption, there are no seeds of corruption, in Him. It is incorruptible life that has come with Him. And the life that He
gives to the child of God is incorruptible life. That is not
ourselves, what we are ; it is a distinct gift which, while
being in us, is apart from us. And mark you, that is the
key to our spiritual survival, in spite of a world of corruption, and a nature of corruption. He has given to us His
own incorruptible life. Life and incorruption have been
brought to light through the Gospel.

Let me say to young Christians : Be very wary of an
insidious deception—partly through unfortunate mistrans-
lations of the Scripture, but more through common language and phraseology about immortality, the ' immortality
of the soul '. The Bible does not teach it ! The Bible word,
where the translators of the Authorised Version have put
' immortality ', is really ' incorruption ' (see R.V.)—and
incorruption is quite a different thing from what men mean
by the immortality of the soul. They lump all men together
in this and by their word ' immortality ' lift us on to a level
to which we do not all belong, and to which we can never
come naturally. Incorruption is the *true* immortality.

But immortality is thought of as continuity of existence,

and we will allow that for the soul; but there is a very great difference between continuity of existence and incorruption, incorruptible life. Eternal life is a different thing altogether from just continuity of life. It is a *kind* of life, a *character* of life. It is the life which we have *in Christ.* You see, this goes to the root of the whole matter. We have got to get right back to Jesus Christ. Christ is different from all other men in the essential nature which is in Him; and, when He gives us His own life, we as Christians are different essentially, with the biggest difference possible, from all other creations—because this is an eternal matter.

THE COUNTER TO CORRUPTION

Now Paul sees corruption coming into the Church. Moral laxity, and all sorts of things which belong to this fallen creation, to this evil world, were creeping into the Church in Paul's day; corruption was manifesting itself in the life of God's people. What is going to be done about it? *"Remember Jesus Christ"!* For just consider: you and I have another life, through Christ, and we have got to live on the basis of that life, and to remember that it is not necessary for us to be corrupted. We have in us a life, the mighty life of God, which in Christ has overcome death and corruption, for man. "Remember Jesus Christ"! Remember that, in Jesus Christ, there is that which went through all corruption untainted, and it is still possible— and blessed be God, it has been proved actual again and again—for a child of God to walk in white raiment in the midst of Sodom and Gomorrah. Where Satan's very seat is you may find saints walking in purity. It is the marvellous miracle of the Christian life that we can be subjected to all the filth and all the horror, all the corruption and pollution of this world around us, and still go on, unstained, untainted.

So, when corruption is assailing, is seeping in, remember: your life is a different life from that. That is not your life, that is not for you ; that is not your way, that is not the way of Christ. *This* life is not one imposed upon you by law—it is something in you by power. Thank God for this miracle. A young man or young woman, without a great deal of knowledge, instruction, or teaching, or experience, has to go out into this world, and, without another Christian anywhere near, be surrounded by people of the lowest type, and that young man or woman can be kept by the power of God unpolluted. This incorruptible life is very practical. Jesus is different. He is not just better than the rest ; He is different, basically different from the rest. That is the truth about Jesus, and that is the truth about the child of God : not only a bit better than other people, but different. The life-principle is different. Is that important? Surely it is, if we are to negotiate this course safely to the end.

"Thou hast a few names even in Sardis which have not defiled their garments" (Rev. iii. 4, A.V.). That is a testimony—"even in Sardis". And it is a throw-back to chapter one of Revelation, where Jesus is seen clothed with a robe down to His feet—the white robe of incorruption. "I am . . . the Living one ; and I became dead, and behold, I am alive unto the ages of the ages" (Rev. i. 17, 18, R.V. mg.). So He says, as clothed in this white garment down to the feet. What does it mean? Surely this : that He has been thrown in His death into the cesspool of human iniquity for us—"He was made sin for us, he who knew no sin" —and has come out undefiled, triumphant, in a white robe. And "thou hast a few names even in Sardis which have not defiled their garments "—what is that? It is just His victory in the lives of these people in Sardis, where things were morally very, very black indeed. " Remember Jesus Christ ".

Young man, if you are shortly going to get your call-up into the Forces, well, you are going into it. You may not find another Christian near to help you. You may be out of touch with all means of grace outwardly ; it may mean a crisis for your spiritual life. Many have lost out at that turning-point. " Remember Jesus Christ ". Remember " Christ in you " is there as the power of an incorruptible life. It is possible for you to go through and come out triumphant because of Jesus Christ. And what is true in that connection is true in all others. You see the difference between Jesus Christ and all other men, even the best. His goodness was a different goodness.

CHRIST'S KNOWLEDGE SPIRITUAL, NOT ACADEMIC

Take a move round to another angle from which to look at Him—His *knowledge*. Now, no one will question or dispute that Jesus had a very wide knowledge, was tremendously well informed, was very rich in His understanding. Everybody in His day had both to recognise and to acknowledge it. Even His critics and enemies raised the question : 'Whence hath this man this knowledge?' He spoke as one having authority, and not as the very knowledgeable men, the Scribes ; there was something extra here. But His knowledge was not the knowledge of the schools. He never went to college or to university. He had to work at home, hard and long, for that pittance to keep mother and brothers in food and raiment. He was not able to earn in order to put aside a nest-egg against a rainy day

—if that is not mixing metaphors!—for, when it came to going out on His life's work, He could not afford a lodging, He had nowhere to lay His head. He had to work a miracle to pay His taxes.

No wonder they asked: "How knoweth this man letters, having never learned?" (John vii. 15). How does He get this knowledge—knowledge which has extended and exhausted all the brains ever since His day? And they are still at it. Look at all the libraries that have been written on Him and His sayings!—and still we come back and wonder what He meant when He said this and that; we still have not fathomed it. So everybody will acknowledge that He had a very, very large knowledge: but whence was it? We say again: It was not the knowledge of the schools; it was something other and something different and something else. Well, we Christians have the answer; we know. But, mark you, that difference is *the* difference between Christ and all others—the 'knowledgeable' people; and the difference between every simplest child of God and the wisest amongst men.

"Remember Jesus Christ". There is a source and a kind of knowledge, by which we can be got through, which all the this world's princes of knowledge do not possess. It is a *kind* of knowledge. I want to enlarge upon that later, but I am making the statement here. Unless we have this kind of knowledge, this spiritual understanding, this spiritual intelligence—this intelligence which is different, which is other, this mind which is the mind of Christ—we are not going to negotiate these critical corners in Christian life and experience and in the work of God. We need understanding more than the best understanding in this world to get round these crises. How are we going to negotiate this situation? It may be that you are facing

such things. You are exercised; you are wondering—
How are we going to get round this, how are we
going to get through this? Well, there is a kind of
knowledge, a kind of understanding, a kind of spiritual
intelligence, available to the child of God, that will get us
through. That is very true in experience and in history. If
we had not known the Lord at certain times, where should
we have been? Our knowledge of the Lord saved us. And
many times our knowledge of spiritual principles has saved,
our knowledge of how God does things has been a tremendous stand-by in times of need.

Yes, remember Jesus Christ. He had a knowledge which
was more than all the knowledge of this world, and different: it was that which He had by the Spirit. These letters
are themselves proof positive of this. Here is the new situation arising, and the big question is, How is the Church
going to get through this crisis without disaster, without
calamity? Well, the letters are just full of a knowledge,
are they not, which meets the need: it is the knowledge of
Christ. Do you know that Christ is mentioned twelve times
in each of these letters? They are very brief letters; you
can read them through in a few minutes, both of them;
and Christ is referred to 24 times. When you get any word
dominant like that, it surely gives a clue to what it is all
about. Paul here is coming back with Christ: it is *Christ*,
it is *Christ*—He is the one upon whom we should draw.

CHRIST'S INFLUENCE SPIRITUAL, NOT PSYCHIC

So much, then, for the matter of His knowledge. A word
about His *influence*. It is indisputable that He had an immense influence. His presence always made itself felt. He
could not be anywhere without it being known that He

was there. Without any need for Him to speak, things began to come out ; His presence was a powerful presence. That does not need proving or enlarging upon. This mysterious influence and impact—what was it? Some people, of course, have tried to explain it psychologically : that He had a powerful psychic effect upon people. They have summed it all up in the phrase, ' a tremendously strong personality '. Well, they may think that if they like, but that is not the answer. His influence, His impact, was something other than the psychic, something other than just a strong personality. It was essentially *spiritual*. Evil spirits recognised His presence—demons cried out in His presence. This is not psychic ; these are actual entities and intelligences. It is a registration upon the spiritual world.

Influence is not just a matter of having a strong personality, or being able to make a strong psychic registration wherever you are. That is a false conception of influence. So far as men and this world are concerned, you may be without the training of the schools and all the values of a rich education ; you may have had nothing in your birth and inheritance and upbringing to make you an important person or a strong character : and yet you may exercise a very great influence, you may count for something more than all that. It is true again—and here is the miracle of it all—that " God hath chosen the weak things . . . and the things that are not ", that He may destroy, may nullify, may bring down the things that are wise, and the things that are strong, and the things that are. It is so often a, humanly speaking, very insignificant little person who is counting mightily for God. There is a great difference between natural influence and spiritual influence.

In the churches in the book of the Revelation, we find that the testimony had lost its power and its influence in the world; and so it is to-day, very largely. What is the remedy? It is, as we have sought to indicate, the recovery and the reinforcement of spirituality. Spirituality is a tremendous power. Really spiritual people, be they what they may from this world's standpoint, are the people that count; they are the people of influence, and they are the people that are needed in this world. God needs spiritual men and women for the preserving and carrying on of His testimony. He needs reinforced spirituality. "Remember Jesus Christ". You can only account for Him—in His knowledge, in His influence, as in every other way—by the anointing of the Spirit. "God anointed [Jesus of Nazareth] . . . who went about doing good, and healing all that were oppressed of the devil; for God was with him " (Acts x. 38). It was the anointing. And we have the anointing—the same anointing. And so His *authority,* to use the word of Scriptures, was not that of personality; it was *spiritual* authority. How we need that! His judgment of things, His insight, His power of discrimination, was not just human sagacity, not just a high level of human shrewdness; it was spiritual wisdom. This is what Paul argued out so thoroughly in his first letter to the Corinthians.

The point is this: Jesus Christ, Jesus the Anointed (for that is the meaning of " Christ "), is different, and superior. What was true of Him then is true to-day. In the way that I have indicated—wisdom, understanding, power, judgment, and everything else—He needs to be brought right into every spiritual crisis. "Remember Jesus Christ". It is all by the anointing. If we have any sense whatever of the real need to-day in the Church, amongst God's people—yes, and in ourselves—because of things as they are, as they have become, or as they are threatened, do not our hearts beat with Paul's in all this? We can take up Paul's concern. You see, this man just poured out his heart in these letters. There is something of a yearning, if not of a breaking heart, in the way in which Paul here says: "O Timothy"— "O Timothy, guard the deposit". That cry, that ejaculation, that bursting forth of his heart which is found through the letters, not just in that language, but in other forms, reveals Paul's tremendous concern about this matter of spiritual life, the reinforcing of spirituality.

We ought to share that concern with Paul to-day; we ought to feel like that. Are you concerned about spiritual things? Are you concerned about the way that, speaking generally, things have taken—the declension, the departure, the diversion, the dropping down, the differences, that have come about since the beginning? Are you concerned? Well, remember that it must be not just a sighing and groaning over it, but an intelligent concern, in the full and clear realisation of what the solution is—the reinforcement of spirituality in ourselves and in the Lord's people. May the Lord give us the concern of His servant in this matter!

CHAPTER FIVE

THE SPIRITUAL BASIS OF THE CHRISTIAN LIFE

We to-day, as christians, live in the full development of that which Paul feared. It is very largely—
though, thank God, not wholly—present in Christianity
to-day. But it is very necessary to recognise that this is always a persistent tendency in all Christian life. You and
I can fall into this peril as easily as anyone else : indeed,
to avoid it constitutes the greatest difficulty that any
Christian has, and certainly that any body of Christians
has—to avoid decline into a merely formal system, merely
outward order, into something organized and institutional.
All unconsciously, often imperceptibly, we move away
from the essential spiritual nature of our life. I think you
will recognise that this is a warning that has a place to-
day, as protective and as recovering.

Let us now, through these letters to Timothy, widen
our horizon a little, and be led out into the larger realm
of this matter. We shall find ourselves moving in a very
large sphere in this particular connection. These letters
will lead us there quite naturally. We take up again the
retrospective feature in these letters, looking back to the
beginnings, to the foundations, to the essentials. In our
last chapter we were occupied with the look back to Jesus :
"Remember Jesus Christ". Now we are going to look
back to the real basis of the Christian life, as Jesus showed
it ; but let us go through Timothy.

BACK TO THE BEGINNINGS

As we look into these letters, we find Paul reminding
Timothy—yes, reminding him very forcefully—of certain things which lay right at the very root of his own life
and of his service to the Lord. We have fragments like
this: I Timothy i. 18: " according to the prophecies which
went before on thee "—literally, ' the prophecies which
led the way to thee ' ; in modern language, ' in accordance
with the prophetic intimations concerning you '. If you
look at the context, you will see that the time referred to
was when Timothy was coming under the anointing for
service, for ministry, for his active part in the Gospel. The
Apostle is calling to remembrance the great principle, the
great truth and foundation, of his life and work. Further,
I Timothy vi. 20: " O Timothy, guard the deposit ".
II Timothy i. 6: "Keep constantly blazing the gift of
God which is in you . . ." ; again it is dated back, as you
see, to a particular time. II Timothy ii. 2: " The things
which thou hast heard from me . . ." ; iii. 14: " Abide
thou in the things which thou hast learned . . . " You see
all this takes Timothy back. Paul is calling up the past,
calling up the foundations, calling up what has been. He
is, in effect, saying: ' Now, Timothy, this has got to be
reinforced, this has got to be consolidated, this has got to
be confirmed, in the face of the present tendencies and
perils, the present course of things. All this has got to be
brought up in a new way, and re-established. We are going round a bend in the road, and that is always a dangerous place and time, and we need on such an occasion to be
reinforced with what has been of God in the past.'

Now, I am not going to dwell upon these passages. I
am simply taking up this factor of retrospect and résumé,

which means confirming that which has been, with the future, this perilous future, in view. What does it all amount to? If you look again more closely, you will find that it all relates to the Holy Spirit. All this means, in effect, that everything at the beginning came by the Spirit ; that everything, to use the other word, is by the anointing. ' Timothy, you stand where you are because of that original anointing, because at the beginning the Holy Spirit did something in you and with you. Timothy, your ministry and service so far have been because of the Holy Spirit. Now the threat and the tendency at this time is to depart from that basis, and for another basis of things to come in which is not essentially spiritual—it is something else.' It is very important that we should recognise that. I may say, in parenthesis, that never before in my own life have I seen such a contrast amongst Christians, and in Christianity, as there is to-day, and it is really the cause and root of all the trouble. It is a difference, not between the Christian and the world, but within Christianity itself, between what is spiritual and what is natural. And it is that that we must look at.

THE GOSPEL OF SPIRITUALITY

Now, in order to be helped, we must take our retrospect much further back. We must go right back to John's Gospel. I said earlier that Timothy naturally leads us into a wider realm : and yet Timothy does not lead us back only. You know that John's Gospel was written long after Paul's two letters to Timothy. Although Paul's second letter to Timothy was the last thing that he ever wrote, it was years afterwards that John wrote his Gospel, his Letters and the Revelation. So that Timothy leads us right into the full development of this other thing. I wonder if you have ever really grasped this. We take up our New Testament in the familiar arrangement as we have it, and we say, ' Well, of course, the first things in the New Testament are the four Gospels—Matthew, Mark, Luke and John : that is the beginning of the New Testament ' ; but have you recognised that at least the fourth of those was written long after everything else in the New Testament? If you were compiling the New Testament chronologically, you would have to put John's Gospel right over near the end.

Now do you see what that implies? Why did John write his Gospel, his Letters, and the Revelation, as the last writings of the New Testament age, the apostolic age? *The Gospel of John was written when this other kind of Christianity had become almost full-grown—this other kind of Christianity that is not spiritual, but natural.* You have got to read John's Gospel in the light of the situation existing in the Church when it was written, otherwise you cannot really get its message, its values. It is a great callback to spirituality. This Gospel of John is, as we know, the spiritual Gospel. It is not just the earthly life of Jesus : everything here is of spiritual, heavenly and eternal significance, not of earth and time at all.

You notice how it begins. Take the third chapter. The third chapter of John was written when the Church had left its first love, when the Church had left its first position ; when Christianity had taken on an altogether different complexion from what it had at the beginning. This chapter is the enunciation of a fundamental principle of the Christian life which needs to be recovered. We know this chapter—or we think we do. Of course, we know the words. Perhaps we are almost wearied with that name,

Nicodemus. And yet—I do not exaggerate ; please believe me—I speak the truth when I say that I come back to that Gospel of John, after having known it, and read it, and studied it, and spoken on it, for many, many years, and feel that we really have not grasped this—the Church has not grasped what is here. It would be impossible for the present situation amongst Christians and in Christianity in general to exist, if what is in the third chapter of John really obtained! I am not exaggerating ; I cannot be too strong about this.

And so, at the risk of touching on things which you think you know, let us look again at these words. We will not read the whole chapter, but consider the following passages. *"That which is born of the flesh is flesh ; and that which is born of the Spirit is spirit. Marvel not that I said unto thee, Ye must be born anew."* (The margin says ' from above '.) *"The wind bloweth where it listeth, and thou hearest the voice thereof, but knowest not whence it cometh, and whither it goeth . . ."* (' This thing is a mystery to you, you don't know . . .') : *" so is every one that is born of the Spirit."*

A NEW ENTITY

First of all, you have an entity : " That which is born of the flesh." That is an entity. That is not difficult to understand on the natural side. Every little new-born baby is an entity of the flesh : it is something quite concrete, something quite definite, and you do not find two in every respect alike. So far as the flesh is concerned, and the natural, that which is born is a definite, concrete entity—we know that. And, in just the same way, " that which is born of the Spirit " is a distinct, definite, concrete entity, altogether different, but absolutely real. That entity, born of the Spirit, is something quite definite and altogether distinct from that which is born of the flesh. With the new birth of every child of God, a spiritual entity has been brought into being, different entirely from the entity and the constitution of the natural, but just as real, just as definite.

I repeat: very, very few Christians seem to understand or know this. We have 'joined' something, we have 'joined Christianity', we have 'gone into the Christian religion'—put it how you will. It is something objective; we have come over into some other sphere of interests and activity and life and conduct. That is the idea about Christianity. The Lord Jesus here is saying—what the New Testament confirms through and through—that this is an altogether different thing; this is not one bit of the order of the natural, this is spiritual; the natural and the spiritual belong to two different orders and kingdoms. That is the context of these words. And therefore every born-again child of God is, in the innermost truth of their being, a different entity. It is not that they have 'taken on' something, or 'gone into' something. I have often used the word 'species'—they are a different kind of person in their very being, with another constitution, something constituted by the Holy Spirit, the Spirit of God, all from above.

People are talking nowadays about visiting the moon. At the end of the century men will perhaps have landed on the moon—but not with their bare earthly constitution! No man, just as he is, will ever do that. He will have to have an apparatus which constitutes him, in effect, a different kind of person, in order to live out there. To go into that realm as he is would be disaster, destruction. And you and I will never be able to go to Heaven without a new constitution—and not an artificial one either! No make-up about this! It has got to be constitutional. There is a clear gulf, broad and unbridgeable, between what we are naturally and what we are as children of God.

If you really are a child of God, if you have come to the Lord, if you have really had the experience of salvation, you know that something has happened to you. This is explaining what has happened. And the Holy Spirit says, 'Look here, things have got off that basis.' We have got to get back there. We have got to recognise again this broad line of difference and division between what is natural and what is spiritual in Christianity. There are few things more important than that we as Christians should be able to recognise the fundamental difference between what is natural and what is spiritual. We have a new constitution, a different constitution, by the Holy Spirit.

NATURAL VERSUS SPIRITUAL

The natural man is always trying to get things on to a natural basis. He must bring everything on to the basis of natural reason. He must be able to reason the thing through, to comprehend, to compass the thing with his reason. A very great deal of Christianity is just man taking hold of the Bible, of Christian truth, Christian doctrine, Christian things, and interpreting and applying by natural reason. And the Word of God is as distinct as anything can be: the door is closed to that, the door is *closed. God* has closed the door. You are not going to get anything through by the power of your reason, however big it is—not a bit! Look at our friend, Nicodemus. He stands for all time as an example. "How can a man . . . ? How can these things be?" A good man, a clever man, an intellectual man, a religious man, but outside the door. The door is absolutely closed. Now, you can apply that everywhere. Man may be most devout, most devoted, most religious ; he may be a red-hot fundamentalist, a champion of Christian doctrine ; and yet it may all be in the realm of his own intellectual power and grip. There is a world that is closed to him, of which he knows little or nothing. He has ' heard the voice ', but he ' knows not '. He has heard the sound, and taken the sound as the sum : but there is a mystery that is still outside of his kingdom ; and the result of this is that there may be good, yes, devoted, earnest, sincere people, who, living in that realm in Christian things, cannot understand spiritual people, cannot understand the things of the Spirit at all. Spiritual things will always be a mystery, an enigma, to the natural mind.

"Remember Jesus Christ". The difference between Jesus and the Jewish leaders, in their radical and almost fanatical devotion to religion, was not a difference of religion at all. It was not that He was more religious than they. It was the difference between the spiritual and the natural in religion. To them He was an enigma, He was a mystery —and, of course, He was all wrong. He *could* not be right, for, you see, natural reasoning says this and that ; but how off the mark they were. Now do you get the point? It is an exceedingly important one. A real walk with God in the Spirit, while, of course, never contradicting Scripture, but always being consistent with the Word of God, is very often a lonely thing amongst Christians. The tragedy is that it should be so, but it is very often like that. What then is spirituality? It is first of all a fundamental change in the being, in the entity, in the person: that is spirituality. After that, it has many outworkings.

THE SOVEREIGNTY OF THE SPIRIT

" The wind bloweth where it listeth, and thou hearest the voice thereof, but knowest not whence it cometh, and whither it goeth : so is every one that is born of the Spirit." A sovereign act of the Spirit. That takes us back to this other fragment : " That which is born of the flesh is flesh ", and to that earlier fragment in this Gospel by John, which makes it so clear, so emphatic : " . . . which were born, not . . . of the flesh, nor of the will of man, but of God " (i. 13). This is something in the sovereign hands of the Holy Spirit and taken right out of the hands of men. You cannot convert yourself, you cannot convert anyone else ; you cannot make yourself into this other creature, this new creation, and you can never make anyone else it. And you can never say when it is to be, either for yourself, or for anyone else. All that is a matter of the sovereign Spirit. If the wind decides to blow, it does not give you notice a day beforehand ! It just blows, and when it blows you cannot say, ' You are out-of-date, you have come at the wrong time—this is not a convenient moment !' It blows, and that is all there is to it.

Now here you are touching a principle : the sovereignty of the Spirit, as represented by the sovereignty of the wind. You know quite well that is useless to stand up against the wind when it really decides to blow. Carry that principle over further into the New Testament, and you will read three times : " And the Lord added to the church those that were being saved . . . ", " there were added unto them . . . ", " there were added to the Lord . . . " Who added? Did the apostles add? Not at all. The Lord added. There is all the difference between our being told to go and join a church, and the Lord adding to Christ, or between our joining what we call a church, and being added to Christ. We cannot join Christ at our own will, just when we want to, or think we will decide to, because being added to Christ involves being re-constituted on a different principle, and that is not in our power at all. It is the Lord who must do it, so that the adding is His sovereign act: and when He decides to do it, it is wonderful, is it not? And if He does not decide to do it, you can work yourself to death, and nothing will happen. This is the work of the Lord.

Look at the day of Pentecost. The wind blew then—a mighty rushing wind. Was it sovereignty? " And there were added unto them in that day about three thousand souls." This was the sovereignty of the Spirit. How wide and far-reaching is the application of that! Oh, that Christianity were on that fundamental basis to-day—the absolute sovereignty of the Holy Spirit! Why is it not so? Because of the present sovereignty of the natural, because of the intrusion into Christianity of the natural man.

A NEW FACULTY

Read again John chapter three. As we have seen, we have here a new constitution, a new entity—" that which is born of the Spirit ". Here, too, we have the sovereignty of the Spirit: He blows where He will, and there is always a mystery, a glorious mystery, about Him and His work. But notice, further, that it is a matter of capacity. To Nicodemus, the Lord says: " Art thou the teacher of Israel, and understandest not these things? . . . We speak that we do know . . . If I told you earthly things, and ye believe not . . . " ' Why, if you cannot understand the secret of the wind—and that is a natural phenomenon, that is an earthly thing that belongs to your world of reason—if you cannot cope with that, what will it be when I tell you heavenly things?' "We speak that we do know".

Do you see the point? Here is a difference of capacity, a new and a different faculty of knowledge, of apprehension and comprehension and understanding. It is a spiritual faculty, for spiritual things. I know how familiar this is to many : it is not new ; but there is an urgent need that we should bring this again to the whole realm of our Christianity. I am sure that it has not yet been grasped by many Christians, even of long standing in the Christian life, that, by their very constitution as children of God, they are supposed to have a faculty which makes them capable of comprehending and understanding spiritual things that no natural mind can understand. The youngest child of God is supposed to have this faculty. It may not be fully developed, but it is a constituent of their very being. Have you grasped that? And the very presence of that faculty is the basis upon which everything in the Christian life is going to be built. The Holy Spirit only builds upon *His own* foundations, upon what *He Himself* puts down as a basis. And that basis is a spiritual one : that which is of the Spirit is spiritual. All our growth, therefore, is going to be along the line of spiritual understanding, spiritual knowledge : not the accumulation of a vast amount of truth, or of religious, Christian information, but what the Spirit teaches us. It will be *through the Word,* but *only what the Spirit teaches,* for He has come for that very purpose.

Now, there must be a link between us and the Holy Spirit, which is in correspondence with Himself ; and the link between the Holy Spirit and the born-again child of God is the renewed spirit of the child of God, with this new capacity, so that the child of God, over against the whole world of merely intellectual knowledge, is able to

say : ' We know '—" we speak that we do know ". It may
be very little, but you know, you know now. As far as you
have gone, it is a knowledge which is yours, which is new
and altogether different. You are able to say : ' I don't
know very much, but what I do know, I know ; and the
way in which I have come to know it is not because it has
been presented to me, but because it has happened in me.
Something has been done inside ; and, although I cannot
put it into words or theories, or compose it into a set of
ideas, I know—*I know !* ' " We speak that we do know ".
There is something about spiritual knowledge which is so
strong, so settled, so satisfying, so rest-giving. It is a new
capacity. What is the difference? " If I have told you earthly things . . . " That is one realm : what about the heavenly
things? ' Now, Nicodemus, with all your wonderful outfit
of birth, upbringing, training, education, you are still in
the realm of earthly things, and even there they are beyond
you. You have not yet come into the realm of heavenly
things.' Therefore, " Marvel not that I said unto thee, Ye
must be born from above."

That is a very, very great need in safeguarding the whole
Christian situation and in the recovery of spiritual effectiveness in this world : a fresh discernment of the fundamental difference between the natural and the spiritual—
yes, even in Christian things. No one thinks that I am
speaking about something that is extra to what is in the
Word of God. I am speaking about the necessary faculty
given by the Holy Spirit, and the necessary work of the
Holy Spirit, in order that we should rightly know the mind
of the Spirit in the Word of God. If we get on to any other
basis than that, all sorts of things will happen, which will
be very sad and very distressing and very wrong. The Holy
Spirit said through Paul to Timothy : " All Scripture is

given by inspiration of God . . . " Paul is saying, in effect,
' Look here, we must get back to what the Holy Spirit has
given, what has come from the Holy Spirit, and what,
therefore, is spiritual. We must get back to what God
means.'

John iii is a tremendous offset, not only to the world of
the unconverted and un-born-again, but to a great amount
of Christianity as we know it, which is clearly not the
Christianity of a different entity, of a different constitution,
of a different capacity. Let us be sure that with us it is the
right thing, and not the false and the imitation.

THE SIGNIFICANCE OF PENTECOST

Let me close with a word of warning. This is not necessarily a special revelation that is given to any particular
persons. Be very careful there. It may sound a fine point,
but it is a very important one. It does not mean that, because we are so re-constituted and have this other faculty,
we get a special revelation. No, it is not a special revelation, but it is a special faculty for knowing what has been
revealed.

This is the inclusive and comprehensive meaning of the
advent of the Holy Spirit. What took place on the day of
Pentecost corresponded, in the history of the Church, to
what took place in the personal life of the Lord Jesus at
the Jordan. At the Jordan He was baptized, signifying that
He was buried, that something was put out of sight. In
type, in figure, the natural man goes out of view. He rises
in type another man. And then what? Heaven opens, the
Spirit descends, and from that point everything is by the
Spirit. " Then was Jesus led up of the Spirit into the wilderness . . . " And then to Nazareth : " And he opened the roll,

and found the place where it was written, The Spirit of the
Lord is upon me . . . " Everything is by the Spirit.

Again, let us be understood correctly. We have not said
that in the baptism of Jesus an " old man " literally was
buried as in the case of all other believers, but that—sin
apart—He was taking representatively the ground that we
all have to take in one particular respect, that is that nothing shall be in life that is not of the Father by the Holy
Spirit. In Him it was wholly true, but in us it is a position
to be taken and then made real as we seek to walk in the
Spirit.

And so we come to Pentecost. Has the Church in its
representation or nucleus been baptized into His death?
Well, look at them! Before they are re-established on resurrection ground, they are baptized into His death right
enough. They have come to an end of all natural resources,
either for understanding anything, for seeing through anything, or for being able to do anything. They are as good as
dead and buried—no prospect, no future. " We hoped
. . . "—we *hoped*, in the past tense—" that it was he which
should redeem Israel ", and that hope has now gone, there
is nothing. Yes, they were indeed baptized into His death.
But now, on the day of Pentecost, what do we find? They
are raised as a vessel, and the Heaven is opened, and the
Spirit comes and fills it, and from that time everything is
by the Spirit. They had a new knowledge—and how their
knowledge grew, even in the Word of God! The Word of
God, which was for them the Old Testament, had been so
largely a closed book, spiritually. They had only got it in
the letter, and they were all wrong in their interpretation
of it, as it came to be proved. Now the Bible is for them a
new, because they are on new ground ; potentially in the
new day of the Spirit.

CHAPTER SIX

THE TESTIMONY OF JESUS

WE HAVE SEEN THAT, at the end of the apostolic age, and with the close of the first Christian century, Christianity had completely changed. It had lost its primal, original character and nature. And it was in the consciousness of the onset of this change that the Apostle wrote these letters to Timothy, and sought to indicate the way—the only way, God's way—of keeping the things of God pure, maintaining them according to their original nature. In God's thought for 'Christianity'—I use that wide term for the moment—everything had been, and was intended to be, wholly spiritual; whereas that which was developing was a system—formal, ecclesiastical, outward and so on, ordered, governed, arranged and carried on by man. These letters are a strong appeal for the recovery and maintenance of that wholly spiritual character in every department and every aspect of the life of the Christian community.

Now I have used the large word 'Christianity' and the term 'the Christian community', and I am coming immediately to what they really mean—the proper term for them —for neither of those expressions is used in the New Testament. There is a term for what they are intended to mean, and that term is " the Church ". I ask you to look at one or two fragments from these letters which intimate the matter.

159

"If a man knoweth not how to rule his own house, how shall he take care of the church of God?" (I Timothy iii. 5). We leave the context and immediate application, and just note that this that is called the Church of God is introduced, is referred to, as something that must have been known and recognised, as something taken for granted. There is such a thing as the Church of God. Again: *"These things write I unto thee . . . that thou mayest know how men ought to behave themselves in the house of God, which is the church of the living God, the pillar and ground of the truth" (I Timothy iii. 14, 15).* Finally: *"Therefore I endure all things for the elect's sake, that they also may obtain the salvation which is in Christ Jesus with eternal glory" (II Timothy ii. 10).*

Here then we have, in both letters, attention drawn to the *Church.* What we have been saying about this turning-point in Christian history, this change which was coming about, this departure from the original character and nature, was a *Church* matter. It was not just ' Christianity ', in that very general term ; it was not only that certain Christians were losing out, that a state of spiritual decline had set in with some believers. It was a Church matter. The departure was the departure of the Church. And so these two letters are essentially Church letters: that will become even more clear to you if you just read them through.

Now it is quite clear, from the verses we have just read, that the Apostle was speaking of the Church in more than one conception. He was not saying to Timothy, who was in the church in Ephesus, and had a great responsibility given him by the Apostle in relation to that church, ' Now Ephesus is the church of the living God.' He was not saying that any local church is *the* Church. But, to turn it round the other way, he was saying that *the* Church as a whole should find its representation in every local church, that what is true of the whole Church, in the mind of God, ought to be true wherever it is found in a local expression. Any local church should be a representation of *the* Church as a whole. And then the Apostle brings it down to the individuals, the persons, and, in effect, clearly says, ' Now, any one of you individuals can show what the Church is meant to be, as a whole, or else you can let it down. You are not just individual Christians—yours is a Church responsibility!'

WHAT IS THE CHURCH?

This matter is of very great importance in the connection with which we are occupied—God's first supreme thought concerning the Church. *What is the Church?* That is the first question. I think Paul very definitely gives us the answer in a particular term that he uses. " Therefore I endure all things for the elect's sake . . ." (II Timothy ii. 10). If you look at the context, you will see that the Apostle takes that back to what he here calls " before times eternal ". So the Church is something which is ' elect before times eternal ', something quite clearly defined as an elect people, an elect body, which has its roots in eternity past, and therefore is not historical. It is eternal, and therefore it must be spiritual. We may just note one other relevant verse in this connection : " Who saved us, and called us with a holy calling, not according to our works, but according to his own purpose and grace, which was given us in Christ Jesus before times eternal . . ." (II Tim. i. 9). " Purpose . . . grace . . . given us in Christ Jesus before times eternal ". So the very first thing is that the Church,

L

according to God's mind, is altogether different from, and above, anything that is historical—anything, that is, that has its beginnings and course and development in time. This is something which has its beginnings in eternity past, and its course is ordered according to the purpose conceived in eternity past. This is something not constituted by man, not brought into being by any human effort whatsoever : this is something which is constituted by the Holy Spirit, the eternal Spirit. And, as we were seeing earlier, that which is constituted by the Holy Spirit is essentially a spiritual thing. "That which is born of the Spirit is spirit."

Now that, as we saw, relates to the new birth of the individual : the individual Christian is essentially constituted a spiritual being by the work of the Holy Spirit. And what is true of the individual is true of the aggregate of the born-anew : the Church is something born of the Holy Spirit and therefore is a spiritual thing. That does not mean that it is abstract. I have heard someone, praying in a meeting, make the petition that the message should not be ' so spiritual that it was hidden and not manifest '. Well, we know exactly what he meant and are in full agreement, and I am not putting him right when I say that it is impossible for anything to be spiritual and not manifest. Can the Holy Spirit be present, active, living, and no one know it? What is spiritual is not just abstract, indefinite ; something intangible, in the air, like a vapour or a cloud. What is spiritual is terrific, it is mighty ; and so, when the Church was really a spiritual body, it was—and the word can be well applied—it was terrific.

I referred earlier to what the Church encountered, which was developing just at the time that Paul wrote these very letters. It caused his own imprisonment and his own execution, and it was the cause of much that Paul wrote to

Timothy about being strong. For Timothy himself had been arrested with Paul and imprisoned, and later released. Paul (or the author of the letter to the Hebrews) wrote : " Know ye that our brother Timothy hath been set at liberty " (Heb. xiii. 23). But Timothy knew something of what was pending. He needed to be encouraged to be strong. I am referring to what the Church had to encounter in those unspeakable persecutions, horrors diabolical, indescribable, going on for many, many years, with the whole Roman world, the greatest Empire that had been, determined to blot out the name of Jesus of Nazareth by liquidating the last Christian on this earth ; and it stood at nothing, human or inhuman, to do it. And when it had done its worst, the Roman Empire went to ashes and the Church rose out of them, triumphant, growing. Yes, anything that is of the Holy Ghost is a tremendous thing ; nothing can stand before it. Spirituality, true Divine spirituality—that which is born of the Spirit and filled with the Spirit and governed by the Spirit—is not something abstract : it is a potent force in this universe.

THE CHURCH A SPIRITUAL PEOPLE

So the Church, according to the Divine conception, consists essentially of—indeed *is*—a spiritual people, and we must somehow get to the place where we see it as God and as Heaven sees it. And that means a tremendous adjustment for us to make. Our practical difficulty is this. In apostolic times, it was quite easy to see the Church as a single entity. Although it was represented in numerous local companies all over the Roman world, yet it was still a single entity : it was not then divided up into the ' -ists ' and the ' -ans ' and the ' -ians ' and the ' -ics ' and the

'-isms' and all the other terminations that we know to-day. When you speak to Christian people to-day, they very soon ask you if you are an '-ist', or an '-ic', or an '-an', or an '-ian', and they say 'I am an . . . ist'. Ah, but there was nothing of that in the Church in the days of the Apostles. Whatever little differences there were amongst the Lord's people locally, the Church as a whole was one entity, everywhere, held together by spiritual ties and by spiritual ministries, but with no central government or sectional government of affiliated bodies. It was just one, everywhere. If you had gone from one province to another, from one country to another, visiting the Christians in every place, they would never have asked you whether you were an '-ist', or an '-ian', or an '-ic'—whether you belonged to some particular group, distinguished by a special name. No, you were a Christian—that was enough. You belonged to the Lord—that was enough.

But, with the closing of the apostolic age, things were changing—changing into what we have to-day. An altogether wrong and false mentality has grown up around the word 'church'. Most people to-day, when that word is used, think of one of these things with a special termination, or of some place or building—a 'church'—and that is the mentality that is common. Let us be quite clear : *recovery of the original demands an escape from that mentality*. Do not misunderstand me : I am not saying you have got to come out of this and that and the other thing—I am saying that you have got to get out of a *mentality*. We need absolute emancipation from this earth mentality about the Church, into the heavenly standpoint ; to see what the Church really is, as God sees it and as Heaven sees it. We must get free of the confusion which has been brought about by the historical institution called 'The Church'.

What is the Church, from Heaven's standpoint? Heaven does not look upon the matter in the light of these titles, and these sections, and these departments, and these bodies, and these divisions; it does not look at it like that at all. Heaven ignores all that, and looks for members of Christ, born-again children of God, spiritual people, in their constitution by new birth and the indwelling of the Holy Spirit. And wherever Heaven sees those—whether it be in an ' -ism ', or an ' -ic ', or an ' -an ', or anything else—that is the Church, and you and I have got to adjust to that. A *congregation* is not the Church, but *within* a congregation the Church may be represented by only two people. Out of 100 people gathered in what is called a church, 98 may be unsaved people, though adherents and communicants and all the rest, and two may be born-again ones. Those two are the Church, and the others are not! That is what the Church is. It is constituted by the Holy Spirit bringing through to new birth spiritually-made people.

I said Heaven ignores the other. In a sense that is true, but maybe in another sense it is not true, because Heaven will judge the other as a false thing. In a sense, however, Heaven ignores, and I say this because it is a thing that you and I have got to do: meet people—no matter in what they are ; you may not agree with it, you may think it is false ; you have got to ignore that—meet people on the ground of Christ, have to do with them, as far as you can, solely on the ground that they belong to the Lord. Our only enquiry has got to be: ' Do you belong to the Lord? are you born again?' That is all. And then, if they say, ' I am a so-and-so-ist: what are you?', we must reply, ' That does not matter ; leave that out. We belong to the Lord : let us be content with this.' Until you and I can do that, we are held in the lifeless grip of a thing that has lost its spiritual power—because it has lost its true identity, its true nature, which was *spiritual*. Yes, we must adjust to Heaven's point of view. I am really only giving you the letter to the Ephesians! That is how it is seen in Heaven.

FOR WHAT DOES THE CHURCH EXIST?

Well, that is the answer, very inadequately, very briefly, to the question, What is the Church? The second question is: *For what does the Church exist?* We have it stated for us by Paul here, have we not, in the very words that we have read: "... how men ought to behave themselves in the house of God, which is the church of the living God, the pillar and stay of the truth "—and there ought to be no full period there, only a pause to take a breath—" And without controversy great is the mystery of godliness; He who was manifested in the flesh, justified in the spirit, seen of angels, preached among the nations, believed on in the world, received up in glory " (I Tim. iii. 15, 16). That is the deposit in the Church; that is the testimony of Jesus. For that the Church exists. It is to that the Apostle refers, you notice, more than once, when he says: " O Timothy, guard that which is committed unto thee ..." (I Tim. vi. 20; II Tim. i. 14). 'O Timothy, guard the deposit, the trust ...' The Church is the repository of the testimony of Jesus.

What is the testimony of Jesus? There are, of course, certain statements about it here, in the passage we have just read. But I am not going to take up these different clauses, because I am not at the moment concerned with Christian doctrine, or with the doctrine of the Church. I am occupied with the Church itself. But I turn you now to the book of the Revelation, for, as we have said in our last chapter, the writings of John, written after Paul had finished his work and gone to glory, related to the full development of this very thing whose beginnings Paul had witnessed. The book of the Revelation is peculiarly appropriate to this state of spiritual departure and declension, and you find that the all-governing thing of the whole book is this one phrase: "the testimony of Jesus".

John said that he was "in the isle . . . called Patmos, for the word of God and the testimony of Jesus" (Rev. i. 9). But there is a Divine sovereignty over the Roman Empire, over the persecutors and over the one who has sent him to Patmos—a Divine sovereignty which says: 'Right, this is what I have brought you here for! They sent you, but I have brought you! This is not their sovereignty that has put you here; this is Mine. I have something to say to the Church, and I have given you a quiet time to say it for Me.' 'I was in the isle that is called Patmos—because the Roman Empire sent me there? because the Roman Emperor sent me there? because the persecutors caught me and sent me there?' Not a bit of it! "I was in the isle . . . called Patmos . . . for . . . the testimony of Jesus". Now that may have been because he had stood for the testimony of Jesus: but it is very impressive, is it not, that that phrase runs through this whole book, and is seen, as we go on, to be the thing by which the Lord is judging, first of all the churches, and then, representatively, the Church as a whole. And, having dealt with the Church on the basis of the testimony of Jesus, He moves on to deal with the nations, and eventually with the Devil himself and his kingdom. It is all related to the testimony of Jesus.

THE LIVING PRESENCE OF JESUS

What is it? Well, the testimony of Jesus is presented to us symbolically right at the beginning of the book, in the

declaration—we will leave the symbolism for the moment
—made by the Lord Himself: " I am . . . the Living one
. . . I became dead, and behold, I am alive unto the ages of
the ages, and I have the keys of death and of Hades. Write
therefore . . . " What is the testimony of Jesus? *The present,
living Person of Jesus in the power of the Holy Ghost.*
That is where it begins: the living Person of Jesus. Not
the historic Jesus of Palestine of centuries ago—no, the
right up-to-date, here-and-now living Jesus, manifested,
demonstrated, proved to be alive in the power of the Holy
Ghost. Is that carrying it too far? Well, then, why, when
the seven churches in Asia are challenged, is there the
seven times repeated " He that hath an ear, let him hear
what the Spirit saith to the churches "? The Holy Spirit
has got this matter in hand. The Holy Spirit is challenging
—not concerning a creed, or a doctrine as such, but concerning the manifestation of the living Christ, there, and
there, and there. The testimony of Jesus, whether it be in
Ephesus, or Smyrna, or Pergamum, or in any other place,
is just this: that the place where that church is—the town,
the city, the province—is to know, in the power of the Holy
Ghost, that Jesus is alive! That is where it begins. By its
very presence, by its very existence, by its very life there
in that place, the one thing that people are to know is that
they have not got rid of Jesus. They have not been able to
put Him out of this world—He is here, alive!

It is very simple; but that is what the Church is here
for, after all. The very basic purpose of the Church is in
the first place to make this world know that Jesus is alive,
not merely declaring the doctrinal fact, but by living in
the power of His resurrection. There are times in some
countries when the Church is not able to preach and proclaim the truth of Christ, but that is not the end of its

power. Even though silenced in words, it can still make
known that Jesus is alive. Yes, the testimony of Jesus is :
" I am he that *liveth* . . . "; " the church of the *living* God,
the pillar and stay of the truth . . . " ; but it is more—it is
the living victory of Christ in the power of the Holy Spirit.
" I became dead, and behold, I am alive . . . ", never to
become dead again. " I have the keys of death . . . ", the
mastery, the authority, the power over death. ' I have absolutely triumphed over death and all that occasioned death
—sin—in the power of the Holy Spirit.' That is the testimony of Jesus: His living victory, present where Christians are.

Are you thinking that this all very wonderful and very
beautiful, but is this practical? Listen ! It is so practical
that, if you are a living member of Christ, and if you are
in a company of believers, born-again believers, constituted
by the Holy Spirit, on this true spiritual basis, you will,
without doubt, be taken into situations, conditions, where
only the resurrection power of Jesus Christ will get you
through ! Your very survival will necessitate your knowing the power of His resurrection. For individual believers,
from time to time, and for local companies of the Lord's
people, just as truly as for the Church universal (as in those
days to which I have referred), survival is a testimony to
the fact that death has no place here. Death cannot swallow
this up—death itself has been swallowed up in victory !
What a glorious assurance that is ! What a ground of confidence ! What an encouragement ! We come to times
when it looks as though the end has come, we are not going
to survive and get through. But never believe it ! The life
of Jesus was not taken from Him by men : He deliberately
laid it down, by His own free will. " This authority ", He
said, " I received from my Father." The life of Paul was not

taken from him by the executioner's axe just outside Rome. " I am already being offered, and the time of my departure is come." Here is a man who knows when it is the Lord's time for him to go to glory: he is just being offered up, and he is handing himself over. Paul never said, ' I am going to be executed, they are going to kill me ' ; he said, ' I am being offered up '.

If you and I are living on the basis of this One, who says: "I became dead, and behold, I am alive for evermore" —if we are living in the power of His resurrection, our end will be God-governed, not man-governed. It will be when the Lord says, ' It is enough ', not when circumstances dictate. God is in charge of this where His Church is concerned. And so, whatever the world does, whatever men do, and whatever the Devil does with the Church, local or universal, if it is really on this basis, it just cannot be brought to nought. Gamaliel is our stand-by here, is he not? ' If it is of God, you had better leave it alone ; you had better not be found to be fighting against God. Be careful! If it is not of God, well, it will peter out sooner or later ; but if it is of God, you can do nothing . . . ' (Acts v. 34 – 39). And that from a non-Christian! You see the point. This is the Church which is to embody the testimony of Jesus in terms of a life that has conquered death, to be the embodiment of a living victory in the power of the Holy Spirit.

EXPRESSING THE NATURE OF CHRIST

And then it is to be the expression of the living nature and character of Jesus in the Holy Spirit. That is far too large a matter for us to consider fully here ; it can only be stated. But it must be stated, because, both in these

letters to Timothy and in the Revelation, much is made of
this matter of the expression of the Lord Jesus in His
character. The decline was from a level of character, the
departure was from an expression of what Christ is in His
nature. We can never, never overcome the world, nor the
Devil and all his powers, if that same Devil has got a foothold right in our being, if there is something there that is
of himself in moral failure or delinquency. In the power
of the same Holy Spirit, you and I have got to exemplify
Christ—the Church must exemplify Christ, express what
Christ is ; not merely give out facts about Christ, but be the
embodiment of Christ's nature.

That is why John, coming back at the end of the apostolic age, has so much to say about this matter of love. 'You
don't know the Lord', he says, ' if you don't love your
brother. It is no use your saying you love the Lord, if you
don't love your brother—that is all nonsense '. In other
words, it is hypocrisy. ' How can a man love God, whom
he has not seen, if he does not love his brother whom he
has seen?' (I John iv. 20). That is John's argument. It is
a matter of ' walking in the light as He is in the light '
(ch. i. 7). So much of John's writings touches upon this
thing. Look at those letters to the seven churches. What
they are concerned with is state, condition, with lost spiritual life, in the sense of expressing what Christ is like in
His nature. That is the testimony of Jesus. The testimony
is lost if you and I are un-Christ-like. It is no use using
phrases, and making claims : these have to be substantiated
by what we are like, and what we are like must be what
Christ is like. The Church is for that purpose. It does not
merely consist of a set of doctrines to be upheld—although
the doctrines must be upheld ; not of a number of ordinances to be maintained and repeated, not of congregations

of Christians having meetings and conferences. It is to be the embodiment of Christ by the Holy Spirit.

THE HOLY SPIRIT GOVERNING FROM HEAVEN

Now, coming back to the matter of the point of change that we mentioned earlier, the Church in which we find ourselves to-day, with all its break-up and division, its sectionalism and so on, is so different from what we have just described. How are we going to get over this? Well, it just depends where the seat of government is, does it not? As things are to-day, there is no one government of the whole Church on this earth, is there? We do not admit the claims of Rome. But it is not true for any section that the headquarters of the Church is any *place*. The headquarters of *the Church* is in Heaven. *The* seat of government of *the* Church is in Heaven ; it is nowhere else. And the Lord will not allow it to be anywhere else. When Jerusalem was beginning to assume the character of a governmental headquarters for the expanding Church, the Lord scattered them to the ends of the earth. No headquarters on earth ! Headquarters is in Heaven.

At this point I would like to take you into the book of the Revelation again, and indicate certain passages, though without staying for much comment on each.

" John to the seven churches which are in Asia : Grace to you and peace, from him which is and which was and which is to come ; and from the seven Spirits which are before his throne . . ." (Rev. i. 4).

" These things saith he that hath the seven Spirits of God, and the seven stars : I know thy works . . ." (iii. 1).

" Out of the throne proceed lightnings and voices and thunders. And there were seven lamps of fire burning be-

fore the throne, which are the seven Spirits of God" (iv. 5).
" I saw in the midst of the throne and of the four living
creatures, and in the midst of the elders, a Lamb standing,
as though it had been slain, having seven horns, and seven
eyes, which are the seven Spirits of God . . ." (v. 6).

This book is, as you know, just full of symbols. Here
you have these four references to the seven Spirits. It does
not, of course, mean that there were seven separate Spirits.
Seven is the number of spiritual entirety, completeness,
fulness. When you come to the number seven, you have
completed something: for instance, the seventh day
marked the completion of creation. I need not go further.
Seven is spiritual completeness: so that the symbolism
here is of the fulness, the completeness, the absoluteness of
the Holy Spirit. " These things saith he that hath the seven
Spirits . . . " This that is going to be said is in the authority
and the power of the Holy Spirit. *He* is in charge of this
matter, He it is that is inditing these things that are to be
said, He it is that is before the throne. The Holy Spirit, in
touch with the seat of government, is dealing with things
down here. Have you grasped that? There are all these
things down here on the earth, but the throne, the seat of
the government of everything, is up there.

Note that the first connection of the seven Spirits is with
the throne and with the " seven stars " which are " the
angels of the seven churches " (i. 16, 20 ; iii. 1). The throne
of government of things down here is in the hands of the
Holy Spirit, in the fulness of His power and intelligence.
The " seven eyes " speak of His knowing all about it, seeing perfectly the truth through all the deception, through
all the masks, through all the pretence and profession,
through the ' name to live ' ; perfect perception, perfect
knowledge, perfect comprehension. The Holy Spirit is

governing in the fulness of His knowledge. And in the fulness of His power—" seven lamps of fire burning ". This is not cold light, this is not just theoretical knowledge ; this is not something abstract. It is a burning lamp, it is something that is alive with fire, with power : He has come to deal with this situation in the burning power of His judgment and of His knowledge. Things are alive with the Holy Spirit.

In order to pass with Him, then, the Holy Spirit requires that everything must be purely spiritual. It has got to be according to the judgment of the *Holy* Spirit, the Spirit of God. The Holy Spirit operates in relation to " The Lamb in the Throne ". That is the testimony in relation to all our sin, and all our failure : it is the Lamb in the throne. But what we are saying is that the Lord's idea of a Church, in any dispensation, in any age, at any time, in any place, is that it is essentially a spiritual thing, essentially a heavenly thing : it is essentially governed by the Holy Spirit. The headquarters are in the throne, and the Holy Spirit administers the Church from Heaven. If He does not, then man will have to administer it himself, and he will make an awful mess of it, as he has done. Oh, for a people, wherever they are—whether local companies or the Lord's people at large—really to be under this government of the Holy Spirit !

I will close by saying this. Every one of us, and young Christians perhaps especially, need to realise this : that, in coming to the Lord, having received Christ as our Saviour, having become a Christian, having been converted—however you may put it—if you have been truly born again, you are not just a Christian individual. You are a part of an eternally foreseen, chosen Body, you belong to a great spiritual, corporate entity, you belong to every other truly born-again child of God. Yours is a related life and not just an individual life. So much depends upon your realising that! You have not *just* 'become a Christian'—you have become something infinitely more than that. You have become a member of this timeless, heavenly thing, conceived "before times eternal", fulfilling its real vocation when time shall be no more. That is what you have come into! And you have come into a tremendous vocation, to be part of that which is to keep alive the testimony of Jesus in this world.

You see, the Devil and his vast kingdom of countless hosts of evil spirits, as Paul puts it, is out against one thing, and one thing only. From the beginning, when Jesus Christ was "appointed heir of all things" (Heb. i. 2), Satan has relentlessly and unceasingly set himself to frustrate and spoil and destroy one thing—the testimony of Jesus. And if he divides us up and gets in between us, he has touched the testimony of Jesus, because the testimony of Jesus is so bound up with our united and related life.

CHAPTER SEVEN

THE RESPONSIBILITY OF THE CHRISTIAN

Our final word will be very simple, but I trust vital. I ask you to look again at the letters to Timothy, with special reference to four very brief series, or groups, of fragments.

Here is the first series :

I Tim. i. 11 : "... the gospel ... which was committed to my trust."

i. 18 : "This charge I commit unto thee, my child Timothy ..."

vi. 20 : "O Timothy, guard that which is committed unto thee ..."

II Tim. i. 12 : "... I know him whom I have believed, and am persuaded that he is able to guard that which I have committed unto him against that day." (You will see that the margin gives the alternative : "He is able to guard that which he hath committed unto me".)

Now the second series :

I Tim. i. 18 : "This charge I commit unto thee ... that ... thou mayest war the good warfare".

II Tim. ii. 3, 4 : "Suffer hardship with me, as a good soldier of Christ Jesus. No soldier on service entangleth

176

*himself in the affairs of this life ; that he may please him
who enrolled him as a soldier."*

The third series :

*II Tim. ii. 5 : " And if also a man contend in the games,
he is not crowned, except he have contended lawfully."*

The fourth series :

*II Tim. ii. 15 : " Give diligence to present thyself approved
unto God, a workman that needeth not to be ashamed,
handling aright the word of truth."*

I wonder what impression those passages make upon
you. Hearing them, reading them, putting them together,
what is the conclusion to which you come? What do they
say to you? Surely they ought to leave one very definite
impression upon us : namely, that *the Christian is a very
responsible person.* Every one of those passages, and indeed,
the much more lying behind them and in these letters, does
really say very, very clearly and very strongly : We are
in a position of tremendous responsibility. The Christian
is, in the Word of God, looked upon as being a very
responsible person.

When the Lord Jesus and His apostles appealed to
people to come along and follow, to be saved, to become
Christians, it was never just for their own pleasure, just
that they might have a good time. The appeal was never
to the pleasure-instinct in people, to the desire for a good
time. They never, never made their appeal on that ground
at all—that if you are saved, if you become a Christian, you
are going to embark upon an endless joy-ride, a whole life
of pleasure and gratification. Whatever there may be of
good and enjoyment and profit to follow, the appeal of

M

Christ, the appeal of His apostles, the appeal of the Scriptures, is always to people who mean business more than pleasure, who really are prepared to take serious responsibility for the interests of their Lord, and, if needs be, to allow themselves to be involved in trouble or suffering for His sake. They are the people He wants.

THE CHRISTIAN AS TRUSTEE

Here, then, we have this many-sided picture of the Christian as in responsibility. Let us take up some of the titles or metaphors used, which give the Divine conception of the Christian, very simply. In the first series, I Tim. i. 11 : " According to the gospel of the glory of the blessed God, which was committed to my trust " ; i. 18 : " This charge I commit unto thee, my child Timothy . . . " ; vi. 20 : " O Timothy, guard that which is committed unto thee . . . " What is this conception of the Christian? The Christian is called to be, has the privilege of being, a trustee for God, a custodian of an infinitely precious deposit, committed to his trust. ' Timothy, you are in trust ; Timothy, you are a trustee ; Timothy, here is something precious put into your custodianship, given you of God to watch over, to guard for Him.' Paul calls it ' the gospel of the blessed God which was committed to his trust ', and he is passing it on. He has kept it intact, he has guarded it, he has preserved it : it has lost nothing ; but he is about to go. ' Timothy, I pass it on to you, I hand it on to you in the Lord's Name. Timothy, guard it. It is for you to see that this Gospel, this wonderful Gospel, suffers no loss by any kind of carelessness, unwatchfulness, indifference, slothfulness, preoccupation or diversion, persecution or suffering, or anything else. Let there come to it nothing to spoil it, no tarnish, no rust, no injury. Timothy, guard it—do not let it suffer loss.' That is the Divine conception of the Christian.

What I want to urge upon you is just this. If you would claim to be a Christian, to belong to the Lord, I would that you would recognise this: that you are put in trust with the Gospel, that you are a trustee of " the gospel of the blessed God ", that there rests upon you this solemn obligation to see that it does not suffer in any way through you, because of you, that on no account does it suffer, but that it is preserved in its pristine glory and in its entirety; and that you at the end do what Paul was able to do—pass it on intact, so that there will be those who come after you who will, in their turn, take it up from you and carry it on. Does that sound very simple, very elementary? Paul put his heart into this. ' O Timothy, my child Timothy—this charge, this *charge* I commit to thee. Guard the deposit, take care of the great trust.' Will you believe, whether you are the youngest Christian or the oldest, or somewhere between, that you are a custodian of the interests of your Lord, and that those great interests can suffer because of you, if you do not take your responsibility seriously?

But that is a very elevating thing—it is a very strengthening thing to realise that, is it not? To feel that God has committed to me His interests, that I stand in this world, not just to be a Christian and try to live a Christian life, but as a responsible trustee of the very interests of God! Whether we like it or not, it is so. If you are a Christian, this great trust, this great Gospel, is suffering or being preserved by you; it is being let down or it is being upheld, whether you like it or not. But why not do what Paul was seeking to get Timothy to do? Realise this, face this, and take it up, as a solemn responsibility before God : ' I am a man with a charge, put in trust, a trustee.'

THE CHRISTIAN AS WARRIOR

The next series of fragments begins with the 18th verse of chapter one of the first letter : " War the good warfare . . ." ; followed by these so familiar words in the second letter, second chapter : " . . . a good soldier of Christ Jesus. No soldier on service entangleth himself in the affairs of this life ; that he may please him who enrolled him as a soldier."

(a) ON ACTIVE SERVICE

There are three ideas bound up with those words. Firstly, of course, the conception of the Christian as a warrior, and of the Christian life and Christian service as a warfare. Perhaps we hardly need to be reminded of that. It may be that you are a really war-scarred warrior : you have been in the fight and the battle has left its marks on you. You know it quite well. And yet it needs to be said—perhaps firstly to those who have newly donned the armour, who have newly come to the Lord. Understand that you have been enrolled in a spiritual *army* ! That is what it says : you have been enrolled in a spiritual army, and your life-business is *war*. You are going to find that out sooner or later, whether you like it or not ; but there is the fact. And that is a very responsible position. One, by failure in this warfare, may let down many and affect the whole campaign.

But, although the older ones may know it so well, and feel that you do not need to be reminded, are you sure that you do not? I think I know something about the warfare from experience; and yet, and yet—there is this subtle truth, this subtle fact, that very often, when we are in a situation, and things are going on, we begin to blame people and cirumstances, and get all worked up, and look for scapegoats, forgetting the reality of this thing—Why, the Devil is after something! Here is the battle on, there is no doubt about it; the air is thick with conflict; and we get our eyes on people and things. We are defeated, we are just beaten, rendered casualties, put out of the fight— simply because we lose sight of the fact, the abiding fact, that we are in a spiritual warfare, and that behind ' things ' there are other, spiritual, forces.

We all need to be reminded. It is no small thing, you know, when we are really in a situation like that, and things are getting worked up to a fine pitch and stress, when someone comes along and says, ' Look here, the enemy is in this ; he is trying to get you, he knows something or other, he is on your track; let us have some prayer about it ' ; and we get to prayer, and the whole thing goes. Sometimes just to remind one another of the *fact* is a tremendous deliverance: we find that it *is* a fact. We have been attributing the situation to things and people, and there is all the time something much deeper than that behind it. We need to be reminded continually that we are in a warfare—for we are.

That is the first thing here—this conception of the Christian life—and we must get hold of it and settle it. And, although I don't like saying it, I don't think we are ever going to be out of this warfare here!

(b) WITH UNDIVIDED INTERESTS

The second thing that is in these statements is that, if we are going to wage triumphant spiritual warfare, we

must be *altogether* in it. " No soldier on active service "
(for that is the literal wording) " entangleth himself with
the affairs of this life." He must be *disentangled*. One of
the enemy's most successful tactics is to get us all tied up,
tangled up with all kinds of conflicting things, or with
some other interests, dividing us in our life and in our
strength and in our application. Now this that Paul says
to Timothy here does not mean, ' Look here, you must not
go into business—you must come out of business, and be
all on spiritual work.' It does not mean that you have got to
leave everything else and come and be a full-time worker,
or full-time soldier—it does not mean that at all. It is
entirely possible—and, though difficult, this is what the
Apostle and what the Lord would say to most of us—it is
altogether possible for you to pursue your daily employment, and do it conscientiously and thoroughly, as you
should, leaving nothing for reproach, while yet at the same
time, whether in it, through it, or over it, your supreme
interests are spiritual. The really governing things in your
life are the Lord's things.

The warfare, then, may be in the daily business. But if
you get all churned up and obsessed, you are put out of
the war, out of the fight. Inwardly in our hearts there has
got to be a disentangled spirit. Now that could be enlarged
upon very much. The Apostle is saying : You must not
have two dominating interests in life ; you can only have
one. You must not be a divided person who has, on the one
side, interests in the things of the Lord, on the other side
interests in the world. That is no good ; you will not be a
good soldier if you are like that. If you have to be in this
world, and do its work, and follow your profession, your
dominating concern must be the interests of the Lord, and
in that part of your life you must be disentangled. In a

word, one thing over all must predominate ; there must be no dividedness of heart or mind. " This one thing I do . . . ", said the Apostle.

(c) ALONGSIDE OF OTHERS

And the third factor or feature in these fragments is something which is not observable in our translation. You notice it says: " Suffer hardship with me as a good soldier of Christ Jesus . . ." There are other translations of that clause, such as: " Take your share in suffering hardship . . . " Neither of them, perhaps, gives the exact sense of the original. This is one of the occasions when Paul uses one of his favourite compounds. You know that Paul was tremendously fond of compound words, and one of his favourite kinds of compound was a whole series of words with the prefix ' *syn* ' to them. ' *Syn* ' means ' together ', and what he is saying here is this: ' Look here, Timothy, we are all in it. You are not alone in this ; this is a collective matter, this is a corporate matter. This is something which, if it only related to you, might not be very important ; you might not think it important enough to be seriously considered. But look here, Timothy, we are together—you must not let me down.'

This fact of the collective or corporate aspect of the conflict is a big thing, is it not? We are fighting alongside of one another and for one another ; the battle is a common battle, and we must not let one another down. If someone else is having a bit of hardship, we must come and share the hardship with them ; and if we are having a bit of hardship, they must come and share it with us. It is a tremendous factor in victory, to keep together in it. So it is the ' togetherness ' of the battle and the warfare that is quite definitely thought of by the Apostle here.

THE CHRISTIAN AS ATHLETE

Our next 'group' consists of just this fragment: "If a man contend in the games, he is not crowned except he have contended lawfully." Here, hidden behind the English translation, is a Greek word—*athleo*—from which we get our English words 'athlete' and 'athletic'. The Greek word means to compete in, or take part in, the public games or contests. The Christian is compared to a Greek athlete. Now that sounds like sport, but it is not! For the word is a very strong word, implying one who engages in a contest for the mastery. That is making a business of things, is it not? We, as Christians, are called to engage seriously in a contest, at the end of which there is a prize, which it is possible for us to lose. That is the conception. Of course, there is a very large background of the Greek games to this word of Paul's; he knew all about it. The Greek athlete was called upon to spend ten whole months in rigorous preparatory discipline and training before he was allowed to enter the contests. And the rules for training were stringent. He must shun many things; he must observe certain regulations; he must discipline himself and put aside all his own preferences and his own likes. He must recognise that this thing is so serious that, should he break one of the regulations of his training, he is disqualified, he is not allowed to enter.

Well, here is a contest, here is an engagement, which calls upon us to be very watchful, and to be in many directions self-denying. But don't mix this up with your salvation—you can never be saved by good works! To be a Christian you don't have to give up this and give up that, and do all sorts of things that you don't naturally like doing! This is not *in order to be* a Christian; but when you *are* a Christian, here is a vocation, here is a responsibility. Paul said: " I buffet my body . . . lest . . . after that I have preached to others, I myself should be rejected " (I Cor. ix. 27), and he is thinking of this very thing—this business on hand, this great responsibility into which he is called, this great contest. ' I must see to it that my body, my fleshly appetites, don't get the upper hand ; I must keep a strong hand upon myself ; I must learn the disciplined life.' To most people that word ' discipline ' is a most hated word. Yes, but this is not just discipline for its own sake—it is because of what is involved. And we can lose so much— young Christians, you can lose so much, and you can be disqualified from the great calling with which you are called, and from obtaining the great prize, the real prize, which is set before you, if you do not learn the disciplined life. Keep under your body. A Christian ought to be a very disciplined person, with a life well ordered and regulated —nothing loose or flippant or careless. We ought to be people girded on a great business.

THE CHRISTIAN AS CRAFTSMAN

And finally, the second chapter of the second letter, and the so well-known 15th verse: " Give diligence to present thyself approved unto God, a workman that needeth not to be ashamed, handling aright the word of truth." The translation that we have in our Authorised Version, "*Study* to show thyself approved unto God . . . rightly dividing the word . . . ", has given rise to a good deal of misunderstanding. Many have thought that this is a picture of the student in his study, taking the Word of God and cutting it up and putting it into all kinds of different watertight compartments and dispensational sections. A whole school of dispensationalism and ultra-dispensationalism has been built upon this word, and it is all wrong. We shall be led astray if we get that idea.

This has nothing to do with the study and with the book. The Revised Version has improved upon the translation : " Give diligence to show thyself approved unto God, a workman that needeth not to be ashamed . . . " It is true that your work is with the Word of God, but the picture here is not of a student, but of a craftsman, and what lies behind the Greek here is the stonemason. The stonemason has the specification before him of the stones that are to be cut and fitted into a building ; and in the specification, or the blueprint, there are all the lines where the cuts are to be made, very finely, so that, when these stones are put together, they exactly fit, they belong to one another. It is the craftsman's job. With all the mass-production and the machine-made things of to-day, I think there are few things better than to see a real craftsman at work : really to find a craftsman, an old-fashioned craftsman, with his genuine hand-work, that is not the work of a machine.

Paul is talking about the craftsman. And he says, ' Now you have got the specification given to you in the Word of God. Don't toy with it, don't play with it, don't be careless about it. See to it that the truths of the Word of God are faithfully observed, that you handle the Word of God absolutely honestly.' In his second Corinthian letter you remember the Apostle used this phrase : " Not . . . handling the word of God deceitfully " (II Cor. iv. 2). What does that mean? Making it mean what it does not mean, for our own convenience—because it suits us so to interpret it ! But " no . . . scripture is of private interpretation " (II Pet. i. 20). Our attitude must be : The Word of God says *this ;* we cannot get round it. Don't try to get round it, don't try to make it mean something that it does not mean, and certainly don't be superior to it and think that you know better than what it says. Be absolutely honest with the Word of God. The Word of God says that; the blueprint, the pattern, the specification gives that as the precise line of things: then take it. Don't think that you can improve upon it; don't be careless about it. Take note of it.

The Spirit, the Holy Spirit, gave the Word. Here, to Timothy, the Apostle says so: "All Scripture given by inspiration of God is profitable for . . ." this and that and that. The Spirit gave the Word. We must be adjusted by the Holy Spirit to the Word that He has given! That is 'rightly dividing', or, as literally the word is, 'cutting straight lines' with, the Word of God. Just be honest with it! Just let it mean to you what it really does mean, and don't try to get round it. "All Scripture is given by inspiration", by the Holy Ghost. Paul was not saying things just out of his own predilection, his own preferences, his likes and dislikes: he was speaking what has become Scripture. Don't get round it. Be honest. You don't stand to lose anything; you stand to gain the blessing of God. Yes, we must be adjusted to the Word of God: neither less than the Word, nor more.

We have been considering some figures, metaphors, similes, of the Christian. They are very clear, very simple; but I come back again to where I commenced. Put together, they do show that a Christian is a very responsible person, or is to be so regarded; one who must say to himself or herself, ' I am not in something that is just optional—my pleasure, my life; not something that does not matter very much—as though I could say, " I am saved, I shall get to Heaven all right!" ' Oh, no! There is more than getting to

Heaven, there is more than just being saved. There are great interests of the Lord to be served, and these are the people required for them.

So—' Give diligence, take your share of the hardship as a good soldier, guard your trust, keep the rules, learn discipline.' " For thus shall be richly supplied unto you the entrance into the eternal kingdom . . . " (II Pet. i. 11). And so we, the successors of Paul in the battle and in the work, may be able to say, as he said: *" I have fought the good fight . . . I have kept the faith : henceforth there is laid up for me the crown of righteousness, which the Lord, the righteous judge, shall give to me at that day : and not only to me, but also to all them that have loved his appearing "* *(II Tim. iv. 7, 8).* We are in the same fight, the same contest, the same calling.

WHAT IT MEANS
TO BE A CHRISTIAN

T. AUSTIN-SPARKS

CONTENTS

CHAPTER ONE

THE IMMENSE SIGNIFICANCE OF THE CHRISTIAN LIFE

THERE ARE MANY MISCONCEPTIONS as to what the Christian life really is. I shall, however, not say very much about this negative side—that is, as to that which is either mistaken, confused or inadequate. The best way of dealing with all such difficulties is to take the positive line, by seeking to present the truth in its fulness, as we may be enabled, and so leave the comparisons to be made by those who read.

Our first phase of this matter, then, is the immense significance of the Christian life. That phrase embodies a principle of very great importance. It is this, that we shall never really appreciate anything presented to us in the Word of God until we see it in its full setting. If we regard it as just something in itself, we miss a great deal. We need to get its great background and its great setting in order to feel the full impact of its significance. That is what we shall seek to do now, as we are Divinely en-

5

abled—to see something at least of the immense significance of the Christian life.

THE CHRISTIAN LIFE BEGINS WITH CHRIST

We shall probably be on the ground of common agreement when we say that the Christian life begins with
Christ, but that means a great deal more than it sounds.
To say that Christianity began with Jesus is true if you
put Jesus in His right setting, and it is just at that point
that an adjustment may be necessary in order to grasp
the immensity of this matter. For neither the Christian
life nor Christianity began with the historic Jesus. They
did not begin when Jesus was born, when Jesus lived
here, when Jesus died and rose again. It is just there, I
say, that we need to make an adjustment. We must know
what it is that the Bible shows as to our Lord Jesus Christ.

CHRIST IN THE ' BEFORE TIMES ETERNAL '

Now you take up your New Testament, and open at
the Gospels. You find that Matthew traces the genealogy
of Jesus back to Abraham. Luke takes Him back still
further, to Adam. Mark begins his life of Jesus at the time
of His baptism, when He was thirty years of age. But
John reaches beyond them all, back through the thirty

years, beyond Bethlehem, back to Abraham and beyond
Abraham to Adam; and he does not stop there, he
goes still further back. " In the beginning "—whenever,
wherever, that dateless time was—" in the beginning was
the Word, and the Word was with God, and the Word
was God." That is a statement—and it is only a statement,
a statement of truth, of fact—as to the Person of the
Lord Jesus; and that, with one or two other sentences,
is all that John gives us.

But we have in the New Testament, through another
Apostle, a much fuller revelation concerning Jesus in that
dateless past. Through the Apostle Paul we are taken
right back and shown a very great deal about God's Son
" before times eternal ", not only before He came into
this world, but before this present world order came into
being. It is the general custom to begin a biography with
something concerning the ancestry of the person in view,
leading up to his or her birth, the whole thing being, of
course, just an account of the human and earthly history
of this person. But the biography of Jesus Christ does not
only go right back long before His own birth into this
world and beyond His human parentage or ancestry. A
large section of the biography of Jesus Christ in the Word
of God relates to that which is called " before times
eternal ". Here are some fragments of Scripture. We hear
Him praying. He is praying to His Father, and He is say-

ing: "Glorify thou me with thine own self with the glory which I had with thee before the world was" (John xvii. 5). That is really a bit of His biography, or autobiography —"the glory which I had with thee before the world was." And then the Apostle Paul, in that matchless description of Him, has this one clause, this mighty clause of only five words: "He is before all things" (Col. i. 17). "The glory which I had with thee before the world was." "He is before all things."

It is right back there, then, that we travel to find the meaning of a Christian, the Christian life and Christianity. Let us contemplate the Lord Jesus there, from the standpoint of definite statements in the Scriptures.

First of all, as to His Person—what He was like then. "God . . . hath . . . spoken unto us in his Son . . . who being the effulgence of his glory, and the very image of his substance . . ." (Heb. i. 2, 3). That certainly does not belong to the days of His humiliation. That goes right back, as we shall see in a moment, in the very connection or context of those words—"the express image of his substance", "the effulgence of his glory". That is what He was like before the world was.

What was His position then? ". . . Who, existing in the form of God, counted not the being on an equality with God a thing to be grasped" (Phil. ii. 6). Though He was equal with God, on an equality with God, He counted not that equality with God as something to be grasped. Equal with God, on equality with God—that was His position then.

Then as to His appointment. Here again is the Scripture context of the words we quoted just now. " God . . . hath . . . spoken unto us in his Son, whom he appointed heir of all things ". "*Appointed* heir of all things ". When did that happen? That was not done in time, that was not at the time of His birth or subsequently. That was right away back there in eternity past. There was something done in the counsels of the Godhead, whereby the Son of God was appointed Heir of all things, when it was determined that all things should be the heritage of God's Son, His rightful inheritance as God's Heir. It was not, of course, that He was to come into it on the demise of God, but God bound up all things with His Son, and made Him their Inheritor. These are things that we know through the Scriptures. How did the men who stated them come to know? Well, they tell us. Paul, who says most about this, tells us quite definitely that it was given to him by revelation: God made it known to him.

That, then, as to the " before times eternal ". And out of that relationship with God, out of that fellowship with God, and out of that appointment of God, came the next move, the creation of the present world: not the creation of the present world condition, but the present cosmic

order ; and again we are given very much information and
light as to the relationship of Christ to this.

CHRIST THE AGENT OF CREATION

We are told in the first place that He was the Agent of
it, God's Agent in the creation. Here is the statement:
" All things were made through him ; and without him
was not anything made that hath been made " (John i.
3). Or again another statement: " In him were all things
created, in the heavens and upon the earth, things visible
and things invisible, whether thrones or dominions or
principalities or powers ; all things have been created
through him, and unto him " (Col. i. 16). And if it needs
another word to bear that out, here it is: " There is . . .
one Lord Jesus Christ, through whom are all things "
(I Cor. viii. 6). He was the Agent in creation.

CHRIST THE OBJECT AND INTEGRATOR OF CREATION

He is the Object of creation. " In him were all things
created ". " All things have been created through him, and
unto him ". And yet another statement: " For of him, and
through him, and unto him, are all things " (Rom. xi.
36). And then a further movement, or a further constituent of this creative activity and purpose, is indicated. It is

found in the little clause which completes that wonderful statement that we have read earlier. " He is before all things, and in him all things consist " (Col. i. 17). The Agent, the Object, the Integrator. " In him all things hold together "—are integrated. He is therefore the very reason for the creation. Remove Him, and the creation will disintegrate. When they crucified Him and He committed His Spirit to God, saying: " Father, into thy hands I commit my spirit ", there was a great earthquake, and the sun was hidden, and darkness was over the face of the earth. The very Object of the creation has been put out of His place by man. The creation knows that its very Integrator has been rejected. These are but tokens of a great fact. Jesus Christ is the very meaning of this creation : without Him the creation has no meaning.

Perhaps, if you are a thinking person, you are saying, ' Well, these are tremendous statements ; they may be a wonderful theory, a system of teaching, wonderful ideas ; but are they facts? how can you prove them?' My dear friend, you are yourself a proof of them. In these talks we are seeking to discover the meaning of the Christian life. Until you find Jesus Christ you have no meaning at all in your own creation. The first thing that is livingly true about one who finds Jesus Christ as their Lord and Saviour is that they are conscious of having found the meaning of their very being—they have discovered why they are alive! Life then takes on its true meaning, and these are no longer just great wonderful truths, suspended in an abstract way for our contemplation, acceptance or rejection. They are borne out in the creation, and you and I are a part of it. There is no unification of our own individual lives; we are divided, scattered people; life is not an order at all—it is a chaos—until Jesus becomes the centre. But when that happens, there is a marvellous integration.

We shall have to come back to that presently. At the moment we are occupied with Jesus Christ, firstly away back before the world was, and then as the Agent, Object and Integrator of the creation. Out of this, three wonderful, though simple, things quite clearly arise. Firstly, His likeness to God—He was the very image, or impress, as the word is, of God's substance; secondly, His oneness with God; and thirdly, that aspect of His Person as the agency of God. I want you to keep those things in mind, because they are carried over and they come very much into this matter of the Christian life. With all this, however, we have to recognise a uniqueness and exclusiveness about Him, and I want to underline that as many times as I can, lest presently it might look as though I were on very dangerous ground. But I want you to extract those three things: likeness to God, oneness with God, and agency of God's purpose and God's work—in the case of Christ something unique and absolutely exclusive.

gathered into the word Deity, ' very God of very God '.

That, in brief—but oh, what a comprehensiveness, what a profundity, what a fulness!—that in brief is what we are told about Jesus Christ before He came into this world. Let us now pass on to what the Bible has to say about man.

MAN MADE TO REPRESENT GOD

What is the very first thing that the Bible says about man? " And God said, Let us make man in our image, after our likeness " (Gen. i. 26). That is the Divine conception, that is the Divine idea. And what does that amount to? Surely it amounts to representation of God. Any image of a thing is supposed to be the representation of that thing, and the idea or conception of man in the Divine mind was that man should represent God. Not, of course, in that exclusive sense—Deity—of which I have just spoken: that does not come into it with man at all; but in this matter of being an expression of God, bearing the likeness of God: so that if you should meet a man who answers to the Divine idea you have a very good idea of what God is like. If only that were more true!—but in a very limited way we do know something of it, when we sometimes meet what we call a ' godly ' man (and ' godly ' is only ' God-like ' abbreviated), and we say to one another,

B

' When you meet that man, you seem to meet the Lord, you seem to find something of the Lord—you seem to touch what you think the Lord would be like.'

Now, that was the Divine intention, conception, idea, as to man ; but the intention was that the representation should be a full one, that the existence of man should convey the knowledge of what God is like in His moral character, in the beauty of His personality, that in touching man you should touch an expression of God, and be led back to God. And therein is a principle, mark you, a principle that we ought to take up, and that is to be carried into this matter of what it means to be a Christian. All our talking about God or Christ is utterly worthless unless we *convey* God and Christ—unless our Lord is found in us. That is the best thing, and sometimes that does its work without any talking, whereas a vast amount of talking will do nothing unless there is the touch of the Lord there. The conception of man in the heart of God is just that HE should be found in a creation.

You see, the Lord Jesus when He was here was always trying to convey, by different means, sometimes by stories or parables, an impression of what God is like. He was speaking to people of very small spiritual apprehension. He could not go beyond illustrations, pictures and figures, such as, for instance, the parable—or was it a life-story?—known as ' The Prodigal Son '. I think it is a misnomer. It

would be better to call the story ' A Father's Love ', and
you would get to the heart of what the Lord Jesus was
after. What He was saying was that when you have contemplated that father, his broken heart and his marvellous forgiveness and restoration, even smothering
confession before it is finished, and lavishing upon that
renegade son all that he had, you have got a faint idea of
what God is like. And man was intended to be endowed
and endued with the Divine nature. Peter even uses those
words. " He hath granted unto us his precious and exceeding great promises ; that through these ye may become
partakers of the divine nature " (II Peter i. 4). Once again,
let me emphasize that we leave Deity out. It is enough that
we may bear the Divine likeness—a likeness in nature—
without aspiring to Deity.

ONENESS IN LIFE

It was God's thought, moreover, that man should become an inheritor of the very uncreated life of God. He
was put on test, on probation, and missed it. It was there
in the symbolic form of the tree of life, to be had on condition, but he missed it : and so man by nature—all the
children of Adam right up to our own time and ourselves
—has never possessed that Divine life outside of Jesus
Christ. But that is the gift. As we shall see later, that is one

of the great things that happen when we become Christians: we become partakers of God's own, Divine, eternal, uncreated life.

FELLOWSHIP IN PURPOSE

Then again, God's idea for man was not only likeness and oneness, but fellowship in purpose: that man should be brought into a working relationship with God in His great, His vast, purposes in this universe. The statement of Scripture is: " Thou madest him to have dominion over the works of thy hands " (Ps. viii. 6)—fellowship with God. Here again we have a vast amount in the New Testament. I think we could probably say that ninety per cent of the New Testament is occupied with this co-operation with God in His great purposes on the part of Christians. The Apostle Paul is so fond of using that phrase, ' according to His purpose '. Fellowship in the purpose of God— that was in God's mind in creating man.

But note, that all this likeness in nature, oneness in life, and fellowship in purpose, is related inseparably to God's Son, Jesus Christ: there can be none of it apart from the appointed Heir. We are said to be " joint-heirs "; that is, we come into things by union with Christ. So the Apostle Paul has as his abundant phrase, found everywhere (two hundred times) in his writings—" in Christ ",

" in Christ " : nothing apart from Christ, nothing outside of Christ. It is all in Christ, inseparably bound up with God's eternally appointed Heir of all things.

THE FAILURE OF MAN

Before we can follow that through into the Christian life, we have to look at that tragic interlude, as we may call it—the failure of man. We know the story, how it is written and how it is put. If you have difficulty in accepting the form in which the story is given, that is, either the actual way in which the test was set before Adam, as to the tree, the fruit, etc., or all this as symbolism, you should be helped in such difficulty by remembering that behind any form of presentation there are spiritual principles, and these are the essential and vital things. It is the *meaning* that matters, not so much the form of conveyance.

We want to get behind that man's failure. The Bible tells us what the source of that failure was. Here again, marvellously, we are taken right back before the creation. The veil is drawn aside and we are shown something happening outside of this world, somewhere where those counsels of God have become known, His counsels concerning His Son and the appointment of His Son as Lord of creation, as Heir of all things. It has become known amongst the angels, the hierarchy of Heaven, and there is one there, the greatest created being of all, Lucifer, son of the morning, who becomes acquainted with this Divine intention. How—this is the mystery—how into that realm iniquity could enter we do not know: we cannot fathom the origin of sin; but what we are told is that " unrighteousness was found " in him (Ezek. xxviii. 15). Pride was found in his heart.

Pride immediately works out in jealousy, does it not? Think of pride again. It always immediately shows itself in jealousy, rivalry. Pride cannot endure even an equal. Pride will always lead to a trying to ' go one better ' in whatever realm it is. And so all the jealousy and all the rivalry sprang into that heart. We are told in the Scripture that that one said: " I will exalt my throne above the stars of God; . . . I will ascend above the heights of the clouds; I will be like the Most High " (Isa. xiv. 13, 14). He was jealous of God's Heir, and a rival to His appointment; Heaven was rent. But that one was cast out (Ezek. xxviii. 16 – 18). We are told that he was cast out of his estate together with all those who entered into that conspiracy with him against God's Son. Those " angels which kept not their own principality, but left their proper habitation " (Jude 6), were cast out.

The next thing we see is the appearance of this one in beautiful guise—not with horns and tail and pitchfork! —but in beautiful guise to deceive; we see him coming into the realm of God's creation, to man and his partner. Now, what was his method? We shall never understand the meaning of the Christian life until we grasp these things. What was the method, what was the focal point, of the great arch-enemy's attack upon the man—this man whom God had created to come into fellowship with His Son in the great purpose of the ages?

The focal point was man's *self*-hood. I doubt whether the man had any consciousness of selfhood until Satan touched him on that point and said, "Hath God said?" The insinuation was—'God is keeping something from you that you might have ; He is limiting you. God knows that, if you do this thing which He has forbidden, you yourself will have the root of the matter in yourself, you will have the capacity and faculty in yourself for knowing, knowing, knowing. At present, under this embargo of God, you have to depend entirely upon Him : you have to consult Him, refer to Him, defer to Him ; you have got to get everything from Him. And all the time you can have it in yourself, and God knows that. You see, God is withholding something from you that you might have, and you are less of a being than you might be—so God is not really favourable to you and your interests.'

It was a maligning of God. But the focal point was this : ' You, *you*—you can *be* something, you can *do* something, you can be " in the know " about things '—self-centred-ness, self-interest, self-realisation, and all the other host of ' self ' aspects. The ' I ' awoke, that ' I ' which had brought the enemy out of his first estate. '*I* will be exalted above the stars, *I* will be equal with the Most High '. To awaken the ' I ' in man—so that, instead of man having his centre in God, deriving everything from God, he aspired to have the centre in himself ; instead of being God-centred, he was self-centred—that was the focal point. And man was enticed into the same pride as had brought about Satan's downfall, leading to the same act of independence—nothing less than a bid for personal freedom from God.

As to the results, well, we know them. The older this world becomes, and the greater the development of this race, the more and more terrible is the manifestation of this original thing. We see a picture of man trying to get on without God, man saying that he *can* get on without God ; man seeking to realise himself, fulfil himself, and to draw everything to himself ; seeking to be himself the centre of everything, not only individually but collectively. That is the story, that is the history. The results? Look at the world—all the terrible, terrible suffering, all the misery, all the horror. We should never have believed, had it not become an actuality in recent years, what man is capable of doing—all because of his break with God. We will not dwell upon it ; it is too awful. If we ask, Why,

why should all this suffering and misery and wretchedness go on in the world?—surely the answer is this. God can never remove from man the consequences of this act of pride and disobedience, independence and complicity with His arch-enemy, without letting man go on in his independence. All this is God's way of saying—the way in which He is compelled to say—It is an awful, awful thing, to be without God, to be in a state of breach with God.

Now suppose you come into the Christian life. That does not remove all the misery and suffering in the creation, and it does not remove the suffering from yourself, but there is a difference. The mighty difference between one who is outside of Christ and one who is in Christ is this: both suffer, but whereas the one suffers unto despair and hopelessness, in the sufferings of the other there is the grace of God turning it all to account to make him or her Godlike again. The others suffer without hope, die without hope, but the sufferings of a Christian are to make that one like their Lord. It is a marvellous thing to see the likeness of Christ coming out in His own through their sufferings.

THE INCARNATION OF THE LORD JESUS

We come now to the next phase of things—the incarnation of our Lord Jesus: for it is just at that point—the incarnation—that all that was appointed for Him, all the

Divine design and conception of God's Son in this universe, all the creative activity through Him and by Him
and unto Him, and all the meaning of man's creation, as
we have been trying to show, is taken up in a definite way
for realisation.

This incarnation, the coming of the Lord Jesus into this
world, is a far, far greater thing than any of us has yet
appreciated. The Word of God makes a great deal of this
coming into the world. You know that, at a certain season
of the year, we are talking all the time about the birth of
Jesus—about Jesus being born in Bethlehem. There is
much about that in our carols and in our talk. It is all
about the birth of Jesus. But the Word of God, while it
uses that phrase, " Now when Jesus was born in Bethlehem . . .", says far, far more than that about His coming.
That was not the *beginning* of Jesus : that was the *coming*
of Jesus. He definitely and deliberately and consciously, in
that full form of His eternal existence with God, made a
decision about this matter, a deliberate decision to come.
Coming in baby form had its own particular meaning—
we cannot now stay with all the details of this—but it was
a coming.

And what the Word of God says first of all about that
coming is that it was a mighty, mighty renunciation on
His part. Listen again. " Who, existing in the form of God,
counted not the being on an equality with God a thing to

be grasped, but emptied himself, taking the form of a servant, being made in the likeness of men; and being found in fashion as a man, he humbled himself, becoming obedient even unto death, yea, the death of the cross" (Phil. ii. 6—8). And there is a clear implication in that sentence in His great prayer: "Father, glorify thou me . . . with the glory which I had with thee before the world was" (John xvii. 5). He has let it go, He has given it up. That was the mighty renunciation by God's Son of His heavenly, eternal glory, of His position of equality—down to what? Servanthood. The word is 'bond-servant': a bond-slave, the form of a bond-slave. You and I cannot grasp all that, because we cannot grasp what it meant for Him to be equal with God. We cannot understand all that He was and had in the eternity past. We know so little about that; we understand less. But here it is: it has all been renounced, and He is now here in incarnation, not as a master, but as a bond-slave. "The Son of man", said He, "came not to be ministered unto, but to minister" (Matt. xx. 28). "I am in the midst of you as he that serveth" (Luke xxii. 27). "He took a towel, and girded himself. Then he poureth water into the bason, and began to wash the disciples' feet" (John xiii. 4, 5). That was the job of the slave, the bond-slave.

The next part of the statement as to this cycle from glory to glory is—"being found in fashion as a man".

This just relates to the central feature and inclusive meaning of the Incarnation: i.e., to all that is meant by the fact that everything was by Man—as man—for man. There were many theophanies in Old Testament times (*theos* = God; *phaino* = to show), manifestations of God to man by actual appearances (some believe that these were the Second Person of the Trinity, but that need not be discussed here). But the Incarnation is something different, and its essential point is that the great work of redemption was not committed to angels, but, as the hymn goes:

> ' O generous love! that He, who smote
>   In man for man the foe,
>   The double agony in man
>   For man should undergo.'

It was Man for man assuming responsibility for this state of things, and for the recovery of what was lost and the reinstating of what had been forfeited, the redeeming of man and creation. For that He became incarnate, and then straight to the Cross. He had no illusions about that —He had come for that. One of His great imperatives was always related to the Cross. " The Son of man *must* be delivered up . . . and be crucified " (Luke xxiv. 7). That imperative was in His heart as overruling and overriding everything else. He knew it, and that is why He repudiated and rejected the cheap offer of the kingdoms of this world at the hands of the Devil: because He had come, not to have them as they were, but to have them as God ever intended them to be, and that could only be by the Cross.

So the Cross was the great repudiation of the world as it was and is, the great repudiation of man as he had become, whom God could not accept, in whose heart was found this pride. For, representatively, in the judgment and death of Jesus Christ God was saying concerning the whole race, ' I have finished with that', and turning His face away. The heart of the Son was broken as He cried, ' Thou hast forsaken Me!' Why? Because He was there as man's representative, the world's representative as it was, and He had to die as it. He " tasted death for every man ", which meant experiencing God-forsakenness, repudiation, and the closed door of Heaven, God's eternal ' No ' to that fallen creation. By that means He redeemed man, He redeemed the creation, and in His resurrection-ascension to the right hand of God He reinstated man, representatively, in the place that God ever intended man to have. This is not all isolated action on the part of Jesus Christ. This is related all the time. He is the inclusive One, and what happens to Him is what God means to happen to man. Until man is in Christ he is repudiated by God. There is no way through. " No one cometh unto the Father, but by me " (John xiv. 6). But in Christ the inheritance which was lost is recovered. In Christ, personally at God's right hand as his representative, man is reinstated. Christ is there as the earnest of what we shall be and where we shall be, by the grace of God. But, mark you, the Christ risen is not now the Christ made sin in our place, but with sin put away, and a new creation instated, though still *man*.

Well, all this is the setting of the Christian life ; this is the background of a Christian. Is it not immense? We struggle for words in order to try to set it forth, it is so great. All I can hope to do is to leave an impression on you. I cannot explain, I cannot define, I cannot set it out, I cannot convey it ; but all this, which is so poor an expression, surely, surely, should leave at least an impression upon us. We should at least grasp this—that a Christian is set in an eternal background. It is a wonderful thing to be converted and to become a Christian ; it is blessed to be saved ; but oh! our conception and experience of the Christian life is such a little thing compared with God's thought. We need to get the eternal dimensions of the significance of Jesus Christ as the setting of a Christian life.

Christianity does not begin when we accept Christ. By accepting Christ we are placed right back there in the eternity of God's thought concerning man. We are brought into something that has been from all eternity in the intention of God, and, as we shall see later, linked on with a realisation unspeakably wonderful in the ages to come.

To become a child of God, to be born again, however you may define or explain it, is to come right into something that is first of all not of time at all—it is of eternity. It is not just this little life here on earth ; it is of Heaven, it is universal in its significance. It is a wonderful thing, beyond all our powers of grasping, to be a Christian. If we could only get some conception of the cost of our salvation, the cost of redemption, the cost of recovering the lost inheritance ; the cost to God, the cost to God's Son—the awful depths of that Cross ; if only we could get some idea of this, we should see that it is no little thing to be a Christian. It is something immense.

What I have said has not been outside the Word of God ; I have been keeping closely to the Book. I have not turned you from passage to passage, but there is a vast amount of Scripture behind what I have said. All that I have given you, and more, is in the Word of God. And the important thing is that what I have said can be put to the test—it can be made true in experience, now, in this life. That is just the wonder of it: a truly born-from-above child of God knows within himself or herself, ' This is true ; this is why I have a being ; now I have the explanation, and much more.'

Now if this is true, if all that is the meaning of being in Christ—and I put the ' if ' by way of argument—what an immense challenge it is to be a Christian, and what a terrible thing it will be not to be in Christ. What an immense thing it will prove to be, not only in this life, but more, infinitely more, in the ages to come, to be in Christ!

If there is one reading these lines who is not yet in Christ, it is a challenge to you. You are not dealing merely with your father's or your mother's beliefs or faith. You are not dealing with something that you call ' Christianity ', or with your own conception of a Christian, which may be all wrong, faulty, or at most inadequate. You are dealing with a vast thing, an immense thing. May God help you, from this contemplation of the setting of the Christian life, to reach out, if you have never yet done so, to embrace God's gift. If we know what it is to be in Christ, let us make sure that we are set upon knowing all that the Christian life means, that we are not going to be content with a little Christian life, with anything less than God's fulness for us ; and if we have a lot of experience and knowledge, let this all lead us to a new determination that we shall not stop short anywhere of God's full and ultimate intention in apprehending us in His Son.

CHAPTER TWO

WHAT HAPPENS WHEN WE BECOME CHRISTIANS

IN THESE TALKS, we are seeking to be pre-eminently practical. That is, we are not occupied with the presentation of Christian doctrine in itself. Christian doctrine will be here, but we are not interested in presenting the doctrines of Christianity in the abstract, important as they are. What we are concerned with is that everything shall be practical and experimental, and capable of being immediately put to the test.

There is, of course, a difference between the facts and truths of the Christian life, and the explanation of them. That is, it is possible for all the facts to be present in the life without the person concerned being able to explain those facts. It is a part of our present business to try to explain the facts, and to challenge as to the facts. Now, any explanation of the Christian life should be corroborated by the experience. That is, it ought to be possible for you to say, ' Well, I could not have explained it like that, but I know exactly in my experience what you mean—

29

C

that does just express my own life.' So that the explanation
must be borne out by the experience: the experience
must corroborate the explanation.

Let us, then, consider what happens when we become
Christians. We shall spend some of our time in seeking
to get behind this matter of becoming a Christian, to get
to certain other facts—facts stated or revealed in the
Bible, and true to human experience.

MAN'S RELATIONSHIP WITH GOD DISLOCATED

When we come to consider man as we know him, man
by nature, the first thing we find is that his relationship
with God is completely dislocated. We say 'dislocated',
because we believe what the Bible teaches: that things
were all right once, and they have gone wrong. If for the
time being you prefer to waive the word 'dislocated' and
substitute 'severed', you may do so. We shall probably
at least agree that things are not in order between man
and God. The relationship between man and God is in a
broken-down condition. That is the fundamental fact. The
relationship is disjointed; it is in a state of strain. There
is distance between man and God. The relationship, or
perhaps we should say 'non-relationship', is a very unhappy thing: it is altogether unproductive; there is nothing coming from it. It is barren and desolate, quite

unfruitful. With many God does not seem to matter, and is quite ignored.

But that is more or less neutral or negative. In most cases the situation is much worse than that—it is positively antagonistic. Man is in a state of antagonism to God in his nature, and often in his mind, in his attitude, and in his reference to God; there is a state of conflict, there is suspicion in man's mind as to God. A great deal of resentment exists in many human hearts. And we can go further —for the Bible goes this far—and say that in some cases, perhaps in not a few, there is even hatred in the human heart for God. We meet that sometimes. So that is the first fact—the relationship between man and God is chaotic, broken-down, dislocated or disrupted.

SPIRITUAL FACULTIES WHICH ARE NOT FUNCTIONING

That is not all. We need to get inside of that and go further. Man has a set of senses belonging to his spiritual being which are not functioning—a set of senses which correspond to his physical senses. The physical senses, as we know, are: seeing, hearing, feeling, tasting, smelling. But man has another set of five senses which are not physical, but which belong to his inner man. They are the counterpart of those five physical senses, and in man by nature these other senses are not functioning. The Bible speaks of all these senses in a spiritual way in relation to God.

The Bible speaks of a *seeing* of God, which is not physical at all; it is not with the natural eye. There is that little fragment known to most: " The pure in heart . . . shall see God " (Matt. v. 8). That is certainly not a physical matter.

Again, *hearing*. There is a spiritual hearing of God which is not audition through the natural or physical ear. It is something in the heart. It is not the hearing of an audible voice, but it corresponds to that in a spiritual way. People are able to say they have heard the Lord speak to them, but they never heard anything with their natural ear.

Tasting? Yes, the Bible says: " Taste and see that the Lord is good " (Ps. xxxiv. 8), and no one thinks that that is a physical matter.

Smelling?—that seems to be difficult, perhaps. But we know what we mean, without any physical factor coming in, when we say that we are 'scenting' something. We go into a room, and somehow we detect that there is 'something in the air'. People have been talking, and when we go in we see embarrassment on their faces, and they suddenly become quiet and look at one another, and we 'scent' something. In an analogous way, we know that it is possible to sense the presence of God.

There are thus a whole set of spiritual faculties which, when they are in proper order and function, serve to relate us to God ; and in the natural man, the unregenerate man, those senses are not functioning at all. There is no seeing God, in that way ; there is no hearing God speak to him ; there is no sensing or feeling God—it is a tremendous thing to feel God, not with your hands, but in an inward way. There is no ' tasting that the Lord is good ' in the natural man. All these things are out of order—and yet the Bible speaks of them a very great deal. The Bible teaches, and man's condition corroborates, that, where God is concerned, man is blind, man is deaf ; man is numbed, has no feelings, is insensitive to God. Is that not so? That is a true description of anyone—it may be you who are reading these lines—who has not had a definite Christian experience. You do not see God in this way, you do not hear God, you do not feel God, you do not sense God ; God is unreal, remote, far away, if He is at all. You do not know Him.

It is no real contradiction of the above and of what follows when we say that in most cases—very, very few exceptions exist—there is a consciousness of the existence of some supreme Object demanding recognition. Our point is that there is no fellowship, understanding, knowledge, or living relationship with God.

MAN BY NATURE DEAD TO GOD

But the Bible goes further still. It says that man by natural birth is lacking in yet another thing, which corresponds to his—may I use the phrase?—biological existence, his life. We have a biological existence which we call life. Now it is a very significant thing that the New Testament puts two different words over two different classes of people. It uses one word (*bios*) for natural life, but it never uses that word of the life of the Christian. For that it uses an entirely different word, with an altogether different meaning. What the Bible says is that man by nature not only lacks the functions of his spiritual senses, but even lacks that which corresponds to his natural existence —life. In a word, the Bible says that man is dead ; not only blind and deaf and insensitive to God, but *dead*. " Death passed upon all men " (Rom. v. 12), says the Word of God. By nature man is dead to God.

DEAD TO THE MEANING OF HIS OWN EXISTENCE

And he is dead to the true meaning of his own existence. Man by nature does not know why he was born, why he has a being. We have all sorts of accounts of his being —wild explanations and excuses, shelving responsibility, and so on, all proving that he is entirely dead to the real

meaning of his own existence. He makes the best of it—
and sometimes it is quite a good best that a man makes of
his life; but, after all, when set in relation to God and
in relation to eternity, he does not know why he is alive,
why he has a being. He is dead to that. He is dead to
eternal and heavenly things and values. What a futile and
hopeless thing it is to talk to man by nature about the
things of Heaven and the things of God! He looks at
you, he gapes at you, he does not know what you are talking about. That belongs to a world with which he is just
not acquainted. It is something foreign, far off, and he is
utterly bored.

He may be a very good man from certain standpoints,
a very educated man. He may be occupying a position of
high esteem and respect amongst men—he may even be
a very religious man. There was such a man who came to
Jesus, an outstanding specimen of the best product of
humanity outside of Christ; but over him was suspended
one big question-mark. He was full of interrogations—
'How . . . ? How . . . ? How . . . ?' And Jesus said, in
effect: 'Well, it is no use talking to you about heavenly
things at all. You do not belong to that realm; you are
just dead to that.'

Now, is that true? I said at the beginning that you can
put everything to the test. This is not just a statement of
abstract Christian doctrine. This is a statement of fact

which is verifiable. Some of you may be actually knowing
the truth of it now, in your own experience. Many of you
did know it in time past, but, thank God, you know it no
longer. According to the Bible, man is dead. It is useless
to speak to a corpse—you will get nothing back. As far
as the things of God are concerned, man makes no response. There is no correspondence, no interchange, no
communion, no fellowship possible. That is what the
Bible and human experience say as to man's condition
by nature.

WHAT HAPPENS WHEN WE BECOME CHRISTIANS

That brings us to a very practical point in approaching
this question: What exactly happens when we become
Christians? There are two fragments of New Testament
Scripture which I think sum this up for us very concisely
and very fully. The one is that statement, so familiar and
yet so little understood even by Christians, the statement
made to the man to whom I referred just now, who came
with his big question—his multiple " How . . . ? " Jesus
simply looked at him, and did not try to answer his question at all, because He knew how hopeless a thing it is to
talk to a dead man. He looked at him, and said: " Ye must
be born anew ", or " Ye must be born from above " (John
iii. 7). The other passage, from one of Paul's letters, is

also very well known: "Wherefore if any man is in Christ, there is a new creation" (II Cor. v. 17). Those two words sum up what happens: "born anew", "a new creation".

(a) A NEW ALIVENESS

I said I would keep off negative ground and on positive, but let me say here in parenthesis that it is *not* becoming a Christian just to accept, or give a mental assent to, the tenets of the Christian religion, or to join some society which has the name of being a Christian institution, even though it may go by the name of 'church'. That is not becoming a Christian in the New Testament sense. The only true 'becoming a Christian' is by way of being born anew, becoming a new creation: which means you become a different species from what you were before, and from what all other people are who have not had that experience.

But when we so become Christians, what happens? Our state of death gives place to a state of life. This other life, this resurrection life, which no man by nature has ever yet had, excepting Jesus Christ; this life—which we will not even refer to in the New Testament terminology—is given in the day of our faith-exercise toward the Lord Jesus as Lord and Saviour. A new aliveness takes place.

It is the first wonderful basic experience of the Christian. The Christian at that time leaps into life: he immediately begins to talk a new language about now knowing what it is to live, knowing the meaning of life, and so on. What happens when we become Christians? Well, we are alive from the dead! We become alive.

But it is not just the resuscitation of something. It is the impartation of what was never there before—a new life, belonging to a new creation: that is, a new order, which is a heavenly order. For this is birth "from above". Jesus never said a truer thing than that. "Ye must be born again." If there is someone reading these lines who has not had that experience, you know, after what we have said about the natural condition, that, if you are going to see God and hear God and feel and sense God, in the way of which we have spoken, something has got to happen to you which is as radical as being born all over again in another realm. Jesus is right at any rate on that, is He not? It is true. "You *must* . . ."—it is not just an imperative of command, it is not just a declaration that you have got to become a Christian to be accepted with God. It is the statement of a fundamental and inescapable fact: that you can never, never know God in a real way, far less have living fellowship with God, until something has happened in you that is absolutely *constitutional*. You have got to have a new life, which is God's own life, to enable you to understand what God is, to know Him.

(b) A NEW CONSCIOUSNESS OF GOD

This new life immediately introduces a new consciousness of God. Immediately you are alive to God—you
sense God. God becomes a reality, a living reality: no
longer remote, far off, indefinite, but now very dear, very
real, very wonderful, indeed the greatest reality in your
whole life. You know God in a new way, you have a new
consciousness of God.

(c) A NEW CONSCIOUSNESS OF THE MEANING OF
OUR EXISTENCE

And then you find you have a new consciousness of the
meaning of your own existence. Every Christian who is
truly founded upon this basis of beginning, of resurrection,
almost immediately leaps into this consciousness: ' Now
I have got the explanation of life, I have got the key to
life. I know that I was born for something! I never before
knew that I was really born for something, but I know
now. There is a sense of meaning in my being here, and of
destiny, wrapped up with this new experience. It gives an
explanation to my own life.' Is that not true, Christians?
It is—it is just like that. ' Now we know why we are here!'

(d) A NEW CONSCIOUSNESS OF PURPOSE AND VOCATION

And to carry that one step further—it is a new consciousness of purpose and vocation. It is not only that there is a meaning in our being alive, but that a purpose has come in with this new life, a sense of vocation. We are called for something. You do not have to have a lot of instruction about that. You do not even have to wait for it. The truly born-again child of God spontaneously, instinctively, begins to talk to other people about it. You can test your Christian life by that. You just must tell them, you must talk about it, you must let them know. That is vocation coming out. You feel you are called for something, that there is business on hand. And that can develop, as we know, to specific vocations. But this consciousness of purpose, meaning and vocation springs up with new life.

(e) A NEW SET OF RELATIONSHIPS, INTERESTS AND DESIRES

And then we find we have a new set of relationships, of interests, of desires. We know that; it happens. It is no use talking to anybody who has not had the experience about these things. They have their relationships, their interests, their desires, and they just despise you for not doing what they do and going where they go and engaging in the things which are everything to them. They do not understand you. They think you have missed the way, that you have lost everything that is worth having. But you know quite well that it is just the other way round. You do not despise them, but you pity them, are sorry for them. This is a transcendent, superlative set of relationships. Christians know the meaning of a little phrase that was used about some early servants of God who were arrested because they were doing this very thing—fulfilling, expressing, the sense of vocation, and not keeping it in and keeping it to themselves. They were arrested and brought before the authorities and threatened. ' And being let go, they went to their own company '—instinctively to their own company (Acts iv. 23). We know what that means. There is a new ' company '—a new relationship, a new fellowship, a new set of desires and interests. No one else can understand or appreciate it, but the Christian knows.

(f) A NEW SET OF CAPACITIES

Further, we have a new set of capacities. This is a wonderful thing about the new creation life, this ' born-anew' life, this true Christian life. We get a new set of mental capacities, something different from, and additional to, and altogether transcending natural mental capacity.

It is a new understanding of things, and it is one of the wonders of the Christian life. You may find a person who has had no great advantages academically, educationally, or in any other realm, a very ordinary person: and yet, when they come into a real experience of the Christian life, it is remarkable how they acquire an entirely new understanding and intelligence. They have an insight into things that a man of the highest education and the biggest brain is—by these means alone—entirely incapable of grasping or understanding.

This is something that the Christian knows to be so true. Very often we may think that a certain person, because of such academic achievements and qualifications, is bound to be able to understand, we are bound to have good interchange and fellowship with them: yet, when we begin to speak about the things of the Lord, we meet a blank—they do not know what we are talking about. But here is this simple man or woman who knows. They have a new mental faculty, a new set of capacities and powers for understanding the things of the Spirit of God, for knowing what no natural man can know—not by the way of study, but by the way of communion with God.

And these wonderful new capacities grow and develop as the Christian goes on. We find that we have new powers of transaction and enaction—of 'doing'. The Christian has the power of doing things that other people cannot do : a power of endurance, a power of overcoming, and a power of working. Many of my readers will understand me when I say that sometimes—indeed very often—it seems that the Lord takes pains to undercut our natural ability for doing, in order to lead us into a life where we can do without ' abilities ', without any natural explanation at all. If you look at much that has been done through true Christians, in this world's history, you will not be able to account for it at all on natural grounds. They were weak things, frail things, things at a discount in this world. But just see what God has done through the " weak things " and the " things that are not " !

(g) A NEW HOPE

A new hope—that is characteristic of the true Christian. An altogether new prospect has leapt into view ; we shall see more of that later. But here it must be stated that the Christian, if a true Christian, is not one characterized by despair, by hopelessness, by a sense of final frustration and disappointment. A Christian is one, deep down in whose very being there is rooted the consciousness that there is something wonderful ahead, something beyond. The final argument for the afterward is not in any system of teaching about Heaven or its alternative. It is found in the heart, in the life—it is found in a mighty dynamic. What is it that has kept Christians going in the face of unspeakable difficulties and sufferings and opposition? What is it? Others capitulate, give up, let go, fall into despair. The Christian just goes on. And it is not because the Christian is of any better natural calibre than others, with more tenacity and doggedness. Not at all. So often they are the weak ones, as counted by men ; but there is this going on. They are gripped by an inward conviction that this is not the end, this is not all, there is something beyond. There is this *hope*, which has come from the " God of hope ".

THE SECRET OF THE "ALL THINGS NEW"

Now what is the explanation of it all—a new life, a new consciousness, new relationships, all things new? We are not exaggerating the Christian life. What does it amount to? What is the inclusive secret of it? You see, it is not just that the Christian receives some abstract *things*. You may call it life, you may call it understanding, you may call it hope, you may call it power, but these are not merely abstract things. The true, born-anew Christian has received, not abstractions, but *a Person*. The inclusive explanation of it all is the gift of the Holy Spirit. God gives His Spirit to them that obey Him (Acts v. 32).

Now, the Holy Spirit is God, no less than God, and the Holy Spirit has all the intelligence and knowledge of God, all the eternal prospect of God ; the elements of eternity, timelessness. All that is true of God is true of the Holy Spirit. If, then, God gives the Holy Spirit to become resident inside a person, and that person learns from the beginning, like a babe, day by day, year by year, to walk in fellowship with the indwelling Holy Spirit, that person is bound to grow in all these characteristics that we have mentioned.

In the first place, they are bound to know Divine life—God's own life within. This is a most wonderful thing, when you think of it. We have not just an ' it ', but Himself, God in Christ by the Holy Spirit, as our very life. I love the way the Bible puts that about God: "He is . . . the length of thy days" (Deut. xxx. 20). Think about that. It means that if God really is our portion, resident within, then our duration, our spell, is not dictated by natural things. *He* is the length of our days. We shall die when He says that the time has come, and not before. You see, all things are in His hand, and until that time comes the threats may be many, but His life persists, and we rise again and rise again and rise again. We thought the end had come, but we rise again and go on—because He is our life. The Holy Spirit is called "the Spirit of life" (Rom. viii. 2). To have such a Person resident within is a very wonderful thing.

And so, if He has all Divine intelligence, and we are

D

in His school, living with Him, keeping fellowship with Him day by day, we shall grow in this intelligence, which no natural man has. We shall be growing in knowledge, growing in understanding, growing in ability to grasp the things of God, which no man, apart from the Spirit of God, can understand. I want to lay emphasis upon that. It is the Holy Spirit *Himself*. I know that Christians as such believe in the Holy Spirit—the majority of evangelical Christians believe in the Person of the Holy Spirit. They put the article there—*the* Holy Spirit—whereas others speak of ' Holy Spirit '. It is a part of our Christian faith to believe in the Holy Spirit as a Person ; to have some knowledge of the doctrine of the Holy Spirit, His work and His power. And yet there is among Christians a lamentable lack of understanding of what it means to have the Holy Spirit really dwelling within. This is disclosed and manifested by the very fact that they can sometimes act and speak so contrarily to the Holy Spirit without seeming to be checked up by Him. It is truly astonishing how many Christians can speak in a manner in which the Holy Spirit certainly cannot acquiesce, and yet seem to be quite unconscious of the fact that the Holy Spirit disagrees with them. Many Christians can believe lies about others, and repeat them, and yet never register the Holy Spirit's disagreement. There is something wrong here in regard to the practical expression of

the indwelling Holy Spirit—for He is the Spirit of truth.
Now the true Christian life means that wherever the
Holy Spirit is in disagreement with anything that we say
or do, or with the way we say or do it, we should be aware
of it. At once we should register—not a voice, but a
sense: the Holy Spirit saying, in effect, 'I do not agree
with you—that is wrong, that is not right, that is not true,
that is not kind, that is not good, that is not gracious.'
There is a very great need for the reality of the indwelling
Spirit to be expressed. It is not that the failure to recognise and sense and discern means that the Holy Spirit is
not there; it simply means that, if it is like that, we are
not walking in the Spirit. There is something needed on
our part by way of adjustment.

But, coming to the positive side, the true Christian life
can be, and should be, like this. With the Holy Spirit resident within, when you or I say or do anything with which
He does not agree, we know it at once. We have a bad
feeling right in the middle of us, and we do not get rid of
it. We have to say, 'Evidently I was wrong in what I said,
or did. Lord, forgive me and put it out of the way.' If it
has done someone any harm, well, let us try to put it
right. That is a life in the Spirit. It is very practical.

That is what happens when we become Christians. It
begins like that. The beginnings are very simple. If you
are still quite young in the Christian life, you surely must

know something of this in simple ways. Perhaps you go to do something that you used to do, and something inside you says, 'Oh, no, not now—that belongs to the past.' That is a simple beginning, is it not? If you go on, you burn your fingers—because you are alive! If you were dead, you would do these things and not feel them. Because you are alive, you are sensitive.

Yes, that is what happens when we become Christians. It is very simple ; many of us know about it from experience. But it is important for the many who are coming to Christ in these days, who are at the beginnings of the Christian life, to know really what they have come into, really what has happened to them. They should be able to say : 'Yes—well, I could not have explained it, I could never have put it into words or defined it ; but I know what you mean. That is true to my own experience.' But, you see, it is something more than just *feeling*. We need to *understand,* we need to be *intelligent* about these things. May God make us intelligent Christians—Christians who are going on in life-fellowship with His Spirit within, and growing all the time. God forbid that any young Christians, reading these lines, in five, ten or twenty years' time should be just where they are now. That is not necessary, because of course—praise God!— being born again is not the end of things—it is only the beginning !

CHAPTER THREE

THE DIVINE PURPOSE AND PRINCIPLES GOVERNING THE CHRISTIAN LIFE

IT IS MOST IMPORTANT that we should be alive to the fact that the Christian life is governed by *purpose*. The thought of 'purpose', indeed that very word itself, is much in view in the New Testament. Most of us are familiar with one statement relating thereto: "To them that love God all things work together for good, even to them that are called according to his purpose" (Rom. viii. 28). Unfortunately it is usually cut in half and only part of the first half taken: "all things work together for good". We might go on: "to them that love God"; but that is not the whole statement, which adds: "to them that are the called according to his purpose". Then we have another word, not so generally known: "Foreordained according to the purpose of him who worketh all things after the counsel of his will" (Eph. i. 11). Again: "according to the eternal purpose which he purposed in Christ Jesus our Lord" (Eph. iii. 11). Yet once more: "according to his own purpose and grace" (II Tim. i. 9). These are sufficient at least to indicate that 'purpose' is a governing idea in the Christian life: that we are not saved just to be saved, we do not become Christians just to be Christians. That is only the beginning of something ; it is with a view to something very much more in the thought and intention of God.

WHAT THE PURPOSE IS

You are asking, 'Well, what is the purpose?' There are many things said about it in the Scriptures, which we cannot stay to cite just now. Without going into great detail, when all things said about it are gathered together, there is one thing which includes and covers them all, of which they are all just parts. The Divine purpose is all-inclusively set forth in a clause in one of Paul's letters : " till we all attain . . . unto the . . . fulness of Christ " (Eph. iv. 13). We are going to spend a little time in looking into that, but you will instantly recognise that that makes Christ very great. Surely, if all the Christians that ever have been and are and will yet be are called with the purpose of attaining unto the fulness of Christ—and the number is just countless in all the centuries, in all the generations since the first Christian—if all this vast, uncountable number are called with that same calling, the fulness of Christ, then Christ must be very great indeed.

Yes, and the Christian life must therefore be something

very great. If it takes its character, its meaning, and its dimensions from Christ, then the Christian life corresponding to Christ must be a very great thing. It must necessarily be something progressive. No Christian at any time in their experience or history here on this earth can ever say that they have reached that end. It means that the Christian life is one of progress and development. It is all moving toward that ultimate fulness. So we find in the New Testament that the Christian life is set forth in three distinct phases: we *are* Christians, we are *becoming* Christians, and we are *going to be* Christians. These three phases are indicated in the original language of the New Testament by three different tenses of the verb.

I believe it was Bishop Handley Moule who was travelling on one occasion, and a Salvation Army lassie entered the same compartment as he. When they had got settled and on the way—he was, I believe, actually a Dean at the time, but of course wearing his canonicals—she interrogated him: ' Sir, are you saved?' Whereupon the kindly old scholar looked at her and said, ' Do you mean . . .'— and then he quoted the three Greek words. He quoted the word meaning ' I was saved ', and then the word meaning ' I am being saved ', and then the third word which means ' I shall be saved '. Of course, she was completely bowled over! It was perhaps a bit hard on her, poor lass: of course she did not know what to say ; but it led to a very

profitable talk about the beginning, the growth and the
end of the Christian life.

Well, there it is in the New Testament. We were saved,
we are being saved, and we are going to be saved. We
were accepted in Christ, we are growing in Christ, we are
to be perfected in Christ. Christ, then, is spread over the
whole life of the Christian, from its beginning, through
its continuation, to its consummation. That is a statement
which needs no labouring.

THE FULNESS OF CHRIST

But what does that mean? What is the "fulness of
Christ"? Well, what is the beginning—the simple, elementary nature of Christ, into which we come at the beginning? When we come into Christ, we say we have
come into *life,* we have found *life* in Christ. The great
secret of the first experience is that we have received "the
gift of God", which is "eternal life". And, what is more,
we know it. There is no doubt about it—we *know* that life
has been given to us.

Then at the beginning we speak of having received
our sight, or of having come into the *light.* Although we
may not be able to define or explain it, everything has
become illumined to us, has become altogether new as
another world. We know our eyes have been opened. We
have come to see ; light has broken upon us. We are able

to say : " Whereas I was blind, now I see." ' I was in the dark—now it is all light.' Put it how you will, the beginning of the Christian life is just that.

Life, light—and then *liberty*. One of the great things of the beginning of the Christian life is a wonderful sense of release, of emancipation, of having been set free. It would need a chapter all to itself, this liberty into which Christ brings us, this wonderful setting free. It is a very great reality.

Lastly, when we come into Christ, we come into *love*, Divine love, and Divine love comes into our hearts.

These are four of the things into which, in an elementary form, we come, and which come into us, right at the beginning. Of course, there is much more that could be said, and there are many other things, but that is enough to provide for the answer to our enquiry. Let us run over them once again.

First of all, *life*—a new life and a different life. I do not mean now the way we live—that follows, of course —but a new dynamic power in us, which is Divine life. It is a new life, another one altogether, and that life has in it another nature. It belongs to another realm, and has the nature of that other realm. It is the realm of God Himself. I do not mean, of course, that we are now at this point altogether other creatures ; but this is the beginning. We are conscious that there is a new nature at work within us, working for certain things and against certain other things—which is something that was never true of us before.

Yes, we have a new and different life—an *energy*. Life is an energy, is it not? See what life will do. Life really demands difficulty to prove its energy. I remember, some years ago, going down into Cornwall and staying on a farm. This farm had fields on a slope, and one of the fields was just strewn all over with large, white stones. It was the time of the year when seed was in, and nothing was appearing. I said to the farmer, ' Surely you will never get a crop of wheat in that field with all those stones!' ' Don't you make any mistake ', he replied. ' I thought that when I first came to this farm, so I cleared them off, and got a very poor crop. So I put them back again, and I got a very much better crop with the stones—much stronger and healthier than I had before.' Life, you see, proves itself by difficulties and opposition. Here is a new life-force, an energy of a different kind, of another kingdom, that is given to us in our new birth. It is different.

Light—a new intelligence, a new understanding, a new clearness about things. Everybody who has had a genuine Christian experience knows that. They see what they could never see before. Up till then, they may have been striving and struggling to see. But now they see, and it is another world that is open before them, just as a new world is given to any person who has been born blind and at some time receives their sight. They are given a world. They have heard about it, talked about it, had it explained to them, but they have never before been able to say, ' Now I see ! '

Liberty—release—and with the release enlargement. What a large thing the Christian life is ! There is something wrong with a Christian life that is small, mean, limited, petty and narrow. The Christian life is a large thing ; it is a " land of far distances ". With every enlargement, there comes a new inward sense of prospect. Things are ever and ever beyond. The further you go in the Christian life, the more conscious you are of how much more there is. You never exhaust this wonderful sense of prospect and future, of a vast, wide-open door.

Love—a new motive power in the life, in the heart. The hall-mark of a true Christian life at its very beginning is love. It shows itself in an instantaneous desire to let someone else know all about it, to share the good things into which we have come. It is a great heart over-flow to all the world. And it is in its character a selfless love. Self goes out. You do anything, you make any sacrifice, you never consider yourself ; this " love of Christ constraineth ", in a great care for the things of others, a deep, warm devotion to their interests. It is a new love. We cannot enlarge upon each of these—least of all, per-

haps, upon this wonderful love of God which is shed a-
broad in our hearts—but you see that these four things
alone are there, in an elementary form, right at the
beginning.

CHRIST FILLING ALL THINGS

What, then, is the fulness of Christ? It is simply the
continuous enlargement and ultimate finality of these
very things. The continuous growth of life—the freshness,
the dynamic force of God within the life—this motive
power—this Divine nature, which is in His life—should
never, never come to a standstill. It is intended, according
to the eternal purpose, to grow and grow and grow more
and more. More life! Let us take this earnestly to heart.
To receive eternal life may be a gift once and for all, but
if you are at the beginning you have yet to discover how
wonderfully full that life is, and how that life can become more and more abundant as you go on. The longer
we as Christians live, the more should we be characterized
by this mighty life of Christ—" the power of his resurrection ", it is called. And the fulness of Christ is the progressive enlargement and development and sum of those
very things which came to us, and into which we came,
at the beginning ; and if we attain unto fulness—which
we shall never do here in this life ; but we shall ultimately

move right into the fulness—it will be the universality of all those things.

Now you can see how vast Christ is, and how vast the Christian life must be. The Scripture speaks of Christ ' filling all things '—" that he might fill all things " (Eph. iv. 10). How is Christ going to ' fill all things '? It just means that, when that comes about, all things—and it is a vast, an infinite ' all '—will be full of His life, full of His light, full of His liberty, full of His love, and there will be nothing else. All that Christ is will be expressed in the whole creation. That is the purpose of the Christian life, and we have failed of the purpose if that is not true, in a progressive way, now. If it is not true that those things are increasing in us, we have missed the very object of the Christian life. Yes, if there is not more love, and still more love, and yet again more love—and life, and light, and liberty—the very purpose of the Christian life has been missed.

ALL THINGS FILLED INTO CHRIST

Christ filling all things—and all things filled into Christ. Perhaps one of the best illustrations of this is provided by Solomon ; indeed, he is in the Old Testament for that very purpose. Everybody knows about king Solomon and his great wisdom. ' The wisdom of Solomon '

is the very synonym for wisdom. If anybody shows particular wisdom or acumen, we often dub them 'a little
Solomon'.

I saw recently in the paper the following story. A class
of boys was being told about the incident of the execution of John the Baptist. You remember that Salome
danced before Herod, and he was so pleased that he said,
'What would you like? What is your request? I will give
it to you, even to the half of my kingdom.' She went away,
and consulted her evil mother, who hated John the Baptist
because of what he had said about her evil ways ; and the
mother counselled the daughter to ask for the head of John
the Baptist. When she did so, Herod was very, very dis-
tressed, and looked for a way out ; but he found none, and
because of the oath that he had made, he commanded that
the head of John the Baptist should be brought. Here the
teacher turned to the class, and said, 'Now, what would
you have done if you had been Herod?' And one bright
boy chirped up, 'I would have said to the woman, "That
belongs to the half of the kingdom that I did not promise"!' And so in the paper the story was headed: 'A
Young Solomon'.

That is just by the way. But Solomon is the synonym
for vast wisdom. Also of vast wealth : we know of the
riches of Solomon. Vast power : for his kingdom reached
beyond all the kingdoms that had ever been in Israel. And

vast glory: even the Lord Jesus referred to that—it was proverbial. He said: "Even Solomon in all his glory . . ." And we read that, when the queen of Sheba came to prove for herself all this, her verdict was: ' The half was never told me! I had heard fabulous stories, but the half was never told!' And Solomon's people were in it—they were in the good of that; and in certain senses it was in them too. Solomon would not have arrogated all this to himself, but it would be seen in the lives and homes of the people. They were in the greatness of Solomon, but the greatness of Solomon was in them also.

Now here, in the New Testament, Jesus says: " . . . a greater than Solomon is here " (Matt. xii. 42). Christ infinitely transcends Solomon, and therefore the people of Christ are in the same measure greater than Solomon's people. His fulness is to be their inheritance: they are to be in it—it is to be in them. The purpose of God is that. What God has purposed is to have a people eventually in great prosperity, great wealth, great spiritual riches, great spiritual glory. We are called, says the Word of God, unto His eternal glory (I Pet. v. 10). That, briefly and very simply, is the purpose.

THE PRINCIPLES GOVERNING THE CHRISTIAN LIFE

Now, there are principles governing the Christian life. It is exceedingly important that we should recognise this :

for, apart from the principles, there can be no realising of
the purpose. The principles are basic and governmental to
the purpose. We shall never move on in the purpose, progressively, or attain to it finally, except by way of the
Divine principles. So, if the purpose lays hold of our
hearts, and we respond and say, ' Yes, it is a wonderful
thing to be called according to that purpose, and I want to
attain to that ', then it is necessary to know some of the
principles which govern it—principles which are indispensable to the development and realisation of the
purpose.

(a)   THE CROSS

The first basic principle of the purpose is the Cross—
the Cross of our Lord Jesus Christ. The Cross has two
sides, or operates in two ways. First, outwardly, as to what
it means *for* us, and then inwardly, as what it means *in* us.
These two sides of the Cross occupy a vast amount of the
teaching of the New Testament.

The Cross is a work which, on one side, is finished. It is
a work fully and finally done : that is, as to our being
allowed to come to God, having access—that is the New
Testament word—access to God, having union with God
and having fellowship with God. All the work for that
has been fully finished. We are ' made nigh through the

Blood of His Cross '. We have been made one with Him by the Cross. The Cross on that side, for our approach to God, our access to God, our union with God, is a fully accomplished work, and there is nothing more to be done apart from our accepting of it by faith. But there is also the other side to the Cross—what it is to mean *in* us. The Cross is to be an abiding power in our lives. It is a principle to be continuously at work in us. On the one side, then, there is what the Cross meant in itself, then and there. On the other side, there is what the Cross requires of us.

What did it mean? Well, all-inclusively and comprehensively, the Cross meant the removal from God's sight of one kind of man. Jesus Christ at one point assumed the capacity of representative of all men, as in God's sight : that is, in sin, under judgment. " Him ", says the Scripture, " who knew no sin he made to be sin on our behalf " (II Cor. v. 21). Again, He was made a curse in our place (Gal. iii. 13). That is where we were, where all men were —*sin*. We were not only doing sins—we were *sin-full* in God's sight, under judgment, under condemnation, in rejection. And Jesus at that given point took that place— your place, my place, the place of every man as in God's sight under that rejection—and entered into an experience of all the conscious meaning of that rejection such as you and I have never known, and need never know. To have the slightest taste, the slightest sense, of having been re-

E

jected of God is enough to disintegrate the very soul. If you and I should have any consciousness of being forsaken by God, it would be devastating to our moral being, utterly unbearable. Jesus took the sum of that in full consciousness. It disintegrated Him—His very heart ruptured under it and broke—because He knew and endured in that one awful eternal moment the reality of being forsaken of God, on our behalf. 'My God, Thou hast forsaken Me!' That was done for you and for me. We never need awake in eternity to that, if we will accept what He has done for us.

You see, what He had voluntarily accepted was the setting aside of a particular kind of man. In that awful hour He had voluntarily allowed Himself to take the place of that kind of man. It was God saying, 'I close the door for ever to that kind of being.' The Cross means that in Christ's death you and I, as to what we are naturally— men and women by nature—have been set aside. God has in Christ disposed of and removed a kind of being, a degenerate species of creation. He has put it out of the way. In the resurrection of the Lord Jesus that is all done: *that* man has gone. It is not *that* man that is raised from the dead: it is a new man—another. Christ has put off the 'old' man, and now assumes the place of a 'new creation' man.

And there the Heaven is opened. God accepts that Man,

and He is installed and instated for ever before God, as
the type of man that God has ever had in mind. The Cross,
on the one side, sets aside a kind of man, and, on the other
side, installs and instates another kind of man. " Wherefore ", says the Apostle, " if any man is in Christ, there is
a new creation : the old things are passed away ; behold,
they are become new " (II Cor. v. 17). The Christian life
is just that, in principle. The Cross has brought about
this—that there is a difference between where we
were and how we were and what we were before, in
God's sight, and how it is now. In Christ, there is a different man ; by faith in Christ there has come about a different creation. In the resurrection of Christ, the old kind of
man has been replaced by an altogether new one.

Now there arises the necessity for our first of all accepting this position. We shall never get anywhere in Christ,
anywhere on the way to the realm of fulness, until we
have accepted that position into which God has put us
in the death of Christ. In effect He says to us, ' Look here :
so far as I am concerned, in yourself you are a dead man, a
dead woman. I want you to recognise that, when My Son
died, you died in Him, and when He rose, you rose in Him
too, and there is now a new creation. Until you do that,
you will never get anywhere at all. When you do that,
then you are in the position to take your place in the reality
of Christ risen.' Sooner or later our growth spiritually will

come up against that principle in the form of suffering and discipline.

You see, first of all it is a matter of *a position to be taken,* deliberately taken by faith. This is something that needs constantly to be underlined. It is the basic principle of the Christian life, that we have got to consent to God's verdict upon us as we are by nature. We are not to dissect ourselves and say, ' This is good and this is bad, and this is not so good and this is not so bad.' God says : ' *All* of you has gone in My Son. I do not make distinctions between what you call good and what you call bad. I regard you as altogether under condemnation.' " There is none righteous, no, not one " (Rom. iii. 10). " In me, that is, in my flesh, dwelleth no good thing " (Rom. vii. 18).

Yes, that is basic, and it is vital that we should get hold of this fundamental principle of the Christian life. Many Christians do not make any progress at all, development and growth is stayed and arrested, because they have not got that basic matter settled. They are still trying to make something of the person, the self, the nature, that God says He will never entertain at all. They are still thinking that they can be something in themselves, and trying to be something in themselves. They have never accepted this utter, ultimate position. God says, ' I have put you in a grave with My Son, and that was the end of that. Now everything has got to be of another kind, from another

source altogether. It must all come from Christ risen, and
not from you at all.'

That is the key to fulness. It opens up the way, throws
wide open the doors. When you get that really settled and
by faith take that position, there is no limit to what can
be done in the Christian life. But then, when once the
position, the utter position, has been taken and accepted,
acknowledged, received by faith, then the other side begins
—the application of the principle. We accept that ultimate position as a basis and recognise it as God's own
verdict, and then the principle of the Cross begins to work
in us. Yes, the tenses again, that we had earlier, are : firstly
past—we were crucified with Christ (Rom. vi. 6 ; Gal. ii.
20). Then *present*—Paul says : " Always bearing about in
the body the dying of Jesus, that the life also of Jesus may
be manifested in our body " (II Cor. iv. 10) ; and again :
" I die daily " (I Cor. xv. 31). And lastly *future*—his as-
piration was : " that I may know him, and the power of
his resurrection, and the fellowship of his sufferings, being made conformable to his death " (Phil. iii. 10).

Here is the principle at work. It was accepted
in a definite act, but now it is being applied as an active thing in the life, on the one side bringing to an
actual reality our death with Christ, and correspondingly,
on the other side, bringing into our experience our
life-union with Christ. As the death works, so the life

works. This is just the meaning of the Christian life.

What is God doing with us? Why all this trouble, all this difficulty, all this discipline—this chastening, this hard way, this difficult school? Why all this? ' I thought the Christian life was going to be one continuous song and picnic and joy-ride!' You find that it is not. It does not mean that joy disappears, but it does mean that we come into a lot of difficulties and into what, to that ' old man ' of ours, is a very difficult way. What is the meaning?

Ah, God is applying the principle—getting the old man out of the way and making way for the new. Is it not true of a Christian, a true Christian, as differing from any other person, that suffering produces beauty, suffering produces the fruit, the nature, of Christ ; suffering just brings out what Christ is? In others, so often, suffering brings out bitterness, resentment. Some of the most difficult people that I have ever met and tried to help have been people who, because of some great adversity in their lives, have turned against God, become bitter, sour. Suffering has done that. But that is not what happens to a Christian. The marvel of the Christian, the miracle of the Christian life, is just this, that you can find some dear children of God, in lifelong suffering and agony, either of body or of circumstances, who are just wonderfully radiant. You go in where they are, and it is the peace of God. The hymns they sing are hymns about the love of God. Such are their favourite hymns, and yet, if they sang at all, you would think, naturally speaking, it would not be about that. I have clearly in mind certain outstanding instances of such people, in my own experience.

What is it all for? Why, the principle of the Cross is at work, clearing the ground for Christ, for this new creation life, making way for the fulness of Christ. That is the first principle.

(b)   RELATEDNESS

The second principle can only be mentioned briefly before we close. This is a very important principle indeed. It is that of relatedness. You see, no individual Christian, and no number of Christians just as separate isolated individuals, can come to the fulness of Christ. Indeed, if you think about it, it goes without saying. If Christ is as big as we have said, how can any one individual come to that? It is nonsense to suggest it. It would be arrogance to think it. It will require a vast, vast multitude to come to that ; but they will never come to it as a multitude or congregation of *individuals.*

You see, the great conception that is given to us in the New Testament is of the aggregate of Christians as the Body of Christ. You have only to think for a moment about your body, and you know quite well that no one member of your body will grow if detached from the others. It requires not only all the other members, but all the members united, to make one body. There can be no development, either of any member or members, or of the body as a whole, without articulation. I believe that one of the first things that a student of medicine has to face is a box of bones—a box of bones is handed to him. It is all the bones of all the members of a human body. 'Now then, put those bones together and make up a skeleton!' That is the first lesson. And the very first lesson of spiritual fulness and growth is the articulation of Christians, the recognition of the fact that we belong to one another.

The second lesson is that we cannot get on without one another. Our spiritual life depends upon our relatedness with one another, and the maintenance of that adjustment one to another is the secret of spiritual growth. You will find that if Satan can carry out his master-stroke of separating Christians, he has effected their spiritual arrest. It is always like that. That is why he is after it. Divisions are the masterpiece of the Devil, who is set against God's ultimate purpose—the fulness of Christ. If we would only look at our divisions—not only the larger ones, but the little ones, between us and somebody else—in the light of how it first of all affects our or their spiritual growth, and then relates to the larger interests of Christ's increase, we should have a motive for getting rid of those divisions, healing those quarrels, and adjusting our relationships. Relatedness is vital to growth. It is first of all articulation, member to member, and then it is mutuality of life, dependence and interdependence, the recognition of the fact that we must have one another, that our very spiritual life depends upon it. Fellowship is essential, is indispensable. It is a principle of growth. You will be greater or smaller in your measure of Christ according to your recognition and observance of that principle.

But, mark you, it is not artificial, it is not institutional, it is not something that we organize: it is *organic*—it is by life and by love. It is not from the outside, by our arranging it, deciding to have it and fixing it up; it comes from the inside—it comes from Christ within. Paul put his finger upon that very thing in the church in Corinth, when he found rival circles there. One circle centred in himself, saying, ' We are of Paul '. Another circle centred in Apollos—' We are of Apollos.' Another circle centred in Peter—' We are of Peter '; and so on. His appeal to them was this: " Is Christ divided?" (I Cor. i. 13). Of course, the answer is, ' No, you cannot divide Christ.' ' Then if Christ is in you and governs, this is all a contradiction to Christ, this is all not Christ! '

No wonder, then, that we find a poor, mean, miserable measure of spiritual life at Corinth at that time. Thank God, we have another side to the story later on. They evidently got over it, on the basis, the principle, of the Cross. Paul's second letter to them gives a very different picture of the Corinthian church. But Christ cannot be divided, and all divisions, from individual differences between two or more Christians, right up to the great divisions between major Christian groups, are a contradiction of Christ, and no wonder there is spiritual poverty, weakness, ineffectiveness, and lack of registration and impact upon this world. The Devil has triumphed there. We must take note of that. It is a great battle is this matter of fellowship, for the very reason that all the evil forces are set against it. Paul says that this is a matter about which we have to be very diligent: " giving diligence to keep the unity of the Spirit in the bond of peace " (Eph. iv. 3).

(c)   PURITY OF HEART

I close by just mentioning a third principle, without enlarging upon it. It is the principle of purity of heart. You and I will not grow at all with the increase of Christ, toward the fulness of Christ, unless we maintain a very pure spirit. By that I mean an open heart: one that is free from prejudice, free from suspicion ; a readiness to receive, an ability to adjust ; no final closure, even though we may have been brought up in a certain way. If the Lord has ' more light and truth to break forth from His

Word ', we are open to it ; we have not come to a final position that we know it all, we have got it all, we are in it all. A pure spirit means an open heart, a ready spontaneity of response to every bit of light that God gives ; obedience instant, without argument. Upon this hangs very much more than we may imagine.

CHAPTER FOUR

THE ETERNAL PROSPECT OF THE CHRISTIAN

WE SAW AT THE BEGINNING that the Christian life is not something which just springs up in this particular era—the Christian era, as it is called—but that it dates right back to eternity past. We saw that it was designed by God in His eternal counsels—the New Testament has much to say about this—and that that eternal purpose and design is pressing into this present dispensation in a very definite and particular way.

Now we are to see that the future eternity is also pressing into this dispensation. The future eternity is governing the present, is shaping and explaining the present. God is not only working onward. Really, the onward aspect of Divine activities is our side of things. God is, so to speak, working 'backward'. From His side of things He is always working back to His full thought in eternity past. He is bringing us on, but from this other standpoint He is really bringing us back.

THE PROSPECTIVE ELEMENT IN THE NEW TESTAMENT

So we come to this matter of the eternal prospect of the Christian. We have to realise—not that it is difficult

72

to do so—that there is a very large prospective element in the New Testament: that is, the New Testament is always looking on. In the New Testament everything is dominated by the ages to come. God's conception was an eternal one, not just one of time; it is something far, far too big to be realised in fulness in any mere period of time. It certainly, therefore, cannot be realised in the life-time of any person. It outbounds time. This is "from eternity to eternity", and it requires timelessness for its full realisation.

This, of course, explains a great deal. It explains the very nature of the Christian life and of Christian service. A very big factor in the ways of God with His people, with Christians, is that of experience. God puts a great deal of value upon experience. Yet it often seems that, just when we are beginning to profit by experience, the end comes, and we are called away from this life, and all the long and full and deep experience has really had no adequate expression. There is something about this that would be a problem. If God puts so much value upon experience, and then when we have got it we cannot use it, it seems like a contradiction. It requires an extension somewhere, somehow, in order to turn to account all that deep experience which God has taken so much pains to produce. And so this eternal prospect explains God's ways with us in the path of deep and deepening experience.

Then as to the work of God. Well, the work is difficult, it is hard; the progress is all too slow; and though you may do much, and fill your life, when you have had all the days that can be allotted you and have spent yourself to the last drop, what have you done? What does it amount to, at most? We have to say—little, comparatively little. There is so much more to be done, and every successive generation of Christian workers has the same story to tell. On we go, on we go, and we never overtake, we never reach anything like fulness in this life. Something more is required to make perfect both our imperfect lives and our imperfect work.

And then another factor, which is not a small one, is that God seems to be so much more concerned with the worker even than with the work. This of course creates the perplexities of Christian life and service. If God were really concerned with our Christian work, surely He ought never to allow us to be laid aside from it, especially repeatedly or for long periods, and He certainly ought not to allow us to die ' prematurely ', as we would say. If the work is everything, then He ought to keep us on full stretch all our days, and extend our days to a full period; but He does not. So many of His choicest are not able to be in action, to serve, in the way in which Christian service is ordinarily thought of; and even those who are fully in action are conscious that the real need in the work of

God is for their own deeper knowledge of God Himself—
that God is concerned with *them*, even more than He is
with their work.

What does this say? All that discipline, chastening,
trial, testing, that we go through under the hand of God :
is all that just for now? Surely He is preparing for something more. He is concerned with men and with women—
with *people*—quite as much as, if not more than, with
what they do for Him. This, of course, will never be taken
as an excuse for our not working to full capacity, but it
does all point to something more. *There is nothing perfect or complete so long as death remains.* You will remember the argument which the apostle develops in the
letter to the Hebrews concerning the priesthood of the Old
Testament. A priest of the old dispensation could bring
nothing to finality because he died and had to hand on to
another ; and in like manner he himself never attained to
finality ; and so it went on. The argument is that, because
of death, nothing was made perfect. But He—Jesus, our
High Priest—has made and does make things perfect, because He " ever liveth ". It requires an endless life—" the
power of an indissoluble life "—to reach fulness. That is
clearly shown in the Scripture.

You see, the picture of immortality which the Bible
gives us is a very wonderful one, and one, of course, which
in our present order of things we cannot understand. The

picture of immortality which the Bible gives us is that of new productions coming about without the dying of the old. Our present order is that everything new comes out of a preceding death. Seed, flower, everything has to die, in order to produce or make way for something new. That has been the natural order of things since Adam fell. And the heart of this present dispensation is the great truth of Jesus Christ, the " corn of wheat ", falling into the ground and dying, that there should be a production on a larger scale. That is the order of this dispensation. But that is not the order of the coming eternity. The picture of immortality there, as given in the Word, is of trees producing new branches, new leaves, new fruit, and yet the old never dying. Fruit is brought to perfection without any death at all. That is rather wonderful, is it not?

And how much there is in the Word in the nature of an urge and an imperative to wholeheartedness, to utterness. All the time the apostles are urging us, bringing upon us the weight of this great imperative to *go on—go on—go on !* By exhortation, by warning, they are constantly saying to us, ' Go on and ever on! Have no margin of life that is not burnt up for God!' And the point of that argument, of that urge and imperative, is the coming eternity. All this is in the light of the afterward. We must, they say, be utter for God because of what is going to follow, because this is not the end. There is that which, coming afterward, will show the justification for having been utter for God.

THE COMPARATIVE ELEMENT IN ETERNITY

Now, that leads us to the next thing in this connection —the comparative element in eternity. There is, I think we agree, a prospective element in the Christian life which occupies a great deal of the New Testament. Cut out that prospective element from the New Testament and see how much you have got left, whether it be Gospels or Epistles. You are not going to have very much left if you take that out. It is there and it is mightily there. But in addition to it, there is in the New Testament what I am calling the comparative element in relation to the coming eternity. I mean by this that things are not all going to be on one ' mass production ' level hereafter. There are going to be differences where the children of God are concerned, and very great differences.

It was to this, of course, that the Apostle was pointing when writing to the Corinthians. Speaking about foundations and superstructure, he said : ' The foundation is laid. Now let every man take heed how he build thereon. If any man build thereon wood, hay, stubble, gold, silver, precious stones, every man's work shall be tried by fire ' (I Cor. iii. 10 – 13). And, he implies, if it is wood, hay or

F

stubble, it will all go up in smoke. And then he brings in this tremendously forceful word (vs. 15): " If any man's work shall be burned, he shall suffer loss: but he himself shall be saved; yet so as through fire." That is, the man may just scrape through, as a kind of ' emergency '—just managing to get in, as we say, ' by the skin of his teeth '. But everything else has gone. The argument surely is that that is not what God intended. Over against that we have a phrase like this: " For thus shall be richly supplied unto you the entrance into the eternal kingdom " (II Pet. i. 11). On the one hand, we see the possibility of just getting in, with our life and nothing more; on the other hand, an abundant entrance into the everlasting kingdom. You see, there are differences, there are comparative features about the afterward.

What about those messages to the seven churches in Asia, which we have at the beginning of the book of the Revelation? I believe that the people in, those churches are true Christians and not merely professors. If you grant that, then you have got to face this, that between Christian and Christian there is a difference, and there are some very distinct promises given to certain Christians there. " To him that overcometh . . .", " to him that overcometh . . .", " to him that overcometh will I grant . . ." Surely logic implies: ' If you don't, then you won't. If you don't overcome, then you won't get what the Lord offers.' There are differences. I do not believe this is a matter of loss of salvation, but it is something more than just being saved, just getting in.

RELATIONSHIP WITH THE LORD FOR ETERNAL VOCATION

What is the nature of the difference or the differences? Some people will say, ' Well, of course, it is reward.' But what does the New Testament show to be the nature of the reward? The answer is quite clearly this. The reward relates to *calling*. It is vocational—it is always vocational. " And his servants shall serve him ; and they shall see his face " (Rev. xxii. 3, 4). It is service, but service without all the burdensome elements that are so often associated with service now : service to Him without limit, without restraint, without opposition, without suffering. To be able to serve Him! Surely there can be no greater joy than just to be able, without all the straitness and limitations and difficulties of the work now, to serve the Lord in fulness.

Now that is where the New Testament puts its finger. It is calling, vocation ; and this, it goes on to show, is a matter of positions in relation to the Lord, different positions for service. Take an illustration of this from one of the messages to the churches. " He that overcometh, I will give to him to sit down with me in my throne " (Rev.

iii. 21). There you have two ideas. One is a very close relationship with the Lord, a very intimate nearness to Him ;
the other, royal service—the service of the throne. What
is your conception of sitting with Him in the throne? Let
us not have pictures of sitting on golden or ivory thrones,
and so on. This simply means union with the Lord in the
administration of His eternal kingdom. That is service. But
that is said to be a special gift to certain people—it is their
reward, if you like. The point is that it is vocational, and
it is a matter of relationship to the Lord.

The final picture that we have in the New Testament,
while so full of symbolism, is an embodiment of these
spiritual principles. It is the picture of the City. Now again
get your mind clear, and do not think of a literal city. It
is only an illustration, a figure, a symbol. This city is undoubtedly the Church. Need I argue that? "The Jerusalem that is above . . . which is our mother " (Gal. iv. 26).
" Ye are come unto . . . the heavenly Jerusalem " (Heb.
xii. 22). "Ye *are* come . . ." We are not coming later on,
afterwards. " Ye are come . . . unto the heavenly Jerusalem
. . . and to the . . . church of the firstborn ". So that that city
which is said to be the " new Jerusalem, coming down out
of heaven from God " (Rev. xxi. 2), is the Church. Now,
like a capital city, it is put into a particular and peculiar
position, and the idea of such a city is that it is an adminis-
trative centre. We are told that ' the nations walk in the

light thereof ' (vs. 24). You see, there is something at the centre for government, and there is much more that is not at the centre. Here is proximity to the Lord, relationship with the Lord for eternal vocation in administration in His kingdom.

THE URGE AND THE IMPERATIVE

That, surely, is enough to bear out the statement that there is a comparative element in the eternity to come. And that is the point of the urge and the imperative, that is the force of the constraint: " Let us press on unto full growth " (Heb. vi. 1, R. V. mg.)—not looking back, but pressing on ; it is the force of all the warnings—not that you may lose your salvation, but that there are positions and there is a vocation to which you are called in eternity, and you may miss that. I think Paul saw that in what he called ' the on-high calling ' (Phil. iii. 14). He saw something of this reigning life in the ages to come.

Now, with God, nothing is merely official. God never appoints officers in His Kingdom. There are not politicians —political officials—in His Kingdom, neither are there ecclesiastics—ecclesiastical officials. With God, I repeat, there is nothing that is merely official. You know, God does not appoint officers in His Church. God's principle of appointment is always according to spiritual measure.

Even now in the Church—where it is a spiritual thing, where it is according to His mind—God indicates those who are to have oversight as being men of spiritual measure; not selected, chosen and voted in by popular vote. That is the principle of the New Testament, and in the Kingdom it is like that. No one is going to have any position just because he is appointed officially to it. Not at all! Every position will be according to our spiritual measure.

Hence we are urged repeatedly—' let us go on to full growth ' (' perfection ' in the A.V. is an unfortunate translation). It is always according to the " measure of the stature of the fulness of Christ " (Eph. iv. 13). It is just how much of Christ there is, how big we are according to the standard of Christ. That is God's basis of appointment, and it will always be so. It is so now and it will be in the ages to come. It will always be that vocation depends upon how much of Christ there is in those concerned. God's whole thought, as we saw at the beginning of these meditations, is that Christ shall fill all things.

Now that explains our discipline, for our discipline is our training for then ; and the nature of our discipline now is just to increase the measure of Christ and to decrease the measure of ' I ', of ourselves, in every way ; to set aside the one man, that occupies the place of Christ, and to put Christ in his place. The one all-inclusive object of the Holy

Spirit in this dispensation is to make Christ everything, and to get as much room for Christ as He possibly can—and that means, where we are concerned, as much as we will let Him have. That throws us back, of course, upon the question : Are we really going to be ' utter '? The measure of our ' utterness ' will be the measure of our usefulness in the ages to come. This will be governed by spiritual measure and by no other principle.

REWARD AND GRACE

Some people find difficulty—a purely mental one—in reconciling reward and grace. Some may want to say, ' Oh, but it is all of grace, and you are making it a work. After all, it is all of grace.' How can you reconcile reward and grace? Well, you have got to find somehow the place of rewards, haven't you? But it is not so difficult as all that. It is all the grace of God that we have a chance to be ' utter ' at all. It is all of grace that I can be a Christian and that I can go on with the Lord, that I can serve the Lord even a little bit. It is all of grace. And if suffering is going to lead to glory, and the measure of the glory is going to be according to the suffering, then it will require all the grace of God for that. You can never get outside of grace. If ever there should come a reward—if you like to visualise such a thing as a reward being literally offered now, I tell you, dear friend, when we get to that point of full understanding and knowledge of all the forbearance and longsuffering and patience of the Lord, we shall fall on our faces and say, ' Lord, I cannot take any reward—it is all of your grace.'

But then remember that grace is spoken of in more than one way in the New Testament. There is grace which gives us access and acceptance. " This grace wherein we stand " (Rom. v. 2). It is all the favour of God, without merit, that we are saved at all, that we belong to the Lord. Yes, that is grace. But then grace is also spoken of as strength— strength beyond initial salvation. It is what the Lord meant when He said to Paul in the presence of his affliction and suffering : " My grace is sufficient for thee : for my power is made perfect in weakness " (II Cor. xii. 9). Grace is acceptance without merit, but grace is also strength to labour, serve and suffer. However you look at it, it is all of grace.

UTTERNESS FOR GOD

So now we have to focus down upon this, that there is in the New Testament a large place for our meaning business with God. It is not all willy-nilly—that you believe, you accept Christ, and that is the beginning and end of it ; you get everything now. Surely all these entreaties, exhortations, beseechings, bear down upon this. Their burden is :

Do not leave anything to chance. Do not say, ' Oh, well, this does not matter very much, this will not hurt, there is not much wrong in this ; I have got salvation, and the grace of God will cover all these imperfections ; I can do this and that, and it will not make much difference ; God is a God of love.' The New Testament says, in effect, ' Do not take any risks.' If it does not mean as to your salvation ultimately, it does mean as to something. The whole force of the Word is : ' Look here, you be utter ; God does not make provision for anything else. You go all the way with the Lord, for it is that to which you are called.' The Lord has never said, ' Well, you only need to go so far, and I will excuse you the rest.' No, it is always fulness that God keeps in view, and He is challenging us all the time as to whether we will mean business with Him. But there will be no place, in the end, for our boasting in our endurance, our success, our utterness. Even though we pour ourselves out to the last drop, at the last it will be ourselves, above all, who will be the worshippers—we shall be the ones who are down before Him most. The most utter people are always those who are most conscious of their indebtedness to the Lord.

THE GREAT CRISIS WHICH DETERMINES EVERYTHING

And now, as we draw to a close, we come to the great crisis which determines everything. It is always there in the Scripture, always kept in view: a great crisis—the coming of the Lord. It is there, it is then, that everything will be determined. Though we may have passed on before He comes, the Word makes it perfectly clear that that makes no difference—we shall be there when He comes, and those who are alive when He comes will not get ahead of us. We shall be there together, and so we shall all be on the common footing; and then it will be determined what the future is going to be—just exactly what will be our place, what will be our function. That is a big factor in the prospective aspect of things. The Scripture always keeps in view the prospect of the Lord's coming. When we are saved, we receive a new hope, but as we go on as believers we find that that hope becomes something very definite and concrete. It is called in the New Testament ' *the* hope ', and the hope is related to the coming of the Lord.

So that all the appeals and all the warnings and all the entreaties focus down to this. The Lord is coming, and at His coming everything will be decided, everything will be settled. It is then that our future eternity will be decided upon. You recall all those appeals, in the light of His coming, for watchfulness, for being fully occupied, being on full stretch, till He comes, and the earnest warnings that, if we are not, something serious is going to happen— something is going to go wrong. I am not putting this into any system of doctrine, crystallizing it into any form of teaching ; but these are the facts, pure, simple facts. At the coming of the Lord, great decisions will take place, and if we are not watching, if we are not occupying, if we are not on full stretch, something is going wrong. The Word makes that perfectly clear in various ways. Something is going wrong—I put it like that. I mean that something is going to be other than the Lord would have had, and what might have been with us.

So we bring the eternity that is ahead right into the present, and say that this is a tremendous motive. It gives a tremendous motive to the Christian life. Oh, the life hereafter—going to Heaven, or however we may speak about it—is not something that is just out there, in a kind of objective, detached way, and we are looking forward to that day, waiting for that day to come. Dear friend, that day is pressed right into the present. That day is here now in all its implications. There is little hope of our going to Heaven, if Heaven has not already come to us. Our place and our vocation in that day (though not our salvation) will depend very largely upon the measure that Christ has had in us in this life.

That, again, explains many things, does it not? It explains, for instance, why the Lord very often presses into a short time a great deal of suffering, much affliction, much trial, that produces a wonderful measure of Christ. You can see the growth in grace. You discern the patience, the forbearance, the kindness, the love of Christ coming out in this suffering child of God. This is preparation for glory, preparation for service. It explains very much. We can go round it, and look at it from many different standpoints, but after all what it amounts to is this. The New Testament keeps the future in view as the great governing thing for the present. The New Testament says that it is going to make a difference in the eternity to come just how far we have gone on with the Lord, and how much room the Lord has gained in our lives now.

And it is going to be definite. The New Testament says the Lord is coming. The Lord will come in His own time, and then all will be decided. You see, so many people are interested in the second coming of Christ purely from a prophetical standpoint, as to events and happenings in the world, and so on, and so few Christians are alive, fully alive, to the fact that in the New Testament the coming of the Lord is always brought to bear upon our spiritual state. " He that hath this hope "—not, ' he that hath this prophetic interpretation of the second coming '—but " he that hath this hope set on him purifieth himself " (I John iii. 3): he gets ready, he seeks that his state shall be all right as well as his standing. It matters, and it will matter, a very great deal. So we must open the door wide in our Christian lives to that far greater life that is before us. At

most this is a brief one, a small one ; it is only the beginning ; but in that day all its meanings are going to come
out in fulness.

Will you hear the appeal? The Christian life, as we
have said, is a tremendous thing, an immense thing. We
are called with an eternal calling, unto an eternal vocation.
Here we are just brought into relationship with the Lord,
and then are dealt with by the Lord. We are allowed to
serve the Lord ; but even in our service we are in school,
we are learning, rather than anything else. Do you not
think that that is how it ought to be? Not just that we
should be doing a thousand and one things, but that we
should be learning deeply in the school of experience. And
it is all related to the calling on-high, and the great vocation afterward.

The Lord move our hearts to be utter for Him, to take
no risks, to leave nothing to chance whatever, but, like
His servant Paul, to go for the highest prize, the fullest
thing that the Lord ever intended.

THE GOSPEL
ACCORDING TO PAUL

T. AUSTIN-SPARKS

CONTENTS

CHAPTER ONE

IN HIS LETTER TO THE ROMANS

" . . . the gospel which I preach . . ." (Gal. ii. 2).

" Now I made known unto you, brethren, the gospel which I preached unto you . . ." (I Cor. xv. 1).

" For I make known to you, brethren, as touching the gospel which was preached by me, that it is not after man " (Galatians i. 11).

" The gospel which I preach ". " The gospel which was preached by me ".

THERE ARE IN THE NEW TESTAMENT four main designations for the basic matter with which it deals, the vital truth with which it is concerned, and those four designations are The Gospel, The Way, The Faith, and The Testimony. That which has now come to be known as ' Christianity ' was then expressed by one or other of those designations. Of these four, the one used more than any other is the first—The Gospel. That title for the inclusive message of the New Testament occurs there at least one hundred times—that is, in the noun form, ' the Gospel '. In the corresponding verb form it occurs many more times, but unrecognised by us, because it is translated by several different English words. The verb form of this very same Greek word appears in our translation

9

as 'to declare', 'to preach', 'to preach the gospel'. It would sound very awkward if you were to give a literal translation to this verb form. It would be just this—'to gospel', 'to gospel people', 'to gospel the kingdom', or, to take the meaning of the word, 'to good-news', 'to good-tidings', and so on. That sounds very awkward in English, but in Greek that is exactly what was said. When they preached they conceived themselves as 'good-newsing' everything and everybody. To preach the gospel was simply to announce good tidings.

It is impressive that this word, this title, for the Christian faith—'the gospel'—abounds in twenty of the twenty-seven books of the New Testament. The exceptions are: the Gospel by John, where you will not find it, nor will you find it in the three letters of John. You will not find it in Peter's second letter, nor will you find it in James or Jude. But these writers had their own titles for the same thing. We mentioned amongst the four, 'The Testimony': that is John's peculiar title for the Christian faith—often, with him, 'The Testimony of Jesus'. With James and Jude it is 'The Faith'. But you see how preponderating is this title of 'the good news', 'The Gospel'.

THE RANGE OF THE TERM 'THE GOSPEL'

So we have to take account quite early of a most important fact. It is that this term, the good news, covers the entire range of the New Testament, and embraces the whole of what the New Testament contains. It is not just those certain truths which relate to the beginning of the Christian life. The gospel is not confined to the truths or doctrines connected with conversion and, in that limited sense, salvation—the initial matter of becoming a Christian. The gospel goes far beyond that. I repeat, it embraces all that the New Testament contains. It is as much the gospel in the profound letters to the Ephesians and the Colossians as it is in the letter to the Romans— perhaps no less profound a document, but often regarded as being mainly connected with the beginnings of the Christian life.

No, this term, the ' good tidings ', covers the whole ground of the Christian life from beginning to end. It has a vast and many-sided content, touching every aspect and every phase of the Christian life, of man's relationship to God and God's relationship to man. It is all included in the good tidings. The unsaved need good news, but the saved equally need good news, and they constantly need good news. Christians constantly need some good news, and the New Testament is just full of good news for Christians. The servants of the Lord need good news. They need it as their message, the substance of their message. They need it for their encouragement and support. How much the Lord's servants need good news to encourage them in the work, and support in all the demand and cost of their labours! The Church needs good news for its life, for its growth, for its strength, for its testimony. And so the gospel comes in at every point, touches every phase.

Now as to our present method in the pages which follow. I would ask you to follow me carefully, and to grasp what I am trying to say by way of the foundation of this word. We are going to pursue what I am going to call the ' resultant ' method : that is, to elicit the conclusion of the whole matter, rather than the particular aspect of any one portion of the New Testament.

Let me illustrate. Take, for instance, the letter to the

Romans, which we are going to consider in a moment. We all know that that letter is the grand treatise on justification by faith. But justification by faith is shown to be something infinitely greater than most of us have yet grasped or understood, and justification by faith has a very wide connotation and relationship. All that is contained in this letter to the Romans resolves itself into just one glorious issue, and that is why it begins with the statement that what it contains is ' the gospel '. " Paul, a servant of Jesus Christ, called to be an apostle, separated unto the gospel of God . . . concerning his Son ". Now all that follows is ' the gospel '—but what a tremendous gospel is there! And we have somehow to sum it all up in one conclusion. We have to ask ourselves : ' After all, what does result from our reading and our consideration of this wonderful letter? ' You see, justification is not the beginning of things, neither is it the end of things. Justification is the meeting point of a vast beginning and a vast end. That is, it is the point at which all the past eternity and all the future eternity are focused. That is what this letter reveals.

THE GOD OF HOPE

Let us now look at it a little more closely in that particular light. What is the issue, what is the result? That result is gathered up into one word only. It is a great thing when you can get hold of a big document like this and put it into one word. What is the word? Well, you will find it if you turn to the end of the letter. It is significant that it comes at the point where the Apostle is summing up. He has written his letter, and he is now about to close. Here it is.

" Now the God of hope fill you with all joy and peace in believing, that ye may abound in hope " (Rom. xv. 13).

If your margin is a good one, it will give you references to other occurrences of that word in this same letter. You will find it as early as chapter v, verse 4 ; you find it again in chapter viii, verses 24 and 25 ; again in chapter xii, verse 12 ; and then in the fifteenth chapter—first in verse 4, and finally here in our passage, verse 13. " The God of hope ". That is the word into which the Apostle gathers the whole of this wonderful letter. This, then, is the gospel of the God of hope ; more literally, the ' good news ', or the ' good tidings ', of the God of hope. So that what is really in view in this letter from start to finish is *hope.*

A HOPELESS SITUATION

Now, quite obviously, hope has no meaning and makes no sense except in the light of the contrary—except as the contrary exists. The Divine method in this letter, therefore, in the first instance, is to set the good tidings over against a hopeless situation, in order to give clear relief to this great word—this ultimate issue, this conclusion, this result. A very, very hopeless situation is set forth. Look at the Divine method in this. The situation is set forth in two connections.

(a) IN THE MATTER OF HEREDITY

Firstly, it is exposed in regard to the race—the whole matter of heredity. If we look at chapter v, with which we are so familiar, we see that there the whole race is traced back to Adam—" as through one man . . ." (verse 12). The whole race of mankind is traced right back to its origin and fountain-head in the first Adam. What is made clear in this chapter is this. There was a disobedient act through unbelief, resulting in the disruption of man's relationship with God. "Through the one man's disobedience" (verse 19), Paul puts it—not only here, but in his letter to the Corinthians (I Cor. xv. 21, 22). And hence all men issuing from that man, Adam, became involved in that one act of disobedience and in its consequences—mainly the disruption of the relationship between man and God.

But that is not all. What immediately followed, as the effect of that act, was that man became in his nature disobedient and unbelieving. It was not just one isolated act which he committed, not just one thing into which he fell for a moment. Something went out of him, and something else entered into him, and man became by nature a disobedient and unbelieving creature. Not only did he act in that way, but he *became* that; and from that moment the very *nature* of man is unbelieving, the *nature* of man is disobedience. It is in his constitution, and all men have inherited that.

This is something that cannot be adjusted, you see. When you have become a certain kind of being, lacking a certain factor, you cannot adjust. You cannot adjust to what is not there. No man can believe unless it is given him of God to believe. Faith is ' not of ourselves, it is the gift of God' (Eph. ii. 8). No man can be obedient to God apart from a mighty act of God in him causing him to be of an obedient nature or disposition. You cannot adjust to something that is not there. So the situation is pretty hopeless, is it not? Something has gone, and something else which is the opposite of that has come in and taken its place. That is the condition of the race here. What a picture of hopeless despair for the whole race! That is our heredity. We are in the grip of that.

You will, of course, agree that in other realms, in other departments of life, heredity is a pretty hopeless thing. We often use the very hopelessness of it as a line of argument by which to excuse ourselves. We say, ' It is how I am made: it is no use you trying to get me to do this—I am not made that way'. You are only arguing that you have in your constitution something that makes the situation quite impossible. And let me take this opportunity of emphasizing that it is quite hopeless for us to try to find in ourselves that which God requires. We shall wear ourselves out, and in the end come to this very position which God has laid down, stated and established —it is hopeless! If you are struggling to be a different kind of person from what you are by nature, trying to get over what you have inherited—well, you are doomed to despair: and yet how many Christians have never learned that fundamental lesson! For the whole race, heredity spells hopelessness. If this needs focusing at all, we have only to consider the conflict and battle that there is over believing God, having faith in God. You know that it is a deep work of the Spirit of God in you that brings you, either initially or progressively, to believe. It is the " so-easily-besetting sin "—unbelief—followed, of course, by inability to obey. We are crippled at birth ; we are born doomed in this matter by our heredity.

(b) IN THE MATTER OF RELIGIOUS TRADITION

Then the Lord takes this thing into another realm. I hope you recognise the meaning of the background, the dark background, against which this word ' hope' is placed. The Spirit of God through the Apostle takes it into the realm of religious tradition, as exemplified by the Jews. Everything now for them is traced back to Abraham and to Moses. What a lot the Apostle has to say about Abraham and his faith—" Abraham believed "—and then about Moses, and the Law coming in. And here is something of tremendous significance and importance that we must note, for here we see the particular function that was in view in God's sovereign choice of the Jewish nation. Have you ever thought of it like this? There are many things that could be said about the Jewish nation, their past, present and future, but what comes out so definitely here is their function in the sovereignty of God. It was, and still is, their function, so far as testimony is concerned, that is, the witness of their history. It was to show just one thing. You can have a grand father—I do not mean a grandfather!—and you may have the best religious tradition ; but nothing of that is carried over in your heredity, that is, it does not pass into your nature.

What a father was Abraham! What a lot is made of " Abraham our father "! What a magnificent specimen of faith and obedience was Abraham! They were all of the stock of Abraham; as a nation, they derived from Abraham. And what a system was the Jewish system of religion, so far as standard is concerned, a moral, ethical, religious standard. There is nothing that can improve upon it in the religions of the world. What a magnificent system of religious precept was the Jewish religion, which came in through Moses!—not only the ten commandments, but all the other teaching that made up the Law, covering every aspect of man's life. And they were the children of that: yet what do you find here? You do not find the faith of Abraham in them, and you do not find the reflection of that great system in them, in their nature. These very people, deriving from such a one as Abraham, and being the inheritors of all those oracles of the Mosaic system, in their natures are devoid of everything that is represented by Abraham and Moses. These people are still characterized by—what? unbelief, in spite of Abraham ; disobedience, in spite of Moses ! What could be more hopeless?

Some people have the idea that, if they have a good father and a good mother, that puts them in a very secure position, but human nature does not bear witness to that. There may be advantages in having had godly forebears—some advantages ; but it is no final guarantee that you are going to escape all the difficulties and all the conflicts and all the sufferings of getting your own faith. The fact is that parents can be utter for God, they can be the most godly, the most pious, and yet their children can be the most renegade. A strange thing, is it not? The disposition to faith and obedience is not in the blood. Religious tradition of the best kind does not change our nature. It may go back for generations—it does not change our nature. We are still unbelieving and disobedient in nature, however good our parents were. You may have prayed from the beginning for a loved child, from the time that it was the smallest babe ; you may have sought to live before it for God : and yet here is that child self-willed, disobedient—everything else.

HOPE IN A DESPERATE SITUATION

How desperately hopeless this situation is ! But that is the way in which the Lord establishes a setting for this tremendous thing that is called hope. And so we come to the transcendent solution, and I use that word carefully at this point, for here is something very great. This is an immense mountain, this mountain of heredity: but there is something that transcends the whole, gets above it all; a solution which rises above the whole hopelessness and despair of the natural situation; and that is what is called 'the gospel'. Oh, that must be good news! Indeed that is why it is called 'good news'! *Good news!* What is it? There is hope in this most desperate situation.

THE GOSPEL IN ETERNITY PAST

Now, if we look at this letter again as a whole, we shall find that the good news, or the good tidings, of the gospel is not only in the Cross of the Lord Jesus—though that is the focal point of it, as we shall see in a moment. The good news, or the gospel, is found to be something very, very much bigger even than the Cross of the Lord Jesus! What is that? It is "the good tidings of God . . . concerning his Son . . . Jesus Christ our Lord". The Cross is only one fragment of the significance of Jesus Christ Himself.

So this letter, what does it do? It takes us right into the eternity of the Son of God. This is wonderful, if you grasp it. If this gospel does not save you, I do not know what will. Here we are taken right back into the past eternity of the Son. "Whom he foreknew, he also fore-ordained to be conformed to the image of his Son" (Rom. viii. 29). He must have had His Son, the Master-Pattern, there in view before ever man was created, the eternal, the timeless, Pattern that the Son was: before there was any need of redemption, atonement, the Cross, the Son was the eternal Pattern of God for man. And, mark you, it is so positive, so definite. It is in that tense which means a definite, once-for-all act. "Whom he foreknew, he also foreordained". It is something which was done before time was. That is where the gospel begins.

Yes, we see the Son in His eternity as God's timeless Pattern; and then we have the eternity or timelessness of the redeeming sovereignty. The redeeming sovereignty is included in that. 'He foreordained, He called, He justified, He glorified'. Now these three remaining things are not subsequent. They all belong to the same time—which is not time at all; it is eternity. It does not say that He foreknew and foreordained, and then in course of time He called and He justified and He glorified. You see what you are committed to if you take that view. Most of us have been called and justified, but we are not glorified yet. But it says 'He glorified', in the 'once-for-all' (aorist) tense.

This must mean, then, that when He took this matter in hand in relation to His timeless Pattern, the Lord Jesus, He finished it all in sovereign purpose and intention. It was all rounded off then, so that the marred vessel is an incident in time; a terrible incident, a terrible tragedy, that the vessel was marred in the hand of the Potter; but, for all that, an incident in time. God's counsels transcend all that has come in in time. Dear friend, when the Lord projected the whole plan of redemption, it was not because something had happened calling for an emergency movement to try to save the situation on the spot. He had already anticipated the whole thing, and had got everything in hand to meet the contingency. The Lamb was "slain from the foundation of the world" (Rev. xiii. 8). The Cross reaches back over all time, right back over all sin, over the fall, over the first Adam—right back to the eternal Son, before times eternal. The Cross goes back there—to "the Lamb slain from the foundation of the world".

What great hope is here! If that is true, if we can grasp that, that is good news, is it not? *We* make everything of the situation in ourselves which is so hopeless ; *God* makes everything of His Son to meet our hopelessness. And God is not experimenting because something has gone wrong—'We must find some kind of remedy for this, we must find something with which we can experiment to see if we can meet this emergency ; man has gone sick, and we must look round for a remedy.' No ; God has already covered it from eternity, met it from eternity, *in His Son*. It is the gospel, the good news, of God "*concerning his Son*". This may raise a number of mental problems, but here is the statement of this book. Hope, you see, is not destroyed because Adam falls : hope reaches back beyond man's sin.

You say, 'Then what about the Cross?' Well, the Incarnation and the Cross are only effecting what was settled in eternity—bringing out of eternity into time in a practical way, making effectual for man in his desperately needy condition, that great purpose, intention, design of God concerning His Son. The Cross is the means which lifts right up out of the trough, the valley, of human sin and failure, on to the level of the eternal counsels of God, and restores the even course of that which ultimately is eternally unaffected by what has happened in time. Tremendous good news, that, is it not? The Cross becomes the occasion of faith by which all this is transcended—of course it provides the ground for our faith—and when faith acts in relation to the Cross, what happens? We are brought into Christ : not brought into the Jesus of three and a half years, or even of thirty years, but brought into

Christ as representing God's timeless thought for man. Faith brings us into that. That is the good news, "the good news concerning his Son"; the gospel, the good news of "the God of hope".

You see, hope is founded upon God's eternal provision outside of time: and that is a very safe rock upon which to stand! Yes, founded upon the eternal rock of Christ's Sonship, not upon an after-thought and an after-measure to meet something that has happened unexpectedly. Hope is grounded and anchored outside of time. The Apostle, writing to the Hebrews, uses a picture, a metaphor. "The hope . . . which we have as an anchor of the soul, a hope both sure and stedfast and entering into that which is within the veil" (Heb. vi. 18, 19); taking you outside of time, outside of this life, anchoring you there in eternity. How great is the Cross! How great is the message of Romans vi! It takes us right back beyond Moses, Abraham and Adam. It takes us right back past Adam's sin and failure, and the whole race's hopeless condition. The Cross takes us back before it all, and there in the past eternity links us up with what God intended. The Cross secures that. And with the other hand the Cross reaches right on into eternity to come, and says, "Whom he foreknew . . . them he also glorified" (Rom. viii. 29, 30). The Cross secures the coming eternal glory. How great is the Cross!

Hope, then, is resting upon the immensity of the Cross. Hope rests upon the fact that Christ, who passed this way, becoming the last Adam, being made sin for us, bearing it all, now raised by God, is seated at God's right hand, and therefore that we, as "in Christ", have been placed beyond any risk of another fall. I always think that this is one of the most blessed factors in the gospel—that Jesus in Heaven now, having been this way and the way of His Cross, says that this Adam will never fail. There will never be another fall. This heredity is secure, is safe, because linked with Him. There is no fear of our being involved in any more falls of that kind, no fear at all. It is indeed a wonderful hope, this gospel of the God of hope!

Do you see how very vividly the dark picture of hopelessness is drawn? I have only given you the outline, but you look at the details—the terrible picture of the Gentiles and the Jews drawn in the first chapters of this letter, and the hopelessness of the situation for both. Yes, despair indeed—and then over it all written, Hope! The good news of hope stands over it all, in spite of it all, because hope rests upon God having before all things determined upon something which He will carry out, and which He has demonstrated by the Cross of His Son, Jesus Christ. You and I know, do we not, that when faith has acted in relation to the Cross of the Lord Jesus, something begins in us which reverses altogether the natural course of things. Now faith is growing, faith is developing; we are learning the way of faith, we are being enabled to trust God more and more. Everything has changed: obedience is now possible.

And there is another life, another nature, another power, in us, which has made for hope. A contradiction of the Christian faith is a despairing Christian, a hopeless Christian; one who is not marked by this great thing which is pre-eminently characteristic of God—hope. He is " the God of hope ". The Lord make this true, that we are filled with hope, " rejoicing in hope ". " Patient in tribulation ", but " rejoicing in hope " (Rom. xii. 12).

CHAPTER TWO

IN HIS LETTERS TO THE CORINTHIANS

WE NOW PASS to the letters to the Corinthians, and, again following our method, we seek to find that which will sum up all that these letters contain. After all the details, all that goes to make up these letters—and it is quite a lot—we ask: 'What does it amount to? What is the result with which we are left?' And once more we shall find that it is only the gospel again—forgive me putting it like that—it is just a matter of the gospel again from another angle, another standpoint.

We may be surprised to learn that the word 'gospel', or, as it would be in the original, the term 'good tidings', occurs in these two letters no fewer than twenty-two times: so that we are not just taking a little fragment and hanging an undue weight upon it. We need some fairly solid foundation upon which to base our conclusions, and I think that twenty-two occurrences of one special word in such a space forms a fairly sound basis. Whatever else these letters are about, they must be about that. Much of what you read in these letters might lead you to think it was not like that at all—it looks very bad ; but what we are after is the resultant issue.

THE SUMMING UP OF THE LETTERS

There is one very familiar sentence which sums up the whole of the two letters. It occurs, naturally, at the end of the second letter.

"The grace of the Lord Jesus Christ, and the love of God, and the communion of the Holy Spirit, be with you all" (II Cor. xiii. 14).

This is sometimes called ' the benediction ' or ' the blessing '. That is, of course, man's title for it. But it is not just an appendix to a discourse—a conventional way of terminating things, a nice thought. Nor was it used by Paul as a kind of concluding good wish or commendation with which to terminate a meeting, as it is commonly used now. I suppose there is a blessing in it, but you have to look much more deeply than just at these phrases. Really it was a prayer, and a prayer in which was summed up the whole of the two letters which the Apostle had written. In Paul's wonderful way of comprehending much in few words, everything that he had penned through these two letters is in this way gathered up.

THE ORDER OF THE SUMMING UP

It is perhaps important to note the order of these three clauses. The grace of the Lord Jesus, the love of God, the communion or fellowship of the Holy Spirit. That is not the order of Divine Persons. If it were the order of Divine Persons, it would have to be changed: ' The love of God, the grace of the Lord Jesus, and the fellowship of the Holy Spirit '. But we have no need to attempt to put God right—to try to improve upon the Word of God and the Holy Spirit's order. This is not the order of Divine

Persons. It is the order of the Divine process. This is the way along which God moves to reach His end, and that is exactly the summing up of these two letters. All the way through God is moving to an end, and this prayer of Paul's is according to the principle, the order, of Divine movement.

Let us now come to the words themselves, and see if we can find a little of the gospel—the ' good tidings ' of these two letters—gathered into these three phrases.

THE GRACE OF THE LORD JESUS

What was the grace of the Lord Jesus? Well, if you look back in this second letter, to chapter viii, verse 9, you have it.

"*Ye know the grace of our Lord Jesus Christ, that, though he was rich, yet for your sakes he became poor, that ye through his poverty might become rich*".

There are three quite simple elements in that statement. The Lord Jesus did something—He became poor ; and what He did was voluntary—for grace ever and always carries that feature at its very beginning. It is that which is perfectly voluntary ; not compelled, not demanded, under no obligation, but completely free. The grace of our Lord Jesus meant firstly a voluntary act. That is grace very simply, but it goes to the heart of things. So that is what He did—He became poor. And then the motive, as to why He did it : ' that we, through His poverty, might be made rich '.

I think that is a simple, and a very beautiful, analysis and synthesis of grace. He became poor—He did it without compulsion—and in so doing His motive was that we might become rich.

Now, you see, you have here in the Lord Jesus a Person and a nature wholly and utterly, fully and finally, different from any other human being ; a nature completely contrary to the nature of man, as we know it. Human nature as we know it is being rich, doing anything to become rich, and anybody else can be robbed to make us rich. That does not necessitate taking a pistol and putting it at people's heads. There are other ways of getting advantages to ourselves, at other people's expense or otherwise. There is really no ' grace ' about man, as we know him. But the Lord Jesus is so different from this ! Christ is altogether different—an altogether other nature.

Now the whole of the first letter to the Corinthians is crammed full of the self-principle. I am assuming that you are more or less familiar with these letters. I cannot take you through page after page, verse after verse ; but I am giving the result of close reading, and you can verify it if you care to. I repeat : the whole of the first letter to the Corinthians is just full of the self-principle—self-vindication, going to law to get their own rights, self-seeking, self-importance, self-indulgence—even at the Lord's Table —self-confidence, self-complacency, self-glory, self-love, self-assertiveness, and everything else. You find all these things in that first letter, and more. ' I '—a great, an immense ' I '—stands inscribed over the first letter to the Corinthians. This is the nature, the old nature, showing itself in Christians. Everything that is contrary to " the grace of the Lord Jesus " comes to light in that letter, and the Lord Jesus stands in such strong, clear, terrible contrast to what we find there.

In our last chapter we sought to show that, in order to reveal the glory of the good tidings as the good tidings of the God of hope, the Divine method was to paint the hopelessness of the picture as it really was and is for human nature. Now, in order to reach the Divine end, the Holy Spirit does not cover up the faults, the weaknesses — even the sins, the awful sins—of Christians. The grace of God is enhanced by the background against which it stands. And so, while we might feel, ' Oh, what a pity that this letter was ever written! What an exposure, what an uncovering, of Christians! What a pity ever to speak about it—why not hide it?'—ah, that is just where the good tidings find their real occasion and value.

You see, they are the good tidings of the benediction. The good tidings here are found right at the very beginning of the letter. God knows all about these folk. He is not just finding out—He knows the worst. Dear friend, the Lord knows the worst about you and about me, and He knows it all; and it is a poor kind of all! Now, He knew all about these Corinthians, and yet, under His hand, this Apostle took pen and began his letter with—what? ' To the church in Corinth ', and then: " sanctified in Christ Jesus, called saints ". Now, is that pretending? Is that make-believe? Is that putting on blinkers and saying nice things about people? Not a bit! I repeat: God knew it all, and yet said, " sanctified in Christ Jesus . . . saints ".

Do you say, ' Oh, I cannot understand that at all!'? Ah, but that is just the glory of His grace, because the grace of the Lord Jesus comes out here in calling *such* people saints. Now, *you* do not call such people saints; you reserve that word for people of a very different kind. We say, ' Oh, he is a saint '—distinguishing him, not from people who are unsaved, but amongst good people. Now, God came right to these people, knowing this whole black, dark story, and said: " saints "; and that other word, " sanctified in Christ Jesus ", is only another form of the same word

' saints '. It means ' separated '—separated in Christ Jesus.

You see, the very first thing is the position into which the grace of the Lord Jesus puts us. It is positional grace. If we are in Christ Jesus, all these lamentable things may be true about us, but God sees us in Christ Jesus and not in ourselves. That is the good tidings, that is the gospel. The wonder of the grace of the Lord Jesus! We are looked at by God as separated, sanctified in Christ Jesus. That is where God begins His work with us, putting us in a position in His Son where He attributes to us all that the Lord Jesus is.

Now, you can break that up in this letter. "Christ Jesus, who was made unto us wisdom from God, and righteousness and sanctification, and redemption" (I Cor. i. 30). *He* is made unto us righteousness, sanctification, redemption. I am afraid that some Christians are afraid to make too much of their positional grace. They think that it will take something away from their Christian life if they make too much of that, because they put such a tremendous amount of emphasis upon the need for their sanctification, actually, as to condition ; and they are so occupied introspectively with this matter of what they are in themselves and trying to deal with that, that they lose all the joy of their position in Christ through grace.

We need to keep the balance in this matter. The beginning of everything is that the grace of the Lord Jesus comes to us—even though we may be like the Corinthians—and sets us and looks upon us as in a place of sainthood, " sanctified in Christ Jesus ". You cannot describe it. Grace goes beyond all our powers of describing, but there is the wonder of the grace of the Lord Jesus. The fact of the matter is that we really only discover what awful creatures we are after we are in Christ Jesus, and after we have been in Him a long time. I think the longer we are in Christ, the more awful we become in our own eyes. Therefore, if we are in Christ Jesus, what we are in ourselves does not signify. Our position does not rest upon whether we are actually, literally, truly perfect. The good tidings first of all has to do with our position in Christ.

Ah, but it does not stop there. This does not introduce any kind of shadow, or it should not. Thank God, it is good tidings beyond even that. The grace of our Lord Jesus can make the state different—can make our standing lead to a new state. That is the grace of the Lord Jesus. It can make our own actual state now correspond to our standing. Grace not only receives into the position of acceptance without merit: grace is a working power to make us correspond to the position into which we have been brought. Grace has many aspects. Grace is acceptance, but grace is power to operate. "My grace is sufficient for thee" (II Cor. xii. 9). That is the mighty word of power in need. The grace of our Lord Jesus is indeed good news—good news for all Christians.

THE LOVE OF GOD

After "the grace of the Lord Jesus", "the love of God". See how God is moving to His end. Now the second letter to the Corinthians is as full of the love of God as the first is full of the grace of the Lord Jesus. It is a wonderful letter of the love of God, and of its mighty triumph, its mighty power. The love of God is God's present-day method of showing His power. If that will not do it, nothing will. What God is doing in this dispensation, He is doing by love. Let that be settled. Not by judgment, not by condemnation. The Lord Jesus said He did not come to

condemn, He had come to save (John xii. 47 ; cf. iii. 17).
Yes, it is the love of God which is the method of His power in this dispensation. The method will change, but this
is the day of the love of God.

Now, Paul has already, toward the end of the first letter,
given that classic definition and analysis of the love of
God—I Corinthians xiii. There is nothing to compare
with it in all the Bible as an analysis of—not your love,
not my love ; we are not interested in that—but the love
of God. " Love suffereth long and is kind, love envieth not,
love seeketh not its own, is not puffed up, doth not behave
itself unseemly ", and so on. There is the love of God set
forth. We shall find that we cannot stand up to it. No man
can stand up to that fully. " Love *never* faileth "—never
gives up, that is. Here is the quality of Divine love.

Now bring it into the second letter to the Corinthians,
and see the mighty triumph, the power, of the love of God.
First of all, see it as working triumphantly in the servant
of the Lord. Look again at the letter. Paul has in different
places in his writings given very wonderful, very beautiful, very glorious revelations of the grace of God in his own
life ; but, considering the setting, I do not think there is
anything anywhere in the New Testament that so wonderfully sets forth the triumph of the love of God in a servant
of God, as does this second letter to the Corinthians. If
ever a man had reason to give up, to wash his hands, to
despair, to be fiercely angry, to be everything but loving,
Paul had reason for such a reaction in regard to the Corinthians. He might have been well justified in closing the
situation at Corinth, and saying : ' I am done with you, I
wash my hands of you, you are incurable. The more I love
you, the more you hate me. All right, get on with it ; I
leave you.' Look at this second letter : the outgoing, the

overflowing, of love to these people—to *these* people—
over that situation. What a triumph of love, the love of
God, in a servant of God! That is how God reaches His
end. Oh, God give us more love, as His servants, to bear
and forbear, to suffer long, and never to despair.

Yes, but it was not left there. You can see it, even if it is
only beginning—and I think it is more than that—in the
Corinthians themselves, as he speaks to them about the result of his strong speaking, his pleading, his rebuking, his
admonishing, his correcting. The terms that he uses about
them are their sorrow, their godly repentance, and so on.
It was worth it, the love of God triumphing in a people
like that; and you know that that is what made possible
the wonderful, beautiful things that Paul was able to write
to them in the second letter. Paul could never have committed himself to write some of the things that are in this
second letter, but for some change in those people, in their
attitude, in their disposition, in their spirit; but for the
fact that he had got this basis of triumphant love.

For this second letter has to do with ministry, with testimony, and Paul would be the last man in the world ever
to suggest that anybody could have a ministry and a testimony who knew nothing about the conquering love of God
in their own nature. Paul was not that kind of man. It is,
alas, possible to preach and be a Christian worker, and
know nothing of the grace of the Lord Jesus in your own
life—to be just a contradiction. There is far too much of
that. Paul would never countenance anything like that. If
he is going to speak about ministry and about testimony in
the world, he will demand a basis, that grace shall have
done its work at least in measure, so that in this way the
love of God is now manifested. There is now humility:
'Oh, what godly sorrow', he says, 'what godly repent-

ance!' Where is the 'I'? Where is the selfhood? Something has broken, something has given way; there is something now of the grace of the Lord Jesus, in self-emptying, in the negation of the self-life. Yes, they are down now, broken. This is the triumph of Divine love in such a people.

That is the gospel, the good tidings! It is good tidings, is it not? The gospel is not just something to bring the sinner to the Saviour. It is that—but the gospel, the good tidings, is also this, that people, Christians like Corinthians, can be transformed like this through the love of God. Good tidings! The glory of the triumph comes following on here, in words that we love so much: "Thanks be unto God, who always leadeth us in triumph in Christ" (II Cor. ii. 14), to celebrate His victory over Christ's enemies. This is the triumphal procession of grace and love. It is a different Paul, is it not?—a Paul different from the first letter. He has got the wind in his sails now, he is running before the wind, he is in triumph. He is talking about everything being a triumphal procession in Christ, a constant celebration of victory. What has made Paul change? Why, the change in *them* ! Yes, it was always like that with Paul; his life was bound up with the state of the Christians. 'Now I live if you stand fast' (I Thess. iii. 8). 'This is life to me.'

"And the love of God". "God, that said, Light shall shine out of darkness . . . shined in our hearts, to give the light of the knowledge of the glory of God in the face of Jesus Christ. But we have this treasure in earthen vessels, that the exceeding greatness of the power may be of God, and not from ourselves" (II Cor. iv. 6, 7). 'We are poor creatures, Corinthians: I am, you are; but God has shined into our hearts. Something has been done in our hearts.

The love of God has come in. Fragile vessels as we are in ourselves, that love shines forth—the glory of the love of God.'

THE COMMUNION OF THE HOLY SPIRIT

"The communion [or fellowship] of the Holy Spirit ". Did ever a people need to know the meaning of fellowship more than the Corinthians? Is Paul touching upon some spot that was a very, very sensitive spot? Fellowship? He wrote: "Each one of you saith, I am of Paul; and I of Apollos; and I of Cephas; and I of Christ " (I Cor. i. 12). Is there any fellowship in that, any communion in that? No. When you stay in the flesh, there is no fellowship, there is no communion; you are all in bits and pieces, all flying at one another. So it was. What is God after? Fellowship, communion, amongst believers; and it must be the communion, the fellowship, of the Holy Spirit, that is, fellowship constituted and established and enriched by the Holy Spirit. This is the result of "the grace of the Lord Jesus and the love of God"—oneness.

Let us clearly recognise that this is the deepest work of the Holy Spirit. Much has been said earlier, in Paul's first letter, about the Holy Spirit. They had made much of spiritual gifts; spiritual gifts attracted them. They were enamoured of power to do things, of signs, wonders, and so on. That was very much after their heart; these gifts of the Spirit, and much more that was just outward, brought a great deal of gratification to their souls.

But when you come to the supreme end and deepest work of the Holy Spirit, you find it in the oneness of believers. It takes the deepest work of the Holy Spirit to bring that about, seeing that we still have a nature that is an old nature. We still can be Christians, and yet Corinthian Christians. There is still lurking—and not always in hidden corners—the ' I ', the self-life in some form or other. Seeing it is there, it takes a mighty work of the Holy Spirit to unite indissolubly even two believers ; but to unite a whole church like that is something stupendous.

Nothing less or other than that is the communion, the fellowship, of the Holy Spirit. Something of that seems to have come about at Corinth. Oh, wonder of wonders, the difference between these two letters ! Yes, it has happened. It is an inward triumph over nature, and it shows real progress. That is the communion of the Holy Spirit. When Paul started his first letter, he said : ' When every one of you says, I, I, I, are you not babes? Do you not have to be fed with milk?' (I Cor. iii. 1 — 4). Babies are always scrapping and fighting. That was the Corinthians. But they had got past the babyhood stage, through "the grace of the Lord Jesus and the love of God". Things changed ; they have grown up.

It takes the Holy Spirit to make us grow up spiritually in this way. The measure of our spirituality can be indicated very quickly and clearly by the measure of our mutual love, our fellowship. We are, after all, little people spiritually if we are always at variance. It takes big people to live with certain other big people without quarrelling. It takes "the grace of the Lord Jesus, and the love of God", to lead to "the fellowship of the Holy Spirit".

This fellowship of the Holy Spirit, then, is essentially corporate. Perhaps you have thought that this last clause, "the communion of the Holy Spirit", meant your communion with the Holy Spirit and that of the Holy Spirit with you. It does not mean that at all. Paul is perhaps just gently hitting back at the old state, touching on that old condition. ' What you Corinthians lacked more than you

lacked anything else was fellowship ; there was no fellowship. Now you have come along the way of " the grace
of the Lord Jesus and the love of God ", and " the communion of the Holy Spirit " is found amongst you '. That
is what it means. It is corporate, and it is a mighty work
of the Holy Spirit. It has to be in more than one of us. Now
you, of course, think it has to be in the other person ! No,
it has to be in more than one of us, not just the other person. It must be in you *and* me—it must be in everyone
concerned. Well, that is the gospel : good tidings to a
people in a pretty bad state ! What good tidings !

Let me close with this. We never get anywhere by recognising the deplorable state and just going for it—beginning to knock people about, wielding the sword or the
sledge-hammer and smashing things, bringing people
down under condemnation. We never get anywhere that
way. If Paul had gone to work that way with Corinth, he
would have smashed it all right, but that would have been
the end of it. But love found a way, and, although there
was brokenness, it was not the end. Something, " beauty
for ashes ", came out of it—because " the grace of the
Lord Jesus, the love of God, and the fellowship of the
Holy Spirit ", was the principle upon which Paul himself
lived and by which he worked.

You and I must be people of good news. We have got
good news for any situation, though it be as bad as that
in Corinth. Believe this ! *Good news ! Good news !* That
must be our attitude to everything, by the grace of God ;
not despairing, not giving up. No, good news ! The Lord
make us people of the gospel, the good tidings.

CHAPTER THREE

IN HIS LETTER TO THE GALATIANS

We now pass into the letter to the Galatians, where we actually have the phrase which is basic to this consideration—" the gospel which I preach ". The phrase is found in the second chapter and the second verse, and in another form in chapter one, verse eleven—" the gospel which was preached by me ". We have noted how many times this word ' gospel ' occurs in the letters of Paul. The word is sprinkled through his letters, indicating by the frequency of its occurrence that that, after all, is what he is really writing about. The same thing is true in this brief letter to the Galatians. In the noun form—that is, where the whole body of Christian truth is called ' the gospel '—it occurs in this letter eight times ; and then in the verb form—which cannot be translated into English correctly, that is, ' to gospel ' or ' to good news ', translated for our convenience into English as ' preach ', ' preach the gospel ', ' bring good tidings ', and so on, but just one word in the original—in the verb form it is found in this letter six times : so that we have here fourteen occurrences in a very brief letter.

THE SITUATION AMONG THE GALATIAN CHRISTIANS

Now, if we could reconstruct the situation presented by this letter, or come upon it in actual reality, what should we find? Supposing that the situation represented here existed in some place to-day, and we visited that place where this thing was going on, what should we come upon? Well, we should find a tremendous controversy in progress, with three parties involved. On the one hand, we should find a group of men who are extremely and bitterly anti-Paul. On the other hand, we should find Paul roused and stirred to the very depths of his being, as we never find him in any other place in his writings or in his journeys. And, in between these two parties, there would be the Christians who are the immediate occasion of this tremendous battle that is going on. Very much bigger issues than the local and the occasional are involved, because it is a matter of the far-reaching and abiding nature of the gospel. Now Paul, in the battle, is committing himself to a re-statement of 'the gospel which he preached', over against these who were seeking to undermine, neutralise and destroy his ministry altogether. What was it all about?

Well, first of all, take the anti-Paul party. What is their trouble? What is it that they are seeking to establish? In brief, in a word, their object is to establish the old, Jewish, religious tradition. They are standing vehemently for the permanence of that system. They are arguing that it came directly from God, and what comes directly from God cannot be changed or set aside. This thing has the support of antiquity. It is the thing which has obtained and has existed for many centuries, and therefore it carries the value of being something that is not, like Paul's teaching, something quite new. It is established in the ages of the past. They

would go further, and say that Jesus did not abrogate the
law of Moses: He said nothing about the law of Moses
being set aside. Well, there is all this argument, and much
else besides. Their position is that Judaism, the Law of
Moses, is binding upon Christians. 'Be Christians, if you
like, but you must add to your Christian faith the Law of
Moses, and you must come under the government of all
the Thou Shalts and Thou Shalt Nots of that tradition and
that system ; you must conform to the teachings and the
practices of the Jewish system, of the tradition of Moses.'
That is their position in brief.

On the other hand, there is Paul. He is no stranger to
Moses, no stranger to the Jewish system. Born, bred,
brought up, trained and very thoroughly taught in it all,
nevertheless here he is found directly and positively opposed to their position. He argues that the Law was given
by God indeed, but it was only given by God to show up
man's weakness. The real value and effect of the Law is to
show what man is like—that he just cannot keep it. How
hopeless man is in the presence of God's demands ! How
helpless he is before this whole system of commandments
—Thou Shalt and Thou Shalt Not ! And though Christ
did not abrogate the Law, set it aside, and say, ' That is all
finished ', Christ in Himself was the only One, the only
One amongst all human beings that ever walked this earth,
who could keep it ; and He did keep it. He satisfied God in
every detail of the Divine Law ; and having satisfied God
and fulfilled the Law, He introduced and constituted another basis of relationship with God, and thus the Law is
in that way set aside. Another foundation of life with God
is brought in by Jesus Christ.

That is Paul's argument in brief. Of course, there are
many details in it, but Paul comes to the opposite conclu-

sion to that which these Judaizers had reached. The Mosaic law is no longer binding upon Christians in the way in which it was binding upon the Jews. The argument of Paul is that in Christ we are freed from the Law. The great word in this letter is liberty in relation to the Law.

From the strong terms used in this letter we can gather how intense are the feelings of those concerned. Of course, these Judaizers are very, very strong. They have pursued Paul wherever he has gone. They have sought by every means, by personal attack and by argument and persuasion, to undo his work and to lead away his converts from him and bring them back to Moses. Paul is found here, as I have said, in a state of perfect vehemence. This Paul, so capable of forbearance and longsuffering and patience, as we saw in our last chapter in the case of the Corinthians, where every kind of provocation to anger was met by him—the wonderful, wonderful patience and forbearance of Paul with those people—yet here the man seems to have become stripped of all such forbearance: here he is literally hurling anathemas at these men. Twice over, with a double emphasis, he says, " Let him be anathema . . . so say I now again, Let him be anathema "—accursed.

Now, when Paul gets like that, there must be something involved. For a man like Paul to be worked up in that way, you must conclude that there is something serious on hand. And indeed there is, and this very heat of the Apostle indicates how serious was the difference between these two positions.

THE ANSWER TO THE SITUATION

Now, in the letter we may feel that there is much mysterious material. For instance, in drawing upon Old Testament types, Paul uses as an allegory the incident of Hagar and Ishmael. We know the details ; we are not going into that at all. There seems to be a lot of mysterious material that Paul is using for his argument. But when we have read it all through and considered it and felt the impact of it, what does it all amount to? When we have studied this and been impressed with its seriousness, what is it that we are left with? Is it just a conclusion about legalism—that the Law no longer holds us in bondage, and we are freed from it? Is it that a dispensation of liberty in that respect has been introduced, and that its principles are no longer binding upon us? Is that just the position? Is it that Christianity is something without obligations as to truth and as to practice? Is it that grace will override all our breaking of laws and violating of principles?—a false interpretation of grace indeed! —but is it that? What is it?

You see, it is possible to grasp very truly the value of a letter like this, but for it to remain, after all, just a theological matter, a mere matter of doctrine. Yes, the letter to the Galatians teaches that we are no longer under the Law of Moses, and that we are free as children of God. Very nice, very beautiful! But where is that going to lead you? What does it amount to? All that is negative.

I wonder—and this is the whole point just now—I wonder how many of us are really living in the enjoyment of the secret and heart of the gospel, as it is presented in this letter. Paul is saying much here about the gospel or the good tidings. What really is the gospel, or the good tidings, as found here in this letter and in this particular connection? After all, it is not just that Christians want to be ' libertised '—freed from all restraints, from all bondage and all obligations, just to do as they like, follow their own inclinations. That is not it at all. You and I want to know something more positive than that. We cannot be satisfied with mere negatives.

CHRIST WITHIN

What does the gospel amount to here? Paul says, ' This is the gospel '. It is summarised in one fragment of this letter, a very well-known passage of Scripture, at which we all rejoice—Galatians ii. 20: " I have been crucified with Christ ; and it is no longer I that live, but Christ liveth in me ". This is the gospel, the good tidings, of *the indwelling Christ*. This is the heart of the whole matter, this is the answer to the whole argument, this settles all the questions, this deals with all the difficulties—the gospel, the good news, of the indwelling Christ.

And, when you think of it, this is the most vital and fundamental factor in Christianity. No wonder Paul saw that, if this was sacrificed, Christianity went for nothing : the Judaizers had carried everything away ; Christianity had become of no meaning at all. He was fighting, therefore, for Christianity on one point only—but one which included the whole. The whole was wrapped up and bound up with this : " Christ liveth *in* me ". If that is true, you do not need to argue about anything at all ; all the argument is settled.

" Christ liveth in me ". *Christ !* What is Christ? Who is Christ? What does Christ mean? What does He embody? Why, everything that satisfies God is found in Christ! In His Son Jesus Christ, God has His full, final, complete answer. Christ can stand up to every demand of God, and has done so. Christ can bring the full and complete favour of God wherever He is. Oh, we could stay long with that— what Christ is, how great Christ is, how wonderful Christ is! And " Christ liveth *in me* "! Christ, that Christ of the eternal glory, that Christ of the self-emptying, humiliation, that Christ of the triumphant life, that Christ of the mighty Cross, of the resurrection, of the return to glory, and of the enthronement now, is in you and in me! What more can we want—what more could we have—what greater thing than that?

THE POWER OF CHRIST WITHIN

Now Christ is an actual, living Person : not an abstract idea, an historical figure, but an actual, living Person. " Christ *liveth* in me ". I do not wear a crucifix of a dead Christ on the outside. I have a living Christ within, the good news of a living Christ inside. You can read that, or hear it said, and you can nod your head and say, ' Yes, Amen ' : you agree with that! But I have known people to hear that for years, and agree with it as heartily as you do —and then one day to wake up to it. ' You know, after all I have heard about that, I have only just come to realise that it is true that Christ really lives in me ! ' It is something more than the doctrine of Christ within—it is the *experience*.

Paul focuses his whole history as a Christian and as a servant of God upon that one thing. ' God has shined in my heart ' (II Cor. iv. 6). ' It pleased God, who separated me from my birth, to reveal His Son in me ' (Gal. i. 15, 16). ' The gospel which I preached was not of man ', " but . . . through revelation of Jesus Christ " (Gal. i. 11, 12). How did it come? Not only objectively and outwardly, but inwardly. ' God has shined within '. " Christ liveth in me ". The most startling thing that ever happened to a man in the course of human history was that which happened to

Saul of Tarsus on that noonday when he realised that
Jesus of Nazareth, who he thought was done with, dead
and buried, was alive, *alive,* actually alive. Remember how
very alive He was. And Paul says: ' That One liveth —
and not only in the glory — He liveth in me, *in me* !' A
living Person, a living actual power within, yes, a real
power inside, is Christ.

THE INTELLIGENCE OF CHRIST WITHIN

Furthermore, He is a real Intelligence, who possesses
the full knowledge of all that God wants, and, possessing
that, dwelling within me, is the repository and vehicle of
God's full will for my life. Full intelligence by Christ within! All the knowledge that Christ possesses is within, and
if that is true, if Christ is within — the Apostle, of course, is
speaking here not only about Christ within, but much
about the Holy Spirit, to which we will come presently —
if the indwelling Christ has His way, then that which He
is becomes actual in the life of the child of God : the fact
that He is a living Person, the fact that He is a mighty
power, the fact that He is a full, Divine Intelligence.

CHRIST WITHIN
THE KNOWLEDGE OF THE WILL OF GOD

We would like to have all understanding in our mind,
all knowledge and intelligence in our reason. We have
not got it, but we have another kind of intelligence. The
true child of God has another kind of intelligence, altogether different from that which is of the reason. We do
not know how to explain and interpret it, but somehow
we know. We can only say, ' We know '. We know what

the Lord does not want where we are concerned. We find it impossible to be comfortable along any line that the Lord does not want, and we come to that position so often. We put it in different ways, but we have to say, ' I know the Lord does not want me to do that, to go that way; it is as deep in me as anything. To do it would be to violate something that relates to my very life with God.'

That is on the negative side. And on the positive, if the Lord really wants something, we know it; in spite of everything, we know it. If only we will wait for that, it will be so sure. The trouble is that we cannot wait for the Lord; we get into such tangles over these problems of guidance. But when the Lord's time comes, there is no question about it at all: we know. How do we know? It is spiritual knowledge, it is spiritual intelligence. It is Christ dwelling within, in possession of all the mind of God.

Now, here are these poor Galatian Christians, torn between the Judaizers and Paul. They do not know what to make of this. These, on the one side, are so strong about their line of things; and on the other hand, here is Paul, saying that they are all wrong! What are they to do? The answer comes: ' If Christ is in you, you will know—you will know what you ought to do '. And that is the only real way of knowing what you ought to do—what is right, and what is wrong: Christ in you. But you *will* know.

CHRIST WITHIN THE POWER OF ENDURANCE

Now you say, ' I have not realised that, I do not feel that, I do not see that; I have not got all that intelligence, I do not sense all that power '. You see, as Paul is always trying to point out, there is such a great difference between

the human kind of knowledge and spiritual knowledge.
We have knowledge of this kind, not by information, but
by experience.

Some of us have been on the Christian way for many
years. If it had been left to us, should we be still going on
with the Lord? If we had had to carry on, struggle
through, fight it out, on our own resources, should we still
be here? I think I can say for you as for myself, Certainly
not! We would not be here to-day ; we should not be rejoicing in the Lord, going on with the Lord. If Satan could
have had his way, we should not be here, for both in ourselves and in Satan we have found every conceivable
thing inimical to Christ, to make it impossible for us to
go on with the Lord. Everything in our own selves is
against us spiritually. Everything in Satan is up against us,
and everything that he can use is thrown into the battle
for our undoing.

But we are here, and that is the proof that Christ in us
is a living power, and it is found—though not yet in fulness—in experience, in fact, and not just in our sensing
it. We would like to have the sensations of this great power, to feel it ; but no, there is often the hiding of His power, and it only comes out in facts—often in quite long-
term facts.

THE DISPOSITION OF CHRIST WITHIN

Power, intelligence, knowledge : and then disposition.
This is one of the realities of the Christian life. When
Christ is within, we have a different disposition altogether.
We are disposed to new things, disposed in new ways. Yes,
our disposition has changed. The things which we once
found to be our life no longer draw us to them. We are
not disposed to them any longer. This is the world's prob-

lem with the Christian: 'Why do you not do this, that and the other?' And the only answer we can give, but which never satisfies them, is, 'I have lost all disposition for that sort of thing: I am no longer disposed that way: I have a disposition in another direction altogether.' It is like that: another disposition—Christ within. That is Christianity!

You see, Moses says, 'You have got to do this, and you have got to do that, and you must not do this, and you must not do that'; and my disposition is altogether against Moses. Moses says, 'You must do this'—I do not want to do it; it may be quite right, it may have come from God, but I just do not find it in my nature, in my disposition, to do it. Moses said, 'I must not do this', and my disposition says, 'I want to do that—that is just the very thing that I do want to do!' Somehow or other, in myself I am just across God in every way.

What is the solution to the Law? Christ in you. If Christ is in you, then you will be disposed to do what God wants you to do, and you will fulfil the Law. If Christ is in you, you will have no disposition for doing what God does not want you to do, and you will again fulfil the Law. But, you see, you fulfil it on another basis altogether. You fulfil it, not because Moses said it, but because Christ is in you ; not because you must, but because Christ gives you another disposition. This is the gospel, the good news, of the indwelling Christ.

THE WORK OF THE HOLY SPIRIT WITHIN

Now, when you turn to the teaching about the Holy Spirit in this letter, you find that it comes to the same thing. Christ in you is the Holy Spirit's standard, and He is working in you on the basis of the indwelling Christ to bring you into line with Christ, to build you up according to the Christ who is in you. The Holy Spirit is the energy of Christ within, the energy to make us Christ-like, to enable us to be like Christ, and therefore to be fulfillers of everything that is right in the sight of God, and shunners of everything that is not right in the sight of God. There is an energy by the Holy Spirit to do this.

The Apostle speaks about the fruit of the Spirit. " The fruit of the Spirit is love, joy, peace, longsuffering, kindness, goodness, faithfulness, meekness, self-control " (Gal. v. 22, 23). The Spirit, you see, is inside, and He is the Spirit of Christ within to cause that the fruits of Christ shall be borne in us, or, shall we say, the fruit of Christ which shows itself in all these many ways. The fruit of Christ is " love, joy, peace, longsuffering, kindness, goodness, faithfulness, meekness, self-control ", the fruit of the mighty energy of the Spirit of Christ within.

And what about law? Yes, the Spirit works according to law. Before he is through, the Apostle says that tremendous thing, that terrible thing: " Be not deceived ; God is not mocked : for whatsoever a man soweth, that shall he also reap. For he that soweth unto his own flesh shall of the flesh reap corruption ; but he that soweth unto the Spirit shall of the Spirit reap eternal life " (Gal. vi. 7, 8). The law of the Spirit, you see, is this. Sow, and you reap ; what you sow, you reap. Sow to the Spirit, and you reap life everlasting. If you sow to the Spirit — that is only saying, in figurative language, If you conform to the Spirit's energy, the Spirit's law, the Spirit's government, or to Christ in you — you will reap Christ, you will reap life. There is a law here, and ' free from the Law ' does not mean that we are set free from any necessity for recognising that God has constituted His universe, our bodies and souls, upon principles; but it does mean this, that Christ in us makes it possible for us to obey the principles, whereas otherwise we should be violating them all the time.

"The gospel which I preach", says Paul: 'after all, it amounts to this—after all your arguments about legalism and Judaizers and the rest, it amounts to this: "Christ liveth in me".' That is good news, that is hope—everything is possible!

CHAPTER FOUR

IN HIS LETTER TO THE EPHESIANS

"... the word of the truth, the gospel of your salvation ..." (Eph. i. 13).

"... the Gentiles are fellow-heirs, and fellow-members of the body, and fellow-partakers of the promise in Christ Jesus through the gospel, whereof I was made a minister ..." (iii. 6, 7).

"... having shod your feet with the preparation of the gospel of peace ..." (vi. 15).

"... praying ... on my behalf, that utterance may be given unto me in opening my mouth, to make known with boldness the mystery of the gospel, for which I am an ambassador in chains ..." (vi. 19, 20).

WHEN WE COME TO CONSIDER 'the Gospel according to Paul' in the letter to the Ephesians, we find that we have the word 'gospel' in the noun form four times. We have it also, on one or two other occasions, in verb form, as in chapter ii. 17 —

"... and he came and preached peace to you that were far off ..."

You notice the margin says "preached good tidings of peace". Now that is just an English way of juggling with a Greek word. The Greek word is the verb of which 'the gospel' is the noun; and, as I have tried to point out before, what it really says—it cannot be translated literally into English—is: "came and 'good-tidinged' or 'good-newsed' peace". That is impossible in English, but it is just the verb of the noun 'gospel'. It occurs again in chapter iii, verse 8—

"... *to preach unto the Gentiles the unsearchable riches of Christ* ..."

—that is, "to good-news unto the Gentiles", "to proclaim unto the Gentiles the good tidings of ...". It is the verb again for 'gospel'. I think that gives us ground for saying that this letter is about the gospel.

Many people have the idea that when you reach the letter to the Ephesians you have left the gospel behind, you are further on than the gospel, you must really now have got a long way beyond the gospel. I do not think we can get further than this letter, so far as Divine revelation is concerned: as we shall see, it takes us a very long way indeed in Divine things; but it is still the gospel. The gospel is something very vast, very comprehensive, very far-reaching indeed.

A LETTER OF SUPERLATIVES

This leads us to note that the letter to the Ephesians is the letter of superlatives. An expressive adjective has come into vogue of recent years, by which people try to convey the idea that a thing is very great, or of the highest quality. They say it is 'super'. Now here, in this letter, everything is—may I use the word? —'super'! The whole letter is written in terms of what is superlative; and I must take it for granted that you can recall something of what is here. Superlatives relate to almost everything in this letter.

There is the superlative of time. Time is altogether transcended: we are taken into the realm of timelessness. By this letter we are taken back into eternity past, before the foundation of the world, and on into eternity to come, unto the ages of the ages. It is the superlative of time— transcending time.

There is the superlative of space. One phrase runs through this letter—" in the heavenlies ". When you come into the heavenlies, you are just amazed at the immensity of the expanse. In the natural realm that is true, is it not, even of the very limited ' earthly heavens ', as represented by the earth's atmosphere. If you travel a good deal by air, you pass through the airports and see the 'planes coming and going, coming and going, every few minutes, all day long and all night long and day after day —and yet when you get up into the air you rarely meet another machine. It is quite an event to pass another 'plane in the air, so vast are the heavens in their expanse. And this letter is written in the realm of the superlatives of space, in the spiritual heavenlies, altogether above the limitations of earth.

Again, it is written in terms of the superlative of power. There is one clause here, so familiar to us, which touches that: " the exceeding greatness of his power to us-ward who believe " (Eph. i. 19). There is much about that power, superlative power, and its operation, in this letter.

Further, this letter is the letter of the superlative in content. How to approach and explain that is exceedingly difficult. You see, some of us have been speaking, giving

talks, giving addresses, about this letter to the Ephesians
—and it is only a little letter so far as actual chapters or
words are concerned—for over forty years, and we have
not got near it yet. I defy you to exhaust the content of
this letter. It does not matter how long you go on with it
—you will always feel, 'I have not begun to approach
that yet'. I know what some of you think about me over
this letter. I am almost afraid to mention the very name
'Ephesians'! Even as I have once again meditated over
this letter at the present time, I have been saying to myself: 'I would like to start now to give a long, long series
of messages on the letter to the Ephesians, and I should
not touch much of the old ground!' It is like that. But
when you look into it and consider it, you find that you
are in the realm of superlatives so far as contents are concerned, and it begins with "hath blessed us with every
spiritual blessing in the heavenlies in Christ" (i. 3). Can
you get above or outside that? You cannot!

Again, it is in the realm of the super-mundane. The
earth here becomes a very small thing, and all that goes
on in it. All its history and all that is here becomes very
small indeed. The earth is completely transcended.

It is super-racial, as we shall see in a moment. It is not
just dealing with one race or two races. It is all one race
here.

It is super-natural. Look again, and you find that everything here is on a plane that is altogether above the natural. You cannot naturally grasp it, comprehend it, explain
it. It is Divine revelation. It is by "the Spirit of wisdom
and revelation". That is super-natural. The knowledge
that is here is super-naturally obtained.

And what more shall I say about the 'super'? The list
could very easily be extended. Have I said enough? Can

I go on pointing out in what a realm this is, what a range? You see, you have some very great words here. I give you three of them.

"*Unto me, who am less than the least of all 'saints, was this grace given, to preach unto the Gentiles the unsearchable riches of Christ*" *(iii. 8).*

This letter is written in terms of the unsearchable, the untraceable.

"*. . . and to know the love of Christ which passeth knowledge, that ye may be filled unto all the fulness of God*" *(iii. 19).*

"The knowledge-surpassing love of Christ". Here we have the incomprehensible.

"*Now unto him that is able to do exceeding a-bundantly above all that we ask or think, according to the power that worketh in us . . .*" *(iii. 20).*

Here it is the transcendental. These are big words, but you need big words throughout for this letter, and I am seeking to make an impression upon you.

THE GREATEST CRISIS IN RELIGIOUS HISTORY

Now, let us come more to the inward side of this. This letter, in its content, represents perhaps the greatest crisis in religious history. That is saying a great deal. There have been many crises in religious history, and very big ones, but this letter represents the greatest of them all. Before the Lord Jesus was raised from the dead and went to Heaven, and the Holy Spirit came on the day of Pentecost, there were only two classes of people on the earth. The whole of the human race was divided into two classes of people, the Gentiles and the Jews. When the Holy Spirit came, a third class came into being which, from God's standpoint, is neither Gentile nor Jew: it is the Church of God. They are taken out of nations of Gentiles and taken out from among the Jews, but, so far as God is concerned, they are neither Jew nor Gentile, or as Paul puts it, "neither Jew nor Greek" (Gal. iii. 28). 'Greek' was a representative word comprehending the Gentiles. When the Lord Jesus comes again, as He is coming, and takes the Church away, the two others will remain here. There will be a reversion in the earth to what was before. The whole world will be divided again into Gentiles and Jews.

So this that came into being on the day of Pentecost, this third and spiritually quite separate class of people called the Church, represents the greatest of all crises in human history for this reason, and in this way—that that Church is not something just of *earthly* history. The Apostle makes it perfectly clear, right at the beginning of this Ephesian letter, that this Church had its existence in the foreknowledge of God before the world was. This Church is a super-temporal thing, transcending all time and transcending the earth. This Church, the Apostle makes clear, will be there in the ages of the ages, still super-temporal, super-earthly, when Jews and Gentiles go on. Yes, there will be saved nations in the earth: but this other goes on in a relationship which is altogether outside of this world and outside of time; and it is concerning this particular class, this people, this Church, that all these things are said in this letter. It is this Church which takes the character of all these superlatives. This is itself something superlative, this is the supreme thing in the economy of God, this is the supreme thing in all God's sovereign activities from eternity to eternity. We live in the dispensation of something absolutely transcendent— God taking out of the nations, both Jew and Gentile, this people called the Church, which is " the body of Christ ".

A SUPERLATIVE VESSEL AND A SUPERLATIVE CALLING

Now this superlative vessel or instrument or people has a superlative or transcendent calling. The Jews had an earthly calling to serve an earthly purpose, a vocation of time on this earth. Many believe very strongly that they are yet to serve such a purpose. There are others, and amongst them outstanding Bible teachers, who believe that the day of the Jew is finished as in the economy of God, and that everything has been transferred to the Church now because of the Jew's failure. I am not going to argue that ; that does not come into our consideration at all. The fact remains that the Jews were raised up to serve an earthly and temporal purpose in the economy of God. But this Church, eternally saved—eternally chosen, as the Apostle says, in Christ Jesus before the world was—this has a superlative calling to serve the purposes of God in Heaven. It is something timeless, superlative in calling, in vocation. It is a tremendous thing that is here.

We have often put it in this way, and indeed it is what the letter to the Ephesians teaches—we have to touch on this in another way presently—that this world, as to its conduct, is influenced by a whole spiritual hierarchy. Even men who have not a great deal of spiritual discernment, men whom we would hardly think of as Christian men, in the essential sense of being born-again children of God, have recognised this and admit it: that behind the behaviour of this world there is some sinister force, some evil power, some wicked intelligence. They may hesitate to name it, to call it Satan, the Devil, and so on, but the Bible just calls it that. Behind the course of this world's history, as we know it—behind the wars, the rivalries, the hatred, the bitterness, the cruelty, all the clash and clamour of interests, and everything else—there is an evil intelligence, a power at work, a whole system that is seeking to ruin the glory of God in His creation. And that whole system is here said to be in what is called " the heavenlies ", that is, something above the earth ; in the very air, if you like, in the very atmosphere. Sometimes you can sense it : sometimes you can almost ' cut the atmosphere with a knife ', as we say ; sometimes you know there is something in the very air that is wicked, evil. You cannot just put it down to people ; there is something behind the people, something about. It is very real—sometimes it seems almost tangible, you can almost smell it—something evil and wicked. It is that which is governing this world system and order.

Now what is here in this letter is this, that this Church, eternally conceived, foreknown, chosen, and brought into existence in its beginnings on the day of Pentecost, and growing spiritually through the centuries since—this Church is to take the place of that evil government above this earth. It is to depose it and cast it out of its domain, and itself take that place to be the influence that governs this world in the ages to come. That is the teaching here : a superlative calling, a superlative vocation, because of a superlative people in their very nature. There is something different about them from other people. That is the secret of the true Christian life—of the true ones in Christ : there is something about them that is different. To this world, Christians are a problem and a conundrum. You cannot put them into any earthly class. You cannot just pigeon-hole a Christian. Somehow or other, they elude you all the time. You cannot make them out.

Now, in this letter Paul speaks first of all of that superlative calling, and then he says that, because of the greatness of that calling, this Church must behave itself accordingly. " I . . . beseech you to walk worthily of the calling wherewith ye were called " (Eph. iv. 1). Conduct has to be adjusted to calling. Oh, that Christian people behaved correspondingly to their calling—to their great, eternal, heavenly vocation! But because of this calling, this destiny, this vocation, this position, that mighty evil hierarchy is set to its last ounce to destroy this vessel called the Church, and therefore there is an immense and terrible conflict going on in the air over this thing, and Christians meet it. The more you seek to live according to your calling, the more you realise how difficult it is, and what there is set against you. It is fierce and bitter spiritual conflict.

SUPERLATIVE RESOURCES

Now, mark you, this is what Paul calls the gospel —all this is the gospel! Did you ever get an idea of the gospel like that? did you ever think of the gospel in such terms? Yes, it is still the gospel, the same gospel ; not another, the same. Now, because all this is true as to the gospel, surely the demands are very great. The reaction of so many, when you say things like this, is : ' Oh, I cannot rise to that—that is altogether beyond me, that is too much for me, that is overpowering, that is overwhelming! Give me the simple gospel!' But I wonder if we realise what we involve ourselves in when we talk like that. For it is just there that the true nature of the gospel comes in, in this whole letter. Yes, the calling is great, is immense ; the conduct must be on a high level ; the conflict is fierce and bitter. And that makes tremendous demands. If that is the gospel, then how shall we stand up to it, how shall we face it, how shall we rise to it, how shall we get through?

Well, we come back to the phrase to which I am gathering the whole of this letter. It is here: " to ' good-news ' the unsearchable riches of Christ ". It is translated ' preach ' in our Bibles, but it is the same word, as you know, in the verb form. " To ' good-news ' the unsearchable riches of Christ ". The good news is that the riches are unsearchable! Oh, this is something for us in which to rejoice, being hard pressed, hard put to it; feeling we shall never rise to it, never go through with it. The superlative riches are for a superlative vocation and for a superlative conflict and for superlative conduct.

" Unsearchable *riches* ". Now that is a characteristic word that you find scattered through this letter. Riches! Riches! In chapter i, verse 7, it is " the riches of his grace ". That phrase is enlarged in ii. 7 —" the exceeding riches of his grace ". And then in i. 18 it is the inheritance—" the riches of the glory of his inheritance in the saints ". That just means that the saints are the inheritance of Jesus Christ, and in them, in His Church, He has a tremendous wealth. Now, if He is going to have wealth in this Church, it is He who must supply the wealth, and it is " according to the riches of his grace " that He will find " the riches of his inheritance " in the Church. There is much more said about that. In iii. 16 the word is used again—" the riches of his glory ". Riches! Riches! Very well: if the demands are great, there is a great supply. If the need is superlative, the resources are superlative. All this sets forth and indicates the basis and the resources of the Church for its calling, for its conduct, and for its conflict.

So what is ' the gospel according to Paul ' in the letter

to the Ephesians? It is the gospel of the "unsearchable riches" for superlative demands, and when you have said that, you are left swimming in a mighty ocean. Go to the letter again, read it carefully through, note it. Yes, there is a high standard here, there are big demands here, tremendous things in view here; but there are also the riches of His grace, the unsearchable riches of His grace for it all. There are the riches of His glory: it is put like this— "according to the riches of his glory". Now, if you can explore, fathom, exhaust, God's riches in glory, then you put a certain limit upon possibilities and potentialities. But if, after you have said all that you have tried to say in human language, as the Apostle did here, you find that you have not got enough superlatives at your command when you are talking about the resources that are in God by Christ Jesus, then everything is possible— according to the riches of His grace and of His glory.

That is a gospel, is it not? Surely that is good tidings, that is good news! And, dear friends, *we shall get through* —and we ought not just to scrape through. If it is like that, we ought to get through superlatively. The Lord bring us into the good of the superlatives of the gospel, of the good news.

CHAPTER FIVE

IN HIS LETTER TO THE PHILIPPIANS

CONTINUING OUR ENQUIRY into what the Apostle meant by his words "the gospel which I preach", we take in our hands the little letter written by Paul to the Philippians. Although this was one of the last writings of the Apostle —it was written from his imprisonment in Rome shortly before his execution, at the end of a long, full life of ministry and work—we find that he is still speaking of everything as 'the gospel'. He has not grown out of the gospel, he has not got beyond the gospel. Indeed, at the end he is more than ever aware of the riches of the gospel which are far beyond him.

Here are the references that he makes in this letter to the gospel.

"I thank my God ... for your fellowship in furtherance of the gospel ... " (Phil. i. 3, 5).

" ... it is right for me to be thus minded on behalf of you all, because I have you in my heart, inasmuch as, both in my bonds and in the defence and confirmation of the gospel, ye all are partakers with me of grace" (i. 7).

60

" . . . *the one [preach Christ] of love, knowing that I
am set for the defence of the gospel : but the other proclaim
Christ of faction, not sincerely, thinking to raise up affliction for me in my bonds. What then? only that in every
way, whether in pretence or in truth, Christ is proclaimed ;
and therein I rejoice, yea, and will rejoice*" (i. 16 — 18).

" *But ye know the proof of him, that, as a child serveth
a father, so he served with me in furtherance of the gospel*" (ii. 22).

" *Yea, I beseech thee also, true yokefellow, help these
women, for they laboured with me in the gospel . . .*"
(iv. 3).

" *I can do all things in him that strengtheneth me. Howbeit ye did well, that ye had fellowship with me in my affliction. And ye yourselves also know, ye Philippians, that in
the beginning of the gospel, when I departed from Macedonia, no church had fellowship with me in the matter of
giving and receiving, but ye only . . .*" (iv. 13 — 15).

You see there is a good deal about the gospel in this
little letter. I say ' little ' letter. This letter is like a beautiful
jewel in the crown of Jesus Christ, or like a beautiful pearl
whose colours are the result of exquisite pain and suffering. It is something very costly and very precious. So far
as actual chapters and verses are concerned, it is small. It
is one of the smallest of Paul's letters, but in its intrinsic
values and worth it is immense ; and as a real setting forth
of what the gospel is, there are few, if any, things in the
New Testament to be compared with it. What we really
come to in this letter is not only a setting forth of what the
gospel is in truth, but an example of what the gospel is in
effect. Look at it again, dwell upon it with openness of
heart, and I think your verdict will be—it surely should

be—'Well, if that is the gospel, give me the gospel! If that is the gospel, it is something worth having!' That surely is the effect of reading this little letter. It is a wonderful example of the gospel in expression.

THE LETTER OF THE JOY OF TRIUMPH

But as we read it, we find that it resolves itself into this. It is, perhaps more than any other letter in the New Testament, the letter of the joy of triumph. Joy runs right through this letter. The Apostle is full of joy to overflowing. He seems to be hardly able to contain himself. In the last chapter we were speaking of his superlatives in relation to the great calling of the Church in the gospel. Here the Apostle is finding it difficult to express himself as to his joy. I leave you to look at it. Look just at the first words, his introduction, and see. But it runs right through to the end. It has been called the letter of Paul's joy in Christ, but it is the joy of triumph, and triumph in a threefold direction. The triumph of Christ; triumph in Paul; and triumph in the Christians at Philippi. That really sums up the whole letter: the threefold triumph with its joy and exultant outflowing.

THE TRIUMPH OF CHRIST

First of all, triumph in Christ and of Christ. It is in this letter that Paul gives us that matchless unveiling of the great cycle of redemption—the sublime course taken by the Lord Jesus in His redemptive work. We see Him, firstly, in the place of equality with God: equal with God, and all that that means—all that it means for God to be God. How great that is! —how full, how high, how majestic, how glorious ! Paul here says that Jesus was there equal with God. And then, ' counting it not something to be held on to, to be grasped at, this equality with God, He emptied Himself '. He emptied Himself of all that, let it go, laid it aside, gave it up. Just think of what He was going to have in exchange. These are thoughts almost impossible of grasping : God, in all His infinite fulness of power and majesty of might, in His dominion of glory and eternal fulness, allowing men of His own creation, even the mean- est of them, to spit on Him, to mock and jeer at Him. He laid it aside ; He emptied Himself, and took upon Him the form of a man, was found in fashion as a man ; and not only that, but still lower in this cycle — the form of a bond-slave, a bond-slave man. A bond-slave is one who has no personal rights ; he has no franchise, he has no title. He is not allowed to choose for himself, to go his own way, and much more. Paul says here that Jesus took the form of a bond-slave.

And then he goes on to say that ' He humbled Himself, became obedient unto death ' : and not a glorious death at that, not a death about which people speak in terms of praise and admiration. ' Yes ', says the Apostle, ' death on a cross ' — the most shameful, ignominious death, with all that that meant. You see, the Jewish world, the religious world, of that day, had it written in their Book that he that hangs upon a tree is cursed of God. Jesus was obedient to the point of being found in the place of one who is cursed of God. That is how they looked upon Him — as cursed of God. And as for the rest of the world, the Gentile world, their whole conception of that which should be worshipped was one who could never be defeated, one who could never be found in a situation which should cause him shame, one who could stand before the world as a success — that was their idea of a god. But here is this Man on the Cross. Is He a success? That is no sign of success. That is no indication of human strength. That is weakness. There is nothing honourable about that—it is disgraceful. That is humanity at its lowest.

And then the cycle is reversed, and the Apostle breaks in here, and says: "Wherefore also God highly exalted him, and gave unto him the name which is above every name; that in the name of Jesus every knee *shall* bow" —sooner or later; either gladly to acknowledge Him Lord, or forcedly to do so; sooner or later, in the determinate counsels of Almighty God, it shall be; "and every tongue shall confess that Jesus Christ is Lord, to the glory of God the Father". What a cycle! What a circle! What a triumph! You cannot find triumph fuller or greater than that: and Paul calls that the gospel. It is the good news of Christ's tremendous triumph. He has triumphed in that circle, and all that is included in the triumph is the gospel. We cannot stay to dwell upon it, as to why He did it, or what He effected by it, what He has secured in it. All that is the gospel. But the fact is that in that way Christ has accomplished a tremendous victory. In the whole circle of Heaven and earth, from the highest height to the lowest depth, He has triumphed. Paul finds unspeakable joy in contemplating that. That is what he calls the good tidings, the gospel—triumph in Christ.

TRIUMPH IN PAUL'S OWN SPIRITUAL HISTORY

Paul then comes in himself, and gives us in this letter quite a bit of autobiography. He tells us something of his own history before his conversion, as to who he was and what he was, and where he was, and what he had. Of course, it was nothing to be compared with what his Lord had had and had let go. But Paul himself, as Saul of Tarsus, had a great deal by birth, by inheritance, by upbringing, by education, by status, prestige and so on. He had quite a lot. He tells us about it here. All that men would boast of—he had it. And then he met Jesus Christ, or Jesus Christ met him ; and the whole thing, he said—all that he had and possessed—became in his hands like ashes, like refuse ! " I do count them but refuse ".

Many people have this false idea about the gospel, that, if you embrace the gospel, if you become a Christian, if you are converted, or however you like to put it, you are going to have to lose or give up everything, you have to give up this and you have to give up something else. If you become a Christian, it will be just one long story of giving up, giving up, giving up, until sooner or later you are skinned of everything. Listen ! Here is a man who had far more than you or I ever had. We cannot stand in the same street with this man in his natural life, in all that he was and all that he had, and all the prospects that were before him as a young man. There is very little doubt that, if Paul had not become a Christian, his name would have gone down in history amongst some other very famous names of his time. But he says—not in these words, but in many more words than these : ' When I met the Lord Jesus, that whole thing became to me like refuse.' Give it up ? Who will find any sacrifice in giving up a candle when they have found the sun ? Sacrifice in that ? Oh, no ! ' In comparison with Christ, I just count it the veriest refuse '.

What a victory ! What a triumph ! You see, this giving up—well, put it like that, if you like—but Paul is very happy about it. That is the point. It is Paul's joy, the joy of a tremendous victory in himself.

TRIUMPH IN PAUL'S MINISTRY

But further, here it is the story of the great victory in his
ministry, in his work. We recall the story of how he went to
Philippi. He had set out to go into Asia, to preach the
gospel there, and was on his way, when, in that mysterious
providence of God which only explains itself afterward
and never before, he was forbidden, checked, prevented,
stopped. The day closed with a closed way, a halted journey. He was in perplexity as to the meaning of this ; he did
not understand it. Waiting on God during that night, he
had a vision. He saw a man of Macedonia—Philippi is
in Macedonia—saying : " Come over into Macedonia, and
help us " (Acts xvi. 9). And Paul said, " We sought to go
forth . . . concluding that God had called us for to preach
the gospel unto them ". So, turning away from Asia, he
turned towards Europe, and came to Philippi.

Sometimes disappointment and upsetting of plans can
be the very ground of a great victory. God can get a lot by
putting aside our cherished plans, and upsetting everything
for us.—But we continue. Paul came to Philippi. And the
Devil knew that he had come, and got to work and said,
in effect, ' Not if I can prevent it, Paul ! I will make this
place too hot for you to stay here ! ' And he got to work,
and before long Paul with his companions were found in
the inner dungeon of the prison, their feet made fast, chains
upon them, bleeding from the lashing that they had received. Well, this does not seem to say much for Divine
guidance ! Where is the victory in this ? But wait. The very
jailor and his household were saved that night. They came
to the Lord and were baptized. And when, years afterwards,
in this other prison in Rome, Paul wrote this letter to the
saints he had left in Philippi, he put in a phrase like this :

" my brethren beloved and longed for " (Phil. iv. 1). I like
to think that the jailor and his family were included in this.
" Brethren beloved and longed for ". And in the same letter
he says: " I would have you know, brethren, that the
things which happened unto me have fallen out rather
unto the progress of the gospel " (i. 12). It is a picture of
triumph, is it not? — the triumph in his life and in his
ministry.

TRIUMPH IN PAUL'S SUFFERINGS

And he triumphed in his sufferings. He says something
about his sufferings in this very letter, the sufferings which
were upon him as he wrote; but it is all in a note and
spirit of real triumph. He says: " As always, so now also
Christ shall be magnified in my body, whether by life, or
by death " (i. 20). No tinge of despair about that, is there?
' Even now, as it has always been, Christ must be magnified in my body, whether by life or by death.' That is triumph. Yes, that is triumph, that is joy.

But more: he said, ' Christ manifested in my bonds '. A
wonderful thing, this! Brought to Rome, chained to a
Roman guardian soldier, never allowed more than a certain measure of liberty — and yet you cannot silence this
man! He has got something that ' will out ' all the time,
and he says it has gone throughout the whole Praetorian
guard (i. 13). If you knew something about the Praetorian
guard, you would say, ' That is triumph!' In the very headquarters of Caesar, and a Caesar such as he was, the gospel
is triumphant. It is being spoken about throughout the
whole Praetorian guard! Yes, there is triumph in his sufferings, in his bonds, in his afflictions. This is not just
words. It is a glorious triumph; and this is the gospel in
action, the gospel in expression.

TRIUMPH IN THE PHILIPPIAN CHRISTIANS

And this triumph was not only in Christ and in Paul, but in the Philippians. It is a beautiful letter of the triumph of Divine grace in these Philippians. You can see it, firstly, in their response ; and you really need to know something about Philippi in those days. You get just a little idea from what happened to Paul. You know about the pagan temple with its terrible system of women slaves, and all that is bound up with that horrible thing. As Paul and his companions went through the streets of Philippi, one of these young women, described as having a spirit of Python, a soothsaying demon, a veritable possession of Satan, persistently followed and cried out after them.

That is the sort of city that Philippi was, and Paul finds it possible to write a letter of this kind to believers in a city like that. Is that not triumph? I think that there should ever be a church in Philippi at all is something, but a church like this is something more. And it is not only in their response to the gospel, which cost them so much. Look again at the letter, and see the mutual love which they had one for another. This is indeed a jewel in the crown of Jesus Christ. This letter has been called Paul's great love letter. The whole thing overflows with love, and it is because of the love which they had one for another. Love of this kind is not natural. This is the work of Divine grace in human hearts. It speaks of a great triumph. If there is anything to add, we may recall that, when Paul was in need, it was these people who thought about his need and sent for his help and his succour. They are concerned for the man to whom they owed so much for the gospel.

Well, all that constitutes this tremendous triumph. It is

a letter of triumph, is it not? We have proved our point, I think. I repeat: This is the gospel! But Paul says that these people at Philippi, these believers, are exemplary—they are an example ; and so what we have to do at the end of this review is to ask: ' Just what is the gospel so far as this letter is concerned? What is the good news here, the good tidings? How can this kind of thing be repeated or reproduced? '

THE SECRET OF THE TRIUMPH

We are not dealing with people of peculiar virtues, a specially fine type of person. It is just man, poor, frail humanity: out of that can such a thing be repeated, reproduced? Can we hope for anything like this now? It would be good news if it could be proved to us that there is a way of reproducing this situation to-day, would it not? Knowing what we do know, it would be good tidings if it could be shown to us that this is not merely something which relates to an isolated company of people who lived long centuries ago, but that it can be true to-day—that this gospel, this good news, is for us.

How, then? Is there in this letter a key phrase? We have sought in our studies in these letters to gather everything into some characteristic phrase from each. Is there such a phrase in this letter that gives us the key to it all, the key to entering ourselves into Christ's great victory and all the value of it? Can we find the key to open the door for us into the position that the Apostle occupied—that everything that this world can offer and that might be placed at our disposal is tawdry, is petty, is insignificant, in comparison with Christ? Is there a key which will open the door for us into what these Philippians had come into?

I think there is, and I think you find it in the first chapter, in the first clause of verse 21 : " For to me to live is Christ ". That is the good news of the all-captivating Christ. When Christ really captivates, everything happens and anything can happen. That is how it was with Paul and with these people. Christ had just captivated them. They had no other thought in life than Christ. They may have had their businesses, their trades, their professions, their different walks of life and occupations in the world, but they had one all-dominating thought, concern and interest—Christ. Christ rested, for them, upon everything. There is no other word for it. He just captivated them.

And I see, dear friends, that that—simple as it may sound—explains everything. It explains Paul, it explains this church, it explains these believers, it explains their mutual love. It solved all their problems, cleared up all their difficulties. Oh, this is what we need! If only you and I were like this, if we really after all were captivated by Christ! I cannot convey that to you, but as I have looked at that truth—looked at it, read it, thought about it—I have felt something moved in me, something inexplicable. After all, nine-tenths of all our troubles can be traced to the fact that we have other personal interests influencing us, governing us and controlling us—other aspects of life than Christ. If only it could be true that Christ had captured and captivated and mastered us, and become—yes, I will use the word—an obsession, a glorious obsession! I think this is what the writer of the hymn meant when he wrote : ' Jesu, Lover of my soul ', and when further on he says : ' More than all in Thee I find '. When it is like that, we are filled with joy. There are no regrets at having to ' give up ' things. We are filled with joy, filled with victory. There is no spirit of defeatism at all. It is the joy of a great triumph.

It is the triumph of Christ over the life. Yes, it has been, and because it has been, it can be again.

But this needs something more than just a kind of mental appraisement. We can so easily miss the point. We may admire the words, the ideas; we may fall to it as a beautiful presentation; but, oh, we need the *captivating* to wipe out our *selves*—our reputations, everything that is associated with *us* and our own glory—that the One who captivates may be the only One in view, the only One with a reputation, and we at His feet. This is the gospel, the good news—that when Christ really captivates, the kind of thing that is in this letter happens, it really happens. Shall we ask the Lord for that life captivation of His beloved Son?

CHAPTER SIX

IN HIS LETTER TO THE COLOSSIANS

As WE COME TO THIS LETTER to the Colossians, by way of laying a foundation we will read some verses from the matchless first chapter.

" For this cause we also, since the day we heard it, do not cease to pray and make request for you, that ye may be filled with the knowledge of his will in all spiritual wisdom and understanding, to walk worthily of the Lord unto all pleasing, bearing fruit in every good work, and increasing in the knowledge of God ; strengthened with all power, according to the might of his glory, unto all patience and longsuffering with joy ; giving thanks unto the Father, who made us meet to be partakers of the inheritance of the saints in light ; who delivered us out of the power of darkness, and translated us into the kingdom of the Son of his love ; in whom we have our redemption, the forgiveness of our sins : who is the image of the invisible God, the firstborn of all creation ; for in him were all things created, in the heavens and upon the earth, things visible and things invisible, whether thrones or dominions or principalities or powers ; all things have been created through him, and unto him ; and he is before all things, and in him all things consist. And he is the head of the body, the church : who is the beginning, the firstborn from the dead ; that in all

things he might have the preeminence. For it was the good pleasure of the Father that in him should all the fulness dwell ; and through him to reconcile all things unto himself, having made peace through the blood of his cross ; through him, I say, whether things upon the earth, or things in the heavens " (Col. i. 9 — 20).

Now, that forms quite a good foundation for speaking about the gospel—and do note that that is the gospel. All that is what Paul calls the ' good news '. It is the thing that Paul preached—" the gospel which I preach ". In this letter, that word occurs not so many times as in other letters, but with a peculiar point. It occurs in this first chapter, verse 5 : " *. . . because of the hope which is laid up for you in the heavens, whereof ye heard before in the word of the truth of the gospel* " ; and then in verse 21 : "*. . . if so be that ye continue in the faith, grounded and stedfast, and not moved away from the hope of the gospel which ye heard, which was* "—and here is the same word in the verb form—" *preached in all creation under heaven* "—" which was ' gospelled ', ' good newsed ', in all creation under heaven ".

GOOD TIDINGS IN AN EMERGENCY SITUATION

Now, if anything is to be good news, or good tidings, if it is to have a really keen edge to it, there must be a situation for which it brings relief, assurance, comfort or gratification. If it does not matter, then it is not good news. For example, supposing someone, with whom your life and heart are closely bound up, lies in a very serious and critical illness, and you call in medical help. You are under a great burden of anxiety : it matters very much to you which way it goes ; and you wait for what seems an eternity for the doctor to come down and give you a report. When he comes down and says, ' It is all right, you need not worry ; things are going all right, they will come through ', that is good news indeed. It has an edge on it, because your heart is bound up with this matter. If there is a great decision in the balances, which is going to affect in some way your future, your career, your life, and a committee is sitting on it, and you are waiting outside with your heart, as we say, in your mouth, feeling most anxious as to how it is going : when someone comes out and says, ' All right, you have got the job, the appointment ', that is good news. It brings to you an immense sense of relief. If there is a battle on, the issue of which will be serious for all concerned, and some-one comes back from the scene of the fighting, and says, ' It is going well, it is all right, we are going to get through ! '—why, it is a tremendous relief. That is good tidings. It touches us, it means something to us. There has to be something in the nature of an emergency situation really to give point to good news.

THE EMERGENCY SITUATION AT COLOSSAE

Now, in the case of almost all Paul's letters, there was an emergency situation. Something had arisen in the nature of a threat to the Christian life of those with whom his heart was closely bound up ; something had arisen which was causing many of those Christians real concern, worry and anxiety. They were in real difficulty ; the future seemed to be in doubt. It was in order to meet such emergencies as these that Paul wrote his letters, and in them all he uses this word ' gospel ', or ' good news '— good news for an emergency, good tidings for this critical situation.

In this letter to the Colossians it is peculiarly so. There was a real emergency on amongst the believers at Colossae. But it was the same emergency which takes different forms at different times—it is present to-day in its own form. What it amounted to was this: that there were certain people, considering themselves to be very knowledgeable, wise, intelligent, learned people, who haa `. -en dipping into a lot of mysterious stuff, and they were bringing their high-sounding ideas and theories to bear upon these Christians. It all had to do with the great magnitudes of life.

First of all, there was no less a matter in view than the very meaning of the created universe. Now that might be, of course, a realm for philosophical speculation; but you know that, in certain ways, that comes very near to the Christian heart. Is there a design for everything, or is everything either just taking a mechanical course, or being carried on by some mysterious powers which are inimical to human well-being? Is there any real design behind this created universe? To push that one step further: Is there a *purpose* in everything? Sooner or later, Christians come up against these questions. Under duress, trial, pressure and suffering, sometimes we do not know what to make of things. This seems to be a topsy-turvy universe, full of enigmas and contradictions and paradoxes, and we have a bad time over it. Is there a plan in it—is there really a Divine control of everything in this universe, in human history and in all that is happening? Is there after all, to use a word which I do not think we fully appreciate, a Providence for everything and in everything? —that is to say, is everything being made to work together according to design and purpose, and to work out toward a great, Divine, beneficent end?

Now, these people were arguing about that, and the Christians at Colossae were being greatly disturbed by it all.

And then it came nearer to their own Christian existence. It touched upon their very life as children of God. Now, if any people in the world ought to be quite sure about these matters—that there is a Divine purpose and Divine pattern and Divine Providence—it is Christians, and the very life of the Christian is affected by whether this is so or not. The matter of our assurance, our confidence, our restfulness, our power, our testimony, rests upon having an answer to these questions. The meaning of this whole universe, the order and the purpose in it, the design and the control of it, the Providence over all events and happenings in the course of human history—these are things that come very near to the Christian. If we have any doubt about them, our Christianity goes for nothing, the very foundations are swept from under our feet, we do not know where we are.

That was the emergency at Colossae. The very life of the Christians, the very life of the Church, was threatened. And if its life is threatened, its growth is threatened. The whole matter of the spiritual growth of the Church and of the Christians is at stake in this—growth, development and maturity. If that is threatened, then something else will be threatened: the whole thing will disintegrate, will fall apart; its unity and cohesion will collapse; the whole thing will be scattered into fragments. And so the very hope of the Church and of the Christian is struck at, their hope and their destiny. These are neither small nor unpractical matters. They may come very near at some time or other, and they require an answer.

THE ANSWER TO THE SITUATION

Now, it was to meet this whole situation, to answer all these serious questions and issues, that Paul wrote this letter: to confirm the Christians, to establish them, to sustain them, to encourage them; and he calls it ' good tidings ', and it is. If you can give something to answer all that, it is indeed good tidings, is it not? That is ' gospel' indeed! You see, the gospel of the Lord Jesus Christ touches the uttermost bounds of this universe, and covers everything within those bounds, including human history, human happenings, world events, the course of things, the design in things, the end of things. The gospel touches it all at every point.

So Paul answers it, and he answers the whole of it in one word. His answer is: *Christ.* Christ is the answer. That answer is found inclusively in those words in chapter iii, verse 11, the last clause: *" Christ is all, and in all."* And what an immense ' all' Christ is if He covers the whole of that ground! If He reaches out and embraces all those mighty issues, what a Christ He is! The all-comprehending fact is emphatically and categorically stated by the Apostle in this letter. He states it in many sentences, but in this one statement he gathers it all up. The answer to all this is Christ. Christ is the explanation of all the happenings in human history. Christ explains this universe, Christ gives character to this universe, Christ stands behind all the course of the events in this universe. Christ is the integrating Person of everything, the One in whom all things hold together.

' Christ is the end, for Christ was the beginning;
   Christ the beginning, for the end is Christ. '

THE EVIDENCE THAT THE ANSWER IS SATISFACTORY

But perhaps you may say, ' It is all very well for Paul to make a categorical statement like that, but what is the evidence?' Well, the evidence is quite real. And it must be said that, if we are asking for the evidence, something has gone wrong with us! *We* ought to be the answer, *we* ought to be the evidence: because the witness to this is first of all the personal, spiritual experience of the child of God. You can leave the vast universe for the moment, if you like, and come to the little universe of your own life — for, after all, what is true in the microcosm is only a reflection of what is true in the great cosmic realm. God brings down His evidence from the circumferential to the very centre of the individual Christian life, and the answer is there. What is the experience of a truly born-again child of God?

Now you can test whether you are born again by this, and, thank God, I know that many of you will be able to say, ' Yes, that is true to my experience '. But I ask you: What is your experience as a truly born-again child of God? When you really came to the Lord Jesus — however you may put it: when you let Jesus come into your heart or into your life, or when you handed over your life to Him; when there was a transaction with Him, a new birth, by which you became a child of God — not by any ' sacrament ' applied to you, but by the inward operation of His Spirit: when you became a child of God in a living, conscious way, what was the first consciousness that came to you, and has remained with you ever since?

Was it not, and is it not, this: ' There is now a purpose in life, of which I never knew before ; there is a purpose in things. Now I have the sense — indeed I know — that I was not just born into this world and grew up, but there was a purpose behind it.' There is design in things; a sense—you may not be able to explain it all, what it all means—but you have the sense now that you have arrived at, or at least begun to realise, the very purpose of your existence. Is that true? When the Lord Jesus at last has His place in our hearts, the big question of life is answered —the big question as to the ' Why ' of our existence. Till then, you wander about, you do all sorts of things, you fill up time, you employ heart and mind and hand, but you do not know what it is all for. You may have a very full life, a very full life indeed, outside of Christ, and yet come to the end without being able to answer the question, What is it all about?

One man, who had enjoyed such a full life, who had become well-known in the schools of learning, a great figure in the intellectual realm, in his dying moment cried: ' I am taking an awful leap into the dark '. He had no answer to the question. But the simple child of God, immediately they come to the Lord, has the answer in consciousness, if not in explanation, in his or her heart, and that is what is called ' rest '. " Come unto me ", said Jesus, " and I will give you rest " (Matt. xi. 28). Rest is in this: ' Well, I have been a wanderer, but now I have come home ; I have been searching—I have found ; I have been in quest of something—I did not know what it was—but now I have it '. There *is* purpose in this universe, and when Jesus Christ comes into His place, as this letter says, then you know there is purpose in your universe, and there will be purpose in the universe of everybody else, if only they will come that way.

And not only purpose, but more—control. The child of God very soon begins to realise that he or she has been taken under control, brought under a mastery; that there is a law of government set up in the consciousness, which is directive: which, on the one hand, says, 'Yes', the glorious 'Yes' of many liberties; on the other hand, 'No—careful, steady, watch!' We all know that. We do not hear those words, but we know that that is what is being said to us in our hearts. The Spirit of Christ within is just saying, 'Look to your steps—be careful, be watchful'. We have come under control. That is extended in many ways over the whole life, but it is a great reality. This universe is under control, it is under government. The evidence of it is found within our own experience when Christ comes to His place. And you can extend that into the future ages, when the whole universe will be like that, under Christ's control.

And then again: " in whom all things hold together ". The wonderful thing about the Christian life is its integration, or, if you prefer another word, its unification. How scattered, how divided, we were before Christ got His place! We were ' all over the place ', as we say—one thing after another, looking this way and looking that; hearts divided, lives divided; we in ourselves divided, a conflict within our own persons. When the Lord Jesus really gets His place as Lord within, the life is unified. We are just gathered up, poised, concentrated upon one thing. We have only one thing in view. What Paul said of himself becomes true: " but one thing I do ..." (Phil. iii. 13). We are people of " one thing ". Christ unifies the life.

What about life itself, the life of the child of God? When the Lord Jesus is in His right place, the life of the child of God is secured, is established, is confirmed, and grows; there is spiritual growth and maturity. It is a wonderful thing. If, in some Christian lives, it is not realised

as a fact, it is for very good reasons—or for bad reasons!
—but if the Lord Jesus really is "all, and in all", in the
life, if He 'in all things has the pre-eminence', it is wonderful to see the spiritual growth. Those who have much
association with, or experience in dealing with, young
Christians, have found this one of the most impressive
things—how, where the Lord Jesus just gets His way,
they go ahead spiritually, they grow. They come to understanding and knowledge which so many of the scholars
seem to have missed. They have come to a real spiritual
understanding. While other people are trying to get on
along other lines—intellectually and so on—these
young ones, who have not, many of them, the background
of intellectual or scholastic training—they are just simple
people—are just leaping ahead spiritually.

This growth in spiritual intelligence and understanding does not rest upon anything natural. It is coming
about because Jesus has such a large place, and He is the
source and centre and sum of all spiritual knowledge.
Over against that, it is possible to have great acquisitions
and qualifications in the academic realm, to be doing big
things in that realm, and yet to find that the simple things
of the Lord Jesus Christ are to you as a foreign language.
You do not know what it is about—you cannot follow
or join in at all. This is sad, but true. There are Christians,
yes, true Christians, who just cannot talk about the things
of the Lord. If there is to be growth, it can only come
about through Jesus being given His place, fully and without question.

And then, as to destiny. The statement is that the
destiny of this universe is with the Lord Jesus, and that
that destiny is universal glory. But that is just a beautiful
idea, an enchanting vista, is it not? How are you going to

prove it? In your own heart! Is it not equally true with
the other matters that we have already been considering,
that, when the Lord Jesus really gets His place, you have
a foretaste of that glory? No one can understand the
Christian who has not the Christian's experience, but there
it is. It is not just that we are making out that we are having a good time. It is something coming from the inside;
it is something of a foretaste of the glory that is to be. We
have got the answer to all these immense questions right
in our own spiritual experience.

THE WITNESS OF THE CHURCH

But then the Apostle moves to the Church, and speaks
about the Church: " And he is the head of . . . the church
. . . the firstborn from the dead " (Col. i. 18). How does
the Church bear witness to the fact, this great fact,
that Jesus is the answer to these immense questions?
I think the Church gives the answer both positively and
negatively.

It gives the answer positively—though not as positively
as it might have done—but it does give the answer in this,
that, after all (and what an ' all ' of these two thousand
years!), the Church is still in existence. Think of that
inrush of the forces of antagonism and hatred and murder
upon the Church in its infancy, with the determination of
the greatest empire that the world had ever known to
wipe it out. After all, it is that empire that has gone; the
Church continues. Think, too, of all that has set itself
during the centuries since to bring the Church to an end,
to destroy it, and still is set upon that. Oh, that men were
not so blind that they misread history! If only those
powers in the world to-day, great kingdoms, great empires,

would rightly read history, they would see they are on an utterly vain mission, a fool's errand indeed, to try to destroy the testimony of Jesus on this earth. It is they who will be destroyed.

Yes, the very continuance and persistence of the Church is evidence that this is true—that Jesus Christ is the key to this universe, that He is the answer to all these questions. I say, the Church does not give the answer as clearly as it might. If only it had gone on as it began, what an answer it would be!

But it gives the answer negatively, as well as positively. It answers it negatively by the very fact that, whereas once it stood up to the world victoriously, weathered the storms triumphantly, it has now moved away from its centre, the Lord Jesus Christ, and brought in substitutes for His absolute headship and lordship. It has made other things its governing interests. The result has been disintegration, division, and all the rest. Yes, the thing is answered in the negative, and it will always be like that.

Let us be quite clear: it is not that the truth has broken down. If these things ever become a question with you, it will not be because they are open to question, but because something has gone wrong with you as it has gone wrong with the Church. It is not in the truth, but in that which is supposed to represent the truth, that the question lies. These substitutes for the headship of Jesus Christ, whether they be men or institutions or religious interests or Christian activities, whatever they may be, if they get in the place of the Lord Jesus Himself, lead to nothing but disunity and division. To put that more positively, if only men, leaders and all the rest, would say, ' Look here, all our institutions, our missions, our organizations, all our interests in Christianity, must be subservient to the abso-

lute lordship of Jesus Christ', you would find a unity coming about, a oneness. We should all flow together on that
ground. It is the mighty tide of His lordship that will cure
it all.

Go down by the sea-shore. The tide is right out, and all
the breakwaters are naked, dividing up the whole coast-
line as it were into sections. But as the tide comes up, the
breakwaters, the dividing things, begin to disappear. You
come back at full flood-tide, and you see nothing whatever
of those dividing breakwaters. The rising tide has buried
them all. And when Christ is *all,* and in all, ' in all things
having the pre-eminence ', all those things which belong
to the low tide of spiritual life, the ebb-tide of spiritual
life, will just disappear. The proof is in the Church.

We had a little taste of it during the recent visit to this
country of Dr. Graham. There was one consuming passion
to bring Christ into His place at the beginnings of life ;
all the different sections were found concerned with that.
Where were the barriers, where were the ' breakwaters ',
where were the departmental things? They had gone,
buried under this high tide of concern that Christ should
have His place in lives. Why should that be for three
months only? Why should it be experienced only in a
convention lasting a few days once a year? No, this position is God's thought for always. The key to it is just this
—Christ all in all.

Perhaps we can see now why mention of the gospel in
this letter is confined to one emphasis—" the hope of the
gospel ". Yes, the only occurrences of ' gospel' or ' good
news' are in that connection—" the *hope* of the good
news ". The hope of the gospel is in Jesus Christ being
all and in all. Hope is a Person, not an abstract nature in
us—' being hopeful '—which does not amount to much

more than a periodical, variable optimism. Hope here is a Person. The hope of the good news is: *He* in all things having the pre-eminence. That is where the hope lies for you, for me, for the Church, for the world, for the universe. That is the hope of the gospel.

CHAPTER SEVEN

IN HIS LETTERS TO THE THESSALONIANS

"... *our gospel came not unto you in word only, but also in power, and in the Holy Spirit, and in much assurance* ..." *(I Thess. i. 5).*

"... *having suffered before, and been shamefully entreated, as ye know, at Philippi, we waxed bold in our God to speak unto you the gospel of God in much conflict*" *(ii. 2).*

"... *we have been approved of God to be entrusted with the gospel* ..." *(ii. 4).*

"... *being affectionately desirous of you, we were well pleased to impart unto you, not the gospel of God only, but also our own souls* ... *For ye remember, brethren, our labour and travail: working night and day, that we might not burden any of you, we preached unto you the gospel of God*" *(ii. 8, 9).*

"... *we* ... *sent Timothy, our brother and God's minister in the gospel of Christ* ..." *(iii. 1, 2).*

"... *rendering vengeance to them that know not God, and to them that obey not the gospel of our Lord Jesus* ..." *(II Thess. i. 8).*

" . . . whereunto he called you through our gospel, to the obtaining of the glory of our Lord Jesus Christ" (ii. 14).

WE SEE THAT THE GOSPEL has quite a place in these letters. We seek now to discover the real meaning of the gospel, that is, the essential meaning of the good tidings, from the standpoint of these letters and the Thessalonian believers, and we shall be helped to that understanding if we take a look at the spiritual history, life and state of these believers in Thessalonica.

THE THESSALONIAN CHRISTIANS AN EXAMPLE

You will at a glance see what a special regard Paul had for them. He repeatedly uses words such as these: " We give thanks to God always for you all ". Both in the first and second letters he speaks like that (I. i. 2 ; II. i. 3, ii. 13). " We give thanks to God for *you* ". And then he says about them a very wonderful thing, which gives us a definite lead in this consideration. He says in the first letter, chapter i, verse 7: " Ye became an ensample to all that believe in Macedonia and in Achaia ". That is something to say about a company of the Lord's people, and it leads us at once to ask the question—How were they an ensample? It was evidently not only to those immediately referred to, in all Macedonia and Achaia, for these letters remain unto this day, and they therefore represented that which is an example for all the Lord's people. If that was true of them, then the gospel must have meant something very much where they were concerned. It must have had a very special form of expression in them, and so we seek to answer the question: How were they " an ensample to all that believe "?

A PURE SPIRIT AND A CLEAN START

We find the answer in the first place here in this very first chapter. It was in their *realism* in reception of the gospel. *" Our gospel came unto you not in word only, but also in power, and in the Holy Spirit, and in much assurance ".* And again: *" when ye received from us the word of the message, even the word of God, ye accepted it not as the word of men, but, as it is in truth, the word of God "* *(ii. 13).* Now that represents a very clean start; and if we are going to come to the place of these Thessalonian believers, if the gospel is to have that expression in us that it had in them, if it is going to be true in our case that we are an example to all them that believe, then it is very important that we have a clean start.

For us, of course, if we have advanced in the Christian life without becoming such exemplary believers, that may mean retracing our steps in order to start again somewhere where we have gone wrong; clearing away a lot of rubbish and starting at a certain point all over again. But I am thinking also of young Christians who have recently made the start. You are really at the beginning, and we are most concerned about you, because you may meet many old Christians who are not by any means an example to all that believe. I am sorry to have to say that, but it is quite true, and we do not want you to be like that. We want you to be exemplary Christians; those of whom the Apostle Paul, if he were present, could say, ' I thank God always for you '. It would be a great thing, would it not, if that could be said of us? ' Thank God for him! Thank God for her! Thank God that ever we came into touch with this one, and that one! I always thank God for them—they are an example of what Christians ought to be!'

Now, that is the desire of the Lord, that is our desire for you, and it should be the desire of our hearts for ourselves. Although we may not have succeeded, let us not give up hope that some may yet give thanks for us, that we may be an example, that in some things, at any rate, it may be true of us as it was of these. Paul says here: "Ye became imitators of us" (I Thess. i. 6). The Lord help us to be such an example that we could invite others, in some respects at least, to imitate us, without any spiritual pride.

Well, if this is to be so, the start must be a clean one. You see, quite evidently, as these Thessalonians listened to Paul preaching the good tidings, their minds and hearts were free from prejudice. They would not have come to the conclusion to which they did come if there had been any prejudice, if they had already closed down the matter in their minds, or come to a set position. They were open in heart from the outset, ready for whatever was of God, and that created a capacity for discerning what was of God. You will never know whether a thing is of God if you entertain prejudice, if you have already judged it, if already you have come to a fixed position. If you are settled in your mind, closed in your heart, harbour suspicions and fears, you have already sabotaged the work of the Holy Spirit, and you will never know if the thing is of God. You must be open-hearted, open-minded, free from suspicions and prejudices, and ready in this attitude—'Now, if there is anything of the Lord, anything of God, I am ready for that, no matter through whom it comes, how it comes, where it comes. If it is of God, I am ready for it'. That creates a disposition to which the Holy Spirit can bear witness, and makes things possible for the Lord.

Now, as we shall see, that is exactly how these Thessa-

lonians were. They received the word, yes, in much affliction, but they received it as the Word of God, not as the
word of man. Because of their purity of spirit, they had the
sense—'This thing is right, this is of God!' That was a
good start. As I said earlier, it may be that some of us will
have to get back somewhere to make that start again. To
any reading these words, who may be of advanced years in
the Christian life, I would say: Dear friend, if you have
anywhere on the road become in any way affected, infected,
by prejudice and suspicion, you have closed the door to
anything further of God. Let us clearly understand that.
It is true that—

> 'The Lord hath yet more light and truth
> To break forth from His Word'.

We have not yet exhausted all that the Lord has to show
us in His Word; but He will only show it to the pure in
heart. "The pure in heart . . . shall see God" (Matt. v. 8).

These Thessalonians, then, had a pure spirit from the
start.

MUTUALITY AND MATURITY

The next thing that we notice about them, after their
realism in reception, was their mutuality and maturity—
two things which always go together. In both these letters,
that which the Apostle speaks about perhaps more than
anything else is the wonderful love between these believers. "*The love of each one of you all toward one another aboundeth*" (*II Thess. i. 3*). He is speaking all the
way through about their mutual love. And going alongside
of that was their spiritual growth. You see, love always
builds up (I Cor. viii. 1). This kind of love, mutual love,
always means spiritual increase. We can see how true that

is if we view it from the opposite standpoint. Little, personal, petty, selfish, separated, individual Christians, or companies or bodies of Christians who are exclusive and closed, and have not a wide open heart of love to all saints —how small they are, how cramped they are. It is true. And it is in this mutual love one for another, and growing and increasing love one for another, that spiritual growth takes place. Do not forget that. If you are concerned about the spiritual growth of your own heart, your own life, and that of others, it will be along the line of love, mutual love, and you are the one to begin it. Mutuality and maturity always go together.

SUFFERING AND SERVICE

And then, in the third place, you will find that they were characterized by suffering and service, and this is a wonderful Divine combination. It is something that is not natural. The Apostle had much to say about it, as you will see if you underline the word 'suffering' in these letters, and note his references to their sufferings and their afflictions. They "received the word in much affliction" (I Thess. i. 6). He speaks about their sufferings, and he describes those sufferings. They in Thessalonica were suffering along the same lines and for the same causes as their brethren in Judaea, he said (ii. 14).

Now, in Judaea, that is, in the country of the Jews, you know how the Christians suffered. Christ Himself suffered at the hands of the Jews; Stephen was martyred at the hands of the Jews; the Church met its first persecutions in Judaea, in Jerusalem, and they were scattered abroad by the persecutions that arose there over Stephen; and Paul says, 'Now you are suffering in that way'. Evidently there was in Thessalonica much persecution, much opposition; threats and all sorts of difficulties—the kind of thing, perhaps, where it was very difficult for them to do business and get jobs, all because the business was in the hands of those who had no room for this Christianity and for these Christians.

But with all that severe suffering, and with all their "much affliction", they did not become introspective. That is the peril of suffering. If you are suffering frustration, opposition, persecution, or if the best jobs are given to someone else, and so on, the natural thing is to turn in upon yourself, to be very sorry for yourself, to begin to nurse your trouble and be wholly occupied with yourself. But here, suffering led to service.

The Apostle says that the Word went forth from them, not only through all the region of Macedonia and Achaia, but throughout the whole country (i. 8). Their suffering —what did it do? It made them turn outwards, and say, ' There are others everywhere in need, in suffering, as we: let us see what we can do for them '. That is the way to respond to the gospel, is it not? That speaks of the glorious gospel! The gospel had become to them such good news that it had the effect upon them of delivering them entirely from all self-pity in the deepest affliction. Let us take that to heart.

PATIENCE AND HOPE

Furthermore the Apostle speaks of their "patience of hope" (i. 3), and that simply means that they did not easily give up. That counts for something, you know. You are having a difficult time; everything and everybody is against you. It is so easy to give up—just to give up; to draw out of the race, or drop your hands in the fight, and say, ' It is no use—better give it all up '. But no : these Christians had patience and hope. They did not easily give up, they ' stuck to it ', and we shall see that they had a hope that kept them sticking to it.

Such were these who were ' an example to all that believe '. In them we see the constituents of exemplary Christians, and they are the true features of the gospel. You see, the gospel is for Christians in difficulty ! It is not only for the unsaved, but for Christians when they are in difficulty or in suffering. It is still good news. If we lose the ' good news ' element in the gospel, if it loses for us its keen edge as ' good tidings ', we become stale ; we come to the place where we ' know it all '. If we lose that sense, then when trouble comes we give up, we let go ; but if to have come to a saving knowledge of the Lord Jesus is still for us the greatest thing in all the world and all the universe, then we get through.

DIFFICULTIES BECAUSE OF TEMPERAMENT

Now, because difficulties always correspond to our dispositions, that is, what we are always gives rise to the nature of our trials, so it was with the Thessalonians. Nothing is a trial to you unless you are made in a certain way. Something that is a trial to you might never be a trial to me at all. Or it might be the other way round. What might be a terrible thing to me and knock me right off my balance, other people could go through quite calmly, and wonder what I am making such a fuss about. Our troubles and our trials very largely take their rise from the way we are made.

Now I want you to follow this. The thoroughness of these Thessalonian believers led them into peculiar testings. And that is always the case. If you are not thorough-going, you will not have thorough-going difficulties. You will get through more or less easily. If you are thorough-going, you are going to meet thorough-going testings. They arise quite naturally out of your own attitude or your own disposition.

Now, you know that human nature and constitution is made in various ways. You know in general that we are not all alike. That is just as well! But we can to a very large extent classify human nature into different categories —what we call temperaments. In the main there are seven different temperaments, or categories of human constitution. I am not going to deal with that in detail, but there is a very useful point here on this matter. These Thessalonians were quite clearly of the ' practical ' temperament, and the keenness of their particular sufferings was largely found because they were like that. I do not, of course, mean that other people do not suffer, but they suffer in other ways.

You see, the standard of life of the practical temperament is quick and direct returns. We must see something for our money very quickly! It is the business temperament, the temperament of commercial life. The things which govern this temperament are quick successes. ' Success ' is the great word of the practical temperament. It is success that succeeds. The successful are the idols of this particular kind of make-up.

There is not much sentiment here. These people cannot stop for sentiment. Things that are not what they call practical are regarded by them as just ' sentimental '. They are not so, of course, but that is how Martha reacted to Mary. Mary was not sentimental, but Martha thought she was, because Martha was so pre-eminently practical. Again, there is very little imagination in this make-up. It rides roughshod over all sensibilities. It does not stop to think how people feel about what is said ; it just goes right on.

And then it sometimes makes terrible mistakes—it confuses things. For instance, it mistakes inquisitiveness for depth, because it has always to be asking endless questions. The ' practical ' people are always asking questions, questions, questions ; they keep you going with questions all the time, thinking that this is an evidence of spiritual depth. They think that they are not just taking things at their surface value, they are being very practical, as well as deep. But there is a good deal of difference between inquisitiveness and depth. It is very possible to confuse things.

Now we want to get to understand these Thessalonians and the effect of the gospel. Can we not now picture them, in the light of what I have said? They responded quickly, and in a very practical way, and in a very thorough-going way. One of the major themes to which they responded was the coming of the Lord. Right at the beginning Paul says: " Ye turned unto God from idols, to serve a living and true God, and to wait for his Son from heaven " (i. 9, 10). It was a big thing with them, this coming of the Lord, and they had concluded that the Lord's coming would take place, at latest, in their own lifetime. That was their practical reaction to the gospel, and it was good in its way. But you know that these two letters of Paul are almost entirely occupied with correcting a false element in that reaction.

Now you find them in trouble—trouble springing out of their own make-up—in this matter. They had been saying to themselves something like this. ' The Lord is coming—we have been told the Lord is coming, we have accepted that " the coming of the Lord draweth nigh ", and we have accepted that to happen any day ; and we were told that, when the Lord came, all His own would be caught up to meet Him. We concluded that all believers would be caught up, be raptured, and enter into the glory like that, together. Oh, what a wonderful thing—all going together into the presence of the Lord ! But some of our friends died, yesterday, last week, and people are still dying. It seems to upset this whole matter of all being caught up together.' They were thrown into confusion and consternation because, instead of the Lord coming and gathering them all up to Himself, there were people amongst them going into the grave. It was a setback for their practical make-up, you see.

Now, the Apostle writes to them. He writes to them the gospel, the good news, for people who are in perplexity and in sorrow because of disappointment in this way, and he says : ' I want you to know, dear brethren, I want you to understand, that that makes no difference in the final issue. When the Lord comes, they will not have gone before us ; and when He comes, we shall not go before them. It just does not make any difference. They that are asleep in Jesus and we who are alive and remain shall all be caught up together. You need not allow this thing to trouble you any more. You must not sorrow as those who have no hope, or who have lost their great hope—as those whose great hope of the coming of the Lord has been struck at by the deaths of these believers. There is really no place for any element of disappointment over this. It is good news for those who have lost loved ones—it is good news concerning the issue of life and death—that we shall all together go up " to meet the Lord in the air : and so shall we ever be with the Lord." It is just wonderful.'

So we see that here Paul was able to bring in the gospel

—the good news, the good tidings—in order to get over a certain difficulty that had arisen because of their make-up, their disposition.

A HELP TO KNOW ONE'S OWN DISPOSITION

Let us pause there for a minute. You know, we should get over a great many of our troubles if we knew what our temperaments were. If only we would sit down for a minute—and this is not introspection at all—sit down for a minute and say: 'Now, what is my peculiar disposition and make-up? What is the thing to which, by reason of my constitution, I am most prone? What are the factors, the elements, that make up my temperament?' If you can put your finger on that, you have the key to many of your troubles. Asaph, the psalmist, was having a very bad time on one occasion. He looked at the wicked and saw them prospering. He saw the righteous having a difficult time —himself included—and he got very downhearted about all this. But then he pulled himself together, he recollected, and he said: " This is my infirmity; but I will remember the years of the right hand of the Most High " (Ps. lxxvii. 10). ' " This is my infirmity "! This is not the Lord, this is not the truth—this is just me, this is my proneness to go down in times of difficulty. It is how I am made; it is my reaction to trouble.'

Now, perhaps that sounds a very naturalistic way of dealing with things. But I have not finished yet. If you and I will understand this thing—that a lot of our trouble comes because we are made in a certain way; it is really in our own constitution—we shall have a ground upon which to go to the Lord. We shall be able to go to the Lord and say: 'Lord, You know how I am made; You know how I naturally react to things. You know how, because

I am made that way, I am always being caught in certain ways; You know how it is that I behave under certain strains. You know me, Lord. Now, Lord, You are different from what I am: where I am weak, You are strong; where I am faulty, You are perfect.'

Do you not see that the Lord Jesus, the perfect Man, is the perfect balance of all the good qualities in all the temperaments, that in Him are none of the bad qualities of any temperament, and that the Holy Spirit can make Christ to be unto us that which we are not in ourselves? That is the great wonder, the great mystery, the great glory, of the meaning of Christ as mediated to us by the Holy Spirit. It is the wonder of His humanity: a perfect manhood without any of all this that troubles us. Look at Him under duress: He does not go down. Look at Him from any standpoint of testing and trial: He goes through. But He is man. He is not going through on the basis of His Deity. He is going through on the basis of His perfect humanity, and that is to be mediated to us.

Spiritual growth means this, that we are becoming something other than what we are naturally. Is it not so? Naturally, we may be inclined to be rather miserable people—always taking a miserable view, always going down in the dumps. Now, when the Holy Spirit takes charge of us, the miserably inclined people become joyful, although it is not natural for them to be joyful. That is the miracle of the Christian life. We become something that we are not naturally. Naturally, we would very quickly go down under some kinds of criticism or persecution, and nurse our troubles, but when the Lord Jesus is in us, we can take it and go on. We do not go down, we go on. He makes us other than what we are. That is the work of grace in the life of the believer.

These Thessalonians suffered very much because of their practical temperament. They expected that that of which they had been told at the first would come about immediately. They were saying to themselves: 'The Lord will come—He may come to-day, any day—and that will be the end of all our troubles. But time is going on, and people are dying, and things are getting more and more difficult. It does not look very much as though the Lord is coming . . .' They may have been almost at the point of breaking and scattering. And at that point a new presentation of the gospel of the Lord Jesus came in, bringing the hope of something different from what they were naturally.

What is true in the case of the practical temperament is true in all other temperaments. We may take this as a principle. If we only understood it, the Lord is dealing with every one of us like that. He is dealing with us according to what we are. It is no use trying to stereotype or standardise the dealings of God with people. God's dealings with me would perhaps not be very troublesome to you, but God's dealings with you might very well throw me right off my feet. He deals with us according to ourselves, in order that there may be that of Christ in us which is not of ourselves. I say again, that is the work of grace. That is the mediation of Christ—that is the very meaning of being conformed to the image of Christ. It is partaking of His nature—something utterly different. But it is a terrible process. Now we have got to get through as these people got through.

Is that good news? I think it is. I think that is the gospel, 'good tidings'. It is good tidings for the man who is always too ready to drop out and give up and be miserable. It is good tidings to those who, because of their own natural expectations and reactions, are disappointed in what is actually happening. It is good tidings that Christ is something other than we are, and that we can be saved from what we are by Christ. It is very practical, you see. How are we saved from what we are? By Christ! Not by Christ just coming and putting out His hands and pulling us up. That is what we are all wanting Him to do. We are appealing to the Lord to come and do something like that, literally lift us right out of where we are. What He is doing is displacing us, and putting Himself in our place in an inward way. It is a process, a deep process, and it is perhaps only over years that you can see more of Christ. That person used to be such-and-such a one, but there is a difference now, you can see Christ now ; they are no longer what they used to be, they are getting over that. They are being " changed into the same image ". That is good news : good news for the Thessalonians, and good news for us.

THE TEST AT THE END

But there is one other thing with these Thessalonians. Things in the world were becoming increasingly difficult ; they were going from bad to worse. These dear people saw things happening, they saw forces at work, and they thought: ' This does not look as though the Lord is coming, as though His Kingdom is coming. It looks as though Satan is having it all his own way. Things are going from bad to worse ; and as to things being changed, as to there being " a new heaven and a new earth " and a new world state, all this that we have thought would come with the coming of Christ and His Kingdom, we do not see any sign of it at all. Rather is it going the other way : the world is getting worse, evil men are waxing worse and worse.

There seems to be more and more of the Devil than ever there was.'

Now, the Apostle wrote his letters on that, and he said : ' Look here, that does not mean things going wrong ; that does not mean disappointment for your expectations. The Lord will not come until those things have happened and come to fulness. " The mystery of lawlessness does already work ". Before He comes, two things must happen.

' First of all, there must take place a great falling away.' A great falling away? Christians falling away? Professing Christians falling away, going away from the Lord, turning back? That is not very practical for these people ! Yes, that is exactly what will happen toward the end. The nearer the coming of the Lord is, the more the test will be finding people out. The sieve will be at work. There will be a falling away ; there will be many people—professors —who say, ' We are not going with this, we cannot go on with this any longer '. They will go back from following the Lord. It always was so. It was so in the days of our Lord's flesh. At the end it will be like that. ' Oh, how disappointing !' Ah, yes, but understand that that is how it will be, and that it does not mean that everything has gone wrong. It is just going to be like that. When the Lord does take away a people, it will be a people who have gone on with Him to the end ; and He is testing, testing. ' Now, you Thessalonians, understand that what He is doing is testing you as to whether you will go right on to the end. It has to be made manifest whether the root of the matter is in believers, or if it is only profession. So do not misunderstand the signs of the times.

And then the second thing. Antichrist, that man of sin, the Devil, seems to be getting more and more of his own way, they thought. And it was so. ' But ', said the Apostle, 'the Lord's day will not come until that man of sin, the Antichrist, has been revealed.' 'Oh, we thought Christ was coming, not Antichrist!' Ah, but Christ will not come until Antichrist has come. Do not misunderstand things. If there is a mighty movement in this world by Satan, the Devil seemingly incarnate, a great incarnation of him—it may be in man form or system form, whatever it is—that is dead set upon obliterating everything that belongs to Christ, that is not a bad sign. That is a good sign—the Lord is about to come! That is the good news in the day when the Devil seems to be carrying everything away. That is portentous. The Lord is at hand.

" But when these things begin to come to pass, look up, and lift up your heads; because your redemption draweth nigh ", said Jesus (Luke xxi. 28). So if suffering increases, if patience is tested; if Satan seems to be having it his way, and getting the power into his hands, do not be deceived—do not allow that to say to you, 'Well, our hope is not being realised.' Turn it round the other way, and say, 'These are the very things that say that our hope is about to be realised.' This is good news for the day of adversity, good news for Christians in suffering, good news when Satan is doing his worst. The Lord is at hand!

THE SUMMING UP OF THE WHOLE MATTER

But where shall we sum it all up? We have always sought to find a little fragment in which it can be all concluded, and I think we have it here:

"*Faithful is he that calleth you, who will also do it*" (*I Thess. v. 24*).

Here is the conclusion and summing up of the whole matter. Yes, beloved ones are dying, going to the Lord.

Time is dragging on. The Devil is apparently gaining power and doing his worst. We, the Lord's people, are in suffering: nevertheless, God is able to see us through. " Who will also do it." What more do we want? Over against everything else—' He will also do it.' That is good news! After all, and in the final summing up, the good news is that it is not left with us. It is the Lord's matter. What is left to us is to believe God, to seek to understand His ways, to be steadfast, to hope unto the end, and then the Lord takes over. " Faithful is he that calleth you, who will also do it." *Good news !*

CHAPTER EIGHT

IN HIS LETTERS TO TIMOTHY

"... the gospel of the glory of the blessed God, which was committed to my trust" (I Tim. i. 11).
"Be not ashamed therefore of the testimony of our Lord, nor of me his prisoner : but suffer hardship with the gospel according to the power of God ..." (II Tim. i. 8).
"... our Saviour Jesus Christ ... abolished death, and brought life and incorruption to light through the gospel, whereunto I was appointed a herald, and an apostle, and a teacher" (II Tim. i. 10, R.V. mg.).
"Remember Jesus Christ, risen from the dead, of the seed of David, according to my gospel ..." (II Tim. ii. 8).

WE COME NOW to our closing thoughts on what Paul called "the gospel which I preach". "The gospel of the glory of the blessed God". We need, in the first place, just to note the correct translation of these words, because the different versions render them in different ways. The Authorised Version has: "the glorious gospel of the blessed God". You will note how different this is from the Revised Version from which I have quoted above. The latter—the Revised—is the correct rendering of the statement, and the point in getting it right is this. Paul is not speaking of what the gospel is about—the content of

104

the gospel. He is speaking of the gospel which has to do
with the manifestation of the glory of God. That may
sound a little technical, but it is very important. Let me
repeat: what Paul has in mind here is the gospel, or the
good tidings, which is concerned with the manifestation
of the glory of God. The glory of God in manifestation—
that is the gospel.

Note another thing: "the gospel of the glory of the
blessed God". There is a translation which changes that
word, and uses the word ' happy ' in the place of ' blessed ':
" the gospel of the glory of the happy God ". But that does
not sound quite right, does it, in our ears? And yet, if we
understood the real meaning, we should realise that that is
not an altogether inappropriate word.

There are two Greek words translated ' blessed ' in the
New Testament. One, which is much the more common,
literally just means ' well spoken of '. That is its literal
meaning, but in the New Testament it is almost exclusively
used in the sense of ' blessed ', and is so translated. That,
however, is not the word that is used here. The word used
here—the second of the two words to which I have referred—is one that occurs far less frequently. It is a word
which expresses that which properly speaking is true of
God alone: that is, the uniqueness of God as to what He
is in Himself, altogether apart from what men think of
Him or say about Him. It is just what He is in Himself.
You may think what you like, and say what you like, but
God is this. This is the word here translated ' blessed '.
The word really means that solemn, calm, restful, perpetual gladness that fills the heart of God. If you can get the
feeling of that definition, you have got somewhere near
understanding the meaning of the word here translated
' blessed '. It is the gospel of the glory of the calm, restful,

confident gladness of the heart of God ; the good news, the good tidings, of that.

THE GOOD TIDINGS OF THE GLORY OF GOD

What is this glory of God which becomes that gospel, that good news? It is the glory of God in the revelation of Himself in His Son Jesus Christ. The revelation of Himself. In the Old Testament the glory of God has symbolic form, as we know. For instance, in the Most Holy Place of the tabernacle, between the cherubim on the mercy seat, the glory was found. The glory covered the mercy seat. It was a light streaming down upon the mercy seat, upon the ark of the covenant ; streaming down and focusing there. It was heavenly radiance. It was but a symbol. That which it symbolized is here—the light of God streaming down upon, and through, His Son Jesus Christ. That is the glory of God. Paul in writing to the Corinthians puts it in this way : " the light of the knowledge of the glory of God in the face of Jesus Christ " (II Cor. iv. 6). It is that which is in the Lord Jesus of God's perfectly restful, calm, tranquil, abiding satisfaction.

THE GLORY OF GOD IN A MAN

Now, here is a very remarkable thing. You hear about the glory of God. Much is said about it, and you are told that that is what you will find in the Bible ; that, if you go to the Bible, there you will find much about the glory of God. When you take up the Bible looking for the glory of God, what do you find? *A Man !* You find that you are confronted with a Man. You cannot get away from that Man : the Old Testament is always pointing, by numerous means and methods and ways, to a Man ; the New Testament, from beginning to end, has one Man in view, a Man always in view. So that you have to say : ' This is the answer to my quest. I am in quest of the knowledge of the glory of God, and God's answer to the quest is a Man.' That is but an exposition of this little phrase, " the gospel of the glory of the blessed God ", which is the revelation of God in His Son, Jesus Christ.

God is here represented as being in a state of perfect tranquillity, restfulness, calm, abiding assurance and satisfaction and joy, and everything that can be summed up in the word ' blessedness '. God is represented as being, God is stated to be, in that condition. What is the basis of that state of God? It is just that God has found a perfect, a complete, expression of Himself in a Man. Yes, we know who that Man was. I am not overlooking or setting aside His Deity, His own Godhead, but I am not thinking about that just now. You see, God created man with very, very high purposes. Indeed, man was created in order to answer to and satisfy the heart of God : and when we say that, we are saying tremendous things. To satisfy the heart of *God !* There are some people who take a lot of satisfying. Indeed, they never do seem satisfied. Things are always falling short of their standard and their ideal. But you can go a long way, you can go as far as it is possible to go with any human conception of satisfaction, and you still fall far, far short, infinitely short, of God's idea. God is so much greater, so much more wonderful.

We have in the fallen creation but a faint reflection of how wonderful and great God is. Yet even when we view this very creation as it is, with all its faults and weaknesses and variations and so on, we have to stand in awe and worship. We can see just a faint indication of what a wonderful God He is, and of how much it must take to satisfy Him. Yet here He is in a state of absolute satisfaction, calm, tranquil, restful, happy, because all those thoughts of His, all those desires of His, all those intentions of His, and all those first undertakings of His, have now been consummated and perfected—not in the creation generally, but in a Man. That Man answers to God to the very last requirement of that infinite Mind. How great Christ is! God finds, therefore, His happiness, His blessedness, His satisfaction, His tranquillity, in that.

A REPRESENTATIVE MAN

Perhaps you may think, ' That is a beautiful thing to say, those are very wonderful thoughts to express, but where is the practical value of it?' Ah, that is just the gospel, you see. Do you think that the Lord Jesus, God's Son, came through and took the position of man, and was made perfect to God's utter and final satisfaction, just in order that God should have that in one Man? No, the gospel is this, that the Lord Jesus is representative of all the men that God is going to have. He is representative and He is inclusive. The old and beautiful beginning of the gospel, which you and I, after long familiarity with it, still often need, for our own tranquillity, to grasp more perfectly, is just this: that Jesus Christ, God's Son, is a sphere into which we are called, bidden, invited to enter by faith, so that we are hidden in Him as to what we are ourselves; God sees only Him and not us. A wonderful thing! You have got to put aside all your arguments and all your questions, and accept God's fact. That this phrase, " in Christ ", occurs two hundred times and more in the New Testament must surely mean something.

GOD SEES US IN CHRIST

The first, and perhaps the all-inclusive, thing that it means, is that, if you are in Christ, God sees Christ instead of seeing you. I have a little piece of paper here. Let that represent you or me in ourselves, what we are. I put it into a book, and that book represents Christ. You do not see the paper any more; you only see the book. That is our position " in Christ ". That is what Christ means. All His satisfaction to God is put to our account. That is the gospel: when you and I are in Christ, God is satisfied with us—tranquil, happy, blessed. Oh, wonderful gospel! You cannot grasp it, or explain it, but there is the fact stated. This is the gospel of the glory of the satisfied God.

Putting again the test that we were applying in other connections in an earlier chapter, it is just this: that, when you and I really come into Christ and find our place in Christ, one of the first things of which we are conscious is that all the strain has gone out ; we have come to rest. A marvellous tranquillity, that is not natural, has come into us. We feel the battle is all over between us and God. It is wonderful ; a blessed, happy condition. Now, that is our experience, but what is the significance of it? It is the Spirit of the happy God bearing witness to God's happiness in our hearts. " The gospel of the glory of the blessed God ". The first stage of that is a position. We are in Christ.

CHRIST IN US

The second stage or the second aspect of that is that Christ is in us. But we must not pursue that to the same conclusion as in the last point. That does not mean that we are seen and Christ is hidden. No, Christ is in us and we are in Christ: an impossible thing to explain, unless perhaps we can put it like this. Dr. Campbell Morgan was asked on one occasion whether baptism was sprinkling or immersion. He said : 'My dear friend, come with me to the Niagara Falls, and stand underneath. Are you sprinkled or are you immersed?' Well, I leave you to answer. But it is like that. Christ is in us. Why is He in us? He is in us as that very satisfaction to the heart of God, in order that the Spirit of God may work in us to conform us to Christ.

And that introduces another aspect of the Christian life : that, if you and I go on continually on the basis of Christ within, our joy increases. That can be put to the test. Stop going on with the Lord, and see what happens to our joy. Get away from the Lord, and see what happens to our blessedness. We shall begin to lament then—

> ' Where is the blessedness I knew
> When first I saw the Lord?
> Where is the soul-refreshing view
> Of Jesus and His Word?'

Ah, but God forbid that it should be necessary for any of us to sing that hymn. It is not necessary. Go on with the Lord Jesus on the basis of God's satisfaction with Him, and the blessedness increases. God's happiness enlarges in our heart. Christ is installed within as the pattern, standard, and basis upon which God works.

Now, here is something fundamental. Oh, how long we take to learn this! It is simple, I know, but it is fundamental, and it is a thing on which we are always tripping up. If we begin to try to go on on the ground of what we are, God stops. If we get on to our own ground, what we are in ourselves—our miserable, wretched self, that God regards as a corpse and a stinking corpse—forgive me for saying that—because it has been dead for two thousand years (that may sound amusing, but really it is exceedingly serious): if you get off the ground of "Christ in you" on to what you are in yourself, God says, 'I am going no further'. All Divine operations cease. We can only continue as we began. We began in faith that Jesus Christ was our substitute, took our place with God and answered to God for us. That was our faith that brought us into Christ. We have to go right on to the end with the same faith in the Lord Jesus, and no faith in ourselves, and God will go on if we go on on His ground. The good news is that God is ready to go right on with increasing blessedness if we will only keep on His ground. His glory is in His Son, and He has no glory in man apart from His Son.

So Christ is our sphere, Christ is our centre, and Christ is our model, and we are being conformed, says the Apostle, until Christ is fully formed in us. Simple, basic: God's glory in Christ being manifested in believers, in the Church, because believers are resting upon God's satisfaction with His Son. That and that only is the way of the glory of God and the expression of God's blessedness, God's happiness. That is the gospel.

You see, it all comes at last to focus upon this. What is the gospel? When you have said all that you can about it, it is included in, and compassed by, this—*God's perfect satisfaction, rest, tranquillity, concerning His Son, made available to us.* Oh, that you and I might live without conflict with God, because we abide in Christ! Brother, sister, when you begin to feel miserable about yourself, repudiate it. 'Yes, I know all about that. If I do not know all about that now, it is time that I did. I know all about what I am; I know where that will lead me if I begin to take that into account. I set that aside. It is a fact—God has done it—that, so long ago, in Christ I was crucified,

in Christ I died, in Christ I was buried, in Christ I have
been raised. It is all in Christ. That is where I stand.' Maintain that position ; abide in Christ. Get out of that on to
any other ground, and the glory departs, the blessedness,
the happiness, is arrested.

GOOD NEWS FOR YOUNG PEOPLE

Paul was speaking to Timothy about the gospel, and
Timothy needed good news, good tidings. To begin with,
Timothy was a young man. A young man who is a Christian has his own personal problems—he has many difficulties and problems in himself. A young man represents
the sum of a life at its beginnings: all the problems of
life are resident there. Timothy was a young man. To such
a young man, the Apostle says: ' It is all right, Timothy :
you may be beset by all these problems and these difficulties, you may be having all this trouble spiritually in these
different ways, but Jesus Christ is equal to the whole situation!' Do remember, young man, young woman, that the
Lord Jesus is God's answer to all the problems of youth.
That is good tidings, is it not?

Timothy was not only a young man, but he was a young
man in difficulties of a specific kind by reason of his position in Christian work. Difficulties were coming at him
from three directions. Firstly, there was the pagan world.
What a challenge that must have meant for a young man
in those days! It was a world that had no place for God,
no place for the Lord, no place for the things of God, and
all the opposing force of that world must have seemed
concentrated upon this young man. Secondly, there were
all the difficulties of the Jewish world. Paul hints at them
here. These Judaizers were pursuing Paul over the whole

world, with the determination: ' This man shall be brought to an end—this man's work shall be utterly wiped out!' By every means these Judaizers were set upon destroying Paul and his work and his converts, and Timothy was associated with Paul. Paul says: " Be not ashamed . . . of me ". Association created a good many difficulties for Timothy. The answer is: ' All right, Timothy ; there is good news for you! The Lord Jesus is equal to that—He will see you through it all '.

And then Timothy was a young man in great responsibility in the work of God—in the Church of God. If you know anything about that, you know that you need a fairly sure ground of confidence. He came up against some very difficult Christians. But Paul said: " Let no man despise thy youth." There were certain wiseacres—people who thought themselves to be something—who were inclined to say, 'Oh, Timothy is only a young fellow, you know—you must not take too much notice of him.' They were despising his youth. That is rather a difficult thing to endure. It takes the heart out of you if you happen to be in that position. I remember so well, when I commenced ministry and became responsible for a church, where most of the church officers were old men, one of them was heard to say, one day, ' He is so young, you know!' But I had a champion among them, and he said, ' Don't worry about that—he is getting over that every day!' Well, that is very kind and nice : but that sort of attitude among fellow-workers may well take the heart out of you, when you have to carry the responsibility. Timothy was in that position, but this is the gospel for Timothy: ' It is all right: the Lord Jesus is equal to that situation—He can see you through that too '.

After all, it is really just this. It is what the Lord

Jesus is " made unto us . . . from God " : God's satisfaction.
Oh, thank God that the Lord Jesus covers our faults and
weaknesses and defectiveness. I once read a story—I think
it was true—of a certain hotel on the Continent, where
people used to go and stay for rest and quiet and detachment. One day a mother arrived with her little girl, and
that little girl was just beginning to learn the piano. Every
morning, first thing, she went to the piano and strummed
and strummed, and all day long she strummed. Morning,
noon and night she strummed, until those people became
almost distracted, and they were counselling together as
to what they should do, when a famous pianist arrived to
stay at the hotel. He at once sensed the atmosphere, took
in the situation, and when the little girl went to the
piano, he went up alongside and sat down, and put his
hands over hers and guided them, and there began to come
forth the most beautiful music. The people came down
from their rooms into the room where the piano was, and
sat down and listened. When the recital was over, the
pianist said to the little girl, ' Thank you so much, dear ;
we have enjoyed it so much to-day '—and all the trouble
was over.

  Yes, the Lord Jesus just puts His hands over ours. We
might make a mess of things ; we do, if we are left to ourselves. We upset a lot, do a lot of harm ; we are so imperfect, so faulty : and then the Lord Jesus comes, in this
blessed way, and corrects our defectiveness, answers to the
Father for us, makes good our deficiencies—how? —with
Himself, just Himself.

  That is the answer ; that is the good news—" the gospel
of the glory of the blessed God ".

WHAT IS MAN?

T. AUSTIN-SPARKS

CONTENTS

PREFACE

To MY READERS I would say that, although the main subject of the tripartite nature of man is such a controversial one, this book is not entered as a part of the controversy. Such a course would only be to contradict its main contention—that Divine things can only be entered into by revelation and never by reason. Indeed, I have no wish that anyone should read this book unless they are really exercised about reality and spiritual things. I would ask for openness of heart as the one concession to the Spirit of truth if, peradventure, He might be ready to use what is written here for enlightenment.

No claim is made to any expert knowledge. The contents represent more the result of observation and experience amongst Christian people over a wide area during a good number of years, than of study of the subject itself.

The book goes out with a prayer which comes from long ago, " that the God of our Lord Jesus Christ, the Father of glory, may give unto you a spirit of wisdom and revelation in the knowledge of him; having the eyes of your heart enlightened " (Eph. i. 17).

T. A-S.

Bible references in this book are taken normally from the American Standard Version, but in some instances from the English Authorized or Revised Versions.

CHAPTER ONE

MAN'S HIGH PROSPECT AND DESTINY

" What is man ? " Psalm viii. 4 – 6. Hebrews ii. 5 – 8.

THAT NOCTURNAL MEDITATION and contempla-
tion of the Psalmist, which led him to ask this question
and to answer it by placing man at the centre of the universe, has bounded all the ages, gone back to the eternal
counsels of the Godhead before the world was, and
passed on to the consummation of those counsels in the
inhabited earth to come, and beyond it. It is a question
as to the Divinely conceived destiny of a specific creation called Man. Those thoughts had phases: "For a
little while lower than the angels"; crowned "with
glory and honour"; " to have dominion over the works
of thy hands ". The question of the Psalmist is taken up
and enlarged upon by an inspired Apostle . " Not unto
angels did he subject the inhabited earth to come ".
" Thou didst put all things in subjection under his
feet ".

But between the Divine conception and its ultimate
realization there is all the tragedy of human disruption,
and all the glory of Divine grace in redemption. What
is before us here is to say something of the nature of
that disruption as to man's own being, and therefore
to see what conformity to the image of God's Son
means as to the overcoming of that disrupted state. It
is the question of man's own person, and what kind of
person can alone inherit the kingdom of God.

For such a high and glorious destiny not only a spiritual or moral state is required, but a certain type or species
of being. As the crawling caterpillar or silkworm has
to spin its shroud and yield that form of life in order to
awaken in a new order, break through into a new world
as a beautiful moth or butterfly, so has man now to pass
out of one order and be constituted anew with faculties

9

and capacities for a higher. Man, according to God's mind, and according to a dim and intangible sense in himself, is of a universal character, with universal interests. But something has happened which, on the one hand, makes the realization of God's intentions impossible in man as he now is, and on the other hand, causes man to persist in a vain effort to achieve such realization. This terrible contradiction of things at the centre of the universe is the occasion of a new intervention on the part of God in the person of His Son. This intervention has several features. It shows what a man is according to God's mind ; it secures the removal of the man that is not so according to God ; it brings in the powers and constituents of a new creation ; and it reveals and secures what man will be when he reaches the mature form which was ever in God's mind as the end and not the mere creation state of even unfallen man. As we see it, this all hangs upon the setting right of derangement in the nature of man whereby his living and full relationship with God is renewed. This, in the main, relates to one part of his being called the *pneuma* or spirit, and it is here that we therefore need to have enlightenment.

AN ALL-IMPORTANT DISTINCTION

On two occasions in his writings the Apostle Paul used a phrase which is of peculiarly important application to the subject which is before us. It is found in his letters to the Romans (ii. 18) and the Philippians (i. 10), and the marginal rendering is,

" distinguish the things that differ ".

We cannot but feel that a very great deal of loss would have been prevented, and gain would have been secured, if that distinguishing had been applied to the matter of soul and spirit.

This is no matter of merely technical interest to Bible students, but one which involves and touches the spiritual life of God's people at almost every point, and governs the whole question of life and death in spiritual things. There are few things more vital to fulness of life and effectiveness of service than this. It embraces so very much of the meaning of the redemptive purpose of God in and by the Cross of Christ. Many of the most perplexing problems which have pressed upon the Lord's people and servants through the years have their solution here. We might just mention one or two of these.

Firstly, there is the essential and basic difference between the New Creation and the Old with which there is bound up that heart-breaking problem of totally or largely unsatisfactory conversions : converts who seem to have given evidence of the big change over, but who—all too early—reveal symptoms that the really radical, regenerative, work is doubtful. This includes that heart-burning enquiry concerning the large numbers who make a profession under all the peculiarly favourable (?) conditions and provisions of well organized and advertized evangelistic missions, and of whom so great a proportion either drop back soon after the mission is over, or are untraceable, or are only kept by a ceaseless provision of evangelistic hot air and high tension atmosphere. It is said of one city in Great Britain, that every second man you may meet has at some time been 'converted', although now, of course, the great majority have nothing to do with such things. This, surely, in turn raises other questions as to what may be God's ways and means in the realm of evangelistic activity, and what are men's.

Then there is the difficult problem of the very slow spiritual growth of those who really have received Christ. That spiritual maturity is a life-long matter is not doubted, but we are thinking of unduly delayed growth, with all the long-continued features of childhood or even of childishness. This is a matter deeply deplored by the writers of the New Testament letters, and, indeed, represents the main occasion of the mass of the New Testament itself. In the letter to the Thessalonians (the earliest of Paul's letters) the distinction

between soul and spirit is just stated without discussion
or explanation (I Thess. v. 23). The letters to the
Corinthians can be said to centre in the same matter,
when we remember that " natural" in chapter ii.
verse 14 is really " soulical ", and then that there is so
much about the " spiritual " and " the spirituals ", i.e.
spiritual gifts. In the letter to the Hebrews, again, the
whole subject matter is to be viewed in the light of
" dividing asunder of soul and spirit " and " the Father
of our spirits ". In every case it is a question of spiritual
progress or arrested progress.

There are many other questions, such as that of the
small degree of real and genuine spiritual value resultant from so great and so long-continued an output of
energy, devotion and resource. And what of that realm
of the prosperity and success of spurious and ultimately
harmful spiritual movements ? Then the whole question
of deception has to be seriously faced. The deception of
Christians so that they are either led completely astray,
or get into some state which renders them non-effectives
in the work of God and, often, a positive denial of the
very foundations of faith—this is, indeed, a branch of
things which cannot be ignored, neither can *every* such
case be wholly a matter for the medical expert.

To the above, many more spiritual difficulties could
be added, and some of them will be mentioned and
dealt with as we proceed. While each may have more
than one explanation because of peculiar governing
factors—and no one will think that we are claiming
to have found the cause and cure of all woes—we do
believe that the failure to discriminate in the matter of
soul and spirit accounts for more of these conditions
than has been recognized by the vast majority of the
Lord's people. Having indicated the importance of this
consideration, let us get nearer to the actual matter.

WHENCE THIS BLINDNESS ?

If all these—and many more—sorry conditions are
largely due to a failure to recognize a vital difference,

we must ask why it is that the failure has been so general. Of course, when we are seeking to trace spiritual deflection we shall always reach back at once to its source. As the one who has ever desired to spoil God's work and to frustrate God's purpose, Satan would find very great gain in hiding *this*, and in keeping God's people in ignorance as to so important a truth. This he has certainly done ; hence the prayer of Paul : " having the eyes of your *heart* enlightened". But Satan has ways and means, and we must recognize these in order to be delivered from the evil one as well as from the evil. So we begin at the end.

THE GENERALLY ACCEPTED POSITION

As to the being of man, the well-nigh universal position is that he is mind and matter, soul and body. Even in those directions where Christians would accept the Bible phraseology—" spirit, soul, and body "—either an inability to recognize the tremendous issues bound up with this *threefold* designation, or a fatal carelessness, results in a going on as though the differences were not there. But there are other and more positive factors to be taken into account.

The teachers of God's people have failed ! Why have they failed ? Primarily because they have not taken God's Word and definitely sought the enlightenment and teaching of the Holy Spirit *direct*. Or may it be that the *indwelling* of the Holy Spirit as Teacher has not been a reality in so many cases ?

There may be a third explanation. Is it because of fear of appearing unusual, singular, peculiar in running counter to so widely an accepted position ? This leads us to ask : Whence this position ? Is it of heaven or of men ? Note the scriptural alternatives.

There are two quarters responsible for the present position and acceptance. Consciously or unconsciously, certain pagan philosophers or ' Christian Fathers ' have influenced the whole course of interpretation in this matter. So far as psychologists go, their basic conclusions

are pagan. The two who laid these foundations were
Plato and Aristotle. We are not stating the teaching of
these, and while we recognize that Aristotle could more
easily be reconciled with the Biblical position (although
still with considerable manœuvring) yet we want to
point out with emphasis that neither of these had a Bible
in hand, nor did they know anything of a basic experience by which, through the Holy Spirit, the inner man
is renewed and enlightened. Theirs was only the light of
natural reason, the wisdom of this world, and only suitable for a realm of its own kind.

Then as to the ' Christian Fathers ', Augustine and
others. They, in turn, flirted with the teaching of the
said pagan philosophers, and came under their influence.
If we could accept the infallibility of these ' Fathers ' on
some other more obvious matters, we might modify our
attitude as to their position on this so much less patent
issue ; but we cannot ! The ' Fathers ' of the Church
would have acted wisely if they had kept clear of the
entangling alliance with Platonism, which seemed to
offer at first such advantages.

Now, the position is, that to be a teacher of God's
people demands some understanding of man, especially
of what he is and what his purpose is. For such a knowledge, either in the schools or in private study, the works
of psychologists have been taken up. All of these are
built up on the aforesaid pagan foundation. Of course,
things have travelled a long way since Plato's days, and
there is a whole world of research and experimentation
extra to those pioneers ; but—again—the basic formula
is unchanged ; man is said to be dual—mind and matter,
soul and body. It may be that in some Bible institutes
the more Biblical interpretation is taught, but how necessary it is that it should come as a revelation and not
merely as a subject. It seems to us a crying shame that
this matter has not been recognized as to its tremendous
and far-reaching consequences. It is difficult to attend a
convention of the most spiritual order, or find some
special effort for God, without perceiving the governing
influence—all unconscious—of the psychology which

is not of the Word of God. What tremendous things would happen—though perhaps unseen (much safer so) —if influences were spiritual rather than soulical !

But what a change in the standard of values is necessary to let go the seen for the unseen, the present for the eternal, the earthly for the heavenly and the 'successful' for the real!

THE POSITION AS IN THE WORD OF GOD,
A COMPARISON

The phrase "the hidden man" is but one expression used in connection with this subject. But let it be seen at once to discriminate between the 'inner' and the 'outward' man in a different sense from what is meant apart from the Scriptures. It is not the discrimination of the psychologists or philosophers as such, whether they be ancient or modern, pagan or Christian. For them the 'inward man' is the soul, and the 'outward man' the body. Not so in the Word of God. There the "inward" or "hidden" man is the spirit, and the "outward" man the soul or body, either or both. These two terms or designations are respectively synonymous with "spiritual man" and "natural man", and these two are capable of being divided asunder by the sword of the Spirit—the Word of God. It is as dangerous to make one what God calls two as it is to put asunder what God makes one. The only oneness of the three—spirit, soul, and body—is that they compose or comprise one man. The literal translation of I Thess. v. 23 is, "your whole person", or "your whole man", or "the whole of you, spirit, soul, and body"; and three distinct words in the Greek are used, as elsewhere. The Spirit of God does not use words at random, just for variety's sake. Basic spiritual principles are involved in words used by God. The very word 'natural', as applied to man, as we know, is the Greek word *psukikos,* the Anglicised form of which is psychical. 'Spiritual' is the adjective of 'spirit', and 'soulish' or 'soulical' the adjective of 'soul'. In James iii. 15, "sensual" is used, but "soulical" is more accurate, and it is interesting and significant to note in passing, that in that Scripture there are two descriptions of *wisdom.*

MAN UNIQUE IN CREATION

That which makes man unique in the whole realm of creation is not that he is or has a soul, but that he has a spirit and a soul ; and it may be that the union in one person of soul and spirit makes him unique beyond this creation in the whole universe.   God is spirit. Angels are spirits.   There are many passages in the Scriptures which indicate the difference between the inner ' I ' of the spirit and the outer ' I ' of the soul. For instance, Paul says : "My spirit prayeth, but my understanding is unfruitful" (I Cor. xiv. 14). Then, in I Cor. ii. 14, he says that "the natural (soulical) man receiveth not the things of the Spirit of God . . . and he cannot know them because they are spiritually discerned ", or, "are discerned by the spiritual (or spirit ones)".

This distinction is very marked in Paul's recounting of the reception of his special revelation :

"I will come to . . . revelations of the Lord. I (the outward man) *knew a man in Christ* (the inner man) *above fourteen years ago, (whether in the body, I* [the outer man] *cannot tell . . . God knoweth;) such an one* (the inner man) *caught up to the third heaven. And I* (the outer man) *knew such a man* (the inner man) *(whether in the body or out of the body, I* [the outer man] *cannot tell: God knoweth ;) how that he* (the inner man) *was caught up into paradise, and heard unspeakable words which it is not lawful for a man* (the outer man) *to utter. Of such an one* (the inner man) *will I* (the outer man) *glory: yet of myself I* (the outer man) *will not glory" (2 Cor. xii. 1 — 5).*

Here, in passing, we note that, unless the Lord gives

B

the gift of utterance, the things revealed to the spirit cannot be expressed by the outer man. In another place the Apostle asked for the prayers of the Lord's people that he might have "utterance" to speak the mystery.

Many other instances might be given, such as "I delight in the law of God after the *inward man*", and Romans vii. as a whole.

Then we draw attention to the following: "*I rejoice at the coming of Stephanas and Fortunatus and Achaicus . . . for they refreshed my spirit*" (I Cor. xvi. 17 — 18). "*The Spirit himself beareth witness with our spirit*" (Romans viii. 16). "*To deliver such a one unto Satan for the destruction of the flesh, that the spirit may be saved in the day of Jesus Christ*" (I Cor. v. 5). "*. . . that she may be holy both in body and in spirit*" (I Cor. vii. 34), etc.

In the New Testament there are very many occurrences of both "soul" and "spirit", and inasmuch as our present and first purpose is to distinguish between these, or to note that they are distinguished by the Word of God, we must define a general rule by which they are divided.

This general division can be marked in this way; the soul (often translated "life") relates to man in his own conscious life here in this world; his good or evil; his power to do, to achieve, to enjoy, to profit, to know and acquire what is of this world, and to live as a responsible, self-conscious being, answering to God for himself and his life, and so taking account of his life as to include the reality of a Divinely intended higher destiny and intention than just to live to himself and for 'the brief span of this life. The soul can be affected by and responsive to something higher, but its *immediate* relationship is not with God. Such relationship is indirect and secondary.

The spirit is that by which—*given the necessary "renewing"*—man is *directly* related to things Divine. He is thereby constituted to be capable of relationship with spiritual beings and spiritual things. This is a broad and general rule, and if some passages seem to contradict it, the difficulty will usually disappear if we remember the proviso that, on the one hand, God holds man responsible as an intelligent, self-conscious being who can at least choose and seek ; and, on the other hand, when the spirit has been renewed and brought into living touch with God, the soul is affected thereby, and both receives from God and gives to God by way of the spirit. All this will be dealt with much more fully as we go on.

A passage from Paul's letter to the Corinthians might well and aptly be cited here :

"Things which eye saw not. and ear heard not, and which entered not into the heart of man, whatsoever things God prepared for them that love him. But unto us God revealed them through the Spirit: for the Spirit searcheth all things, yea, the deep things of God. For who among men knoweth the things of a man, save THE SPIRIT OF THE MAN. WHICH IS IN HIM ? even so the things of God none knoweth, save the Spirit of God. But we received . . . the spirit which is from God ; that we might know the things . . . of God" (I Cor. ii. 9 — 12).

Each kingdom is governed by and limited to its own nature. A beast and a man cannot go far in mutual intercourse. What is a Handel oratorio to a dog?

So far we have but been paving the way for our real business, and now we must come immediately to grips with it. But may we repeat, before commencing a new chapter, that ours is no academic or technical undertaking. For this we have neither ability nor inclination. We are burdened with a great desire to see a real change in the spiritual condition which exists to-day, and our object is wholly spiritual, and for God's pleasure and satisfaction in His people.

CHAPTER TWO

MAN NOW ANOTHER SPECIES THAN GOD CREATED

THE ABOVE HEADING may be a little startling, but it will be as well for us at an early stage to realize that we are dealing with a matter of the most serious character. It is not merely that at some point man had a lapse, took a wrong turning, or became a delinquent, an offender. Neither is it only that he became a sinner, or even a sinful creature. All of these may be true, but they are not the *whole* truth. Man is not just on the wrong road and needing to be re-directed or put on to the right one. Neither is man just the victim of an evil mood, or a fugitive from law running free, sowing wild oats, and estranged from his better self. The restoration of man to God and to his Divinely purposed vocation and destiny is not merely the transference of his interests and energies from one direction—self, sin, the world—to another—God, good and heaven. When Christ, in speaking of the prodigal, used the words, "When he came to himself", He did not mean just that he recollected and reverted to another course. There is overwhelming evidence in Scripture that salvation is something infinitely more radical than all this.

It is here that there lies the fatal flaw in so much evangelical effort, and even in convention ministry. Surrender, consecration, yielding, and such-like words or terms, are used as though they meant far more than just a first, initial step which only represents an attitude taken. *God does not want, and the Bible does not teach, that the " old man " should be consecrated to Him.* The " old man " has to be crucified, not consecrated! So often the young are exhorted to consecrate to the Lord their talents, their energies, their abilities, their enthusiasm, as

19

' Young, strong, and free ;
To be the best that I can be,
For God, for righteousness, and Thee . . . '

But in the long run they discover a fatal lack, an inade-
quacy and a breakdown, the greatest proof of which is
the convention movement itself. This movement is ever
growing, and year by year, in all parts of the world,
hundreds of thousands of disappointed *Christians* are
found together with a view to finding the solution to
the problem of non-victorious life, or non-effective service. Those of us who have anything to do with convention or conference work cannot smile upon these
great audiences and speak about them as though they
represented a great success instead of declaring the
greatest and most heart-breaking of tragedies. If the
messages given are to be taken as the indication as to
what conventions are for, then there is no questioning
what we have just said.*

But this is the negative side of the question, and we
must come to the positive. It is not a change of sides,
or interests, or direction, nor a reviving of energy and
zeal that is called for. Nothing less than a constitutional change in the being will answer the questions and
meet the need. To carry over *natural* abilities (inherited
or acquired) or energies to the things of God, and to
make them the basis or means of doing His work, is
most certainly and inevitably to put the worker and
the work into a false position, with sooner or later any
one or more of the many possible seriously compromising and disastrous results.

Before we can move back to the beginning and see
what had happened as to man, there is one thing to bear
in mind. It is always important that matters of Divine
truth should never be taken up just in themselves, as
isolated subjects, but that their full range and relatedness should be recognized. Truth is a whole. There is
no plural in Scripture as to truth, that is ' truths ', but

* Of course, we recognize another side of Christian conventions, that
of happy fellowship. But we are referring to the original and still
advertized object of such conventions.

there are aspects of *the* truth, and no one of these can stand alone. It is essential to observe the beginning, occasion and ultimate issue of every phase of the truth.

Then it must be definitely remembered that truth in the Scriptures is progressive. In the early parts, matters are not stated in completeness and preciseness, but there is much in the nature of inference. Only as we get well on toward the end do we get more complete statements, in the light of which all that has gone before has to be considered. For instance, take the doctrine of the Divine Trinity. It is not really until Christ's time that we have this definitely and fully revealed, as in John's Gospel (Chapters xiv — xvi); and not until the advent of the Holy Spirit was this known experimentally. So it is with the matter before us. Man's nature or being as spirit, soul and body, is not definitely stated thus until we are well on in the New Testament. But there are plenty of inferences as well as frequent fragmentary statements to this effect much earlier. The explanation of this delay is a very part of our whole subject, for it means that not until the era of the Holy Spirit as an indwelling reality—with all that that implies—is it possible for man to *know* the things of God in any adequate or vital way. Hence the futility of making the Bible a text-book or manual of subjects to be studied as such. So now, with all the fuller revelation of the New Testament before us, we can work back to the beginning.

MAN AS CREATED AND CONSTITUTED

When we really see with enlightened eyes *the Man,* Christ Jesus, and when we see what a child of God really is as in the New Testament, then we see two things; one, what God's man is as from the beginning, and what a fundamental change is represented by a man being truly born anew.

As to his constituting, we shall see that he was, and is, spirit, soul and body. But to say this is only one half of the matter. That is the fact as to man's components. The other half is that that represents *order and function.*

It was in the upsetting of this order that function was affected fatally, and man became other than God intended him to be.

We have already said, in a word, what the function of the human spirit is, but more is needed.

THE FUNCTION OF THE HUMAN SPIRIT

The all-governing fact is that " God is spirit " (John iv. 24). Then certain things follow. " We are his offspring " (Acts xvii. 28 – 29). He is " the Father of our spirits " (Hebrews xii. 9).

If it is a fixed law that " That which is born of the flesh is flesh, and that which is born of the Spirit is spirit " (John iii. 6), then it is only in his spirit that man is the offspring of God. Fatherhood presupposes offspring ; and there is no fatherhood without offspring. God is spirit. God is also Father. The fixed law of progeny demands a spirit ancestry for spiritual offspring. But as Father — differing from Creator — God is the Father of our spirits *only*.

God is not soul. This we shall see more fully when we deal with soul-function. Therefore, God is not the Father of our souls. God is not body ; therefore our bodies were not begotten of God, but created. The Word of God is clear and emphatic that only spirit can know spirit (I Cor. ii. 9 – 11). That is why the disciples of Christ really did not know Him, in a living and true way, until something had happened in them, and the Holy Spirit had joined Himself with their spirits. It is ever so.

Only spirit can worship spirit (John iv. 23 – 24 ; Phil. iii. 3). In this former Scripture, the words " true " and " truth " are very discriminating words. If the soul is — as the psychologists truly teach — the realm of the reason, will, and emotions, then surely the worship of Jews and Samaritans was not devoid of these. Would it be quite right to say that it was so mechanical and meaningless as to have not even an animal's feeling or sense in it ? But granted all the feeling, reason and will possible, it would still be other than what Christ meant by " true ", for soul is soul and spirit is spirit yet! Only spirit can serve spirit (Rom. 'i. 9 ; vii. 6 ; xii. 11). Only spirit can receive revelation from God, Who is spirit (Rev. i. 10 ; I Cor. ii. 10). We shall return to this later. Let it be understood that God determined to have all His dealings with man, and to fulfil all His purpose through man, by means of that in man which was after His own likeness, that is, his spirit. But this spirit of man for all such Divine intentions must be kept in living union with Himself, and never for one moment infringe the laws of its Divine union by crossing over to take counsel with, or be influenced by, his own soul or self-conscious life — the reason, desire or will—as an independent thing.

This goes to the heart of our Lord's temptations, as it does to the temptation of Adam. When this happened in Adam's case, death entered; and the nature of death, in the scriptural meaning of the word, is severance in the union of the spirit with God. This does not mean that man no longer had a spirit, but that the ascendency of the spirit was surrendered to the soul. (This is borne out by all the New Testament teaching on the spiritual man, with I Cor. ii. 11 – 16 as an example.)

THE NATURE OF ADAM'S TEMPTATION

Let us briefly state what was at the heart of the temptation. By his union with God in spirit, man was conditioned to have everything in relation to and by dependence upon God. His knowledge and his power were to be essentially spiritual, and the absolute lordship and headship of his life was to remain vested in God. A *spiritual* relationship and a *spirit* organ and function made this possible.

The temptation was to have everything in *himself*. This, it was suggested, was possible, and he could be a self-directing, self-possessing, self-sufficient, independent being. To gain this end, it would be futile to appeal to the spirit in man, for this would only mean that the matter would be referred to God. So the *self-conscious* organ must be approached. Thus reason, desire and will — the faculties of the soul — were assailed. Instead of allowing his spirit to bring God in, man acted independently, with several of the most terrible results of which it is possible to conceive.

Firstly, God was set aside in His absolute headship and lordship as to man, and Satan was given His place, as one more to be hearkened to. This was what Satan wanted above all things, i.e. to be "the god of this world".

Then the spirit of man, being so seriously violated, ceased to be the link between himself and God. Fellowship with God, which is always spiritual, was destroyed, and the spirit sank down into subjection to man's soul. So far as that man is concerned, he died to God. "Dead, through . . . trespasses and sins" (Eph. ii.1). So the soul came to dominate the spirit.

Then again—as though this were not bad enough— by an act of spiritual fornication, that bridal spirit which was to be wedded to God was used by man to let in Satanic elements, which are extra to the soul but are— since the Fall — so much a part of it that God looks upon them as one in the unregenerate man. This is what is meant by the terms "fleshly" and "carnal" in the New Testament. Thus we can see that man has become an altogether other type or species than God intended. The main difference is that he is now a soul-man rather than a spirit-man pre-eminently.

It does not require much intelligence to see how utterly this creation is now a soul order. The whole system of running this world is psychological. Everything is based upon desire, emotion, feeling, reason, argument, will, choice, determination. What a large place is held by the various forms of soul activity! In one direction we have fear, grief, pity, curiosity, pride, pleasure, admiration, shame, surprise, love, regret, remorse, excitement, etc.; in another direction, imagination, apprehensiveness, fancy, doubt, introspection, superstition, analysis, reasonings, investigations, etc.; in a third direction, desires for possession, knowledge, power, influence, position, praise, society, liberty, etc.; and, in still another direction, determination, reliance, courage, independence, endurance, impulse, caprice, indecision, obstinacy, etc. We are not saying that this is all wrong, but by these things, which are all forms of soul-life, we can see that we live in a world that is almost entirely a soul-world. But we are not stopping there. Think how much of this has a place in Christian life and service—from the first step in relation to the gospel, through all the course of Christian activity. It is here that we ask for patience in pursuing the subject, when we make the tremendous affirmation that all this —the sum-total of human reasoning, feeling and willing—may be placed to the account of the matter of salvation, either for ourselves or for others, and yet be *utterly unprofitable,* and of *no account* at all.

Multitudes have come to regard themselves, and to be regarded by others, as Christians because of some decision made or step taken under the impact of an argument—a reasoning, an appeal to mind or emotion. In the same way great missionary meetings, with their atmosphere, their stories and their appeals, have led many to believe that they had a call from God to His service. But time has proved, in a great many cases, that this was *not* born of the spirit, but of the soul-force of man. We do not say that God never comes through, or uses His word, at such times, but we have to explain tragic facts and to correct popular fallacies.

The soul of man is a complex and dangerous thing, and is capable of extraordinary things. It can entirely mislead us and play us many tricks, as we shall see. Man is now a disrupted and disordered creature, and we must remember that the creation, including man, because of this disruption has been deliberately subjected to vanity. That is, it has been rendered incapable of realizing its originally intended destiny, or coming to full fruitage. For the unregenerate man, life is indeed a mockery, for *he* can never reach his intended objective. This is God's answer to his assaying to have all in himself in independence (Rom. viii. 19—23).

There are certain questions which will arise from what we have been saying. One will have to do with the point in his probation at which Adam fel!. Another will be concerning the creation formula. A third will be as to the right place of the soul. A fourth arises in connection with more modern psychology. Let us consider these.

ADAM'S PROBATION

It is important to realize that although Adam, when created, was sinless and innocent, he was not perfect, as God intended he should be. There was something to be added if he was to attain to all that God meant, in his nature and destiny. The link with God through his human spirit carried with it a potentiality or a possibility, not an absolute and final one-ness. Hence, he had to obey God along the line of commands and orders—more in the position of a servant than a son ; or let us use the New Testament distinction between " child " and " son ", and express the difference as between one born, and one come to maturity. That which would *in Adam's case* have made the great advance upon this position, from childhood to sonship, from the outward to the inward government, from the incomplete to the complete, was eternal life through obedience of faith.

So that at that point the whole significance of the tree of life has its place. That tree was a type of God manifested in Christ as the life whereby alone man reaches his intended destiny, even the sharing of Divine life and nature. Adam, because of unbelief and disobedience, did not attain unto eternal life ; therefore, that life is reserved for such as believe on the Lord Jesus Christ, and are thus in Christ and also have Christ in them. " Christ in you, the hope of glory " (Col. i. 27). In eternal life is found all God's secret of all His eternal purpose in and through man.

Then it must be kept in mind that eternal life is a gift. The special object for saying that here is to counter another error. There are two interpretations of new birth, one the true, and the other the beautiful lie which subverts the truth. This latter interpretation is that spiritual life is a kind of renaissance, an inner quickening brought about by the play of mystical forces which hover round the soul, rousing it from torpor as the spring sun wakens the sleeping seed, stirring already existent but dormant energies into activity—a lifting up of what we already possess to a higher plane, or tide, and a consequent flooding of hitherto unvisited, unvitalized areas, whose inhibited forces and functions it straightway releases and relates to consciousness within and to service without. The other, and true, interpretation is that new birth is the reception of an entirely new and different life, required to be generated from above by a specific act of Divine impregnation—a quite new and original endowment which has never before been in our human life, and which remains an altogether other life that is not in us by nature, but a unique and miraculous generation—as Christ is.

As every error has some element of truth in it, which is like its claw for catching hold, so this one, which we have mentioned, has its catch in a failure to discriminate between three things ; one, the soul ; two, the spirit ; three, eternal life. Eternal life raises the spirit from death, and energizes the soul. But neither soul nor spirit is of any avail Godward—so far as man's Divinely intended destiny is concerned—apart from the ' altogether other ' eternal life. This life is God Himself, in Christ, by the Holy Spirit. The Holy Spirit is " the Spirit of life " (Rom. viii. 2), and Divine life, even when given to indwell the believer, is still retained in the Divine Person . " God gave unto us eternal life, and this life is in his Son " (I John v. 11). The presence of the Divine Person in the believer or in the Church is expressed by life. Lest Adam should act with the same object of having life in *himself* as out of relation to God, the tree of life was deliberately protected from him and he was driven forth. The symbolism is clear. This is something which is so other than man—so Divine—and it can only be had in God and by spirit-union with Him.

All this will gather into itself much New Testament truth concerning Christ's representative life, temptation, death and resurrection, and also concerning the nature of new birth and the life of the believer.

It will have been observed that innocence in Adam was but a negative thing. This can also be true, therefore, of sinlessness in *his* case. It may, in one sense, throw some light on the life-long testing of Christ, although we say this with some reservations, which we will not make a divergence now to explain.

Holiness is positive, and Adam's innocence was accompanied by a capacity for holiness. Holiness is the result of faithfulness under testing, in man's case. He may go into testing innocent, but the very essence of testing is a capacity to choose between two courses, his own and God's.

Faith, obedience, loyalty to God, resisting evil by resort to God, issue in a positive state which is something more than innocence, i.e. more than the fact of not yet having sinned in a specified way. The faculty which governs and regulates in this is the spirit. Hence the issue is either *spiritual* holiness, or *spiritual* wickedness. They both represent a relationship respectively to God the *Holy* Spirit, or to Satan and *evil* spirits. Hence we see what the issue of Adam's probation and failure is.

THE CREATION FORMULA   (GENESIS II. 7)

In taking up the statement as to man's constitution in Gen. ii. 7, we would recall you to what has been said about the progressiveness of revelation. For here we have a precise instance of things being but in germ form in the first reference, needing the reflex of the later and fuller light. We would not say that this passage is a positive assertion, but more an implication. Later Scriptures bear out the implication. It will be noticed that we are not dealing with the account of man in Gen. i. 26, which rather describes God's intention for him than what actually is the case; that is, his place and office more than his being. Here is Gen. ii. 7 :

"*And the Lord God formed man of the dust of the ground, and breathed into his nostrils the breath of lives ;* and man became a living soul*".

On the face of it, the statement appears to contradict all that we are saying, and to support the contention that man is dual or bipartite.

If we pass over to Paul's exact quotation of this passage in I Cor. xv. 45, we find that it is used to describe a difference between the first Adam and the last Adam. The former was made "a living soul", the latter "a life-giving spirit". This will help us. But first let us note the synthesis. There are three things:

(1) The material elements: "the dust of the ground".

(2) The formative factor: "the breath of lives".

(3) The final issue: "man became a living soul".

We need not discuss the first; most people will accept the material side of man's being. 'Adam', from *adamah,* means 'of the earth'. (It also includes a colour element: *red* earth.)

The second point brings us immediately to our present object. Here we have two sides or aspects.

(*a*) "The Lord God"—the One Who effects.
(*b*) "The breath of lives"—the means He uses.

Creation and emanation are not to be confused. When the animal part of man is in view there is nothing said which would support the idea that there is a oneness of nature between the created and the Creator. But when we are considering that part of man's being in which he is the image and likeness of God, we have a higher nature, and this is communicated, not created;

* The word here is in the plural. We do not propose to enter upon a discussion or enquiry as to the meaning of this and so add considerably to detail, but merely point this out for the present.

the method is different. The spirit of man is not an act
of creation, but rather in the nature of procreation. This
breath of lives is not man's soul, but his spirit. We
shall see later that this is not merely the abstract animating element which marks the difference between man as
a living organism and inanimate matter, but something
which, being out from God, is an organ, or faculty,
as well as a function. From the general teaching of
Scripture we conclude that it was the Holy Spirit, the
Spirit of life, who breathed into man, and by this breathing not only made him animate, i.e. put the body-soul,
physio-psychical life, into him, but formed the link
with God, for ultimate Divine purposes.

In Zech. xii. 1, we have the phrase "... the Lord ...
formeth the spirit of man within him". The word
"formeth" is the Hebrew word *yatsar*, which means
'to mould into form'. God formed man's body out of
the dust of the ground. He also formed man's spirit
within him. (There must have been a 'him' there
first.) Along with this must go the words of Heb. xii. 9,
"The Father of our spirits". It is here that we are the
offspring of God.

We must remember that the *pneuma*, or spirit, is
vested with the powers of a definite and independent
entity. Look at the following instances.

"Jesus perceiving in his spirit".	Mark ii. 8.
"He sighed deeply in his spirit".	Mark viii. 12.
"My spirit hath rejoiced".	Luke i. 47.
"Jesus rejoiced in spirit".	Luke x. 21.
"... worship the Father in spirit".	John iv. 23.
"He groaned in the spirit".	John xi. 33.
"Troubled in the spirit".	John xiii. 21.
"Paul was pressed in the spirit".	Acts xviii. 5.
"Whom I serve in my spirit".	Rom. i. 9.
"Serve in newness of the spirit".	Rom. vii. 6.
"The spirit of the man which is in him".	I Cor. ii. 11.
"Absent in body, present in spirit".	I Cor. v. 3.

"That the spirit may be saved in the
    day of the Lord Jesus ".   *I Cor. v. 5.*
" My spirit prayeth, but my under-
    standing is unfruitful ".   *I Cor. xiv. 14.*
" I will pray with the spirit ".   *I Cor. xiv. 15.*
" The spirits of the prophets are sub-
    ject to the prophets ".   *I Cor. xiv. 32.*
" Spirits of just men made perfect ". *Heb. xii. 23.*

There are those who contend that spirit, or *pneuma*, is just the life of the soul and body, the animating factor. We are aware that ' breath ', ' wind ', etc., are sometimes used of the same original word as ' spirit ', but so they are of ' soul '. The usage in that case is because of the *invisible* power and action which is represented. No one will substitute ' wind ' or ' breath ' for any of the above usages of ' spirit ' ; it would at once be meaningless and absurd.

The relationship between soul and body is one which is well beyond our power to explain. The Bible makes many definite statements on the matter, but never explains it. For instance, soul and life are often interchangeable terms, and these are repeatedly said to be in the blood. " The life is in the blood . . . The blood . . . is . . . the life thereof " (Lev. xvii. 11, 14). Science has not helped us at all to understand this, but, of course, the fact is irrefutable. One thing is established—that while life properties and qualities are in the blood, after a given time they cease to be there, although the blood may still be retained. But, when we come to the matter of soul and spirit, not only are two so distinctly different words used, but these are said to be separable without either perishing, and each is vested with its own responsibility, set of faculties and destiny.

At least by inference, as the marrow is deeper than the joints, the spirit is more inward than the soul (Heb. iv. 12). As it is easier to reach the bone through the body, or flesh, so it is easier to reach the soul through the body than it is to reach the spirit through the soul. Much soul-piercing and -cleaving has to be done before the spirit is really reached and dealt with. In other words, the physical senses are an easy way to the soul, but it requires the mighty energy of the Spirit of God to reach the spirit. But note, the difference between soul and spirit is only made manifest when the Word of God is driven in by the Holy Spirit's energy and might.

But, to touch definitely on point three—" man became a living soul ". First, the animal being out of the dust; then the spiritual life by the breath of God; and then the soul is mentioned. What did man become? " A living soul ". Was that *all*? If that were all, then what of the body? But this " living soul " has a body. Is that all? No! This living soul with a body has a spirit. This phrase, " living soul ", well sets forth the nature of man's soul as in that first order as midway between matter and spirit; " lower than the angels " (pure spirits), higher than the brute. The quotation in I Cor. xv. 45 we said would help us. It does, in two ways. " The first man Adam became a living soul ". The original of the last four words is *egeneto EIS psuchen zōsan*. The *eis* is interesting; it is local, and implies that the soul is the meeting place of two opposite natures, the body and the spirit. The added clauses in Paul's statement make it clear, or strengthen the conclusion, that in the first Adam the soul is the terminus of body and spirit. The statement helps us in a second way by showing that in the last Adam the spirit is the terminus, or governing factor. Thus the soul is the nexus between the higher and the lower natures, not merely the difference between physical and metaphysical; it is the *ego*.

Nothing that is said in this book is intended to infer that soul, as such, is a wrong thing, i.e. that it is wrong for man to have a soul, and that therefore it has to be destroyed. What we are saying is that the soul of man has become poisoned with a self-directive interest, and has become allied with the powers which are opposed to God. This is not known, nor imagined, to be so until a real awakening has taken place in the spirit. It is therefore wrong to live wholly or pre-eminently on the soul side of our being—now. The truly spiritual people will find their chief enemy in their own souls, and God finds His chief enemy in the soul of man. When the *spirit* is renewed, and Christ dwells and reigns within—in other words, when we are " filled with the Spirit "—then the soul can come to serve the Lord as a handmaiden of the spirit to real but governed usefulness.

So man awoke—so to speak—" a living soul ". He came to a threefold consciousness ; a world-, or sense-consciousness through his psycho-physical body ; a self-consciousness in his soul ; and a God-consciousness by his—what? Does man arrive at the knowledge of God as a Person, a living Person, by his reason, feeling and volition? The Word of God denies this, and, in the matter of living union with God as an experience, man's history denies it. " Canst thou by searching find out God? " (Job xi. 7). Philosophy gives a positive answer, inasmuch as it is the most deadly thing to faith ; and philosophy is an intense activity of the *soul*, mainly on its reasoning side. Multitudes have been lost to a true and vital Christian experience through taking up philosophy as a subject. When God had breathed into the already fashioned man, something more than body and soul was there, and it was this that determined everything in relation to God's purpose through man. The soul was the meeting place of body and spirit. Let the soul surrender to the body and all is lost. Let it surrender to the spirit and all is well.

To sum up. Man became a living soul, having a body and a spirit. By asserting *himself*—the *ego*—in favour of the body and not of the spirit, he became a sinful soul. It is what he *is*, not just what is in him.

He has got to be saved from himself. This is accomplished in two ways. Christ's death in its representative nature is a potent thing to be entered into by the " natural " man, so that, by a crisis and a process, the power of Christ's death is wrought and established in the soul-consciousness of man. He becomes aware that he is forbidden to live and move on the basis of the self-, *ego-*, life. On the other hand, the resurrection of Christ is also a mighty power in man's spirit, and by its introduction by the Holy Spirit into man's inner being, he is made a *spiritual* man, as over against a merely natural. His position henceforth is most perfectly stated by the Apostle Paul thus :

" I (the natural man) *have been crucified with Christ ; and it is no longer I that live, but Christ liveth in me: and that (life) which I now live in the flesh I live in faith, (the faith) which is in the Son of God, who loved me and gave himself up for* (in place of) *me " (Gal. ii. 20).*

This is what Christ meant when in the undeveloped truth He said: *" If any man would come after me, let him deny himself, and take up his cross daily, and follow me " (Luke ix. 23).*

Before taking the third of the questions mentioned earlier it may be more helpful to take a fourth.

CHAPTER THREE

WHERE PSYCHOLOGY FAILS

MANY WHO READ THIS will be familiar with the position of psychology, and it is just here that we find that point which makes all the difference between the natural, which keeps God out, and the spiritual, which gives Him His full place. For here we find that the scriptural description of man runs entirely counter to the conclusions of 'scientific' psychology. We have observed that the psychologist will not allow the three-fold description of man as spirit, soul and body, but only soul—or mind—and body. But still, the psychologist has to confess to the existence of a third element. He recognizes it, finds his chief interest and occupation with it, builds up a whole system of experimentation around it, and often borders on calling it by its right name. But to do so would be to give too much away; and Satan, who has the mind of the natural man well on leash, sees to it that in this, as in other matters, just *the* word is not used. The psychologist, therefore, recoils and calls the extra factor 'the subconscious mind', or 'the subjective mind', or 'the subliminal self', or 'the secondary personality', etc. Listen to some of the things which indicate the length to which such teachers go :

'The soul consists of two parts, the one being addicted to the truth, and loving honesty and reason ; the other brutish, deceitful, sensuous'.

Or again :

'There is a schism in the soul '.

'The existence of a schism in the soul is not a mere dogma of theology, but a fact of science'.

35

' Man is endowed with two minds, each of which is capable of independent action, and they are capable of simultaneous action ; but, in the main, they possess independent powers and perform independent functions. The distinctive faculties of one pertain to this life: those of the other are especially adapted to a higher plane of existence. I distinguish them by designating one as the objective mind, and the other as the subjective mind '.

' Whatever faculties are found to exist in the subjective mind of any sentient being, necessarily existed potentially in the ancestry of that being, near or remote. *It is a corollary that whatever faculties we may find to exist in the subjective mind of man must necessarily exist in its possibility, potentially, in the mind of God the Father '.* (All italics ours.)

When we read things like this, two things press for exclamation: first, Oh, why not call it by its right name! The other: What a tragedy that pagan philosophers should have been their sphere of research and that the Bible should have been set aside! It may be thought that it does not matter much what you call it if you get hold of the thing itself. But we hold that it is vital to recognize that we are dealing with two things which are absolutely distinct and separate, and not with two sides of one thing. It is error to speak of *soul*-union or -communion with God, for there is no such thing. Divine union is with spirit. " He that is joined unto the Lord is one *spirit* " (I Cor. vi. 17), and however highly developed the soul-life is, there is no ' Divine union ' until the spirit has been brought back to its right place and condition.

This opens a further big question :

WHAT IS IT THAT IS BORN AGAIN ?

This experience is said by Christ to be imperative (John iii. 3, 5, etc.).

Nicodemus stumbled over the physical question, but was soon told that "that which is born of the flesh is flesh, and that which is born of the Spirit is spirit". Firstly, then, and obviously, it is not the body that is born anew. But neither is it the soul! "The sinful body of the flesh was destroyed" (Romans vi. 6), and "they that are Christ's have crucified the flesh with the *affections and lusts*" (Gal. v. 24). The passages similar to these are too many to quote, but look up "flesh", "old man", "natural man", etc. The answer to the question is emphatically that new birth is the requickening of the human *spirit* by the Spirit of God, an imparting to it of Divine life, and thus a re-uniting of man with God by one life in the inward man. This, of course, is solely on the ground of Christ's resurrection, and is the believer's union with Him therein; implying that all the meaning of His death as atoning, substitutionary and representative, has been accepted by faith, although perhaps not understood. From that time it is "in newness of the spirit" (Rom. vii. 6). The soul may still be capable of its erstwhile fears, doubts, questionings, feelings, etc., showing that it is *not* a new soul: but there is something deeper than all this, and God is greater than our souls. That which is the truest thing about the new-born is often deeper than consciousness, and although the soul, and even the body, may derive good and enjoy the blessing, God will seek to wean us as babes from the sensations to the fact and to Himself. Such as *must* have, and *demand,* in the senses continuous evidence of their new life will not grow up spiritually, but will remain babes. More on this later.

Seeing that we have seemed to give the soul such a completely secondary place, we must hasten to the third question.

WHAT IS THE PLACE OF THE SOUL ?

What have we said and inferred as to the soul ? We have indicated that it was with his soul that Adam sinned. The result of this was that it is with the soul

that the evil powers have become allied. Further, a consequence is that man has become pre-eminently a
soulical being as against a spiritual ; that is, soul dom-
inates. Thus man is in a disrupted state, and represents
an upsetting of a Divine order. This is only one part
of a much wider derangement through Adam's sin. In
the new creation in Christ the principles of the true
Divine order are re-established. The spirit quickened,
raised, indwelt and united with Christ is set to be the
organ of Divine government over the rest of man, soul
and body. In a truly spiritual or born-anew person, the
soul and body will not have a place of pre-eminence,
but in their right place will be very fruitful and useful
servants and instruments. By his soul, man functions
in two directions—from within to without, and from
without to within. The soul is the plane and organ of
human life and communication. Even Divine things,
which cannot in the first instance be grasped or known
by the soul, if they are to become *practical* in human
life, must have an organ constituted to interpret, translate and make intelligible to humans. Thus, what is
received by the spirit alone with its peculiar faculties
(see later) is translated for practical purposes, firstly to
the recipient himself, and then to other humans, by
means of the soul. This may be by an enlightened mind
for truth (reason) ; a filled heart, with joy or love etc., for
comfort and uplift (emotion) ; or energized will for
action or execution (volition). But it must ever be borne
in mind that to really serve *Divine* ends and to be of
eternal value this does not come in the first instance
from our own souls, but from God to, and through, our
spirits. It must be truth by revelation (Eph. i. 17, 18.
R.V.) not firstly of our own reasoning ; joy and love
by the Holy Spirit, not our own emotion ; energy and
strength in Christ, not our own drive and force of will.
When these latter obtain, then again the Divine order
is upset, a false position exists, and the fruit will perish,
although it may seem very good for the time being.

Then, as to the opposite direction. The soul can recognize, appreciate, register and apprehend everything

of this world in the measure of its capacity, natural or acquired. All this can stop there and be exhausted upon itself, or it can be brought on to the higher ground and regulated so as to be transmuted into spiritual value (which is eternal), made completely subservient in life, or rejected. The spirit will thus, by its touch with God, dictate as to what is good or evil, or only seemingly good. *The soul does not know this of itself.* It must have a spiritual organ with *spiritual* intelligence, conveying Divine standards.

Why is it that so many of the most artistic, poetic and soulish people have been and are so morally defective, degenerate, lustful, jealous and vainglorious ? Why is it that dictators, whose *ego* is so all-else-obscuring, are so godless and God-defiant ? Why is it that so many great intellectuals are so proud, arrogant and often infidel ? Well, the answer is obvious. All this is *soul !* They know nothing of a balancing, adjudicating spirit-union with God, and therefore their own souls are the last word in every matter. It is not that they all dismiss God from the universe, for they sometimes refer to Him. But there is no correspondence between Him and them, and He exists to no practical moral purpose where they are concerned. We leave this just for the present.

We have sought to show that the soul as a servant— not a master—can, and should, be very fruitful and useful in relation to a superior organ. And thus, when we speak of people being ' soulish ', we only mean that soul predominates, not that soul is wrong or necessarily evil. Divine order is always a law of Divine fulness. *

At the same time, we would be careful to point out that the soul is a very responsible servant. Indeed, the human *ego*—the ' I '—as a conscious and rational self-life, has to answer to God for its submission or vaunting of itself ; its ' laying down of its own life ', or its exalting and asserting of itself beyond its measure and province. Hence " the soul that sinneth, it shall die " (Ezek. xviii. 4) was God's dictum, and still is. Altogether apart from a renewed spirit by new birth, there is a responsibility for God's Word.

* See Appendix—note on " Natural Man " and " Old Man ".

In this connection, certain things must be made clear, or as clear as possible. While it may not be possible for an unregenerate person to do the revealed will of God, because for this the enablement of the Holy Spirit is essential, yet to such and all others that revealed will makes an appeal and a demand. This may only be to the extent of taking an attitude to be made willing and able. But, as morally responsible creatures, that obligation rests upon us whenever the word of God is presented.

Then with regard to those who are the Lord's people, there is no such thing as an extra spirituality or revelation, which sets God's Word on one side or transcends it. If God says a thing in the Scriptures, that thing stands, and we stand or fall by it. By spiritual illumination we may come into much fuller meaning of the Scriptures and see God's thoughts and intents behind them. But that does not suspend their practical obligation, *provided that we are in the dispensation to which they apply practically.* We have met a certain type of Christian who, claiming to be acting according to the spirit in relation to the will of God, has been guilty of the most flagrant contradiction of the most obvious and elementary obligations of honesty, righteousness, good faith, trustworthiness and humility.

Sometimes a subtle mental evasion is betrayed by the attempted justification of a course contrary to the Word of God in 'Yes, but the devil can quote Scripture'. It seems incredible; had we not been met by this sort of thing we would feel it too unbelievable to mention. It is, however, something which touches our very subject. Let us ask, How often does Satan try to turn an unregenerate person away from Christ by using Scripture? Have you *ever* heard of his doing so? It must be the most remote case if you have. No; it is those who are truly God's children with whom he employs the method of using the Word of God. Why is this? It is because he has something very much deeper in view. Let us get at it by taking Christ's own case.

When Satan assailed Christ, our Lord met him with

" It is written ". In effect, Satan said (within himself):
' Oh, that is your ground, is it ? Very well, then—" It
is written, he shall give his angels charge concerning
thee ",' etc. He at once sought to defeat Christ on His
own ground. What was his real point of attack ? The
Lord Jesus had definitely and deliberately taken up the
position that He would have and do nothing for or of
Himself, but that all should be held in relation to the
Father and therefore only by the Father's permission ;
yes, all things utterly and only for God, and self-interest,
soul-gratification, utterly set aside. The thing most
likely to move Him from such a position of abandonment to God would be to support any proposed movement or course by the very Word of God itself. It would
be useless to say to the Son of God, the last Adam :
" Yea, hath God said ? " But to say " God *hath* said "
is much more subtle. It is the question of spirit (in
union with God) or soul (in self-direction) that is ever
the point of Satan's efforts. If *Satan* quotes Scripture,
it is to destroy inward union with God. But the Word
of God itself never leads to that ; and no one would
ever defend a course contrary to the clear Word of God
with the rejoinder that ' the devil can quote Scripture ',
or even have such a thing in their mind, unless they
were in themselves wanting to go a certain way. How
our soul-life will defend and save itself ! But how
necessary it is for our own deliverance from our deceitful heart that we are so subject to God that we are
alive to the nature and implication of the snare. We
have here touched the key to the whole question of the
place of the soul. Two things have got to happen to
it. Firstly, it has got to be smitten a fatal blow by the
death of Christ as to its self-strength and government.
As with Jacob's thigh or the sinew thereof after God
had touched it and he went to the end of his life with a
limp ; so for ever there has to be registered in the soul
the fact that it cannot and it must not : God has broken
its power. Then, as an instrument, it has to be " won ",
mastered and ruled in relation to the higher and different ways of God. It is spoken of so frequently in the

Scriptures as being some *thing* over which *we* have to gain and exercise an authority. For instance :

" In your patience ye shall win your souls ".	*Luke xxi. 19.*
" Ye have purified your souls in your obedience to the truth ".	*I Pet. i. 22.*
" The end of your faith, even the salvation of your souls ".	*I Pet. i. 9.*

We must be careful that, in recognizing the fact that the soul has been seduced, led captive, darkened and poisoned with a self-interest, we do not regard it as something to be annihilated and destroyed in this life. This would be but asceticism, a form of Buddhism. The result of any such behaviour is usually only another form of soulishness in an exaggerated degree ; perhaps occultism. Our whole human nature is in our souls, and *if nature is suppressed in one direction she will take revenge in another.* This is just what is the trouble with a great many people if only they knew it. There is a difference between a life of suppression and a life of service. Submission, subjection and servanthood in Christ's case, as to the Father, was not a life of soul-destruction, but of rest and delight. Slavery in its bad sense is the lot of those who live wholly in their own souls. We need to revise our ideas about service, for it is becoming more and more common to think that service is bondage and slavery ; when really it is a Divine thing. Spirituality is not a life of suppression. That is negative. Spirituality is positive ; it is a new and extra life, not the old one striving to get the mastery of itself. The soul has to be taken in charge and made to learn the new and higher wisdom. Whether we are able yet to accept it or not, the fact is that if we are going on with God fully, all the soul's energies and abilities for knowing, understanding, sensing and doing will come to an end, and we shall—on that side—stand bewildered, dazed, numbed and impotent. Then, only a new, other, and Divine understanding, constraint, and energy will send us forward or keep us going. At such times we shall have to say to our souls, " My soul, be thou silent unto God " (Ps. lxii. 5) ; " My soul . . . hope thou in God " (Ps. xlii. 5) ; and ' My soul, come thou with me to follow the Lord '. But what joy and strength there is when, the soul having been constrained to yield to the spirit, the higher wisdom and glory is perceived in its vindication. Then it is that " My *soul* doth magnify the Lord, and my *spirit* hath rejoiced in God my Saviour " (Luke i. 46). The spirit *hath*, the soul *doth*— note the tenses.

So that unto fulness of joy the soul is essential, and it *must* be brought through the darkness and death of its own ability to learn the higher and deeper realities for which the spirit is the first organ and faculty.

No ; do not live a life of suppressing your soul, nor despising it ; but be strong in spirit, so that your soul may be won, saved and made to serve your fullest joy. The Lord Jesus desires that we should find rest unto our souls, and this, He says, comes by way of His yoke— the symbol of union and service.

The soul, like some people, will find its greatest value in service, not as a master. It wants to be the latter, but it is blind to the limitations which God has imposed upon it. It thinks that it can, but God says it "cannot ". But, in its place, with the self-interest lying under the ban of Christ's death, it can be a very useful servant.

D

CHAPTER FOUR

THE NATURE OF SANCTIFICATION

WHILE WE CANNOT EXTEND ourselves to a comprehensive consideration of the subject of sanctification, we are sure that a very great deal of confusion through false conceptions would be removed if it were seen in the light of the difference between soul and spirit. For, indeed, this *is* the key of the matter. As sanctification is but the continuation of regeneration, because regeneration is but sanctification begun, it has to be seen as in the same sphere as new birth. We have said that in new birth it is not the soul but the spirit that is born from above—or born again.

The soul remains prone to evil to the end. This fact constitutes the basis for the whole doctrine of sanctification, inasmuch as the New Testament is one big exhortation to spiritual progress by spiritual ascendency. There is ever an enemy to holiness in man's own nature, and holiness in us is not fixed and static, it is progressive. All trial, testing, chastening and suffering lose their meaning if there is no ground or fear of failure. Enlargement has ever been, and ever is, by conflict. There has only been One in Whose nature there existed no actual and positive evil or sin.

The question of sanctification has been greatly confused because certain Scriptures have been made basic which really were not meant primarily to deal with sanctification in itself.

THE PROBLEM OF ROMANS VII AND I JOHN, ETC.

For instance, we have Rom. vii, and the first Letter of John. We cannot quote the entire text, but we extract the salient parts.

" . . . the law is spiritual: but I am carnal . . . For that which I do I know not: for not what I would,

that do I practise ; but what I hate, that I do . . . I know that in me, that is, in my flesh, dwelleth no good thing: for to will is present with me, but to do that which is good is not ".

". . . I delight in the law of God after the inward man: but I see a different law in my members, warring against the law of my mind, and bringing me into captivity under the law of sin which is in my members. O wretched man that I am! who shall deliver me out of the body of this death? (or, this body of death). I thank God through Jesus Christ our Lord. So then I myself with the mind serve the law of God ; but with the flesh the law of sin. There is . . . no condemnation to them that are in Christ Jesus. . . . that the ordinance of the law might be fulfilled in us, who walk not after the flesh, but after the spirit. . . . They that are after the spirit (do mind) the things of the spirit . . . the mind of the spirit is life and peace . . . But ye are . . . in the spirit, if so be that the Spirit of God dwelleth in you. . . . If Christ is in you . . . the spirit is life because of righteousness . . . If by the spirit ye do mortify the deeds of the body ye shall live ".

(Romans vii, viii.)

" If we say that we have no sin, we deceive ourselves, and the truth is not in us ".

" If we confess our sins, he is faithful and righteous to forgive . . ."

" If we say that we have not sinned, we make him a liar, and his word is not in us ".

" Everyone that doeth sin doeth also lawlessness ".

" Whosoever abideth in him sinneth not: whosoever sinneth hath not seen him, neither knoweth him ".

" He that doeth sin is of the devil ".

*" Whosoever is begotten of God doeth no sin,
because his seed abideth in him: and he cannot sin,
because he is begotten of God ".*

               I John i. 8, 9, 10 ; iii. 4, 6, 8, 9.

On the face of it, these last Scriptures appear to present a contradiction of the first magnitude, but as the Word of God cannot contradict itself there must be some way in which they are all true.

But first let us repeat that these Scriptures were not written in the first instance in connection with sanctification. Rom. vii was written in relation to justification and deliverance from the law. I John was written in relation to a true and a false Christianity, the genuine new birth, and the claim of some to be Christians. The two categories are represented by two clauses or phrases: " We know "; " He that saith ". One indicates living experience, the other the unsubstantiated claim. Apostasy was in view with John.

But in both cases one thing is common; it is the nature of the new birth and its outworking in life afterward. Sanctification comes up as one with regeneration in nature, but as the issue and progressive outworking of regeneration. We cannot therefore read Rom. vii without going on into Chapter viii, and we cannot read I John without noting all of its governing words, such as " walk ", " abide ", " practise ". We will touch that again.

THE PLACE IN EXPERIENCE OF ROMANS VII

We must first of all place this chapter. To what part of man's history or experience does it belong? Is it the experience of one who has no inward work of the Holy Spirit, or is it that of one who has been spiritually quickened? We think that it is the latter. There are several reasons for this conclusion. Firstly, the letter was written to believers, amongst whom were Jewish converts whose clean cut with the law had not been made, and who, on the one hand, were in a state of unsettled and restless or uncertain spiritual life, really neither one thing nor the other as to daily experience, failing and repenting, failing and repenting in monotonous repetition, and almost despairing of victory; and, on the other hand, needing further enlightenment and instruction as to what being "in Christ Jesus" really means. They were not in liberty or deliverance because of an inadequate apprehension of the death and resurrection of Christ; that is, of its representative aspect as in addition to its substitutionary. Secondly, Paul, having already stated what identification with Christ really means (Chapter vi), goes on to show that its result is to draw a line between the flesh and the spirit in the believer, and makes the demand that the "walk" shall be in the spirit. Failure to do this always produces the state set forth in Chapter vii. It was a condition not uncommon amongst Christians even in New Testament times, as see I Corinthians and Galatians, and which drew out the mass of New Testament writings.

THE EFFECT OF SPIRITUAL AWAKENING

Thirdly (and this is a fairly strong point) writing many years later the Apostle said that in his unregenerate days his position as to the righteousness which is of the law was "found blameless" (see Phil. iii). He puts himself into Rom. vii and there says that the law was too much for him; it smote him; it slew him; he could not stand up to it. Under its burden he cried "O wretched man", not "found blameless". Something must have happened to disturb his complacency and make him such a divided man with civil war raging within. In the unregenerate man conscience was hiding behind the ritual and observance of the law. Rigid observance of its forms and rites made conscience play deceiving tricks; saying peace, peace, when there was no peace. But when the time of spiritual awakening comes, this kind of thing can go on no longer. It cannot play deceit any more, and, while there may be some flirting with sin on the part of the *soul*, the awakened

and quickened spirit hates and loathes its own soul and
calls a spade a spade—that is, calls sin sin ! Instead
of treating the ceremonial law as an offset to the moral,
it sees that the latter is the important one, and that " to
obey is better than sacrifice, and to hearken than the fat
of rams " (I Sam. xv. 22).

TWO POSSIBLE EVILS—
ROMANS VII, OR ANTINOMIANISM

Unless the meaning and value of the death and resurrection of Christ is known, and the truth of identification by faith therewith, one of two terrible things
will follow. Either there will be a history such as is set
forth in Romans vii, a history of struggle, longing and
defeat: fear of going back on faith in Christ, and yet
deep disappointment with the Christian life: leading
ever nearer to despair and gloom ; or else there will set
in that terrible, conscious-searing, spirit-deadening evil
known as antinomianism. It might be useful to state
here what that doctrine is. The word is—*anti*, against,
and *nomos*, law. The term was first used by Luther as
a designation of the followers of John Agricola, who
maintained that the moral law was not binding, as such,
upon Christians. But the thing itself existed long before
Luther's time or the name given to it. From the earliest
Christian times, there have been those who have denied
that the law was of use or obligation under the Gospel
dispensation. It would appear from several passages in
the New Testament (Rom. iii. 8, 31 ; vi. 1 ; Eph. v. 6 ;
2 Pet. ii. 18, 19), that the principle was at work even in
Apostolic times, for in those passages the Apostles warn
their converts against perversions of their teaching as an
excuse for licentiousness. At the heart of this doctrine
there lies a mistaken interpretation of the doctrine of
justification by faith. Some have in the past even taught
that, being spiritual, their nature could not be corrupted,
whatever their moral conduct might be ; or that an elect
person did not sin even when he committed actions in
themselves evil.

Now, no one would sponsor such a doctrine deliberately, but the principle may operate all the same. Justification by faith: having finality and fulness of perfection *in Christ*: Final Perseverance, i.e. once in grace always in grace: and suchlike beliefs, can—strange to say—produce a hard and legal kind of Christianity if wrongly held, and result in many things which may be either positively evil, questionable, or other than according to the graciousness of Christ.

TWO DOCTRINES OF SANCTIFICATION

From the Scriptures it is possible to frame two mutually exclusive doctrines of sanctification. One is that our sanctification is in Christ Jesus, complete and perfect, and, having taken Him as our holiness objectively, we must just trust that He answers for us in all Divine demands and requirements. We in ourselves are not holy, and it can only be contrary to faith, and an unhealthy introspection or subjectivity, if we become intensely occupied with the matter of personal holiness. We must believe that His Cross has done something which holds good in the sight of God in spite of our state, and " looking unto Jesus ", or the attitude of faith, is the way, and the only way, of deliverance from despair or unrest. We have no hesitation in saying that such is a mixed and indefinite position. It uses certain glorious truths to obscure other equally glorious truths. This is a position which makes it necessary for those who hold it to keep ever on their guard lest their defences are broken down. They are always having to go round to see if their position is intact. It really does not settle the question when they either fall into sin and its resultant shame, or meet another and more desirable position in teaching, or those who have it. They know that they cannot accept an alternative position which to them goes to the other extreme, and so they have to dig themselves in to that which is not perfectly satisfactory.

The other doctrine is that which, with varying forms of words and phraseology, and minor shades of differences, means that sanctification is the rooting out, eradication, cleansing, destroying of all sin, so that a sanctified person does not sin, and cannot sin ; the sinful nature has been fully dealt with. To those who hold this view sanctification—in this sense here mentioned —is an act, a conclusive experience at a given moment, just as is new birth ; and it is to be taken as such by faith.

Here, again, we have to say that there is mixture and a position which has brought a very great number of believers into confusion and despair.

We say that both of these positions have Scripture used for their support, and when you look at the Scriptures, on the face of them, there *seems* to be such support.

The passages cited from John's Epistle appear to present a contradiction :

" *If we say that we have no sin, we deceive ourselves, and the truth is not in us* ".

" *He that doeth sin is of the devil* ".

" *Whosoever sinneth hath not seen him, neither knoweth him* ".

" *Whosoever abideth in him sinneth not* ".

" *Whosoever is begotten of God doeth no sin* : . . . *he cannot sin* ".

These words *must* be regarded as all addressed to Christians. This seems proved by Chapter i. 7 : " *If we walk in the light . . . the blood of Jesus his Son cleanseth* (*Gk.*, cleanses, or is cleansing ; present active tense) *us from all sin* ".

Here, then, is the position. A child of God has to walk in the light, confess his sins, acknowledge sinfulness, and, *as he does so,* the Blood keeps on cleansing. At the same time " *He that doeth sin is of the devil* ", and " *Whosoever sinneth hath not seen him, neither knoweth him* ". And yet, again, at the same time " *Whosoever is begotten of God doeth no sin . . . he cannot sin* ".

The usual way through the apparent dilemma is to correct the translation, and this is certainly a help ; but it does not give anything like a final clearance. Let us get the help that lies in that course by trying to retranslate the passages more accurately and literally. The reader of the English wil! understand that different Greek words are used for one common English word in certain places, and certain Greek words mean more than the English word employed for them.

I John ii. 29.   " Everyone that practiseth (or, is practising) righteousness is begotten of him".

I John iii. 4.   " Everyone who practiseth (or, is practising) * iniquity practiseth lawlessness ".

I John iii. 6.   " Whosoever abideth in him does not wander from (or, miss) the right path " (" sinneth not ", Gk. harmartano = to miss the mark or the right way). Or, " Whosoever abideth in him is not missing the mark ".

I John iii. 7.   " He that doeth (or, is practising) righteousness is righteous ".

I John iii. 9.   " Whosoever hath been born of God is not practising sin (or, is not missing the mark) because a seed of him abideth in him and he cannot be practising sin " (moral aberration).

The help given by a knowledge of the actual words employed lies mainly in the word ' practise ' as representing both an habitual course and a present—ever-present—conduct.

THE REAL KEY TO SANCTIFICATION

But all this does not settle the whole matter. We therefore submit that the key to this dilemma is the difference between soul and spirit. We have said that what begins in regeneration proceeds in sanctification. The carry-over of the atonement as a sanctifying power is thus: there is in the born-again spirit a striving after holiness as well as a new desire for the Lord.

* A. T. Robertson says: "The present active participle (poiōn) means the habit of doing".

When the spirit is renewed and quickened, something happens. That spirit itself is that in man which is the image or likeness of God (spirit). It has been dead —that is, it has been severed from its life in God, and has ceased to function in any Divine way. The Holy Spirit, in virtue of the atonement, first renews *it* by cleansing and quickening, and also imparts Divine life (eternal life) in Christ to it, thus making it one in nature and fellowship with God. The spirit, when thus dealt with, is that seed or has that seed of God which is said by the Apostle to be unable to practise sin—" cannot sin ". This new ' inner man ' cannot be committing or practising sin. The dilemma of many is that there *are* two natures and two springs of life in believers. One gives forth sweet water and the other bitter, and the Bible says that *a* fountain cannot do this. " Can the Ethiopian change his skin, or the leopard his spots ?" (Jer. xiii. 23). Therefore there must be *two* fountains.

The soul, which is the fountain of the natural life, is poisoned and impure. It is ever prone to evil, like the " flesh " in it. The soul is that which has to be continually subdued, won and *eventually* saved (Heb. x. 39, etc.).

The renewed spirit is prone to good ; its course is naturally upward. The life in it makes it gravitate to its source—God. It judges and condemns all the motions of the flesh. It strives, as energized by the indwelling Holy Spirit, to make the whole man go Godward. Its *nature* is Divine, although it does not become the Divine *Person*. It is here that " there is a new creation " (2 Cor. v. 17), and that which " is being renewed . . . after the image of him that created him " (Col. iii. 10).

As we have pointed out elsewhere, this is all a deeper reality than the life and motions of the soul, and registers itself continually against *ourselves* in the natural. There are stages in spiritual experience, more or less pronounced in different cases for certain reasons. The first phase may be a great and overflowing joy, with a marvellous sense of emancipation. In this phase extravagant things are often said as to total deliverance and final victory. An earnest of the ultimate is often given with the incoming of the Holy Spirit. He is that earnest, and His advent in the human spirit is celebrated with glory.

Then there may, and often does, come a phase of which inward conflict is the chief feature. It may be very much of a Romans vii experience. This will lead under the Lord's hand to several things; firstly, to the fuller knowledge of the meaning of identification with Christ, as in Rom. vi. Happy the man who has been instructed in this from the beginning.

SANCTIFICATION AND EDUCATION GO TOGETHER

Then it will introduce to the way of spiritual education. Sanctification and spiritual education are one, as Heb. xii. 1 — 13 makes clear. The advance in this double course is marked by the growth of the spirit. When the spirit is first quickened, it is barely able to show its existence. It is far from able to show its mastery over soul and body. The advance of sanctification is marked by a growth of the spirit. It begins to assert its supremacy, to compel the physical and animal life to know their bounds, and to obey God. The more sanctification advances, the more marked is the spiritual intelligence, power and life, until at last it reaches its coming-of-age in " the revealing of the sons of God, . . . conformed to the image of his Son " (Rom. viii. 19, 29). This education and sanctification is the result of walking, " not after the flesh, but after the spirit ". Such a walk leads away from carnality and babyhood, as I Cor. iii. shows.

There may be crises in this course marked by definite and tremendous experiences. But no such crisis is final : every one has to have an outgrowth leading to greater fulnesses. It is fatal to relate everything to a crisis or experience of years ago, and to stop there.

So the distinction between soul and spirit is the true key to sanctification, for sanctification must not be

negative like innocence, but positive in the sense that
it goes along with spiritual understanding and responsibility. Sonship, which is all of a piece with sanctification (see Rom. viii) is a matter of spiritual and moral
responsibility in God's house. We are born "children"; we are adopted "sons". "Adoption" in the New
Testament is not bringing an outsider into the family,
but the born one reaching his majority and being made
his father's responsible representative with 'rights'.

Rom. vii has to do with condemnation by the law,
and the big question is that of deliverance from the
death which has become such a real, terrible and intoler-
able thing because of spiritual awakening. Rom. vi
shows that such deliverance from death and condemnation, is by union with Christ's death and resurrection.
Rom. viii transfers the law from the outside as an obligation imposed, to the inside as a power imparted. Thus,
in the spirit, the new covenant is written by the Spirit
of the living God (see 2 Cor. iii., iv).

It will help us if we get Paul's mental picture again.
He had in mind the gladiators in the arena. (Remember, the letter was to the *Romans,* and familiar scenes in
Rome were drawn upon.) When the victorious gladi-
ator had been given the 'thumb-down' signal from the
judge, which meant 'kill', it was incumbent upon him
to drag his victim's body round the arena for the specta-
tors to applaud. It was a horrible and loathsome thing,
and the one who had to do it would be longing to reach
the exit. Paul imagined such an one saying to himself,
"O wretched man that I am! who shall deliver me from
this dead body?" and then, espying an exit, he cried,
'Thank God, through here!' This was carried over
into Christian truth, and the way out for the "wretched
man" was "through our Lord Jesus Christ". This has
been more fully explained as being through His death,
burial and resurrection. So then, the death of Christ is
something to be made good in a believer's life by the
Holy Spirit, through faith's deliberate identification.
Then the resurrection of Christ is likewise proved to be

a present, mighty, delivering power ; or the power by which the believer, by the spirit, puts to death the doings of the flesh.

CHAPTER FIVE

WHERE CHRISTENDOM IS DECEIVED

PERHAPS THE GREATEST FAILURE to make the great discrimination with which we are concerned is in relation to the difference between mysticism and spirituality. It is here that not only the world is mistaken but Christendom is deceived. Indeed, an overwhelmingly large proportion of those who would regard themselves as Christians are unable to distinguish between æstheticism (pertaining to the sense of the beautiful) or asceticism (the practice of self-denial) on the one hand and spirituality on the other. The fact is that these belong to two entirely different realms, and the Word of God cuts clean in between them, dividing them asunder.

When we speak of Cain and "the way of Cain", we are accustomed to recall immediately his act of murder, born of jealousy and malice. We remember his peevish, querulous, petulant, ill-tempered or even insolent manner with God. But there is another side to remember, and we must be fair to Cain, or we miss the whole point. Cain did not exclude or ignore God. He was not in the usual sense of the word a godless man. He acknowledged God. Then he built an altar to God. Further, he no doubt selected the best of the products of his hard toil as worthy of God, and brought them. Here was devoutness in religion. Cain worshipped with his whole æsthetic sense, and Cain—murdered his brother ! The Jews did the same in Christ's day. Christendom is largely constituted by this sense—its architecture, its ritual, its music, its adornment, its lighting (or lack of it), its tone, its atmosphere, its vestments and so forth. All are of the soul. But Cain did not get through to God ! Neither did the Jews ! Spiritual death marks that

E

realm, and while there may be intense emotions which make for resolves, 'high' thoughts and desires, there is no genuine change in the nature of those concerned, and repeated doses of this must be taken to maintain any measure of soul-self-satisfaction which makes them feel good. All religions have this soulish feature in common, more or less, and it is here that the fatal blunder has been made by many *religious* people who contend that other religions, which are undoubtedly devout and sincere, should not be interfered with, but the good in them should be recognized and accepted. It is the confusing of religion with what the Bible means by being spiritual. Religion can rise to high levels and sink to terrible depths. It is the *same thing* which does both. But that thing never rises above the human level; it never really reaches God. Religion can be the greatest enemy of God's true thought, because Satan's best deception. Asceticism is no more truly spiritual than æstheticism. There is no more a brief with God for rigours, denials, fastings, puritanic iciness, etc., as such, than for the opposite. Simplicity may give God a chance, but it is not necessarily spiritual. It may be a matter of taste. What sublime thoughts and ideas, in poetry, music and art often can go hand in hand with moral degeneracy and profligacy!

How near to the truth in perception and interpretation can the mystical go! What wonderful things can the imagination see, even in the Bible! What thrills of awe, amazement, ecstasy, can be shot through an audience or congregation by a master soul! But it may all be a false world with no Divine and eternal issues. It may all go to make up this life here, and relieve it of its drabness, but it ends there. What an artificial world we live in! When the music is progressing and the romantic elements are in evidence—the dress and tinsel —and human personalities are parading, see how pride and rivalry assert themselves, and what a power of make-believe enters the atmosphere! Yes, an artificial world. We have been in it and know the reactions afterward.

How hollow, how empty; Dead Sea fruit! The tragedy
in this melodrama is that it is 'real life' to so many.
This soul-world is the devil's imitation. It is all false,
wherever we may find it, whether associated with religion or not.

Those of us who have tasted of this world's springs
have recognized the kinship between what is there and
what is in religion so far as that soul-nature is concerned.
It is only a matter of difference of realm, not of nature.
What the music and drama of the world produce in one
way—the soul-stirring, rousing, craving: the pathos,
tears, contempt, hatred, anger, melancholy, pleasure, etc.
—are all the same, only under different auspices and in
a different setting, and the fact is, that it passes and we
are really no further on. A little better music, a change
of preacher, a less familiar place, a few more thrills, will
perhaps stimulate our souls, but where are we, after all ?
How Satan must laugh behind his mask! Oh, for reality,
the reality of the eternal! Oh, that men might see that,
while a highly cultured soul with a keen sense of the
beautiful and sublime is immeasurably preferable to a
sordid one *so far as this world is concerned,* it is not
necessarily a criterion that such has a personal living
knowledge of God—of God as a Person—and has really
been born anew! Occultism—the power to see deeper
than the average, to sense what most do not sense, to
handle the abstruse, to touch unseen forces—is not spirituality in the Divine sense. The soul realm is a complex
and dangerous one, and can take most people out of their
depths, but then land them into moral, mental and
physical ruin, with all hope gone.

When we pray for 'Revival' let us be careful as to
what we are after and as to what means we use to pro-
mote it, or carry it on.

Having been more precise as to the functions of the
soul, we must go a little further at this point, as to those
of the spirit.

THE ATTRIBUTES OF THE HUMAN SPIRIT

As the soul is a trinity of reason, affection, and volition, so is the spirit a trinity. Its attributes are conscience, communion (worship) and intuition.

"The spirit of man is the lamp of the Lord" (Prov. xx. 27).

"Gentiles that have not the law do by nature the things of the law, these, not having the law, are the law unto themselves ; in that they shew the work of the law written in their hearts, their conscience bearing witness therewith, and their thoughts one with another accusing or else excusing" (Romans ii. 14 — 15).

When Adam sinned, he did so as the result of what seemed to him a sound and right argument and reason, and a judgment of what was good and desirable. But immediately he had so acted he became aware of a faculty within, which rose up and condemned his judgment, reason and ' good (?) motive '. Henceforth he lived under a sense of condemnation. The conscience which accused him and caused him to excuse, could not restore him to God's favour, but for ever kept God in his consciousness. Thus it is that to live in and to be governed entirely by our souls is not to have rest and real life. It *is* possible to put our wills so strongly behind our reason and thought and desire, or so to surrender our wills to our emotions and affections, as to muffle the voice of conscience so that we have little or no conflict within. But should God come into " the garden in the cool of the day ", or, in other words, should we at any time seek a living knowledge of God, we are in for a very bad time with regard to this former mentality, these former reasonings, and this former affectional life. But we are not saying that the human conscience is infallible and always right. Most certainly it is not. We can have a sense of right and wrong which is altogether misinformed and false, and Satan can play tricks with conscience. We are only pointing out what conscience is as an attribute of the spirit. For conscience to fulfil *all*

of its Divinely intended purpose in relation to God—
not merely to keep man aware of something beyond his
own way—conscience must (as with the whole spirit)
be renewed in God and united with the Holy Spirit.
Christ is God's perfect standard for conscience, and
union with Christ is the only ground of life in the spirit.
" Christ . . . was made unto us wisdom from God, and
righteousness and sanctification, and redemption " (I
Cor. i. 30), and when Christ is received by faith, so that
our standing before God rests upon what He is and not
what we are, then we " find rest unto our *souls* " in this
" yoke " (Matt. xi. 29), for we have our " hearts
sprinkled from an evil conscience " (Heb. x. 22). With
the whole human spirit, conscience must be quickened
from above, raised, enlightened, adjusted and related.

Having already spoken of worship in spirit and in
truth, we can pass on to see the function of spirit by intuition. Here the difference between soul and spirit is
very clear and definite. The spirit is the organ of spiritual knowledge, and spiritual knowledge is very different
from natural or soul knowledge. How does God know
things, and by what means does God come to His conclusions, decisions ? On what basis of knowledge does
He run the universe ? Is it by reasoning inductively,
deductively, philosophically, logically, comparatively ?
Surely all this laboriousness of brain is unknown to God.
His knowledge and conclusions are intuitive. Intuition
is that faculty of spiritual intelligence by which all
spiritual beings work. Angels serve the will of God by
intuitive discernment of that will, not by argued and
reasoned conviction. The difference between these two is
witnessed to by the whole monument of spiritual achievement. If human reason, the natural judgment and ' common sense ' had been the ruling law, most, if not all,
of the giant pieces of work inspired by God would never
have been undertaken. Men who had a close walk with
God and a living spirit-fellowship with Him, received
intuitively a leading to such purposes, and their vindication came, not by the approval of natural reason, but
usually with all such reason in opposition. ' Madness '

was usually the verdict of this world's ' wisdom '. Whenever they, like Abraham, allowed the natural mind to
take precedence over the spiritual mind, they became
bewildered, paralysed, and looked round for some
' Egypt ' way of the senses, along which to go for help.
In all this we are " justified in the spirit ", not in the
flesh. The spirit and the soul act independently, and
until the spiritual mind has established complete ascendency over the natural mind, they are constantly in conflict and contradiction. In all the things which are out
from God and therefore spiritual, " the mind of the
flesh is death ; but the mind of the spirit is life and
peace " (Rom. viii. 6). This, then, is the nature of
spiritual knowledge.

The only knowledge of God which is of spiritual
value for ourselves, or for others by our ministry, is that
which we have by revelation of the Holy Spirit within
our own spirits. God never—in the first instance—explains Himself to man's reason, and man can never know
God—in the first instance—by reason. Christianity is
a revelation or it is nothing, and it has to be that in the
case of every new child of God ; otherwise faith will
be resting upon a foundation which will not stand in
the day of the ordeal.

' The Christian Faith ' embraced as a religion, a philosophy, or as a system of truth, a moral or ethical doctrine,
may carry the temporary stimulus of a great ideal ; but
this will not result in the regeneration of the life, or the
new birth of the spirit. There are multitudes of such
' Christians ' in the world to-day, but their spiritual effectiveness is nil.

The Apostle Paul makes it very clear that the secret
of everything in his life and service was the fact that he
received his gospel " by revelation ". We may even
know the Bible most perfectly as a book, and yet be
spiritually dead and ineffective. When the Scriptures
say so much about the knowledge of God and of the
truth as the basis of eternal life, resulting in being set
free, doing exploits, etc., they also affirm that man cannot by searching find out God, and they make it abund-

antly clear that it is knowledge in the spirit, not in the natural mind.

Thus, a rich knowledge of the Scriptures, an accurate technical grasp of Christian doctrine, a doing of Christian work by all the resources of men's natural wisdom or ability, a clever manipulation and interesting presentation of Bible content and themes, may get not one whit beyond the natural life of men, and still remain within the realm of spiritual death. Men cannot be argued, reasoned, fascinated, interested, 'emotioned', willed, enthused, impassioned, into the kingdom of the heavens; they can only be born; and that is by spiritual quickening. The new birth brings with it new capacities of every kind; and amongst these, the most vital is a new and different faculty of Divine knowledge, understanding and apprehension. As we have said earlier, the human brain is not ruled out, but is secondary, not primary. The function of the human intellect is to give spiritual things intelligent form for ourselves and for others.

Paul's intellectual power was not that which gave him his knowledge of truth; but it was taken up by the spirit for passing that truth on to others. He may have used his intellect well, as he certainly did, to study and acquire knowledge of the Scriptures; but his spiritual understanding did not come that way. It was the extra thing, apart from which even his Bible (Old Testament) knowledge had not kept him from a most mistaken course. The spirit of man is that by which he reaches out into the eternal and unseen. Intuition, then, is the mental organ of the spirit. It is in this sense—that is, the deadness of the spirit in the matter of Divine union and the going on with religion in its manifold forms of expression merely from the natural mind—that God says, " For my thoughts are not your thoughts, neither are your ways my ways " (Isa. lv. 8); and the measure of the difference is as the height of the heavens from the earth, of the heavenly from the earthly.

One of the chief lessons that we have to learn, and which God takes pains to teach us, is that spiritual ends demand spiritual means. The breaking down of the natural life, its mind, its energies, *so far as the things of God are concerned,* in the bitterness of disappointment through futility, failure, ineffectiveness and deadlock in real spiritual fruitfulness, is a life work: but the truth mentioned above is the explanation and key to the matter.

How important it is that every fresh undertaking in work for God should come by revelation to those chosen for it. Because God has so spoken and given revelation to some chosen instrument and a truly spiritual work has been done, others have taken it as a model and have sought to imitate it in other places. The result has been, and is, that they are called upon to take responsibility for it—find the resources of workers, funds and general support. This, in turn, issues in many sad and pathetic, if not evil and worldly, methods and means being employed, and those concerned find themselves in a false position. Conception, not imitation, is the Divine law of reproduction. Anointing, not human selection, is the Divine law of succession. The fact is, that the work of God has become a sphere for so many *natural* elements to find expression and gratification. Man *must* do something, see something, have something. Ambition, acquisition, achievement, etc., have found their way over to Christian enterprise, and so, very often (let us be quite frank) things have become ' ours '—' *our* work ', ' *our* mission ', ' *our* field ', ' *our* clientèle ' ; and jealousies, rivalries, bitterness and many other things of the flesh abound.

It is a very difficult thing, a crucifixion indeed, for the natural man to do nothing and have nothing, and especially to *know* nothing. But in the case of His most greatly used instruments, God has made this a very real part of their training and preparation. The utter emptying of all self-resource is the only way to have " *all* things of (out from) God " (2 Cor. v. 18). On this basis, even Christ elected to live. We need not remind you of Moses' " I am not eloquent " (Exod. iv. 10), and Jeremiah's " I am a child " (Jer. i. 6), and Paul's " that we should not trust in ourselves " (2 Cor. i. 9). These were of a school in which the great lesson of the difference between natural and spiritual was taught experimentally.

GOD'S SPECIAL CONCERN

This will help us to see that God's special concern is with the spirit in the believer.

Firstly, we must realize that His quest is for sons of His Spirit. The underlying and all-inclusive truth of what has come to be called the parable of the Prodigal Son is the transition from one kind of sonship, i.e. on the ground of law, to another, i.e. on the ground of grace ; from the flesh to the spirit. There is a sonship of God by creation on the basis of law. In this sense, all men are the offspring of God, and Paul used this phrase in quite a general way to the Athenians (Acts xvii. 28, 29). But by the Fall—the "going astray ", or " deviating " (Gen. vi. 3)—all the Divine purposes and possibilities of that relationship have broken down, and that relationship is no longer of value. " He is flesh ", hence he is separated from God—"alienated" (Eph. iv. 18), in a "far country ", " lost ", and " dead ". Here grace enters and the Spirit through grace. The Spirit begins operations in that realm of death and distance, convicting of sin " against heaven " (Luke xv. 21) (the only adequate conviction), compassing the end of the works of the flesh in despair and destruction, constraining, assuring, producing penitence and confession, and at length bringing to the place of forgiveness and acceptance : from death unto life, but not the same life as before. " That which is born of the Spirit *is spirit* " (John iii. 6). This man is the product of the travail and energizing of the Spirit, and everything in the relationship afterward is new ; a "robe", the robe of Divine righteousness ; " shoes ", a walk and a way in the Spirit (Rom. viii. 2, 4) ; " a ring ", the symbol of authority, the right or jurisdiction of a son (John i. 12, 13) ; " the fatted calf ", food such as was not his before, the best of the father's house.

Each of these points in the Scriptures has a whole system of teaching.

The spirit of man, being the place of the new birth and the seat of this only true sonship (Gal. iv. 5, 6), is also therefore " the new man ", for it is " in newness of the spirit " that we are to live (Rom. vii. 6, etc.). Here it is that all the operations of God in our education, fellowship and co-operation have their base.

The ' prodigal's ' knowledge of the father after his new birth ' was such as he had never possessed before. He really did not know his father until grace came in. His spirit had been brought from death, darkness, distance, desolation, chaos, and he then had not just an objective knowledge of one whom he had termed ' father ', but a subjective and experimental understanding and appreciation of him, because the spirit of sonship had been born within him or given to him whereby he cried " Abba, Father ". There is no saving relationship to, or knowledge of, God except through grace and by new birth.

So, then, those who by being born anew have become " little children " (Matt. xviii. 3) or " babes " in spiritual things (1 Cor. iii. 1)—not wrong if we do not *remain* such—have to learn every thing afresh, because " all things have become new " (2 Cor. v. 17, 18). Such have to learn a new kind of knowledge, to live by a new kind of life, " newness of life " (Rom. vi. 4). Paul says that we are to act as those who are " alive from the dead " (Rom. vi. 13). We have to learn that our life, our natural life, cannot do God's will, live as God requires, or do God's work. Only by His risen life is this possible. An element of offence in this truth is that it demands a recognized and acknowledged weakness ; it requires that we have to confess that, in ourselves, for all Divine purposes, we are powerless and worthless, and that of ourselves we can do *nothing.* The natural man's worship of strentgh, efficiency, fitness, ability, meets with a terrible rebuff when it is confronted with the declaration that the universal triumph of Christ, over hierarchies

more mighty than those of flesh and blood, was because
" he was crucified through weakness " (2 Cor. xiii. 4);
God reduced to a certain impotency ! And " God chose
the weak things . . . to confound the things that are
mighty " (1 Cor. i. 25 — 27). To glory in infirmity, that
Christ's power may rest upon him, is a far cry from the
original Saul of Tarsus; but what an extraordinary
change in mentality ! God has, however, always drawn
a very broad line between natural " might " and
" power " on the one hand, and " My Spirit " on the
other (Zech. iv. 6), and for evermore that distinction
abides.

This ' new-born babe ' has to learn a new walk, now
in the Spirit as different from nature. There may be many
slips and perhaps tumbles, but such are not altogether
evil if they are marks of a stepping out in faith rather
than sitting still in fleshly disobedience or fear. We
have shown that the nature of this walk is that reason,
feeling, and natural choice are no longer the directive
laws or criteria of the spiritual man. For such an one
there are frequent experiences of a collision and contradiction between soul and spirit. The reason would dictate a certain course, the affections would urge in a
certain direction, the will would seek to fulfil these
judgments and desires; but there is a catch somewhere
within—a dull, leaden, lifeless, numbed something at
the centre of us which upsets everything, contradicts us,
and all the time *in effect* says No ! Or it may be the
other way round. An *inward* urge and constraint finds
no encouragement from our natural judgment or reason,
and is flatly contrary to our natural desires, inclinations,
preferences or affections: while in the same natural
realm we are not at all willing for such a course. In this
case it is not the judgment against the desire, as is frequently the case in everybody's life, but judgment, desire
and will are all joined against intuition. Now is the
crisis ! Now is to be seen who is to rule the life ! Now
the " natural " man, or the outer man of sense, and the
" inner " man have to settle affairs.

To learn to walk in the Spirit is a life-lesson of the

new man, and as he is vindicated—as he always will be *in the long run*—he will come to take the absolute ascendency over the " natural " man and his mind ; and so by the energizing of the Holy Spirit in`the spirit of the new man, the Cross will be wrought out to the nullifying of the mind of the flesh (which, in spiritual things, always ends in death) and in the enthronement of the spiritual mind which is " life and peace " (Rom. viii. 6).

This, then, is the nature of the walk in the Spirit, and its application is many-sided. But we must remember the law of this walk, which is faith. We walk *in* the Spirit but " we walk *by* faith " (2 Cor. v. 7).

To walk by faith there must, in the very nature of the case, be a stripping off of all that the outer man of the senses clings to, demands, craves as a security and an assurance.

When the spiritual life of God's people is in the ascendent, they are not overwhelmed by either the absence of human resources on the one hand, or by the presence of humanly overwhelming odds against them on the other hand.

This is patent in their history as recorded in the Scriptures. But it is also true that when the spiritual life is weak, undeveloped, or at an ebb, they look round for some tangible, seen resource upon which to fasten. Egypt is the alternative to God whenever and wherever spiritual life is low. To believe in and trust to the intuitive leadings of the Holy Spirit in our spirit, even though all is so different from the ways of men, and even though such brings us to a Canaan which for the time being is full of idolatry and where a mighty famine reigns: where all is so contrary to what our outer man has decided must be in keeping with a leading and a promise of God ; to leave our old sphere of life in the " world ", to break with our kindred, our father's house, for *this— this !* and then to have to wait through much continuous stripping off of those means, and methods, and habits, and judgments, which are the very constitution of the natural man—this is the law of the spiritual walk, but this is God's chosen and appointed way of the mightiest

vindication. Spiritual children and riches, and fruitfulness, and service, permanence, and the friendship of God,
are for such Abrahams of faith or such children of Abraham in the spirit. God has laid a faith-basis for His
superstructure of spiritual glory, and only that which is
built upon such a foundation can serve spiritual ends.
Let this be the test of our walk in all personal, domestic,
business and Church affairs. Here, again, we have a
principle which, if applied, would be revolutionary, and
would call for the abandonment of a tremendous amount
of carnal, natural, worldly stuff in our resources and
methods. " Faith apart from works is dead " (James ii.
26). True, but the works of faith—of the spirit—are
not those of the flesh ; the two realms are not compar-
able. The walk in the flesh is one thing, but the walk
in the Spirit is quite another. The things of the Spirit
are foolishness to the flesh. Men of faith see what others
do not, and act accordingly. This also being true of men
who have lost their reason, the two are often confused,
and the children of the flesh think the children of the
spirit mad or insane. They are unable to discriminate
between even the insanity of men and " the foolishness
of God ", which is " wiser than men " (1 Cor. i. 25).

Abraham was fortified by his faith, but his walk by
faith was intensely practical, though so different from
the walk in the flesh. A writer has said that faith brings
us into difficulties which are unknown to men who walk
in the flesh, or who never go out in faith. But such
difficulties place us beyond the power of the flesh to
help, and make special Divine revelations necessary, and
God always takes advantage of such times to give such
needed education of the spirit. It is thus that the men
of the spirit are taught and come to know God as no
others know Him. Thus, faith is the law of the walk of
the new man—the inner man—which brings him by
successive stages into the very heart of God, Who crowns
this progress with the matchless designation, " my
friend " ! (Isa. xli. 8).

One other thing in general has to be mentioned. The
new man of the spirit has to learn a new speech. There

is the language of the spirit, and he will have to realize increasingly that speech with " enticing words of man's wisdom ", or what man calls " excellency of speech " (1 Cor. ii. 1, 4), will avail nothing in spiritual service. If all the religious speech and preaching and talking about the gospel which goes on in one week were the utterance of the Holy Spirit, what a tremendous impact of God upon the world would be registered ! But it is obviously not so and this impact is not felt. It is impossible to speak in and by the Holy Spirit without something happening which is related to eternity. But this capacity belongs only to the " born of the Spirit " ones, whose spirits have been joined to the Lord, and even they have to learn how to cease from their own words and speak as they are moved by the Holy Spirit. It is a part of the education of the inner man to have his outer man slain in the matter of speech, and to be brought to the state to which Jeremiah was brought—" I cannot speak ; for I am a child " (Jer. i. 6). Not only as sinners have we to be crucified with Christ, but as preachers, or speakers, or talkers. The circumcision of Christ, which Paul says is the cutting off of the whole body of the flesh, has to be applied to our lips, and our spirit has to be so much in dominion that, on all matters where God cannot be glorified, we " *cannot* speak ". A natural facility of speech is no strength in itself to spiritual ministry ; it may be a positive menace. It is a stage of real spiritual development when there is a genuine fear of speaking, unless it is in words " which the Holy Ghost teacheth " (1 Cor. ii. 13). On the other hand a natural inability to speak need be no handicap. To be present " in weakness, and in fear, and in much trembling " (1 Cor. ii. 3), may be a state which befits an apostolic, nay, rather, a Holy Spirit ministry. The utterance of God is a very different thing in every way from that of man. How much is said in the Scriptures about " conversation ", " the tongue ", " words " etc., and ever with the emphasis that these are to be in charge of the spirit, and not merely expressions of the soul in any of its departments !

If it is true that only the quickened spirit can receive Divine revelation, it is equally true that such revelation requires a Divine gift of utterance in order to realize its spiritual end. It is possible to preach truth without the preacher having any *spiritual* apprehension of it; that is, from a merely *mental* apprehension. The preaching may be just natural ability; but the grievous fact may be that neither the one who preaches nor those to whom he preaches will be in the good of the living and working values of the truth. The spiritual results are hardly worth the effort and expenditure. The virtue of speech resulting in abiding fruit to the glory of God, whether that speech be preaching, teaching, conversation, prayer, is not in its lucidity, eloquence, subtlety, cleverness, wit, thoughtfulness, passion, earnestness, forcefulness, pathos, etc., but in that it is an utterance of the Holy Ghost.

" Thy speech betrayeth thee " may be applied in many ways, for whether we live in the flesh or in the spirit, in the natural man or in the spiritual man, will always be made manifest by how we speak and the spiritual effect of the fruit of our lips.

Oh, for crucified lips amongst God's people, and oh, for lips among God's prophets, touched with the blood-soaked, fire-charged coal from that one great altar of Calvary !

CHAPTER SIX

THE SOUL AND DECEPTION

ONE MATTER UPON WHICH the Bible is unmistakably clear throughout is that of man's deception. All God's methods with man have had this fact behind them. With and ever since the Fall the race is regarded as being a deceived race. Not only was the race initially deceived in Adam, but it is ever led on in its deception to deeper depths. Rather than escape from this deception by what is called ' enlightenment', i.e. civilization, education, culture, etc., these are only making the deception stronger. This is seen in the fact that the most ' enlightened' and ' advanced' nations are, at this late hour of the world's history, locked in the grip of a force which compels them to use all their enlightenment for producing the means of mutual destruction on such a scale and by such devilish and barbarous ways as have never been known before. Let us here introduce one or two passages of Scripture.

" *Now the serpent was more subtil than any beast of the field. . . . And he said unto the woman, Yea, hath God said . . . ? (Gen. iii. 1).*

" *But the Spirit saith expressly, that in later times some shall fall away . . . giving heed to SEDUCING SPIRITS and doctrines of demons* " *(1 Tim. iv. 1).*

" *This wisdom is not a wisdom that cometh down from above, but is earthly, sensual* (soulical), *devilish* " *(James iii. 15).*

" *And the great dragon was cast down, the old serpent, he that is called the Devil and Satan, the deceiver of the whole world ; he was cast down . . . and his angels . . . with him* " *(Rev. xii. 9).*

" *And cast him into the abyss . . . that he should*

71

deceive the nations no more" (Rev. xx. 3).

"And the devil that deceived them was cast into the lake of fire . . ." (Rev. xx. 10).

In these passages, Satan is seen to be the deceiver, first of the woman and finally of the whole inhabited earth. Deception was his first method, and deception was the very heart of the Fall.

Man is by nature now a deceived creature. Deception *is* deception, and the deceived never know it until they are enlightened or delivered. It is like a disease. There are forms of mental sickness which cause those who are so suffering to believe certain things which to the healthy mind are ridiculous and impossible. It is useless to argue with them, and futile to try to convince them of the untruth of their beliefs. Indeed, it is cruel at times to oppose them. If you are to live with them in any measure of peace and be at all helpful you have to take the attitude of agreeing with them and deal with the situation along some other line. Otherwise it is going to be continual clash. The only way to change their convictions is to heal their sickness.

So it is with man. He believes many things as to himself, his ability, potentialities, destiny, about God and about the world, which are not true. He mistakes certain things for other things, but he cannot see that he is deceived. It is useless to hold objects before a blind man, and to tell him to see them ; and it is foolish to be surprised or annoyed that he does not do so. So the Scriptures say, " The natural (soulical) man receiveth not the things of the Spirit of God: for they are foolishness unto him ; *and he cannot know them . . ."* (1 Cor. ii. 14). And again, " The god of this world hath blinded the minds of the unbelieving " (2 Cor. iv. 4).

Now, when we go to the source of this deceived condition, we find that it originated in the soul. The Deceiver assailed the soul—desires, reason, will—and drew this out as a basis of life apart from and independent of God. The motive was to have things in the *ego,* the self, instead of in God by dependence. Having succeeded in getting man to so exalt the *ego* to independence and superiority, he captured man as now a suited instrument for his purposes. Man ceased to be suited to the purposes of God, for his very nature was changed. This man, changed by complicity with Satan, is a false man, not a true man according to God's mind; and is now suited to Satan's false kingdom. The history of man in his natural state is the history of a lie, a false nature, a false expectation, a false hope, a false faith and a false world. The end of *that* man and *that* world is sorry, tragic disillusionment. By the aid of a spirit which, while still existing, is no longer in the place of living fellowship with God, this man faintly glimpses or senses something more of intention and purpose in his being than he can grasp. It eludes him, he cannot come into real touch with it; and so life mocks him, and he seeks satisfaction in other and further deceptions and illusions. Thus he is a part of the creation which the Word of God says is " subjected to vanity " (Romans viii. 20). Conscience still is more or less active, but always accusing or excusing, never approving.

As we have said, not only was deception an initial work of the enemy in the soul of man; he presses this advantage, or works on this vantage ground; and wherever he has this ground of nature he seeks to advance his own government and power thereby. As we shall see, the stronger the soul-life in a person, the greater the peril to that one, and the greater the advantage to Satan and the evil powers. The pursuit of this course is by a multitude of ways, always adapted to the people with whom he has to do. With the ungodly he employs one method; with the religious, who recognize God, another. With the spiritual he resorts to yet other ways, and for them his whole system of deception is by counterfeiting God's system of truth.

He counterfeits God Himself. He " fashioneth himself into an angel of light " (2 Cor. xi. 14). He counterfeits the Church of God with his " synagogue of Satan "

(Rev. ii. 9). He counterfeits the works of God with his "signs and lying wonders" (2 Thess. ii. 9). There is a counterfeit life, and there are counterfeit "gifts" (as of the Holy Spirit). There is counterfeit Divine (?) power. There are counterfeit conversions, spiritual (?) experiences, guidance. He uses Scriptures in a false way to counter God's meaning by them. There is counterfeit worship of God, counterfeit teaching, "doctrines of demons". There is a counterfeit baptism of the Holy Ghost with "tongues", etc. To those who know the Word of God, all these things are not strange, but are exposed therein.

The point is this. Satan, as the Deceiver, could not bring all that upon man from the outside. Man must first be constituted so that Satan can find in him that which responds to his deception. There must be, for all that, something in man which is the organ to be used. The play of Satan upon the soul of Adam drew that soul out as the ground of procedure. It stretched itself beyond its legitimate measure, and Satan impinged upon it. Thus an alliance came about between man's *psuche* (soul) and the powers of evil, "deceiving spirits". The object was gained—the ability to know good and evil—and God admitted this. "The man is become as one of us, to know good and evil" (Gen. iii. 22). But at what a cost ! Knowledge in itself is not evil, although it would be well for man if he did not know some things. It is knowledge *apart from God* that has rendered man a prisoner, a slave, and has cost him that knowledge which is eternal life. "This is life eternal, that they should know thee the only true God, and him whom thou didst send, Jesus Christ" (John xvii. 3). The cost was a "darkened understanding" (Eph. iv. 18). The Apostle Paul, who said that "it pleased God ... to reveal his Son *in* me" (Gal. i. 15, 16), also placed on record that that revelation was intended by the Lord to constitute him an instrument "to open their eyes, that they may turn from darkness to light and from the *power of Satan* unto God" (Acts

xxvi. 18). As to this, he further said: " God, that said, Light shall shine out of darkness . . . shined in our hearts, to give the light of the *knowledge of the glory of God* in the face of Jesus Christ " (2 Cor. iv. 6).

Whenever God in Christ is revealed in the inner man, deception and Satan's power are destroyed, and the man is set free. Against this inshining, Satan works by every conceivable means, ranging from open assault to destroy the messengers, to beautiful substitutes for the truth. But let us return to the principle.

To extend and consolidate his work of deception, and to build his rival and false kingdom, the Deceiver must have *ego-*, soul- or self-life. Herein lies the greatness of the peril of *believers* leaning toward their own self-life, for his occasion against God is greatest in their case. Herein, also, lies the explanation of many other things, as that called ' spiritualism ' or ' spiritism ' and dictatorship, etc.

Children of God who lean to the soul on any or all of its sides—reason (intellect), emotion (feelings) or will (volition)—will be a ready prey for deception. First of all, such people are already a contradiction of their essential nature as now—by new birth—spiritual. It becomes clear at the outset that they are locked up and a law unto themselves. *Their* way is *the* way, and they see no other. As to further light, they are largely unteachable ; as to further experience, they are content ; as to another course, they cannot conceive of it.

Christians who live in their own mind will often be found occupied with a question. They cannot live without a question or a problem. If one is shattered, they will soon have another. Thus they go ever round in a circle, and come back to their starting point, making no real spiritual progress. Like a horse in the ring, they are whipped and driven, and there is no expanse of life or vision. Or they lash others with their ideas and seek to subject other minds to their own. It may eventuate in some very weird, unsound and untrue conclusions. At length somewhere in this occult position—for it is nothing less—a deception will be found, and Satan's hand will be seen.

The same thing is true with regard to Christians living on the emotional side of the soul. This side demands experiences, evidences, manifestations. Indeed the whole realm of sense-life governs here. If we intensify and project our emotional side sufficiently, we can have *any* experience that is possible. The whole body and mind can be involved. Vocal cords or solar plexus may be affected. There may be facial distortions, rigidity, ' second sight', visions, extra capabilities, prodigious strength, mirth, ecstasy, etc. All these, from simple beginnings, may come through the psychical or soul-life as extended and strained along the line of intense desire.

If this is true in these two directions, how true it is on the side of the will. A forceful, dominating, assertive soul, not under the government of the Holy Spirit, is a terrible menace to the interests of God. Decisions will be made, courses adopted, objectives secured, positions occupied, in the name of devotion to God, which will be Towers of Babel, Pyramids of Egypt, Ishmaels of Abram (not *Abraham*). There will be a good deal of remorse bound up with these achievements eventually, and a wish that they had never been. The result will be something false, and many may be involved in the tragedy.

If there is a combination of a strong soul-life with an acute and needle-like brain the supreme peril is that of grasping the deeper implications and meanings of Divine truth, so that it seems to be revelation. Thus, through the soul there is an imitation revelation, which is really only keen natural insight. Usually, when the soul is strong along one line, we shall find it strong in other directions, and so the craving for a sense of power will not be far away. This keen insight, this quick or acute grasp of things, will demand as its complement an opportunity to exhibit itself, and this in its outworking will be to bring others under its influence. The test of genuine revelation is as to whether the one concerned is manifestly well crucified to a desire for power, position, influence. Can that one be resisted, assailed, thwarted, rejected, without in some form *seeking* to come out even or on top ? An element of personal domination or self-vindication will destroy the ministry and discredit the ' revelation ' of such an one. Oh, the peril of getting hold of Divine truth in order to *use* it !

God has laid down every safeguard against this kind of thing in what is truly of Himself. Fellowship, relatedness, interdependence, in the Church which is His Body, are not only privileges or extra factors in a Christian life ; they are basic laws for safeguarding Divine interests from the dangers of independence and personal dominance. This is why one who is in a doubtful position is called upon to " hear the church " (Matt. xviii. 17). That means ultimately the surrendering of their own judgment and way to the spiritual judgment of a spiritual church. This in turn—provided the church is walking in the light—is coming under the headship of Christ as " head over all things to the church, which is his body" (Eph. i. 22, 23). " Subjecting yourselves one to another in the fear of Christ" (Eph. v. 21) is something which cuts the ground from under Satan's feet. In keeping with this principle, *the Holy Spirit never made an individual the sole overseer of a church.* Elders, not an elder, were made in *every* city and church. God will not have anyone lording it over His heritage. This opens up the whole subject of Divine order which would require too extensive a deviation for our present intention. But let us emphasize that the law of mutual subjection is but the outworking of that subjection of Christ to His Father which led to the complete nullification and discomfiture of Satan in His own case. All of Satan's temptations of Christ were intended to seduce Him by deception, even to quoting Scripture. If Christ had asserted Himself, instead of referring and deferring to the Father, Satan would have triumphed. What a great deal there is in letting go to God !

What we have said has been mainly on the positive side. The soul can be passive ; but this is only another form of soulishness. There is the weak passivity of soul which makes it easy for Satan to just play with those concerned ; or which means that, being altogether neg-ative, they count for nothing, and it may be that, sooner or later, he will crush them out of simple trust by pro-ducing an inferiority complex. On the other hand, there is that more positive passivity—if we may put those two words together. This is that deliberate rendering of the mind and will negative, so that a mediumistic state is produced. It is not necessary to say what the results of this are in the direction of deception.

When all has been said about the peril of soul-life as such, we have to recognize that the end is *death*. In-jury is done in the mind, in the nerves, in the spiritual life, in the work of God. A counterfeit spiritual experi-ence, when it has passed or been withdrawn by Satan, or exposed, may result in the black darkness and despair of ' the unpardonable sin ', the ' sin against the Holy Ghost ', Satan's master-stroke in the whole deception, for here even the all-efficacious blood of Christ is robbed of its virtue, so far as the faith of those concerned goes. How necessary, then, it is that the Cross should have done its work in relation to *ourselves* as well as our past sins ! How tremendous a principle is embodied in Paul's words, " *I* have been crucified with Christ, and it is no longer *I* . . ." (Gal. ii. 20) !

Strong-mindedness may be thought to be a praise-worthy or excellent thing, but let it be recognized as an infinitely dangerous thing if the one who has it is not a crucified man or woman so far as self is concerned. " The heart is deceitful above all things, and it is exceed-ingly corrupt " (Jer. xvii. 9).

Many movements have swept over this earth with the name of Christ attached to them. They claim to be for Him, and multitudes are swept into their nets. There are ' conversions ' and experiences. There are super-natural features connected with them. But they are psychical in their foundation. Physical persons with psychical experiences and powers, abnormal and un-canny personal influence, are behind them ; and a cult is developed by certain methods being standardized. These methods or soul-tactics are employed to draw out *soul*-expression in certain forms. It may be a religious form of psycho-therapy or psycho-analysis, and it has remarkable effects upon those who respond to it.

The infallible test of all such things is as to what place they give to that fundamental aspect of the Cross of Christ which sets man by nature wholly aside and gives him no place at all—that is, the death of the man, not only the remission of his sins. Try this truth in such movements and they will collapse, and be popular no longer.

It is a matter of very great importance to be able to discriminate between what we have just mentioned and spiritual understanding.

SPIRITUAL UNDERSTANDING

Paul prayed for saints that they might " be filled with the knowledge of his will in all spiritual wisdom and understanding " (Col. i. 9).

Understanding implies a sense or apprehension of the fuller meaning of what is known, with the ability to apply that knowledge to adequate value. It is a matter of intuitive recognition or perception of the hidden nature and trend of things, and differs from the merely outward impression made upon the senses which calls for thought and reasoning. There may be something of this, as we have seen, in people of good and quick intelligence naturally, but spiritual understanding is something more. It is that faculty of the renewed spirit —an insight, perception, sense, appreciation in relation to Divine matters—which is the work of the Holy Spirit. It is the faculty which makes its possessor assured in an inward way of what is of God and what is not so, when very fine questions are at issue and when things are not by any means obvious. This ' discernment ' or ' judgment' cannot always at first be explained or given a reason ; it is just there, and very real to those who have it. Spiritual understanding is one of the most important things in the equipment of any Christian for responsibility. To put anyone into a position of responsibility in the things of God, or for anyone to take such a position, without this qualification will be to jeopardize the work of God and to put all related thereto into a false and dangerous situation. Something much more than just good 'common sense' and natural judgment is required in things eternal and spiritual. The one pre-eminent object and goal of this spiritual faculty is the knowledge of God, and it does not matter how great and complete may be a man's knowledge otherwise, the one indispensable requirement for responsibility in spiritual work is that he knows God in a measure beyond all natural capability or possibility. No efficiency can substitute for spiritual understanding !

It must be possible for all who are affected by what is said and done to find in the one who speaks and works a personal, living and true knowledge of God, a deep spiritual understanding.

It is significant how much people themselves are brought into the limelight by some forms of Christian work ; but it is not the Christianity of Romans vi !

Any movement which would make for self-consciousness is missing the way. Self-consciousness, whether it be bad self or good self, big self or little self, is weakness and evil. While all that we write here is necessary, we believe, to enlighten as to a great fact, it is not to turn people in on themselves for self-analysis, introspective occupation. This would be fatal ! Christ is our only safe and healthy occupation ; and He is the deliverer from ourselves. A basic and crisic thing must have taken place, so that we know by an established law and an inward government when we cross the line from Christ to self in our own souls. A simple, humble and selfless way is safe ; so let us *not refrain from stepping out on the Lord in conscious weakness, for fear of moving in the soul and not in the spirit.*

CHAPTER SEVEN

WORLD DOMINATION OR DOMINION ?

In the course of our lifetime we have beheld a new phenomenon, or the return of an old one. It is the meteoric rise of dictators. We say truly when we say that this has been phenomenal. In a few short months, from nowhere and nothing, from ostracism, ridicule, and almost general suspicion, such have risen to a place where not only their own nations are at their feet, but all nations are holding their breath while these dictators speak. How is it explained ? What is the principle basic to it ?

It dates back to the eternal counsels of God. In those counsels God determined to gather up the dominion of this world under the headship of His Son. (Adam was " a figure of him that was to come " [Rom. v. 14]).

"... *He hath appointed a day in which he will judge the world in righteousness IN A MAN whom he hath ordained ..." (Acts xvii. 31).*

" *And he charged us to preach unto the people, and to testify that this is he who is ordained of God to be the Judge of the living and the dead " (Acts x. 42).*

" *For there is one God, one mediator also between God and men, himself MAN, Christ Jesus " (1 Timothy ii. 5).*

(See also Eph. i. 9, 10 ; iv. 10 : Col. i. 16 — 19 : Heb. i. 8 ; ii. 6 — 10.)

Thus it has been made known that the dominion of this world and of all which, being beyond it, relates to it is eternally vested in a *Man*: the One Who is known to be the Son of God, Who became Son of man. He is the " heir of all things ". The inheritance is the " inhabited earth to come " (Heb. ii. 5). But there is

G

another who has assumed the rôle of rival to God's Son, and whose ambition has ever been world-dominion. The background of this world's history, that is, the spiritual and unseen background of the cosmos, can be summed up in a few quotations from Scripture.

"... *Cain was of the evil one, and SLEW HIS BROTHER*" (1 *John iii. 12*).

"*Ye are of your father the devil. ... He was A MURDERER from the beginning*"(*John viii. 44*).

"*Which of the prophets did not your fathers persecute? and they KILLED THEM WHICH SHEWED BEFORE OF THE COMING OF THE RIGHTEOUS ONE ; of whom ye have now become betrayers and murderers*" (*Acts vii. 52*).

"*A man planted a vineyard, and set a hedge about it, and digged a pit for the winepress, and built a tower, and let it out to husbandmen, and went into another country. And at the season he sent to the husbandmen a servant, that he might receive from the husbandmen of the fruits of the vineyard. And they took him, and beat him, and sent him away empty. And again he sent unto them another servant ; and him they wounded in the head, and handled shamefully. And he sent another ; and him they killed : and many others ; beating some and killing some. He had yet one, a beloved son : he sent him last unto them, saying, They will reverence my son. But those husbandmen said among themselves, This is THE HEIR ; come let us kill him, and THE INHERITHANCE SHALL BE OURS. And they took him, and KILLED HIM, and cast him forth ...*" (*Mark xii. 1 − 8*).

The emphasis is ours, for the purpose of indicating the connecting thoughts. The governing matter is that of the inheritance vested in God's Son. The next thing is a long history of jealousy working out in murder wherever that Son is in view in type, prophecy, or reality.

We next come to Satan's means, or instrument, of domination. It is also in *man*. As God's Son is the Man according to His mind and after His heart (using human language of God) so, as we have sought to point out, Satan sought to adapt, and succeeded in adapting, man to *his* thought for *his* purpose. The history of man is a long-drawn-out effort to reach to heaven independently of God, the course of Cain : power, rule, domination, worldly glory, reputation, etc. It is the story of *man* coming to the fore and occupying the place of honour. It is the pride of Satan working through the poor, worthless, ruined human race (as viewed from God's standpoint). Oh, what an indictment of so much that is brought into Christian work to make a success of it, even by those who mean to be so consecrated ! Think of the value that is attached to degrees, titles and orders in the propaganda work of the Christian organizations.

To carry weight, have influence, attract interest, make an impression, we find a feverish quest for people of degree, title, of standing as amongst men, and when we see these letters and qualifications on the announcements, advertisements and programmes of Christian effort, we may well ask, ' But what has that to do with the work of God ? What place does that have in Holy Ghost activity ? ' Degrees, titles and honours may be all right in their own realm, if they are really earned and the result of genuine qualification as before the best standard of honourable men ; but it is of the essence of antichrist to make them currency for profit in the things of God ! These are strong words, but we will prove our point. It would be well for all Godly men to suppress and hide their degrees when they come into the presence of holy things, and so holy a God. Here, only spiritual values are recognized. But let us proceed.

Satan has ever in his mind world-domination through man, and the full-grown expression of this mind will be antichrist. Now let us see several things which are said about antichrist.

> " *Little children, it is the last hour: and as ye heard that antichrist cometh, even now have there arisen many antichrists* ".
>
> " *Who is the liar but he that denieth that Jesus is the Christ? This is the antichrist* " (1 John ii. 18, 22).
>
> " *Every spirit that confesseth not Jesus is not of God: and this is the spirit of the antichrist* " (1 John iv. 3).
>
> " *Let no man beguile you in any wise: for it will not be, except the falling away come first, and the man of sin be revealed, the son of perdition, he that opposeth and exalteth himself against all that is called God or that is worshipped; so that he sitteth in the temple of God, setting himself forth as God...* "
>
> " *Whose coming is according to the working of Satan with all power and signs and lying wonders ...* " (2 Thess. ii. 3, 4, 9).

From these passages we learn four things:

(1)　Antichrist is firstly a spirit.

(2)　Antichrist is the expression of a principle.

(3)　Antichrist is a type of man.

(4)　Antichrist has a kingdom or world-domination in view.

No. 1 relates antichrist directly to the evil powers, "not of God".

No. 2 means that the glory of man is ever the factor which governs.

No. 3 means that this spirit and principle operate by way of a dominant *ego*, and intense soul-force.

No. 4 indicates what it is antichrist is after.

Now we are able to understand the times and world-happenings. Steadily the world is coming under the domination of a handful of dictators. The probability is that they will suffer one another until other forms of world-government are weakened. But in time they will have to eliminate one another until one is left supreme. (That is, one *representative* of a human system.) Leaving prophecy aside as not being our present subject, there are however two or three things that need to be said in summarizing the whole matter.

Firstly, may it not be a significant thing that in the realm of what speaks of God there are no outstanding giants in spiritual leadership to-day ? Some of us came into our ministry just at the tail-end of a generation of such. We will not mention names, but Bible teachers, missionary leaders and mighty preachers were in the earth in no sparsity for a generation or more. There was a galaxy of them, and their works stand to-day. But we have seen the last of them pass off this scene, and there are few, if any, successors. Sometimes we almost cry that God would raise up men adequate to the present spiritual need. Why are things as they are ? May it not be that as Satan is bringing his antichrist in so manifestly along the lines of the power and glory of *man*, God, in His things, is keeping man as such hidden and largely at a discount because He is going to bring in His Man with heavenly glory ? May not dictatorship then be one of the most powerful signs of the times ?

But then what of the phenomena ? We cannot wholly account for this power, influence and domination on human grounds. There are greater forces at work which operate in spite of the will of the people. It is uncanny. And yet is it not perfectly true that the connecting link between the instrument and the supernatural powers is an intense and terrific soul strength ? A will is asserted which will brook no resistance. A mind is projected which is agile, subtle and tireless in the extreme. An emotional force is poured forth like a tidal wave carrying all before it, and working people up to uncontrollable frenzy. Yes, it is the consummate demonstration of that selfhood, that *ego*, which first drew things away from God and cast His Son out of His world. All this is with the accompaniment of pageantry which makes *man* its object of glory and almost worship. Is this not enough to make Christian men shun everything and anything which would make them to appear something before men ?

But, ' behold *the* Man ! ' How has world-dominion been secured in Him ? —for it has been secured. The answer is in the Scriptures :

"*. . . this mind . . . which was . . . in Christ Jesus: who, being in the form of God, counted it not a thing to be grasped* (margin) *to be on an equality with God, but emptied himself, taking the form of a bondservant* (margin), *being made in the likeness of men ; and being found in fashion as a man, he humbled himself, becoming obedient even unto death, yea, the death of the cross. Wherefore also God highly exalted him, and gave unto him the name which is above every name ; that in the name of Jesus every knee should bow, of things in heaven and things on earth and things under the earth, and that every tongue should confess that JESUS CHRIST IS LORD, to the glory of God the Father* " (*Phil. ii. 5 — 11*).

So that what counts before God and in His work is not man's attainments, achievements or abilities, but just the measure of Christ. What an infinitely higher level of spiritual life would be represented by God's people if the only consideration in the matter of their leadership, and the ministry, were that of the measure of Christ !

We have moved into a new phase of things. ' Revival ' is being sought earnestly, and certain great names in revival history are in mind, on lip, and much used to stimulate revival-mindedness or -mentality. But it may be that God is not going *now* to allow a great work of His to be related to men's names. Try as we will and may, we shall not produce anything adequate and living if God is not doing it. It has got to be *His* work, and manifestly His alone. Pentecost in its meaning and value for any time stands over against the background of the Cross—the Cross in which Christian disciples and apostles lost everything of this world.

They lost their Christ *after the flesh ;* they lost their kingdom of God *after the flesh.* They lost their own lives, reputations, hopes, expectations and faith so far as anything of God being bound up with this earth was concerned. They recovered all only in a heavenly and spiritual way. Their own *souls* were crucified when Christ died. But what a mighty recompense in the spirit !

There may be too much *soulishness* about for God to commit Himself, and He will not until there is more emptiness and despair.

There is one other thing which is apropos of what we have been saying. This introduces another set of Scriptures, such as :

" *And he put all things in subjection under his feet, and gave him to be head over all things to the church, which is his body, THE FULNESS OF HIM that filleth all in all* " *(Eph. i. 22, 23).*

" *Having abolished in his flesh the enmity . . . that he might create in himself . . . ONE NEW MAN . . . and might reconcile them both in one body . . ."* *(Eph. ii. 15, 16).*

"Unto him be the GLORY IN THE CHURCH and in Christ Jesus unto all generations for ever and ever " *(Eph. iii. 21).*

These, and other suchlike Scriptures, make it clear that " the church, which is his body " is the " one new man " which is destined to be the instrument of Christ's world-dominion.

This " man " is the fruit of His Cross. This Church was born of His travail. This is a crucified, buried, and risen Church in union and identification with Christ. What glory can it know save the glory of its Head ? In this Church there is no place for antichrist in principle. It is in and by the Church which is His Body that the fulness of Christ will be displayed, and God will come into His rights. " Unto him be the glory in the church *and* in Christ Jesus for ever and ever ".

In this connection, there is much said in the Scriptures as to measurement in relation to the Church. In type we have it in Solomon's Temple, but even more so in that of Ezekiel. There every aspect and phase is strictly measured by a heavenly standard. That which is represented by the types is brought out in the spiritual reality of the Church in " Ephesians ". There we have:

" *The breadth and length and height and depth* " *(iii. 18).*

" *The measure of the stature of the fulness of Christ* " *(iv. 13).*

" *The measure of the gift of Christ* " *(iv. 7).*

" *The working in due measure of each several part* " *(iv. 16).*

So that what governs in this spiritual Church or Body is the measure of Christ. We are told that in this Body no earthly factors have any place. " There cannot be Greek and Jew " (not, there is both Greek and Jew) ; no nationalism or national distinction ; no denominationalism, inter-denominationalism, or undenominationalism. All of these represent only human distinctions and differences from one another. Christ is other than all this, and, when Christ predominates, natural elements and features become subjected, whether temperamental, social, educational, national, or of any other kind. The ascendency of Christ is the only way to one-ness and spiritual power. It is in this " one new man " that " the exceeding riches of his grace " will be shown forth " in the ages to come " (Eph. ii. 7).

We have been careful in our use of the words ' dominion ' and ' domination '. The latter speaks of force, assertiveness, despotism and suchlike features. These belong to antichrist. The former is by Divine right with all the universe agreeing and co-operating eventually.

" *His dominion shall be from sea to sea, and from the River to the ends of the earth* " *(Zech. ix. 10).*

" *To him be the glory and the dominion for ever and ever* " *(Rev. i. 6).*

Spiritual power and soul-force are very different things, and they belong to different kingdoms, the kingdom of the heavens and the kingdom of men. Man's destiny, according to the thought of God, demands that he be born of the Spirit, walk in the Spirit, and come to *spiritual* maturity.

Chapter Eight

THE CROSS AND THE NEW MAN

The History of Man, from God's Standpoint, and His Own

By THE SIMPLE DIAGRAM herewith inserted, * we have attempted to set forth the inner history of man both from God's standpoint and his own.

Firstly, we have man " in the day that God created " him (Gen. v. 1). His threefold nature is defined.

i. Spirit: with three faculties, Conscience, Communion and Intuition ; the main value of which is spiritual apprehension.

ii. Soul: with Reason, Emotion, Will or Volition ; the function of which is interpretation for human life.

iii. Body: of flesh, blood and bone ; for executing or transacting the business of spirit and soul.

Then we have the relationship to God by the spirit. This is fivefold :

1. Likeness (basic, " spirit ").
2. Fellowship.
3. Knowledge (spiritual perception).
4. Co-operation.
5. Dominion.

Secondly, we have the ' Fall '.

The results and effects of this were, and are :

1. The human spirit subjected to the soul.

2. The soul the seat of the Satanic attack and triumph, having come under the power of evil forces.

3. The body, the instrument of the soul, under the influence of Satan, especially for purposes of pro-

* At end of book.

90

creation in man's own likeness, after his image (Gen. v. 3).

Then, by the spirit severed from God in what is meant by spiritual death, the fivefold relationship was disrupted—the likeness marred; the fellowship destroyed; the knowledge obscured; the co-operation made impossible; the dominion forfeited. So man is severed from God, alienated, darkened, spiritually paralysed and " subjected to vanity " (Rom. viii. 20).

From this point he is called flesh—" in their going astray they are flesh " (Gen. vi. 3)—and we know from the New Testament that this does not only mean mortality, but the presence of an active principle which is inimical to spirit and to God. Moreover, he is thenceforth known as the " natural man " (soulical). But, above all, he is actuated by " the god of this world " inasmuch as he chose—in his will—to believe in Satan in preference to God.

From this point a double history begins. This is represented in our diagram by the two sets of lines, one narrowing, the other broadening.

The narrowing lines set forth man's history from that time according to God's mind. From being the masterpiece of God's creative activity, God has " concluded " him under sin because of unbelief (Rom. xi. 32). So God introduces in type and symbol the principles of the Cross of Christ. Along this line nothing of man himself is ever accepted by God. Certain things—three mainly—are always kept clearly in view:

1. The fact of man's sinful state, under judgment.

2. Death, being the end of the natural man, to be the due of all, and to be accepted.

3. The perfections of Christ the only basis of all, or any further, relationship with God.

This is what is inherent in the instance of Cain and Abel. This is why death has such a large place in the whole Divine economy. And—wisdom, power and wonder of God !—herein He is seen taking hold of the very tail of the serpent, the very sting of death, the works of the devil, and making death the way of a new life, the pathway *to* His purpose in the resurrection of Christ and the spiritual resurrection of believers in Him. This, again, is why every offering acceptable to God, to bring man nigh, is to be without blemish. The expert eye of a priest, after the most thorough scrutiny, must be able to say ' It is perfect '. (This is actually what Christ cried on the Cross as to the conclusion of all His testings and fiery ordeal—" It is perfect ", not merely concluded or finished.)

On then, ever on, with unvarying, unchanging conclusiveness, God's mind leads to the Cross of Christ. Whenever a man or a people comes under immediate government of God, in relation to His eternal purpose, they will have one thing brought home to them. It is that in themselves " dwelleth no good thing " (Rom. vii. 18), that they are accepted only on the ground of a righteousness which is not of themselves, nor of works, but by faith—it is the goodness of Another. This realization will smite the natural man hip and thigh, that out of the smiting there may emerge one such as the Lord can look to, " even to him that is poor and of a contrite spirit " (or " heart ").

So we see that the Cross of Christ is God's mind as to the natural man, for there the Son of man took not only our sins but ourselves in His representative person, and died under the judgment of God in our stead, or as us (Rom. vi. 2 – 10 ; Col. ii. 12 ; 2 Cor. v. 14, 15, etc.). This Cross throws its reflex back to the hour of Adam's sin. It is for want of a complete or adequate realization of the meaning of the Cross, that so many Christians are " carnal ", or try to live for God out of themselves. This goes to the root of the ever-present weakness and poverty of spiritual life. There is much prayer for ' revival ', and much effort for ' the deepening of the spiritual life '. The only answer to this is a new knowing of the Cross, not only as to *sins* and a life of victory over *them,* but as to Christ as supplanting the natural man.

The conditions at Corinth which caused Paul to write, " I could not speak unto you as unto spiritual, but as unto carnal, as unto babes" (unduly so), were explained in the opening chapters of his first letter as being due to their living so much on the basis of the soulical ("natural") man; and his only remedy was "Jesus Christ, and him crucified". Yes, believers, "called saints" (1 Cor. i. 2) can do this, and can even bring spiritual gifts into the realm where they are soulishly valued and exploited. It is something to make us very sober and steady when we recognize that what is called the 'baptism' of the Holy Spirit, with 'tongues' and other 'gifts' following, does not necessarily carry with it the knowledge of the *major* things of the spiritual life. Hence Paul had to teach those who had such experiences the real meaning of baptism, the Cross, the Lord's Table, the Body of Christ, and Sonship. Revelation is something more than gifts or experiences. The manifestation gifts are no marks of spiritual maturity; often the reverse. Herein lies Satan's most subtle snare. The mistaking of such experiences for deep and real spirituality provides him with his most desired opportunity to lead the most sincere children of God into a false experience. The Cross as deeply applied to the soulical man is the only safeguard against the presentation of what is psychical as a marvellous imitation of what is spiritual.

To continue with our diagram, there is the other aspect. Man has ever refused to recognize and accept God's verdict about him. Hence he pursues a course of self-expression and self-realization. From his beginning, even when the way of God in Abel's offering was so definitely enunciated, he pursued his own course. He went out to build a world, to create a civilization, and to constitute a kingdom. Babel or Babylon is its name. It is the expression of and monument to man's power, ability, and glory. "Let us make *us* a *name*" (Gen. xi. 4). "Is not this *great* Babylon, which *I* have built . . . ?" (Dan. iv. 30). Thus, he inflates, expands and asserts himself. Yes, it *is* a wonderful world which he has produced, and it has got quite beyond him. He cannot manage it. Full of wonders, yes—but full of tragedy ! It is fast leading to his undoing, and his own productions will wipe out his civilization. He has set something going which, by its own momentum, has got out of his hands. God will have to step in to shorten the days of this issue, or no flesh will be saved (Matt. xxiv. 22). That is what is immediately on the horizon. What an amount we could write on this line ! but we refrain. Only fools, blind fools, Satan's dupes, see Utopia as the natural outcome of this present world course. Civilization has only accentuated soul-sense or -sensibility, and we already know something of the meaning of " men's hearts failing them for *fear* " (Luke xxi. 26).

Yet still God's position is unchanged. Man may build his kingdom, and build it to the clouds, but heaven is closed to him. The Cross of Christ proclaims that God settled the end of all that long since. So that ' Calvary ' is *zero* ! So far as God's eternal purpose is concerned, there is no way past the Cross but by death, in identification with Christ by faith. When that place has been taken and all its implications accepted, then a New Man is brought in as by resurrection-union with Christ. " If any man is in Christ, there is a new creation: . . ." (2 Cor. v. 17).

From that point another double process begins. There has to be a definite crisis in which *all* the meaning of God is accepted, *whether wholly understood or not*. The crisis involves and potentially carries with it everything.

The twofold process is, on the one hand, the ascendency of the new man, the spiritual man ; and on the other hand, the subjecting of the natural or old man. This is a life education. It is necessary to understanding. Were God to *actually* blot out, ' eradicate ', the old man, then the whole basis of spiritual training would be removed. We have elsewhere pointed out what this " newness of life " means in learning everything anew, in a different world, with new spiritual faculties. This new man is the "hidden man of the heart" (1 Peter iii. 4) and the training of him by "the Father of our spirits" (Heb. xii. 9) will be in keeping with the earlier statement in the same letter, "the dividing of soul and spirit" (Heb. iv. 12). If the remainder of the diagram is studied, the meaning of this will be clear; for here is a new and altogether other law— "the law of the Spirit of life". This life has its own law or laws, which have to be known.

It is a faith life. "That life which I *now* live . . . I live in faith . . ." (Gal. ii. 20). So, knowledge is the fruit of faith. We need go no further, but return to a final emphasis upon the crisis of the Cross. God has nothing to say to man, but there only. Every new development in the life of a child of God will in some way be by a new expression of the meaning of the Cross; deeper death unto fuller life. God keeps the balances with a steady hand, and eventually the last phase of our self-emptying here will issue in enthronement with Christ there.

CHAPTER NINE

THE RESURRECTION OR SPIRITUAL BODY

THE ORIGIN OF THE LIFE of a child of God as such is spiritual—"*that which is born of the Spirit is spirit*" (*John iii. 6*). The sustenance also of the life of such is spiritual. "*As the living Father sent me, and I live because of the Father; so he that eateth me, he also shall live because of me. This is the bread which came down out of heaven . . . he that eateth this bread shall live for ever . . . the words that I have spoken unto you are spirit, and are life*" (*John vi. 57, 58, 63*).

So also, the consummation of this life is spiritual, and is found in a spiritual body. We are not allowed to take the resurrection of Christ as a type of our resurrection physically, but we are allowed to take the nature of His resurrection body as the type of our resurrection body. There was something different from all others in Christ's resurrection. His body was sinless, and it therefore did not see corruption. " Thou wilt not . . . give thy Holy One to see corruption " (Acts ii. 27). His, in its particles, was preserved and resuscitated, so that it was recognizable as the same body after resurrection, bearing the marks of His crucifixion. And yet so other ! Our bodies will see corruption, for they are already corrupted. " This corruptible must put on incorruption " (1 Cor. xv. 53). But there is that difference about the pre- and post-resurrection body which is in keeping with the whole principle of the believer's life. This principle is set forth in the following familiar words :

"*That which thou sowest, thou sowest not the body that shall be, but a bare grain; . . . but God giveth it a body even as it pleased him, and TO EACH SEED a body of its own . . . it is sown a natural* (soulical) *body; it is raised a spiritual body. If there is a natural*

H*

body, there is also a spiritual . . . Howbeit that is not first which is spiritual, but that which is natural; then that which is spiritual . . . we shall bear the image of the heavenly" (1 Cor. xv. 37 — 49).

By the Spirit were we first quickened and made spiritually alive. By the Spirit of life were we made free from the law of sin and death. So, by the Spirit of life is the consummation brought about when what is mortal is swallowed up of life.

In some way the human soul-life is bound up with the blood. So that body and soul have a special or peculiar relationship. The Old Testament statement, with repeated emphasis, is " The life (or soul) is in the blood ". This is also seen in the interchange of " life " and " soul " in the New Testament, especially in John's Gospel (e.g. xii. 25). Thus the present body of man is a physio-soulical, or a psycho-physical, body having a spirit. But the statement is that " flesh and blood cannot inherit the kingdom of God ; neither doth corruption inherit incorruption " (1 Cor. xv. 50). Any physician will say that the blood is the seat of disease. This is only another point of evidence in what we have been saying, that corruption lies ever in the soul. In Christ's resurrection body, there is no blood. " Handle me and see ; for a spirit hath not flesh and *bones,* as ye see me have " (Luke xxiv. 39).

This is, in the first place, the proof and vindication of His Sonship, and of His having lived and triumphed in His spirit, and having not yielded to the soul or self-life.

" Declared to be the SON OF GOD with power, according to the SPIRIT OF HOLINESS, by the resurrection from the dead " (Rom. i. 4).

The resurrection body therefore is not a blood-soul body, but a spirit body. This is the consummation of the spiritual life. Paul refers to this when he says,

" Whom he foreknew, he also foreordained to be conformed to the image of his Son, that he might be the firstborn among many brethren " (Rom. viii. 29).

H

This follows his earlier words:

> "*The earnest expectation of the creation waiteth for the revealing of the* `SONS` *of God . . . ourselves also, who have the FIRSTFRUITS OF THE SPIRIT, . . . groan within ourselves, waiting for our adoption* (majority) *to wit, the redemption of our body*" (*Romans viii. 19, 23*).

We are totally unable to understand what a spiritual body is, but we see that it is free from many of the limitations of our present form of existence. Our present purpose is not to attempt a description of life beyond the present order, but just to point out and emphasize the principle. There is all the difference between a bodiless spirit and a spiritual body, between a disembodied spirit and a spiritualized body. It is here that our mentality breaks down.

Then, again, all resurrection is not *this* resurrection. Our Lord has said that some will be raised unto a judgment resurrection ; others unto a life resurrection. The life resurrection is that of a spiritual body, the consummation or full fruit of a spiritual life. In the light of this, how important it is to know the difference between soul and spirit ; between religion as a thing of the soul, and true spirituality as from the Christ within, Who alone is the " hope of glory ".

> "*Behold, I tell you a mystery. We shall not all sleep, but we shall all be changed. . . ."*

It is, indeed, a mystery how a physical body can exist without all the features of this blood system. But we are told that it is so, and certain other statements in this connection indicate that it is so. For instance, in the resurrection they " neither marry, nor are given in marriage " (Luke xx. 35). This does away with a very great deal in soul and body. The whole procreative power and system as to this order of life will have gone.

But we have seen that the spirit has its own faculties and functions for knowing and doing, for sustaining and energizing.

There is one thing very evident; that Satan hates resurrection. He would obscure it by spreading a false report as to that of Christ. The one pre-eminent testimony and attestation of God is resurrection. The supreme note in the apostolic proclamation was " God raised him ! " The supreme note in a believer's experience is resurrection. Hence Satan is allowed to bring a servant of God into " deaths oft " (2 Cor. xi. 23), and we are suffered to have " the sentence of death within ourselves, that we should . . . trust in God who raiseth the dead " (2 Cor. i. 9).

This is not the evidence in which the soul rejoices. It prefers success, achievement, progress, reputation etc., according to man's standards. But heaven's standard measure of power is the resurrection of Christ. Hence Paul will cry, " that I may know him, and the power of his resurrection " (Phil. iii. 10). " The fellowship of his sufferings " and " becoming conformed unto his death " are the platform upon which this supreme power is demonstrated. But it takes a spiritual man to see this, and much more to desire it !

We have " the earnest of the Spirit " (2 Cor. i. 22) ; yes, the earnest of our resurrection body. This earnest is even in our mortal bodies. " *If the Spirit of him that raised up Jesus from the dead dwelleth in you, he that raised up Christ Jesus from the dead shall quicken also your mortal bodies through his Spirit that dwelleth in you* " *(Rom. viii. 11).* There is possible a present testimony in prospect of the resurrection of the body, even in mortal bodies.

CHAPTER TEN

THE SOUL, THE SPIRIT AND THE EVIL SPIRITUAL POWERS

THIS IS NOT A TREATISE on demon-possess-
ion, although reference will be made to the unhappy
reality.

At one point we have said that, in the Fall, the
powers of evil entered into alliance with the soul of man
by his complicity with Satan. Then we have sought to
show how those powers of evil take full advantage of
any undue projecting of the soul in order that they may
further the interests of Satan's false kingdom. We have
also, on the other hand, tried to make it clear that the
innermost reality of new birth and spiritual union with
God is something much deeper than the soul and all
soul-sense. It is this, for one thing, that we now wish to
follow up a little more closely.

First of all we must refer to that very real and painful
experience into which many—even of God's children—
pass by reason of physical and mental injury. There is
the ' nervous breakdown ', and there is neurasthenia ;
there is anaemia, and blood-pressure. Not invariably,
but more often than not, these maladies are made an
occasion for the enemy to make cruel assaults. There
is the terrific sense of—is it too strong to say ?—devil-
ishness *within*. The most wicked person alive could not
be more wicked than such sufferers feel and believe
themselves to be at times. Not only do they feel this,
but at times they speak and act out of harmony with a
truly Christlike disposition. Then, with one of these
maladies at least, there is an extra factor ; it is that of
secondary personality—the sense of another presence
as being in the immediate offing. We need not enlarge
upon this. Many, sadly enough, know all about it ; and
if any who read this have no experience of this kind or

100

with such sufferers, let them thank God, but not pass hasty judgment. Then what of that *fact,* which it is not pleasant to mention, but has to be recognized—the drive to self-destruction, which, alas, has not always been overcome ? We *cannot* say with truth that these are conditions which lie outside of the experience of true children of God. We have known the most godly and saintly to suffer thus.

Well, in the first place, the soul *is* the soul, and the stark reality is that it has these possibilities, capabilities, and tendencies bound up with it. At such times, and in such conditions, when the helpfulness of good health and a balanced physical system is no longer present, we see what is possible to *any* mortal under the same conditions. This is only a matter of the degrees in which a basic fact is manifested. Much can be done to relieve this condition and produce amiability and a more happy frame by physical readjustment and renewal, but good health with its attendant good demeanour never was saintliness in its essential nature. A man is not made really more Christlike in his *nature* by being relieved of certain nervous and mental aggravations, pressures, or sicknesses. Perhaps the greatest value of such relief is that he loses the melancholic beliefs about his *spiritual* state. *But what we may believe about ourselves under certain conditions, and what is actually the truth, may still be worlds apart.* Satan has led many children of God to extremes of despair, and even to self-injury, by the lie that their own soul-life is the criterion ; whereas, for the child of God, *Christ is the criterion.* Be the most self-assured, self-complacent, self-possessed, self-composed person imaginable, and you are not necessarily therefore a child of God. Be the most pressed, harrassed, tortured, devil-assailed person possible, but this need not alter the fact that you *are* a child of God.

DEMON DOMINATION AND DEMON POSSESSION

But before we go further with this there is another aspect of the matter to note. There is a difference between demon domination and demon possession.

This difference might be the salvation of many if they recognized it in time. It is far from our thought or intention to imply by anything that we have said that all men by nature are demon-possessed. An alliance is not a possession, and it need not be domination in the full sense. No two allied nations would agree to that. But we are now going further than just alliance, while stopping short of the possession. There are those who, because of a strength of soul-life being asserted on any of its sides—reason, emotion or will—become deceived and dominated by the evil spiritual fórces. In time they show signs of something extra to human wit and perception. They develop an uncanny power of mind in giving interpretations and explanations. These are often unanswerable along ordinary lines of reasoning. But, of course, this acuteness of mind is always in support of their own course, and it is so deeply and terrifically set in their conviction of right that even though their course cuts right across the precise Word of God they either do not see it or will not have it. Other symptoms also show themselves, in looks, conduct and voice. Here is domination. It is in the realm of the soul, and although it is on the high road to possession, it is still short of that. This kind of thing can clear up without demons being cast out, but it comes by much suffering and humiliation.

Surely, this was the history of Judas Iscariot. He will ever remain a mystery from some points of view, but we do know that his was a progressive course. He first allowed his own soul, or self-life, in avarice to govern him. Then, having capitulated to it, the ever present evil powers made their suggestion—to his gain ! (?) Playing with fire, he became *dominated* by those forces and plotted. At length—the inevitable issue of such a course being pursued—" Satan entered into Judas " (Luke xxii. 3). This is something more than soul. An evil spirit may be allied to a *soul*, but it can possess a *spirit*, like to like. * This is " spiritual wickedness ".

* Of course evil spirits can *inhabit* bodies, as in the case of the swine, but this is not in the same realm of things as spiritual possession. The incarnation of Satan in human life is something more than inhabiting a beast's body, which has no spiritual basis.

Satan's supreme and final object is to capture for possession the whole man—spirit, soul and body. We know that the disembodied evil spirits revolt against their condition of 'nakedness' more than anything. Perhaps this was their penalty when they "kept not their first estate" (Jude i. 6). Hence came Satan's eye upon man—God's creation—and hence his wish to sever man's spirit from God and possess it himself. But even before this he would use it.

THE KEY TO SPIRITUALISM

And so we must point out that it is because man has a spirit that he can have intercourse with fallen spirits. We believe that this explains the whole system of spiritism (spiritualism) and that the supposed departed with whom spiritualists communicate are none other than these " spiritual hosts " impersonating the departed, whom they knew in lifetime. Leaving the many phases of this thing in its outworkings and issues at the end of the age, let us note the terrible nemesis in wrecked minds and bodies; haunted, driven, distraught, reason-bereft souls; crowded asylums, prisons; suicides, moral and spiritual wrecks, etc.; all because that which was given to man specifically for union, communion and co-opera- tion with God, namely the spirit of man, has been used as the medium and instrument for this demon invasion and control of his life. The tremendous warnings and terrible judgments associated with all kinds of spiritism —necromancy, witches, " familiar spirits ", etc.—are because of the spirit complicity, dalliance, consorting, with fallen spirits whose purpose is always to capture men and women through their spirits. This they will do even by adopting the guise of an angel of light, and talking religion. Strange, isn't it ? that fifty years ago men threw off the belief in the supernatural in the Scriptures, and to-day they and their school so strongly embrace spiritism. Surely this is the " working of error " sent that they who received not the truth for the love of it " should believe a lie : that they all might be judged " (2 Thess. ii. 11, 12).

It was the spiritual background of their life which led to the destruction of the Egyptians, Canaanites, etc., and this was spiritism in different forms. But it was their being joined to demons that involved them.

THE DEEPEST REALITY IN THE CHILD OF GOD

Now, to return for a moment to the thing that is deeper in the true child of God than all else. We have devoted a whole book to this matter in *The Battle for Life,* but our present purpose would lack something vital if we omitted the particular point. We must always seek to realize that what has taken place in the new birth, that is, the renewing of our spirit and the imparting to it of eternal life, with the Holy Spirit and sonship, is far deeper than all surrounding conditions and circumstances ; and far deeper than our physical or our soulical life. Unless we hold on to that we have no ground of victory. It is possible for a child of God to pass into great soul-darkness, mental darkness, even to lose the reason and have to go to a mental home ; yes, and for things worse than that in the outer life ; and yet for the real relationship with the Lord to be unbroken. These extreme conditions may be no part of a Divine plan, but it is true that a part of God's ways with His children in their education is to cut off their sense-life at times. When this happens they have nothing to prove that they are His children: that is, nothing in all the realm of their own human consciousness. What is left is God, His Word and the *fact* that they have put their trust in Him. The real battle of faith is joined here. Not what *we* are, but what *He* is ! Not what we feel, but His facts.

> ' He cannot fail, for He is God.
> He cannot fail, He's pledged His word.
> He cannot fail, He'll see me through ;
> 'Tis God with Whom I have to do '.

It may please God to risk being misunderstood, and, to our way of thinking, seem to contradict Himself.

The education of ' sons ' is important above all things in this one respect, that they are to represent the reversing of the unbelief, and disobedience thereby, which led to man's spirit-separation from God. That spirit-union has to be established without the help of the soul, so that the soul will once more be put back into the place from which it so forbiddenly asserted itself.

This is the forming of Christ fully in us—that is, in our spirit.

SPIRITUAL SERVICE OR WARFARE

Having seen that the basis of all fellowship and co-operation with God is spiritual, in and through the born-again spirit, we must realize that this at once defines the real nature of our service. The background of all cosmic conditions is spiritual. Behind the things seen are the things unseen. The things which do appear are not the ultimate things.

"The whole world lieth in the evil one". There is a spiritual hierachy which, before this world was, revolted against the equality of the Son with the Father in the Throne, and in spite of the hurling out of heaven and the eternal doom which followed, has been in active revolt and antagonism to that " eternal purpose " right through the ages. A certain judicial hold upon this earth and the race in Adam was gained by Satan through the consent of that first Adam, through whom the purpose of God should have been realized on this earth.

Thus, we have Paul telling the members of the Body of Christ—the last Adam—that their warfare " is not against flesh and blood, but against the principalities, against the powers, against the world-rulers of this darkness, against the spiritual hosts of wickedness in the heavenly places " (lit. heavenlies) (Eph. vi. 12).

What a lot is gathered up into that inclusive phrase " this darkness " ! How much is said about it in the Scriptures ! The need for having eyes opened is ever basic to emancipation (see Acts xxvi. 18). The cause of all " this darkness " is said to be " spiritual hosts of wickedness in the heavenlies ". Literally translated the words are " the spiritualities " or " the spirituals ", meaning spiritual beings. " Wickedness " here does not just mean merely inherent wickedness or evil, but malignance ; destructive, harmful.

" In the heavenlies " simply means inhabiting a realm beyond the earthly ; not limited to earthly geographical localities ; moving in the realm surrounding the earth and human habitation.

" World rulers " means that these malignant spiritual hosts are directing and governing the world wherever the government of Christ has not been superimposed through His Body—the spiritual Church.

" Principalities and powers " (authorities) represent order, rank, method, system. Satan is not omnipresent, hence he must work through an organized dividing of the world under these principalities and authorities, and he himself goes " to and fro in the earth ", and has his " seat " here and there (Job ii. 2 ; Rev. ii. 13 etc.).

The Apostle declares that the explanation of situations is to be looked for in the unseen, behind the actual appearance.

What looks like the natural has its rise too often in the supernatural. Man is always trying to give a natural explanation and therefore to put things right by natural means. But when he comes up against a situation in which interests of the Christ of God are involved, he is floored and beaten. Such situations have become the commonplaces—nay, more—the overwhelming order of the day amongst ' Christian workers ' in these days, both abroad and at home. We have no intention of dealing with the subject at length here, but state the fact, and remind the Lord's people especially, that in more realms than that of Divine activity, " What is seen hath not been made out of things which appear " (Heb. xi. 3) ; but that multitudes of the things in daily life which are inimical to spiritual interests must have their explanation from behind. Let us emphasize that this spiritual union with God in the super-cosmic significance of the Cross of Christ means that our supreme effectiveness is in the spiritual realm. We who are the Divine "spirituals" are to be energized by the Holy Spirit to take ascendency in Christ over the Satanic "spirituals", and thus know something more than mere earthly dominion. Seated together with Him "in the heavenlies" (as to our spirit) we are to learn to reign in that greater "kingdom of the heavens" of which the earthly millennial kingdom is only an earthly counterpart.

Again, let us affirm that all the energies of God in our spirit are toward a corporate spiritual union with Christ, whereby the impact of His victory and sovereignty shall be registered among and upon the "principalities and powers", etc., and their domination paralysed, and ultimately destroyed.

CHAPTER ELEVEN

"THE SPIRIT HIMSELF"

"The Spirit himself beareth witness with our spirit" Rom. viii. 16.

WE HAVE SAID MANY THINGS about man's spirit, but, when we have said all that can be said, we really get nowhere until we give the full place to the Holy Spirit. The most perfectly articulated and adjusted man would be no more than a fine piece of machinery without power, but for the Spirit of God. He is the " Spirit of life ", " light ", " truth ", " wisdom ", " grace ", " supplication ", " power ", and " understanding " ; and indeed of all that God is for us in Christ Jesus. While it is necessary that he has an organ (spirit) in man of the same order as Himself, that organ cannot function in relation to Divine things without Him one whit more than the body can function without its animal life. When we have fully recognized the nature and faculties of the human spirit, we must ever be watchful against making *our* spirit the governing factor in our lives. We do not keep our ears open to *our* spirit. Such procedure would lead us into serious dangers. We must " abide in Christ ", not live in our own spirit. For the child of God the Holy Spirit is the Divine indweller of the human spirit, and He has the direction and government of our lives. We shall not escape confusion and confounding if we make anything apart from the Lord Himself our court of appeal or sphere of life. There are several matters in relation to the Holy Spirit which are very vital to a life in any real measure of fulness. One such matter is that of the corporate nature of the anointing and operation of the Spirit. We have dealt with this in other writings, so will do no more than refer to it here. But one far-reaching, and, we might say, all-inclusive consideration is that of the Holy Spirit's supreme object in this dispensation. This is—to make Christ all-in-all.

Pentecost was a movement from heaven to make real and true in men and women here (as the Church) what had taken place in heaven. There Christ had been exalted at the right hand of God. He had been " crowned with glory and honour ". " All things " had been put " under his feet ", etc. He had been installed as the pattern of man in full accordance with God's thought and intention. This exaltation and installing was to be a *governing* reality in all God's dealings with man. Conformity to the image of God's Son was to motivate all God's practical relationships with believers. Everything, from new birth to glorification, was to have Christ as its power, its nature, and its goal. He, and He alone, was to be the resource for living, being, and serving. What had been true in principle as to His own life on earth in relation to God had to become true in the case of all related to Him after His exaltation. " Nothing of (out from, *Gk.*) himself " (John v. 19) was a rigid law of all His movements, works, words, times, ways. He would commit Himself in no way that would make it impossible for Him to quickly change His course if the Father intimated the desire. He would care nothing for publicity or public opinion. In everything and everywhere the Father's will and way ruled His life. This was the great " even as " which embraced both Himself and His Own afterward (John xv. 10 ; xvii. 16 etc.).

For all this—the setting aside of all of self in every way and consideration, and the enthroning of Christ as absolute Lord—the Holy Spirit came. The soul is the seat of the human *ego,* the spirit is the sanctuary of the risen and exalted Christ, and there He has to rule all that is personal in us, so that in all things He may have the pre-eminence. This is the all-embracing work of the Holy Spirit.

" For this cause I bow my knees unto the Father.
. . . that he would grant you, according to the riches

of his glory, that ye may be strengthened with power through his Spirit in the inward man; that Christ may dwell in your hearts through faith; to the end that ye, being rooted and grounded in love, may be strong to apprehend with all the saints what is the breadth and length and height and depth, and to know the love of Christ which passeth knowledge, that ye may be filled unto all the fulness of God" (Eph. iii. 14—19).

Appendix

"Natural Man" and "Old Man" (page 45).

A distinction has been made by a certain writer between the "Natural Man" and the "Old Man". It is said that the "Old Man" is totally depraved, without 'a single feature that is of God', but that the "Natural Man" bears traces of that which is of God, e.g. 'natural affection, kindness, and often a great measure of truth and uprightness in dealing with his fellows'. This distinction or division of man is the basis of the contention between the humanist and the 'total depravity'-ist. Our point in what has been written here is that, while the soul is not necessarily evil as a part of man's being, there are two things about it which put it altogether outside of the humanistic realm of self-salvation or merit before God: —

(1) It is under the rule of "vanity" (Rom. viii. 20) and the great "cannot" of 1 Corinthians ii. 14.

(2) The soul is the point in man which, through its complicity with them, has become allied to the evil powers ; and only when man's spirit is quickened and renewed does he really know how terrible that alliance is.

"His Great Love"

T. Austin—Sparks

Contents

CHAPTER ONE

The Creation Motivated by The Love of God

". . . *but God, being rich in mercy, for HIS GREAT LOVE wherewith he loved us, even when we were dead through our trespasses, made us alive together with Christ (by grace have ye been saved)*" (Eph. ii. 4-5).

"*And as Moses lifted up the serpent in the wilderness, even so must the Son of man be lifted up; that whosoever believeth may in him have eternal life. FOR GOD SO LOVED the world, that he gave his only begotten Son, that whosoever believeth on him should not perish, but have eternal life*" (John iii. 14-16).

There is a great weight made to rest upon that little word "for"—"*For* God so loved the world." We say that John iii. 16 is the heart of the gospel: but it is much more than that, it is the heart of the universe. There is back of all things in this created universe a heart; not just a mind or a will, a design, a reason, a power, a fiat, but a heart. We are familiar with the attempts to prove there is a design in creation, that there is a mind behind the universe, and that a will brought it into being. That is all quite good and right; but we are not so often asked to consider that behind it all there is a heart—and more heart than anything else. The reason, the will, the design, come from the heart. Everything takes its rise in the heart of God. We have said much about the thoughts of God, the counsels of God. The nearer we get to the very centre of things, the more we shall become affected by this fact, that right there in the centre is a heart. It is a heart that we shall come to eventually; not an explanation to satisfy our reason, not a demonstration of power, but just a heart—but a mighty heart: and when we use that word rightly, we simply mean love. We speak of people being heartless. That means that they are without all that love means. Love is not the governing thing in their thoughts, actions, and motives; they are strangers to love. Heart then for us means love, and when we say that back of all things and at the centre of all things there is a heart, we mean there is love.

All the dealings and ways of God with His own people will have a twofold result—but mark well that this is with His Own, who have come into some very real and vital relationship with Himself in an inward way.

THE TWOFOLD EFFECT OF GOD'S DEALINGS

(a) A DEEPENING EXERCISE TO KNOW HIM

Firstly, a deepening exercise to understand Him, to know Him. Think about that. Is it not true that God's dealings with us and God's ways with us have the effect of causing us to reach out longingly for a knowledge, some better understanding, of Himself; when things have got beyond us, nay, the Lord has got beyond us. For all that we know, for all that we may have learned, He has got beyond us now. He is too deep, too hidden for us now; He is

defeating all our efforts and all our ability to understand Him. But we are not just prepared to leave it
there and throw up our hands and say right away,
"Well, I do not understand the Lord, I do not know
what He is after, what He means; I give it up."
Those in whom the Spirit of God is at work find
that, although they may be in such a position as to
be completely helpless and hopeless in the matter of
knowing and understanding the Lord, at this juncture they find they *have* to know, they *must* know,
they cannot just leave it there and give up. Everything depends now upon knowing the Lord anew.
And it is a very big everything—far more than our
life here on this earth as mere human beings. If that
were all, we should cut it short and seek the way out
through the forbidden door. But we know that
something very much more is at stake than just the
finishing of the tenure of our days on this earth.
Everything that matters over and above this
earthly life, all that we have said and professed and
claimed and hoped for, is bound up with this crisis.
There has to be a discovering of the Lord in some
new way. That is the first effect of the Lord's dealings and ways with His Own.

(b) THE RESULTANT KNOWLEDGE OF HIS HEART

The second thing, as issuing from that, is the
resultant knowledge—not in the first place of His
mind, not an explanation to our reason, a solving of
our problems, a satisfying of our enquiries, but the
knowledge of His heart. Any of you who have
known anything of a life with God can test it by
your experience. You have these deep crises, you
come to an impasse by reason of the ways and deal-

—7—

ings of the Lord with you, and the one thing, the only thing, to save you is a new knowledge of the Lord. I ask you, has He *explained* Himself to you in the first place? Has He ever come to you and said, "Now this is exactly why I have taken you, and am taking you, this way"—and so solved your problems and satisfied your mind? Has He done that? Not in the first place. No, the first effect of this deep exercise of your heart is the knowledge of His heart; that is, arrival in a new way at the fact and the reality of the love of God. We shall come to the wisdom of God through the love of God. We shall come to the understanding of God only along the path of the love of God. Everything is revolving upon this pivot of the universe—the heart of God.

Is that not proved in many ways, and not least by spiritual conflict? Upon what does spiritual conflict turn and hinge? Well, when we get into the vortex of a great spiritual warfare, where the pressure is almost unendurable, where everything is going against us, when the heavens are as brass over us and our prayers seem to get nowhere, when the Word of God seems a sealed book, when adversity and disappointment follow on in quick succession, what is the upshot? The upshot is the love of God every time. When the evil forces create conditions like that, and when the Lord is giving them so much liberty for the time being, those forces are always near to whisper about His love, to turn for us His love into hate. "This is not His love, this is the opposite of love!" Is that not true? You have only to get right down, really down, to have that issue of the love of God presented to you. The heart of the universe is this matter of God's love.

THE LOVE OF GOD THE KEY TO THE
SCRIPTURES

Having said that, are we not able with this key to unlock the whole of the Scriptures? Is not this the key to the Bible?—for the Bible is one continuous and growing revelation of this central and basic fact, that love is the motive of all things. What was the motive back of the creation, and of man as the very centre of the creation? It was love. All the rest of the Bible is an unfolding of God's love for man. Man was made for the heart of God. It is a mystery. The mystery deepens and grows as we go on; but there is always a mystery about love, even amongst humans. Love is a strange thing. Very often you cannot for the life of you explain why some people love certain other people—why it was that So-and-so fell in love with So-and-so; it defeats every attempt to explain. Well, if that is so in the human realm, the Divine is infinite in its range above the human. To explain in terms of love why God, with all His perfect knowledge, knowing the end from the beginning, set His hand to make man, is not the easiest thing. Indeed, I think we are at the depth of mystery. You follow that through the Bible. As we proceed, we are coming on to that again and again.

GOD AND ABRAHAM—
A HEART RELATIONSHIP

You can only explain and understand the drama of Eden by recognizing that it was a love matter between God and man, and that the enemy's activity from then on to the end was, and ever is, to cheat God of that on which His *heart* is set, to take from

God the object of His love. From that tragedy of the garden, you find God moving again in sovereign love, choosing that which is called "the seed." You see Him fastening mysteriously, inexplicably, upon certain individuals. Let Abraham stand out as a very strong and full example. God fastened upon Abraham, and brought him into a relationship with Himself which was a relationship of love. Mark the progressiveness of God's dealings with Abraham as a representative one in bringing that man right into His very heart. Step by step, stage by stage, Abraham was being brought more to the inward side of the heart of God. I am not going now to trace those steps: they are familiar to you. In His dissatisfaction and disappointment with man, and yet in His hunger to have man all for Himself (which was the first motivating activity of God) God chose this man Abraham, brought him in love to that relationship with Himself, one with His heart in His disappointment over man and in His desire to have man according to His own mind; right through those successive stages to the final step—"Take now thy son, thine only son, whom thou lovest . . . and offer him" (Gen. xxii. 2). It was the last step of a spiritual journey where finally, in one magnificent, triumphant step of faith, Abraham went right into the heart of God. *"For God so loved . . . that he gave HIS only begotten Son."* He became one with God's heart in its passion to have man. That is the essence of John iii. 15-16. So the end of that journey sees Abraham as the friend of God, *"Abraham, my friend"* (Isa. xli. 8). You can have all other kinds of relationship without having that. You can be parents and children; you can be husband and wife; yes, you can be on the basis of any known relationship, and yet not just come to that—"my friend." If a

—10—

man's son is his friend, or if a son's father is his
friend, you have something extra, the climax and
the crown of the relationship. And so with every
other relationship. Said the Lord Jesus to His disciples, *"No longer do I call you servants . . . but I
have called you friends"* (John xv. 15). Abraham,
the friend of God! Is it not perfectly clear that, in
the choosing of this seed, what God was after was a
heart relationship? It was a matter of God's heart.
The climax of all was not merely some world, some
creation, some race of very wonderful people objective to God upon whom He had conferred many
wonderful blessings and benefits, that the universe
could look on and say, "Well, God thinks a lot of
those people, He has done a lot for them." That is all
true, but something far more than that is involved.
The end which God has in view is a race of friends,
the expression of mutual love; God's love begetting
love, destroying that evil work when God lost what
He was after in the first place—a potential friend.
You cannot understand that; He is speaking in
human language, to express a Divine mystery; but
the Bible is full of it.

GOD AND ISRAEL—
LOVE THE ONLY EXPLANATION

From the individual seed you come to the
nation. Again the mystery deepens. Why choose
that nation, Israel, the seed of Jacob? But here is
the nation chosen. It would take us a long time, but
it would be well worth doing, to trace the love of
God in the history of that nation. We find ourselves
very near the heart of God when we touch Israel.
You think of all the words the Lord used, the titles
He employed, concerning that people. He called

Israel His child. *"When Israel was a child, then I loved him"* (Hosea xi. 1). He called Israel His son. *"I . . . called my son out of Egypt"* (Hosea xi. 1). He spoke of Israel as betrothed unto Himself, His wife (Hosea ii. 19, 20 etc.); His daughter—*"virgin daughter of Zion"* (Lam. ii. 13 etc.) He spoke of Himself as Israel's mother—*"Can a woman forget her . . . child, . . . yea, these may forget, yet will not I forget thee"* (Isa. xlix. 15). Have you not read the prophecies of Hosea? There, within a very small compass, you have this whole story of God's love for Israel in such terms of strength and passion and longing and yearning and heart-brokenness as cannot be found anywhere else.

"When Israel was a child, then I loved him . . . I drew (Ephraim) with cords of a man, with bands of love; and I was to them as they that lift up the yoke on their jaws; and I laid food before them. They shall not return into the land of Egypt; but the Assyrian shall be their king, because they refused to return to me. And the sword shall fall upon their cities, and shall consume their bars, and devour them, because of their own counsels. And my people are bent on backsliding from me: though they call them to him that is on high, none at all will exalt him. How shall I give thee up, Ephraim? how shall I cast thee off, Israel? how shall I make thee as Admah? how shall I set thee as Zeboim? my heart is turned within me, my compassions are kindled together" (Hosea xi. 1, 4-8).

That is God speaking; and note the setting of that eleventh chapter of the prophecies of Hosea. It is the time when Israel's sin had filled the cup to overflowing, the time when they had reached the climax of iniquity and idolatry, practicing such wickedness as I would not dare to mention here. It would be a scandal in the presence of decent-minded people to say what was going on in the streets of Jerusalem in the name of religion. It is at such a time, when His wrath might most justly have been poured out upon them, that God says about those people—"How shall I give thee up?" You know the story of Hosea's life—how he was commanded by God to go and love and marry a harlot, all to set forth in the life of the prophet the great truth that however deeply buried in iniquity these people were, God loved them. Oh, the mystery of God's love! Will you tell me it is not true that the universe has at its very center a heart that loves? Well, think again and go back to your Old Testament.

GOD'S LOVE EMBODIED IN HIS SON

We pass to the New Testament, and what do we find? We find there that the heart of the universe is now embodied and revealed in One Who is God Himself incarnate. This One gathers up into Himself—and far transcends—all the past. If Israel has so direly sinned and so stricken the heart of God, that heart has gone beyond Israel now. Here, in the person of His Son, God is showing it is not only Israel that is in His heart, but the whole world. *"God so loved the world". ". . . the Gentiles are fellow-heirs"* (Eph. iii. 6). And then you read the first chapters of Romans, and see the state of the world. Horrible things are said about the state of man in those chapters; and yet how does that letter break out? It breaks out in a matchless revelation of the grace of God, which is only another word for love. In this One—His Son—the love of God, far transcending all the wonderful revelation of it in the past, is now embodied and manifested.

You can see the link of the Lord Jesus with all

the Scriptures of the past; and let this be the key to them. It is not just that He was foretold—though that is true: He was the theme of the Old Testament writers and they were all pointing toward Him. But it is something more than that. What have they all been dealing with, what has been the substance, the essence, of all the Old-Testament writings? Is it not God's love for man? The Lord Jesus embodies in Himself all the Old Testament on that point; He includes everything.

Oh, but you say, there is another side to the Old Testament. There is the awful story of God's wrath. Ah yes, but what is God's wrath? Rightly understood, wrath, anger, only exists because of love. There is no such thing as anger or wrath if there is no such thing as love. In the fallen creation, if we are angry, it is so often because of some self-love. There is very rarely that crystal-pure essence of wrath which is utterly selfless. We are angry because in some way we are cheated or defeated or robbed; something is happening to us, and we are angry. There is very little of that pure wrath of God in this creation, that which is apart from any selfish consideration whatever, when we are angry in a disinterested, detached way, angry with pure anger. If you can get that, then it is that because you love so strongly, therefore you hate so strongly. Wrath is only the other side of love. If God is angry, it is His love in reverse expression. That comes out at the end of the Bible. It is seen to be anger because of all that Divine love means—the very *nature* of God.

But to return to our point. The issue of the Old Testament is—"God so loved the world that he gave his . . . Son." The Scriptures have all been pointing to that, but it is love that is behind all. The Lord Jesus is the succession of all that has gone before showing the love of God.

—14—

THE LOVE RELATIONSHIP OF THE SON
TO HIS FATHER

You see Him in His relationship to God His Father. Oh, if the Lord Jesus does reveal God, how does He reveal Him? Well, I do not see any fuller way in which He reveals Him than in terms of love, through His devotion to the One Whom He always calls "My Father." The Father says, once, twice— *"This is (Thou art) my beloved Son"* (Matt. iii. 17; xvii. 5; Mark i. 11). He could have said, "Thou art my loved Son," but He did not. He said, "Thou art my beloved Son." It is not making something out of nothing. Look at some words with that little prefix. "Betrothed"—that is your relationship of a troth to a person. "Besiege"—the direct, immediate relationship of an investing army to those invested. "Beseech"—there is something more in beseeching than just asking. When you beseech, you give yourself, you pour yourself out, you let yourself go, you hold nothing back. And so, "Beloved." The point is that God has come into an immediate heart-relationship with this One, He has taken Him into His heart, He has related to Him in terms of love. His relationship with this One is not just that He loves Him, He has given Himself to Him. He is *"Be-*loved"!

See the relationship of the Lord Jesus to God's will. Oh, yes, it was a blood conflict, even unto death, sweating as it were great drops of blood, but His love for the Father bore Him through. *"The cup which the FATHER hath given me, shall I not drink it?"* (John xviii. 11). *"FATHER . . . not my will, but thine, be done"* (Luke xxii. 42). This love relationship to His Father went down so deep, was so tremendous. Words with us have become so com-

—15—

mon as to be robbed of a great deal of their strength. I was going to say, it was terrific, that love for the Father, when you see what the Son went through. Do you notice that when He had fought through the battle, that battle of His relationship with the Father in terms of love, from that moment He was so calm and steady and tranquil that everything was going down before Him? The battle is over, the situation is established. They come to take Him, with torches gleaming in the night; with sound of hurrying feet, of swords being drawn from their scabbards; a traitor betraying a leader, a traitor who has said, "I know where He goes, I know because I have been with Him, I will take you to Him; and in case you might mistake one of His disciples for Him, I will give you a sign as to which is He, I will kiss Him." Thus they came, with all the hatred that lay behind on the part of the High Priest and the rulers; and He is as steady as a rock, they fall back from before Him. "Whom seek ye?" "Jesus of Nazareth." "I am"—and "they went backward, and fell to the ground." Again He says, "Whom seek ye?" "Jesus of Nazareth." "I told you that I am he"; "if you seek Me, here I am; take Me, let these others go free." See how tranquil, steady, rocklike, He was right to the last, before the rulers, the High Priest, before Pilate. Oh, there is something about triumphant love that settles a great deal of conflict and hate and fever and anxiety, and makes you very steady. That was the Lord Jesus.

THE SON'S LOVE RELATIONSHIP TO HIS OWN

See His relationship to His Own. It is summed up in one word—"*having loved his own that were in*

the world, he loved them unto the end" (John xiii. 1).
Perhaps He loved Judas. You notice that when
Judas led that band to Him, He did not look at him
and say, "Traitor! You scoundrel! You wicked
man!" He said, "Friend"! I think that was enough
to send Judas to suicide. "He called me friend, and
yet He knew what I was doing!" He loved His Own
to the end. And, knowing ourselves, shall we not
agree that there is a mystery about this love? Oh,
yes!

I am going to stop there, because at that point
you have to go right on from the persons here in the
days of His flesh, through the rest of the New
Testament, and all the teaching that was given to
the Church, and so at length to the Revelation, and
you find it is all turning round this one point—the
love of God. I think I have said enough to give some
ground, at least, for believing it is true. Oh, there
may have been times in your experience, and there
may yet be—if you have not yet come there, do not
worry, go on with the Lord—when you wonder
whether you will ever again speak about the love of
God. Everything seems to argue to the contrary,
and Satan has struck such a blow as to have made
your faith rock. What the Lord is, I think, trying to
say to us is this, that that may very well be just the
way to a new discovery that it is all in love, and just
the opposite to what the devil is trying to say.
"Whom the Lord loveth he chasteneth" (Heb. xii. 6).

Well, to sum all that up again; at the center of
this universe is a heart. That is God's side. Our side
has yet to be contemplated. But oh, it is wonderful,
inexplicable love, and I, for my part, am one of those
who believe that if only we could present the love of
God aright, we should never have to speak of the
wrath of God in order to persuade men—and even if
we did, we should have to show that His wrath is
love in reverse.

—17—

CHAPTER TWO

God's Beloved

". . . but God, being rich in mercy, for HIS GREAT LOVE wherewith he loved us. . . ."

In our previous meditation, we were seeking to point out that, although this whole vast universe has behind it a mind, a reason, a design, a plan, a will, a fiat, yet back of all that there is a heart, and that means love. We sought first to see that the very creation of man was dedicated by the heart of God for purposes of His own love, and then that the whole Bible is a progressive and growing unveiling of that fact. It is God's love for man that lies behind all His dealings with man. We traced that fact from Adam, through the chosen seed, particularly citing the case of Abraham, and then of the chosen nation, Israel. How full, wonderful, altogether inexplicable, was the love of God! We went on into the New Testament and pointed out how that eternal, mighty, mysterious love of God became fully embodied in the person of His Son, Who lived His life, did His work, gave Himself, all on the basis of love for the Father and that the Father might have in man that upon which His heart has ever been set. We dwelt at some length upon His love for God His Father, and we marked it also in connection with His disciples, whom, having loved, He loved unto the end; and we saw at what infinite cost to Himself all was at length accomplished, all in the strength of that love.

GOD'S LOVE FOR THE CHURCH
IN THE BELOVED

Passing from the days of His flesh over into the next part of the Bible, beginning with the book of the Acts and running on to the book of the Revelation, we have the love of God from eternity as now seen to be centered, in the first instance, in something called "the Church": *"the church of God which he purchased with his own blood"* (Acts xx. 28). *"Christ . . . loved the church, and gave himself up for it"* (Eph. v. 25). It is quite impossible for us in a brief time to go right through all that section of the New Testament, but I think we shall be agreed that this unveiling is brought to us, not exclusively but in its fullest and richest form, in the ministry of the Apostle Paul, who himself was a wonderful embodiment of God's love. It was the one note deepest in his own heart, breaking out from time to time in nothing short of utter amazement. He *"loved me, and gave himself up for me"*! (Gal. ii. 20). *"O the depth of the riches . . . "* (Rom. xi. 33); they are the riches not only of wisdom and knowledge but also of His love. And this man, who could never understand why that eternal love should light upon him and single him out, has given us such a marvellously full, deep, rich revelation of that love. We are just helpless and hopeless when we try to cope with this revelation through and in Paul. We can only do the best the Lord enables us to do in thinking about it and bringing it to the notice of others.

We remember, as we pointed out in our previous meditation, that, when the Son of God's love stepped out into His great public ministry at Jordan, the Father's word from heaven was—*"This is my beloved Son, in whom I am well pleased"* (Matt.

iii. 17). "My beloved Son." You will recall what we said about that little prefix—"*be*-loved"; not just "My loved Son," but "My beloved Son," that is, one to whom I am utterly given. Now this Apostle of the eternal love of God—with what would be frightful audacity were it not the whole doctrine of the love of God—dares to use that same phrase of the believer, "*hath made us accepted in the beloved*" (Eph. i. 6. A.V.). "Us in the beloved"; God giving Himself to us in the same way as He gave Himself to His Son. Oh, I do hope you do not just take that as a kind of play upon words, a little touch of interest, when I stay to underline the beginning of the word "beloved." I pointed out that it is the beginning of many words and every one of them has to do with a complete thing. If it is "*be*trothed," that is the complete giving. If it is "*be*seech," that is something more than asking. When I come to you concerning something with which my life is wrapped up, something which is of very great importance, I do not just simply and casually ask you about that matter; my whole being goes out to you; I beseech. God is very particular about that, and He very often heads us up to something more than easy asking—to beseeching; not because He is reluctant or unwilling, but because He wants us to get right into the matter. It is of paramount importance. "I beseech," said Paul—that was how he approached men. "*We beseech you on behalf of Christ, be ye reconciled to God*" (II Cor. v. 20). It is a life and death matter. Or take "*be*siege." If you are going to besiege anyone or anything or any place, you do not just walk up to them or it. You give yourself to that thing, you are all in on that matter. That is where God is over His Christ—the Beloved; and that is transferred to us.

CHOSEN IN THE BELOVED

Here, in this letter to the Ephesians, right at the beginning everything is put on that basis. *"He chose us in him before the foundation of the world, that we should be holy and without blemish before him in love"* (i. 4). An alternative rendering to that is, *"He chose us in love before the foundation of the world that we should be holy." "Having foreordained us unto adoption as sons through Jesus Christ unto himself, according to the good pleasure of his will, to the praise of the glory of his grace, which he freely bestowed on us in the Beloved: in whom we have our redemption."* (This is the R.V. reading of Eph. i. 5, 6). It is all *in the Beloved*, in the *Be*-loved. Do you catch the emphasis? It is not just that He chose us, or that He chose us for this or that. It is *where* He chose us. Nor is it just that He chose us in Jesus Christ: He chose us *in the Beloved*, giving the character and the quality of the basis of our relationship to God. That being so, our very existence in relation to God is a love existence, a love relationship. It is what Christ's relationship was to the Father that is ours; and you know how in the New Testament this very word 'beloved' is frequently used concerning believers.* Paul was tremendously fond of using it. Here he says it inclusively—"in the Beloved," but again and again he will say to the saints, "beloved of God." That is not just a pleasant thing said. We can use that language to one another, we can address people in those terms;

*Note. Let it be clearly understood that nothing said here or elsewhere means that the unique and exclusive nature of Christ as "the only begotten of the Father," the eternal Son, is infringed or overlooked. The peculiar nature of the Person of Christ is preserved and jealously preserved. We are here dealing with our calling in Christ.

but Paul was not just saying a nice thing, calling them beloved of God to make them feel comfortable. For him, the whole doctrine of grace was wrapped up in that. He comprehended the eternities past and future in that; "in the Beloved," "beloved of God." If you think that is just language and words, do remember that Paul's horizon, his whole world, beyond which for him there was nothing, was what he so frequently called "in Christ." You have little need that I remind you of the way in which Paul used that phrase. I have managed to find 128 occasions in Paul's writings alone in which he uses that phrase, or what corresponds to it. "He chose us in him." "In whom we have our redemption." Now you go on and see all that he has to say about "in Christ." It is in the Beloved.

UNION WITH GOD IN THE BELOVED

Now, what does that mean? As I see it, it means that the sum of Paul's ministry, which was the outflow of his own life and experience and understanding, was and is *union with God in Christ,* and that, *living* union, *organic* union. I would have to take you back to the Old Testament again to indicate how much that was so in the terms used. We saw in our previous meditation the terms used by God concerning Israel, calling Israel His child, His son, His daughter, His betrothed, His wife. All these are organic, vital conceptions. It is not the relationship of one brick to another in a building, inanimate, cold, however closely connected. It is the throbbing life of a love union, so strong and deep that Paul will cry in one of those inexpressible utterances of his— *"Who shall separate us from the love of Christ?"* (Rom. viii. 35). Then he tabulates and catalogues all the things that do effect separations—life and death, things present, things to come, and all the rest, and he says, But none of these *"shall be able to separate us from the love of God, which is in Christ Jesus our Lord."* The union is so much a part of Himself that it would be dividing God and dividing His Son.

I am not stepping over now to the obligations and responsibilities of this love where we are concerned, but at once you will glimpse something when I quote that passage from Corinthians—"Is Christ divided?" That is only one way of saying, that you cannot divide Christ, you cannot make Christ into parts without destroying His very Person. So this love makes for such a oneness with God, of an organic and vital character, that to separate would be to destroy an organism. Oh, that we had a right conception, God's conception, of the Church and of relatedness! What a tremendous statement that is—*"I am persuaded that neither death, nor life,"* nor this and that and that (tremendous things) *"shall be able to separate us from the love of God, which is in Christ Jesus our Lord"* (Rom. viii. 38, 39). What a pity it is that the chapters should have been broken there (Romans viii and ix). We need to read on to get the full force of it. But we must not be too detailed now.

Paul's whole conception and unfolding of the purpose of God from eternity is in this little phrase —"in Christ," "in the Beloved." Here, in the letter to the Ephesians, you have the summary of it all. He goes right back before ever we were formed, and before ever this world existed in its present order— before the recreative activity of God. It was back there God chose us in the Beloved. Looking right down through all the ages, He chose us in Him.

CALLED INTO THE FELLOWSHIP OF THE BELOVED

Then Paul passes from the eternal choice of love and speaks about our being called into the fellowship of God's Son. Chosen, now called. I wonder what weight you give to your salvation, your conversion, your coming to the Lord, however you may put it? Is it no more than just that one day you met the Lord Jesus, one day you were saved, one day you came to the Lord? Have you recognized that was the day of a call, concerning something related to you and to which you were related, which goes right back before time? It is as though God in eternity past chose you in love, and then called you according to His purpose. He had to wait until you were here to actually call you; and the call came; but that call was wrapped up in something vast, and the vast thing was union with God Himself in His Son in the terms of eternal love.

What is God after? And when He gets what He is after, what will things be like? We talk about the testimony of Jesus. We have a lot to say about the fullness of Christ, of the Church which is His Body, of identification with Christ. All these are great truths, great conceptions. But what I find is this, that we have not come to an end of God's thoughts yet. I am very glad of this; but it is the most painful thing we can know, that we never come to an end here, and in order to go on a further stage something has to happen to us that knocks the bottom clean out of all that has gone before. That is to say, we go through a new experience of death and desolation and emptiness, of hopelessness, in order to come to something further on in the Divine revelation. We thought, "Oh, now we have come into the fullness of God's thought! Now at length we are seeing what God is after!" We get on with that for a time and it fills our whole vision; and then everything is as though it were nothing, and we go through a terrible time. Oh, yes, it was right, it was true, but it was not God's end. My experience is that it is through just such a history with God, of repeated desolations and emptyings and despairings after wonderful unveilings and times when you feel there cannot be anything more, that you are brought up again into something further on, with your vision enlarged. I do not know whether we have come to the last point of God's movements, but what I am saying now is this, that when God gets His end, everything will be only, but absolutely, a manifestation of His love.

I think that is what Paul means here in the letter to the Ephesians, for this is a wonderful revelation. But look at the place of grace in this letter, look at the place of love. "... *the breadth and length and depth and height; And to know the love of Christ, which passeth knowledge,* " (Eph. iii. 18, 19). That is the object. Paul holds it up into view, that we may come to that in the end.

Well then, if you and I are going on to God's end, what will characterize us? This one thing—abounding more and more in love. I state that and leave it for the time being.

ALL-SUFFICIENT PROVISION IN
THE BELOVED

He called us, but, blessed be God, His calling of us is on to and into a perfectly prepared ground, to an all-sufficient provision. It is in Christ. What a terrible thing it would be if He called us with so great a calling, and we had somehow to attain to it of ourselves and to find all that is required for attaining. Why, it were better that we had never been called! We know how utterly impossible it is for us to provide the smallest degree of anything that can attain to God's end. Can you find in yourself this love of God, this kind of love? Why, we have only to read one section of this whole revelation to find ourselves defeated at every point. I refer to I Cor. xiii. There is not a fragment of a sentence there that does not knock us to the ground. *"Love suffereth long, and is kind; love envieth not; love vaunteth not itself, is not puffed up, doth not behave itself unseemly, seeketh not its own, is not provoked, taketh not account of evil."* And to sum up all—*"Love never faileth"*; that is, love never gives up. Where are we? Can you stand up to that? No! But He called us in the Beloved, and in Christ is a perfectly prepared ground. "In whom I am well pleased"—an all-sufficient provision.

That causes Paul to go out along one wonderful line, and he says, *"I have been crucified with Christ; and it is no longer I that live, but Christ liveth in me: and that life which I now live in the flesh I live in faith, the faith which is in the Son of God, who loved me, and gave himself up for me"* (Gal. ii. 20). (Paul is not saying that when we died in Christ we lost our individuality. We ought to have lost our individualism, but not our individuality.) There is some difficulty in translating the verse just quoted. "I live by the faith of the Son of God," or "which is in the Son of God." It seems to me that, in keeping with so much more that Paul says, it means this— "It is Christ Who is providing what is necessary for this new life the other side of the Cross. I live by Him, I live by the provision that He makes." Yes, and God, in calling us into His Son, has called us into an all-sufficient provision. You say, "I cannot love, especially in certain directions." But Christ can, and He has proved it in your case. Do you think everybody loves you? There are some people who do not love you, but Christ loves you whatever you are. You might be unloved for very good reasons by everybody else; He loves you, God loves you now with that love that can and does love the unlovely. He can provide us with a love to love.

Is not this the wonder of the whole evangel? Have we not many times heard missionaries who have come home saying, "When I was called of God to go to such and such a country and people, they were the very people I felt I could never love; everything about them stirred up in me only bad feelings; but I have come to love them, they are my people." Well, that is simple enough. My point is that to be called into Christ is to be called into a provision for what that very word "beloved" means. You have the great example of Paul and the Corinthians. If ever a people deserved the opposite of love from a man, those Corinthians deserved it from Paul. They owed everything to him, and they treated him, to say the least of it, most shabbily, so that he could say that the more he loved them, the less they loved him (II Cor. xii. 15). When you read about them your uppermost feeling is that it requires a great deal to love these people. Yet what is Paul's attitude? His heart is going out in brokenness over them. This is love that is not natural; it is in Christ, it is the provision in the Beloved. Do you catch the thought? I need not labour it. In Christ is an all-sufficient provision.

Well, Paul has many aspects to this great reality of "in Christ." As you know, he says that God put us all into Christ in the Cross. When Christ died and was judged of God, in Him we, too, were judged and death passed upon us all. We are in Him also risen; and not only so, for we are not just left here on this earth as risen: we are in Him seated in the heavenlies. How many aspects of this "in Christ" matter there are! What does it amount to? It amounts to this, that only Christ is the sphere of the believer, and in Christ that great heart intention of God in the creation is realized—a people in the Beloved, beloved of God, the objects of that love, and who should be filled (the Lord forgive us for our failure!) with that same love of God. It is in that sphere of Christ that God proceeds with His love purpose.

CONFORMITY TO THE BELOVED

What is God doing with us in Christ? Inclusively, He is seeking to conform us to the image of His Son in terms of love. What is your idea of the image of God's Son? He is the Son of His love, and the very word "Son" is a love term, than which there is no higher and fuller, and in the revelation of God, Son, Sonship, is the embodiment and exhaustion of love. "Conformed to the image of his Son" in terms of love. I am putting something on you and on myself when I say these things, but there it is. You must ask the Lord to write the force of this in your heart and do not just take it as an address. The Lord will have to help us after this, for there will have to be some very real dealings with Him. We are going to be challenged and found out on this. It is well that we are very much occupied with the word "grace." "Oh, to grace how great a debtor daily I'm constrained to be." We love that word. Do we realize that is only the other word for love, and that it speaks of the initiative of God in this whole matter? In grace He chose us. The initiative of God was in love.

Then what is true of our position in the Beloved is put upon us as our obligation, and when we are bidden to love one another we are bidden to show to others the grace that God has shown to us. In I John iv. 19 there is a fragment which is so often quoted—or misquoted when it is quoted from the Authorized Version—"We love him, because he first loved us." It is a misquotation because the "him" should not be there, and to put it in really does not make sense with the context. *"We love, because he first loved us."* That is the whole of John's argument in that letter. *"If God so loved us, we also ought to love one another"* (I John iv. 11). "God *so* loved"; He gave the all that He in heaven possessed. We therefore love one another, because He loved us first.

That is a tremendous test of the reality of our being "in Christ," and a tremendous challenge, and we need something with which to meet and answer that challenge. Paul says that provision is all in the Beloved. That does not get us close enough. It is not as though the beloved Christ is a kind of sphere and God has put everything inside there. It is Himself. *"It is no longer I, but Christ liveth in me."* Christ is the supplier. Oh, how much Paul dwells upon that! Right through to the end, to the ultimate realization—*"Christ in you, the hope of glory"* (Col. i. 27). If there is anything beyond what I have said, it might be summed up in that word "glory". ". . . *hath called us unto his eternal glory"* (I Peter v. 10). But what is the glory? There is no glory except the glory of perfected love. Perfected love is the glory of God. The glory of God is His love.

Well, if you forget all that has been said, do get the impression upon your heart of the one thing— *"His great love wherewith he loved us."* This whole matter of a Christian's life is gathered into that. That love in us is the satisfying answer to the heart of God. It is not how much truth and doctrine we possess, how much teaching we have or give; it is not a matter of the mysteries of the Gospel; it all resolves itself into this—the love of God shown to us and then shown by us; that is all. The Lord help us!

CHAPTER THREE

Love Serving

Reading: Eph. ii. 4; John xiii. 1-17.

"Jesus ... having loved his own that were in the world, he loved them unto the end ... he ... riseth from supper, and layeth aside his garments; and he took a towel, and girded himself. Then he poureth water into a basin, and began to wash the disciples' feet, and to wipe them with the towel wherewith he was girded."

THE DISCIPLES—PERSONAL INTERESTS DOMINATING

Here is the great object lesson of Divine love. We must get the setting of this scene in order to obtain something of its real effect. The atmosphere at this time was a high-tension atmosphere. It was charged with a sense of pending crisis. It was full of expectation mingled with wonder—wonder as to exactly what was going to happen. The kingdom was in everybody's thoughts; Jesus was being hailed by the multitudes as the Messiah, palm branches were being waved, people were shouting *"Hosanna: Blessed is he that cometh in the name of the Lord"* (John xii. 13). All the Messianic thoughts and expectations now for many centered in Him, and especially so in the case of His disciples. Some great event in relation to the kingdom was on the point of taking place, and this had given a great impetus to their personal expectations. They were, of course, very much in the grip of the Jewish expectations of the kingdom on this earth, the ousting of the Roman power, and the setting up of the Kingdom of the Messiah. All that was in the air and in their minds, and they were beginning to see their respective places in this kingdom. The mother of Zebedee's children had come to Jesus and, worshipping Him, had said, in reply to His interrogation of her, *"Command that these my two sons may sit, one on thy right hand, and one on thy left hand, in thy kingdom"* (Matt. xx. 20). You see the expectation: and the two sons were not ignorant of the ambition and request of their mother: they were parties to it. The other disciples were terribly provoked that this thing should have taken place, and as they went on in the way, they talked about this and discussed who should be greatest in the kingdom.

Now that is a statement, but we cannot leave it with just the thought that they were saying to one another "I will be greater than you." They were clearly going into more detail than that, and saying, "In the kingdom, I am going to be so-and-so;" all thinking in terms of place and position, and vying with one another, each trying to go one better than the others. This is indicated in what is recorded as having taken place. It is also recorded that Jesus knew their thoughts, and understood what was going on. So in this wrangle about place, position, personal importance and advantage in this kingdom that was about to come, they were all jangled and on edge with one another, and out of temper. Such was the atmosphere.

So they come to the upper room which Jesus had taken. In every nicely-appointed guest house or guest chamber in Jerusalem, just inside the door was a little table, and upon it a basin, with a jug of scented water and an apron and a towel. If it were the house of a wealthy or well-to-do person, there would be a servant in attendance. But when Jesus took the room He did not employ a servant, and only the things were there. And the disciples arrive in this spirit, with this mentality, in the upper room—annoyed, irritated, eyeing one another; and they pass in through the door. They look up at the ceiling, or somewhere else, but none of them sees the basin! They are not in a mood for that sort of thing at all. The supper is ready, and they sit down to supper with unwashen feet. Now when I was a young man, there were two cities which were said to be at that time the two dirtiest cities in the world, and one of them was Jerusalem; but even that had a semblance of sanitation. But there was no such thing in the days when the Lord was there. All the garbage and refuse was pitched out into the street. Think of a hot day in the east, the dust and the mess and the smell! They had come through that and gone in. That basin was not a thing that you could just pass by as though it did not mean anything— some quite unnecessary thing. There was a real need for it and for that scented water. But no, they had carefully not seen it!

That is the very strong setting of the whole scene. It is not exaggerated, it is only bringing out the details that are here, a matter of reading between the lines. They had all passed by and sat down to supper.

THE SERVANT SPIRIT LACKING

Now, let us look at these men themselves. Their feelings had been irritated and accentuated; and you know, when we get like that, what excuses we make and how we argue and bring up all we can to support our position. Is that not human nature?

There was Matthew. Now Matthew had taken on service with the alien government in occupation and had made a lot of money out of it, so much so that when Jesus called him to discipleship, he made a great feast for all his friends. He could not have made a great feast without having money, and he could not have had an expensive feast without having servants. So Matthew was doubtless a man who had always someone to wash his feet, and who thought of himself as the big man. No servant, he!

There were James and John. They were friends of the High Priest and had access to the High Priest's court; so they were somebody in the social world, in the world of public influence and importance.

And there was Peter; and Peter could, under these conditions, argue like this—"I am one of the inner three; I have always been privileged above the rest; I have been recognized as something more than the others. Whenever the Lord has wanted something special, I have been one of the three with Him; so it is not my place to wait on the others."

THE LORD—PROMPTED BY LOVE TO LOWLY SERVICE

I am not saying all this merely to draw an entertaining or vivid picture. It is by way of getting the right setting for our Lord. In that atmosphere, in the presence of that mentality, that attitude: false, artificial, unworthy, and oh, so petty, so mean, so contemptible: *"He . . . riseth from supper"*—to perform Himself the task they all avoided. What a significance there is in John's statement in that connection!—*"knowing that the Father had given all things into his hands, and that he came forth from*

God, and goeth unto God." This One it is who rises from supper, and (following, no doubt, what was the usual custom) goes quietly over to the door and takes off His outer robe and lays it down, takes the apron (the servant's apron) and puts it on, ties the towel round His waist, pours water into the basin, and comes to wash His disciples' feet. *"Having loved his own that were in the world* (and just now, at any rate, so very much of the world), *he loved them unto the end* (unto the uttermost)."

The question immediately arises, and is answered here, What is love to the uttermost? What is the love of Christ? What is the love of God? It is not in sentimental words. No, this is it. It is not love for the lovely and the lovable only, for those whom you cannot help loving. *This* is the love to the uttermost.

OUR CLEANSING THE OUTCOME OF SELFLESS LOVE

The rest of His explanation, His comment, His message founded upon what He had done, does bring us all up short for He said, *"What I do thou knowest not now, but thou shalt understand afterward."* And what did they know afterward? They came to know that the world itself was a filthy place, deep-dyed in sin's degradation, with all the muck and refuse of hell spread over it—worse than the streets of Jerusalem—and men had to be saved from that degradation, cleansed from all that filthiness; and it was going to be done, not by a haughty Matthew nor a self-important Peter, but by the Lamb of God becoming *"obedient unto death, yea, the death of the Cross"* (Phil. ii. 8). It was going to be done by stripping, by humbling, by emptying, by the spirit of uttermost service—service of this kind, Christ's service to us. Oh, what humiliation, what emptying, lies behind our cleansing! What it has cost! That is what He calls love—not the finding of a place for ourselves in the Kingdom, being something important, giving ourselves airs. Moffat translates that fragment in I Cor. xiii.—*"Love . . . doth not behave itself unseemly,"*—as "Love giveth itself no airs." We look at the Lord Jesus, and there we see love. To think for a moment of what any given thing is going to mean to our pride, to our influence, to our position, to our prestige, never comes in with love. Love, this love, never leaves room for such a thing as standing up for our rights, for saying they are not being recognized, that we are not being given our place. Oh no, there is none of that here. If the Lord Jesus had taken that position, He certainly would never have enacted this object lesson of love, and would never have gone to the Cross at all; and we should never have been cleansed and saved from this world. It is a sad picture, from one standpoint.

THE CALL TO FELLOWSHIP WITH HIM
IN SERVANTHOOD

I do not know how you feel about it. I confess to you that, as I have been thinking about this, I have wondered whether I ought to pass it on to anyone else. I know by long experience that it is possible to turn the edge of something the Lord says to one's own heart by giving it out as a message. Have you found that, those of you that minister? The Lord brings some thing strongly to you and you give it as a message, and it has gone from you. I take this to my heart. And as I see that my salvation and yours, in the infinite love of God, was through the spirit of lowliest service, servanthood, I have to say, Is there any other kind of service? Can we hope to see anything done by any other kind of movement of the Spirit? Oh, this is more an appeal than a profound message! It all centres in this—*"having loved his own which were in the world, he loved them unto the uttermost"*—such men as they were, and as we are. I do not see them objectively, I see them subjectively. I can see a Peter, a Matthew, a Judas, in my own heart. Thank God, He loves unto the uttermost, and His love unto the uttermost is of this kind, that He does not stand on His rights and dignity and position and demand that I come down in an abject slavery to acknowledge His lordship. He comes to serve you and me. He is Lord, but for the time being a serving Lord. As He is seen in the glory, mark you, He is still girded. He is Lord, but still the great heavenly Servant, serving us, washing away our sin, delivering us from this present evil world. All he does is in the spirit of the servant. Oh, how the spirit of service and servanthood is despised today! Everywhere you hear it. No one wants to be a servant today. That word "servant" is hated. The spirit of service has almost gone from the earth. The spirit of Christ is a rare thing, but, when it is found, it is a heaven-blessed thing, a mighty power. Oh, do not despise the servant position! Be not ambitious for place, for recognition, for name, for reputation. Be not ambitious to have your rights recognized. God fill us with this spirit, that we are not all the time waiting for others to do something for us, but looking to see what we can do for them in Christ's name—being busy in the right sense to find out how much we can do for the Lord's people because they *are* the Lord's people, and for the unsaved because He died to save them, and for the unclean because He died to cleanse them. The Lord fill us with this spirit!

CHAPTER FOUR

The Challenge of Love

"... *his great love, wherewith he loved us*" (Eph. ii. 4).

"*The love of God hath been shed abroad in our hearts through the Holy Spirit which was given unto us*" (Rom. v. 5).

"*Beloved, if God so loved us, we also ought to love one another. . . . We love, because he first loved us*" (I John iv. 11, 19).

The challenge of love, Divine love—"Beloved if. . . ." then . . . "*If God so loved us, we also ought to love one another.*" There is a tremendous challenge in that. We have, I trust I can say, been seeing that Divine love, the love of God, is the key to everything from Genesis to Revelation; and if that is true, as we have said before, that the sum of all Divine revelation is vital union with God in Christ, if it is a matter from first to last of relationship with God as Father, then here in this fragment in John's letter, we are at once brought face to face with the test of our relationship with God. The test of that relationship is here resolved into a matter of love. There follows immediately another of the several "ifs" of John's letter—"*If a man say, I love God, and hateth his brother, he is a liar*" (I John iv. 20), he does not love God. The test of our relationship with God is this matter of love. It all hangs upon "if."

The love of God is shed abroad in our hearts through the Holy Spirit. The relationship with God in Christ is brought about by an act of the Holy Spirit's incoming, in our receiving Him. He is given to us, and He brings about the relatedness, and the immediate result and seal of that relationship by the indwelling Spirit is that the love of God is shed abroad in our hearts. It is the test of relationship. The very basis of our organic spiritual and vital union with God is this matter of the Divine love in us, and John will challenge us with this in his letter and say, *"We know that we have passed out of death into life* (i.e. that we are in vital union with God) *because we love the brethren"* (I John iii. 14). The Word of God makes this love a test of our having received the Spirit.

DIVINE LOVE DEMANDS LOVE OF THE BRETHREN

Well, of course, on the simple basis of our conversion we know that to be true at the beginning —that whereas, before, we had no particular love for Christians, afterward, when we had come to the Lord, we found we had an altogether new feeling toward other children of God. That was the simple beginning. But it is the beginning, the basis. John is carrying us beyond the beginning. He is speaking to us, as in the case of those to whom he wrote, as to people who know the Lord, to people of God who have the Spirit. He says, *"The anointing which ye received of him abideth in you, and you need not that any one teach you; but . . . his anointing teacheth you concerning all things. . . ."* (I John ii. 27). He is writing to those who are getting on in the spiritual life. When we come there, it is possible that in some way a root of bitterness may spring up in us toward our brother. It is possible that you may fail of the love of God. It is possible that this very basic nature of your relationship with the Lord should be numbed for want of love, that your whole spiritual life should come under arrest and be paralyzed, and you cease to be a vital factor and have a real living communion with your Lord day by day, all because the basic love in some way has been arrested or injured. What was the mark of your initial relationship with the Lord? It was the love of God shed abroad in your heart, and you loved other Christians tremendously. That can be changed in such a way that you do not love other Christians as at the beginning. You thought then that all Christians were very wonderful: no questions were asked; they simply belonged to the Lord and that was all that mattered. Since then, you have begun to have questions about Christians, and not only Christians in general, but sometimes Christians in particular. You have come to know that Christians are still human beings and not angels, not that consummate thing you perhaps thought Christians were at the beginning. You have come to some disappointment about them and are really up against something now in them, and your basic relationship with God is being touched. If you do not somehow get over that and find a way through, if you do not have a new accession of Divine love, your very walk with God is going to be arrested, you are going to lose your precious and joyous communion with your Lord, and there will come a shadow between you and your Father. You will find that the only way to get rid of the shadow is to get victory over that un-love toward those of His children who are concerned.

HOW WE KNOW GOD'S LOVE FOR US

How do we know God's love for us? Well, that is

a pertinent question. There are many difficulties and much mystery connected with His love—why, in the first place He should love us at all. But then He has said that He does love us. He has given us exceeding great and precious promises and assurances. We have, in what He has done for us, a very great amount of proof from God's side that He loves us. But even so, with all the doctrine of the gift of God, the great redemptive activity of God, with all the words that tell us that He loves us, there are times when all that is just something in the Book, something of the doctrine. But is it true? Does He love me? It may be true everywhere else, but does He love *me*?

Now come back to that word in Romans v. 5 and you have the answer in principle and in substance. Let us ask the question—How can you and I know that God loves us, know in a way extra to our being told, to having an intellectual presentation of the truth of the love of God for man? I will tell you of one way in which you can know, and know very surely. If you are a child of God and have received the Holy Spirit in you (and remember that the Holy Spirit is the Spirit of Divine love) then if you should have a reservation of love toward another child or other children of God, some attitude of criticism, suspicion, or prejudice, within you something dies or seems to die. Your joy goes, you feel something has gone wrong, and within you there is a sense of grief. You know what it is to grieve, to have that awful feeling of grieving somewhere inside. But in this case it is not you at all who are grieving over that unlove, but there is Someone within you who is grieving: there is a sob at the center of your being. That is how we know that God loves us, that "the love of God hath been shed abroad in our hearts."

When we grieve that love, we know that in us the Spirit says, "I cannot go on in happy fellowship with you, I am grieved, I am pained." It is only love that can be grieved. People who have no love never grieve, they are never pained, never hurt. You need to have love, and the more sensitive the love the more you register and are grieved when things are not right. The Holy Spirit is exceedingly sensitive in this matter of love, because that is His supreme characteristic. Remember, that is His inclusive characteristic. Paul wrote, "The fruit of the Spirit is love" (Gal. v. 22). He put it in the singular. It would have been wrong grammar to have said, "The fruit of the Spirit is love, joy, peace, longsuffering," etc. He would have had to say, "The fruits of the Spirit are love, joy, peace. . . ." But he said, "The fruit of the Spirit is—love" and then he went on to tell you what love is—"joy, peace, longsuffering, kindness, goodness, faithfulness, meekness, self-control." Kill love and you kill all the rest; injure love and you injure all the rest. You cannot have the others, without the inclusive thing—love.

The Spirit, therefore, is inclusively and pre-eminently the Spirit of Divine love, and as such He is very sensitive and easily grieved. *"Grieve not the Holy Spirit of God"* (Eph. iv. 30) is the exhortation. That is how we know that God loves us—that the love of God in us by the Holy Spirit suffers grief when love is injured.

Again, there is so much that the enemy points to and tells us is a mark that the Lord does not love us. For my part, I have to have some inward proof, a living proof, something right inside of me that proves He loves me; and this is one of the ways in which I have learned that God loves me—that if I say or do anything that is contrary to love, I have a terribly bad time. God's love for me is touched, grieved, when I violate that love, and I am at once conscious of the fact. Everything is bound up with that. We do not get anywhere until we say, "Lord, forgive me that, I go back on that, I confess that sin"; and so get it all cleared up and have no repetition of it. It involves the whole walk with God, it touches the very relationship with God. We need to be made sensitive to the Spirit of love so that our lips and hearts are purged by the fire of love, and so that it is not easy for us to be superior and pass superior judgments and to be of a criticizing and suspicious spirit. We shall never get anywhere with God if there is anything like that.

THE PRAYER LIFE AFFECTED BY
LACK OF LOVE

It touches every aspect of our lives. It touches our prayer life. We cannot get on in prayer if it is like that; and what a need there is today of men and women who can pray; not of people who say prayers and yet do not pray. One does not want to despise any prayer, but oh, we do need men and women who can pray through, who can lead us into the presence of God, and take right hold on Him, and get a situation established by prayer. We shall never be able to do that unless this basic relationship with God is established, expressing itself in love for all those whom He loves, no matter what they are nor who they are. Prayer life will be interfered with, and the Word of God will be closed to us. The Lord will not go on if the foundation is hurt.

WE LOVE BECAUSE HE FIRST LOVED

"If God SO loved . . ." Can you fathom that

"so"? Can you understand that "so"? No, we cannot. *"God so loved"*—then *"we also ought to love"*; and we love, says John here, because He first loved us. As I pointed out earlier, the putting in of the word "him" in the Authorized Version is unfortunate. It is not in most of the original manuscripts. I am not sure that it would not be bad doctrine; it certainly is out of keeping with the context. John did not say that in his letter. He said, *"We love, because He first loved us."* You say you do not quite grasp that, and that it would be quite true to put the "him" in and to say, "We love him, because he first loved us." There are literally teeming millions in this world whom God first loved and they do not love Him; there are multitudes of the Lord's people whom He so loved but they do not love Him as they would. Is not the cry "I have not the love I ought to have, even for God, to say nothing of His people and the unsaved"? Not necessarily do we love Him, because He first loved us. When we come to a fuller apprehension of His love for us, then love for Him does flow out, but here the whole emphasis is upon the fact of love—*"We love, because he first loved us."* The challenge is there. The measure of my love for others is the measure of my apprehension of God's love for me. I could never have anything like an adequate apprehension of His love for me, and not love others. Oh, if we were really overwhelmed with the greatness of God's love for us, how could we take an attitude of judgment toward some other erring, mistaken, perhaps sinning, child of God? Not at all! It is herein that we know the love of God, in that we love the brethren. There is the test of our apprehension, the test of our relationship, and it is the basis of everything for the child of God.

GROWTH ON THE BASIS OF LOVE

If I am going to grow spiritually, I shall only do so on the basis of love. I shall never grow because I get a lot more teaching. You do not grow by teaching. That is the tragedy of attending conferences —that you may attend them for years and years and still be of the same spiritual measure afterward, and never grow: still making no greater contribution to the measure of Christ in the Church, still not counting any more than you did years ago in the spiritual battle. No, all the teaching does not necessarily mean that you grow. It is necessary as a background, but we grow by love. Do not let anybody think we can dispense with the teaching and have the love and get on all right. That would be a contradiction of the Word altogether. The teaching has its place, it is absolutely necessary; but though I have everything and have not love, I am nothing (I Cor. xiii). So all is based on this.

THE LOVE OF GOD, NOT NATURAL LOVE

But lest you should inadvertently misapprehend what I am saying, I must emphasize that I am talking about the love of God. You must not think I am talking about a generous disposition, a magnanimous temperament, of the kind of people who are made that way, and who cannot bear to be across someone else, even if there is a tremendous spiritual issue at stake. Such never "truth it in love" (Eph. iv. 15) for fear of anything unpleasant. That is not the love I am talking about. This love is not temperamental love. The people who may be of that kindly, magnanimous, large-hearted disposition may find that they have to have that smashed up and broken by coming up against a spiritual situation for which no natural temperament is sufficient. They may have to be provoked to get on their feet. People who have never been angry may have to be stirred to anger. People who are always compromising rather than have unpleasantness may have to make a clean cut. The love of God may demand something like that. On the other hand, those who may not be at all of that generous, magnanimous disposition, by the love of God and an altogether new heart and nature become what they are now temperamentally. This of which we speak is not on a natural ground at all— what we are or what we are not.

THE LOVE OF GOD TRIUMPHANT OVER EVIL

What I am trying to say is that God's love is a mighty, triumphant love that has triumphed over something immense. The love of God which now comes to us from Christ comes from Him as crucified. It flows to us from the Cross, from His wounds, from His riven side. That love came up against the most awful things in this universe which withstood it, and overcame them. It was not just a nice disposition that looked benignly upon everything wrong and excused it. Oh no! It came up against the fierceness of anti-love, anti-love of God in this universe, and overcame it. Calvary was the mighty triumph of God's love over everything contrary to it, and it is that kind of love we are to have, an overcoming love, a triumphant love.

It is, in a sense, an awful love. Come up against that, and it breaks and shatters; things have to go down before it. Things will not go down before our human niceness, things of the devil, things that are positively evil and antagonistic to God; but they will go down before tested, proved, enduring, patient, longsuffering love. You may have to wait a long time, suffer a lot, put up with a lot, have your love ignored, even resisted. Give it time, and all may go right down before Divine love. It is the longsuffering love of God that has won us. Is not that the deepest thing in your heart?—it is in mine—the infinite patience of Divine love, the bearing and forbearing of that love. It is a tremendous love. It is a power, it is a conquering love—something so much more than this (may I use the word?) sloppy kind of "love" which is always smoothing things over. Oh no, that is not God's love. God's love is overcoming love.

NO TRUE MINISTRY WITHOUT LOVE

There is challenge in this love of God to us. "We also ought. . . . " It is a challenge. Nothing can be except as the love of God is shed abroad in our hearts by the Holy Spirit.

Let us come back to where we started. If you have ever had exercise with God on any matter, do so on this matter. If you are concerned about being of any use to the Lord at all, in any capacity,—as a preacher, a teacher, a personal witness, as a life lived here without any public place at all—let me tell you (and it is the ripening knowledge of a life that has not much further to go but has for forty years been concerned with this matter of being useful to the Lord) let me tell you that nothing of usefulness to the Lord is possible except on the basis of God's love shed abroad in our hearts. It must be this Holy Ghost love for the people to whom we would minister: love for them even to the laying down of our lives for them, suffering unto death for their sakes: love to the point of being brokenhearted—I use that word quite deliberately—over people for whom you have spiritual concern and in whom you have spiritual interest; love like that. No ministry will be ministry to the Lord that is not born of that; no testimony, no life, except as rooted and grounded in the love of God. You can have all the rest, a mass of Bible knowledge, a wealth of Biblical instruction and doctrinal information and all that, but it is all without any value unless its exercise is in a love, a passion, a heart beating with the heart of God for His great love wherewith He loved us.

CHAPTER FIVE

God's Everlasting, Unchanging Love

We have been moving round a center and viewing it from different angles, in different relationships. The center is given to us in Eph. ii. 4—*"His great love wherewith he loved us."*

GOD'S GREAT DECLARATION

We are now coming to look at one of the most amazing statements ever made.

"The Lord appeared of old unto me, saying, Yea, I have loved thee with an everlasting love: therefore with lovingkindness have I drawn thee" or, as the margin gives the alternative rendering, *"therefore have I continued lovingkindness unto thee"* (Jer. xxxi. 3).

I repeat, that is one of the most astounding statements that has ever been made. To verify that, to realize something of that fact, you need to read all that leads up to it and that follows afterward. That is to say, you need to read the prophecies of Jeremiah throughout, and then to add to them some of the prophecies of other prophets. For the work of the prophet was very largely to point out how far, how terribly and tragically far, those being addressed had gone from God's mind, God's thought, God's will, God's way, and in what a terrible state of hardness of heart and rebellion—and worse than that—they were toward God. All that—and it is a terrible and dark story—gathers round this statement. "I have loved thee." At the time when they were in the very worst condition that ever they had been or would be in spiritually and morally, it was then He said *"I have loved thee with an everlasting love."* Viewed in its setting, you must agree it is one of the most amazing statements ever made.

"His great love wherewith he loved us." We are baffled and almost rendered silent when we try to fathom and comprehend the word "grace" in reference to the love of God. How great is God's love? Were we to spend our lives trying, we could never utter its depth or content. Yet here is a statement, and we have to do something about it. We have to approach it, to try to grasp something, be it very small, of this incomprehensible love of God, the mystery of it. So I shall adopt the very simplest method of trying to get into this word, just breaking up the statement into its component words.

THE ONE WHO MAKES THE DECLARATION

We will begin then: "I." You notice here the statement is really governed by the words "Thus saith Jehovah" (verse 2). Who is it speaking? To begin with, it is the One whose name is Jehovah. By that name He made Himself known to the Hebrews through Moses. But later that name became so sacred to Israel that they would not use it, and it was mentioned but once in the year, the great day of atonement, by the High Priest, as he went into the Most Holy Place by the High Priest the name was pronounced, so great, so awful, was that name to them. But what does it mean? Jehovah, the unchanging One, the eternal One, the self-existent One, existing not by anybody else's act or power or support, perfectly self-existent—that is Jehovah, that is the One who says, "I have loved thee with an everlasting love."

But look again. It is the name of the One of infinite holiness, whose eyes are too pure to behold iniquity, whose nature is too pure and holy and altogether right to have any association with sin. You see how helpless we are when we try to deal with God and explain Him and define Him. These are statements, but if you and I, apart from some great provision of God to cover our sinfulness, were to come into the presence of that infinitely holy God, we should be shattered beyond repair. The infinitely holy God! It is He who says, *"I have loved thee with an everlasting love."*

It is the name of infinite majesty, glory, might, dominion, power. He is very terrible in majesty, in glory, in power; and that One says, *"I have loved thee with an everlasting love."*

And still we press in to this name. It is the name of infinite self-sufficiency. From time to time He has found it necessary to state that in various ways. *"If I were hungry, I would not tell thee"* (Ps. 1. 12), He said to them of old. *"Every beast . . . is mine, and the cattle upon a thousand hills"* (Ps. 1. 10). *"I have made the earth, and created man upon it: I, even my hands, have stretched out the heavens"* (Isa. xlv. 12). *"The nations are as a drop of a bucket"* (Isa. xl. 15). "Do I need anything or anyone? Am I, the creator of the universe, in need? Am I suffering want? Am I not utterly and absolutely independent, self-sufficient, the only One in this universe who is self-sufficient?" And that One, out of it all—His holiness, His majesty, His self-sufficiency—says, *"I have loved thee with an everlasting love."* It is a mystery. Can you explain that? Can you understand that?

"I have loved"

"I have loved." The very essence of love is "I must have, I cannot do without." Here the word "love" is just the common word that was used in all true human relationships. It is the word used of parents for children, of children for parents, of husband for wife and wife for husband, of friend for friend. Of the classic instance of the love between David and Jonathan, it says, *"Jonathan loved him as his own soul"* (I Sam. xviii. 1). *"Thy love,"* said David of Jonathan after his tragic end, *"thy love to me was wonderful, passing the love of women"* (II Sam. i. 26). That is the word here. Jehovah, infinitely self-sufficient, used that word concerning Israel. As the friend's love for the friend must have the friend, and, as in every other true relationship, true love must have the one loved, must have the companionship, the fellowship, the nearness, so is Jehovah speaking about Israel. *"I have LOVED thee."* Amazing love!

"I have loved thee"

Ah, but still more inward—*"I have loved THEE."* Now we are at the end of wonder. At the beginning I pointed out the state of these people. Not only were they in a deplorable state morally and spiritually, deeply in sin; not only were they in this tragic plight; but they were in positive antagonism, rebellion, repudiation, killing the very prophets of the Lord who would tell them of their wrong. *"I have loved THEE."*

Without anything positive in the way of opposition or antagonism or rebellion or stubbornness on our part, it is still the greatest mystery and wonder that He should love us. But think of this—*"thee"*! Think again of whom that is said, to whom it applies. *"I have loved thee"*; and that, moreover, coming at the point where it did and at the time it did.

"An everlasting love"

"I have loved thee with an everlasting love." You can never translate that word "everlasting" into English. It simply means that you have got into the spaceless, boundless realm, you have fallen out of time to where time is no more. You have gone out into that mysterious something where nothing can be taken hold of as tangible, it is all beyond you, beyond your grasp, beyond your calculation, beyond your power to cope with it and bring it into some kind of dimensions. That is the word: beyond you, beyond your time, beyond your world, beyond all your ways of thinking and working. "I have loved thee with an everlasting, timeless, spaceless love."

Did you notice the alternative marginal reading to the phrase? "Jehovah appeared of old unto me"? It is, "from afar appeared unto me"—outside of our world altogether. He says, "I have loved you with a love altogether outside your dimensions of time and space."

"I have loved thee with an everlasting love." And strangely, the repetition of the word "love" here adds an extra feature or factor. It is in the feminine, and it means mother-love. "I have loved thee with an everlasting mother-love." Now, mother-love is one of the most mysterious things with which in ordinary human life we have to deal. You cannot always understand mother-love. You may look at a baby and you may see much that is not lovely about the child, but the mother of that child simply adores it. That is mother-love. That is the word the Lord is using here. The world would see

everything to the contrary—but the Lord says, "I have loved thee with an everlasting mother-love."

HIS LOVE FOR THE PEOPLE OF THE NEW COVENANT

Well, we are touching the fringe of this thing, but you are perhaps asking a question. You are not gripped yet, because you say, "That may be quite true as to Israel, but can we rightly and properly appropriate that? Can we step into that and say it is ours; that this same One says that to us?' You have only to read on to verse 31 of this same chapter to find your answer.

"The days come, saith Jehovah, that I will make a new covenant with the house of Israel, and with the house of Judah: not according to the covenant that I made with their fathers in the day that I took them by the hand to bring them out of the land of Egypt; which my covenant they break, although I was a husband unto them, saith Jehovah . . . I will put my law in their inward parts, and in their heart will I write it" (Jer. xxxi. 31-33).

Now do you not know that is taken up in the New Testament, in the letter to the Hebrews, and applied to the Church in this dispensation? Its fulfilment is there said to be not in the Jewish dispensation, but in the New Testament dispensation. That applies to those to whom the gospel of the grace of God has been preached, the new covenant; and it is the new covenant, not in the blood of bulls and goats, but the blood of the Lamb of God, God's Son, who said, in the night in which He was betrayed, when He took the cup—*"This is my blood of the new covenant, which is shed for many unto remission of sins"* (Matt. xxvi. 28). Are we in this? Oh yes, it is for us, the people of the new covenant in the blood of Jesus Christ. Oh, if He could say such a thing to Israel, then if it is possible to say it with fuller meaning and greater strength at all, so He says it to us.

We have so much to confirm this in the New Testament. *"God so loved the world, that he gave his only begotten Son, that whosoever believeth on him should not perish, but have eternal life"* (John iii. 16)—that mysterious word, that age-out-lasting life. *"His great love wherewith he loved US"*—that word was said not to Jews only but to Gentiles, and comes in the letter to the Ephesians, the letter for all men, Jew and Gentile alike. Or again, *"who delivered us out of the power of darkness, and translated us into the kingdom of the Son of his love"* (Col. i. 13). I could go on piling up Scripture to show that it is the same love as that love in Jeremiah xxxi. 3. It is the same God and it is the same love, and now it has expanded beyond Israel to embrace us.

Listen again then. This same God, no less holy, no less majestic and glorious, no less self-sufficient, says to you, to me, *"I have loved thee, I have LOVED THEE with an everlasting love". "His great love wherewith he loved us."* Are you impressed, do you believe it?

HIS CONTINUED LOVINGKINDNESS

What then? There follows the second half of the statement—*"therefore with lovingkindness have I drawn thee"* or *"therefore have I continued lovingkindness unto thee."* 'I have borne with you all this time because I love you; anything could have happened to you, but I have not let it, I have shown you infinite longsuffering and patience, and earnest solicitude for your eternal well-being: because I love

—55—

you, I have kept you alive, and have brought you to this time and to this place; I have not let you go." Oh, that this might come home to us! We may, all unconsciously be hearing this message now simply because of this infinite love of God which has been preserving us unto this hour to let us know it. You may think it is quite fortuitous that you are hearing it—just one of the chance happenings of life; but if you knew the truth it is this infinite love of God which has held you to this time in relation to the infinite purposes of that love to let you know it. There is nothing casual about it, there is sovereign love here. "Because I have so loved, because, self-sufficient as I am, I cannot do without you"—oh, mystery of Divine love!—"because I so much wanted you I created you, and now at this moment I am drawing you." We cannot take that in, but that is the teaching of the Word of God.

We started these messages by pointing out that behind the universe, behind the mind, the reason, the plan, the design, there is a heart. The universe exists as an answer to that heart. Today that heart in its love is bleeding. It has suffered a great deal of disappointment, deprivation; it has been robbed of its object—the wife has been unfaithful. But the Lord comes out in the presence of it all and says, "I loved you and I still love you; My love is an everlasting love: therefore I have kept, I have preserved, and I have brought you to this very hour and I am telling you now that this is the position; there is no breach of love on My part."

LOVE PERSISTING THOUGH SPURNED

But Israel went into a great deal of suffering and distress because they did not respond to that love of God thus expressed, and it looked very much as though the everlasting love was lasting no longer. But not so, it has never changed. You see, love has sometimes to change its form of expression, although in itself it does not change, and so we have another side to the revelation of God's ways with wayward and wilful man. Suffering, affliction and adversity to individuals and to nations and to the world is not because of a contradiction of the statement that God so loved the world. It is the only way in which that love stands any chance of getting a response of the kind God wants. God does not want that kind of love that is not love at all because it gets everything that it wants to satiate its own lusts. That is not love. This love of God must make us like itself, it must be after its own kind.

And so, strangely enough, many have come to find the love of God through the dark way of suffering—to discover that God was not their enemy but their friend, when they thought that He was pursuing with the object of destroying them. But I am not going to follow that out just now.

I want to be content now with making that great declaration with which we started, doing the little I can to try to bring it home to you—who it is that says it, what it is that He says, the people to whom He says it, with the assurance that, so far as He is concerned, He will never take another attitude but love, even if it is disappointed love and we ourselves should lose all that that love meant for us. To lose that and to know it would be our hell of hells. There could be no deeper hell than to discover all that was meant for you by infinite love, and to realize that by your own folly and your own stubbornness it has gone beyond your reach forever. What more of a hell can you imagine than that? I think that is the only kind of hell we need contemplate, whatever may be the full truth about it. For any one to wake up and have to say, "Oh, what might have been, if only, if only I had done so and so! If only I had taken the opportunity! It is too late now!"—that is agony of soul, that is misery, that is despair. You see, it is the effect of love, Divine love's immense purposes, and we discover that it is now all impossible because we have foolishly rejected, refused, repudiated, gone our own way, stubbornly said No! to the Divine love. That is the dark side of this, but I am not going on to the dark side now. Listen again, whoever you may be. If you know yourself only a little you must be amazed at this statement, but if it does not come to you as the most wonderful thing that ever was or could be, there is something grievously the matter with you; that such a One should say to such as *we, "I have loved THEE, with an everlasting love."* May God Himself bring that home to us with something of its implication, something of its meaning and value, its glory, its wonder. If He should graciously do that, we shall be worshippers for the rest of our lives; there will be something about us that is in the nature of awe and wonder and we shall go softly. The realization of it will smite all our pride to the dust. There is no room for pride here. This will remove all those horrible things—pride, avarice, covetousness, self-interest, worldly ambition—and we shall be very humble, very grateful people, full of a great longing somehow to requite that love, somehow to win for that One His rights. This has been the motive and passion of many who have given themselves in the far places of the earth in a daily suffering for their Lord's sake. Love—a little return for this so great love wherewith He loved us.

CHAPTER SIX

Love the Supreme Test of the Church

"His great love wherewith he loved us" (Eph. ii. 4).

We come now to the close of the New Testament, the consummation in the book of the Revelation. A great deal of reading ought to take place at this point for which we have not the time. Will you open the Word at the beginning of the book of the Revelation and glance down through the first, second and third chapters as the first main part of this book, hurriedly recalling what is there, and helping as best you can as we go on by noting details also?

We have said that we are here in the consummation, and I think I shall have no difficulty in having your agreement that, when we come to the book of the Revelation, we do come to the consummation of all that is in the Word of God; that is, it is a gathering up of all at the end to a final settlement. That at least we can say about the book of the Revelation. Whatever may be our ideas of interpretation of the many things here, we are all agreed that here we are at the end and everything is being gathered up to a final settlement. At this point we must just ask a further question. Have we not much to go upon that we are now nearing that final settlement of all things, that we are in the days of the consummation of the ages? Is it necessary for me to gather up all the proofs and evidences and signs to prove that? But I think there again I have your agreement. We certainly are in the end times.

If that is true, then it is a matter of supreme importance that we should recognize what are the primary and ultimate factors with God; and if those factors are at all at issue in our considering them together at this time, then our meditation must take on a significance which is altogether beyond our own. It must be a very solemn and consequential time, and it must demand and receive from us a definite act of putting away every other kind of thought and consideration. There should be an open-hearted seeking of the Lord, with no prejudices, no suspicions, no curiosity, nor anything that is casual or indefinite. We must come, and, with all our hearts, take the attitude that if God is going to say to us that which with Him is of primary and ultimate consequence, we must note that and we must be in it.

I tarry to lay emphasis on one further matter. I am intensely concerned that we should not be just occupied with a lot of Bible matter. This is not just a theme that is being taken up, a subject, with all the subject matter about it being brought out. No, a thousand times no! If this is not God's message to us, well, we had better cut it short and go and do something else.

Well then, let us come to this book of the Revelation. We take chapters i to iii. I have many times made great efforts to resolve these three chapters into one clear meaning, but I have always finished with a sense of defeat. There has been something true and right, but in the thing that I was after I have had a sense of defeat and frustration; and when we come to certain details in these messages to the churches, such as Jezebel, Balaam, the Nicolaitans, somehow we seem to have got into a realm of the technical. The thing has not become a concrete, definite, positive message, it has escaped me. I knew what those things meant in principle, but what I so much wanted to do was to find one resolving thing which gathers them all up and makes of them as a whole a single message for the Lord's people. Until now, as I say, I have felt defeated every time, all through the long years. I am wondering if I have got it now; we shall see.

LOVE THE MASTER-KEY TO THE
WHOLE BIBLE

It seems to me at length that the master-key to the whole Bible is in our hands when we come to this. The master-key to everything is love; and if you will look, I do not think there is any doubt but that you will come to see that all that is here is gathered into that one matter of Divine love. We are in the consummation of love in this book, and it begins and ends with the Church.

LOVE THE KEY TO THE VISION IN
REVELATION I

You take, then, the first chapter, and what is the key? The key to the first chapter and also to the whole book is to be found in the words, *"Unto him that loveth us, and loosed us from our sins by his blood; and he made us a kingdom, priests unto his God and Father."* You can see love in almost every word of that great sentence.

But alongside of, or following on, that statement, you have the presentation of the risen and glorified Lord, and He presented at once in that marvelous designation "Son of man," the title of kinship, the redeeming kinsman. *"Unto him that* loveth us, and loosed us from our sins"—the title, you see, belongs to One who has come right into our estate, and eventually into our state. That is the theme of love. Oh, how great, how comprehensive, is that Son of man, flesh of our flesh, bone of our bone, to redeem us unto His Father! He is described in that matchless presentation, verse by verse, step by step, and when you have read it all and noted everything that is said about Him, every detail of His person and of His adornment, you find it is the sum total of love.

He is "*girt about at the breasts with a golden girdle.*" Every word speaks of Divine love, the breasts, the gold, the girdle. The girdle is the symbol of strength, of energy, of intention, of purpose. You mean business when you gird yourself. The robes are no longer flowing for leisure, loose for reclining. The girdle is golden, symbolic of the very nature of God who is love. Above the rest that girdle seems to me to include all the other features, give meaning to everything else.

I am not going to mention in detail all the features of this Son of man as given to us here. What I am trying to convey to you is that this inclusive presentation of the risen and glorified Christ is the comprehensive presentation of love. "But," you say, "is that true?—because some of the terms used are terrible, awful. John fell at His feet as one dead when he saw Him. Is that the effect of love? Would it not be truer to say that this is the Lord All-terrible, rather than the Lord All-loving?" But think again. It is love, but not our idea of love. We have to reconstitute our conception of Divine love. This One here is described as "the faithful and true." Have you never been in the hands of the Lord in discipline, in breaking, yes, in shattering, being poured out like water on the ground, and afterward have had to say, "Thou wast right, Lord; it was the only way. It was a terrible experience, but Thou wast faithful with me, faithful to all the highest and deepest principles of heaven. It was not in anger and judgment, but in faithfulness and mercy to my soul that Thou didst do it." We have to reconstitute our idea of love. Here John says, *"When I saw him I fell at his feet as one dead. And he laid his right hand upon me, saying, Fear not."* This is not judgment, this is not destruction, this is not death and condemnation. The right hand is the token of honour, of favour. *"Fear not; I am the first and the last."* "Everything is in My hands and in the end it will be all right; I took it up and I am going to finish it; fear not."

I was saying that John fell at His feet as one dead. There was another man who, travelling on a road with the positive intention of blotting out from this earth, as far as it lay in his power, every remembrance of Jesus of Nazareth, was met by this same Lord of glory. All-terrible? Well, certainly Saul of Tarsus went down, he was broken, the encounter overpowered him and left its mark upon his very physical body to the end of his life. For three days he had no sight, and they had to help him into the city. But do you tell me that was God the All-terrible? Oh, listen to the conversation! *"Saul, Saul, why persecutest thou me?"* What is the tone of that? It is not, I am sure, the tone of anger. It is a pleading tone of entreaty, of sorrow, of solicitude. *"Who art thou, Lord?"* "I am God the All-terrible, and now I have brought you to book"? No—*"I am Jesus whom thou persecutest . . .What shall I do, Lord? . . . Rise, and enter into the city, and it shall be told thee what thou must do."* The Lord went ahead

—63—

of him, prepared the way for him (Acts ix. 1-9; xxii. 4-11). Do you tell me that terrible revelation was not love? Well, ask Paul himself what he thought about it, and see in after years what he had to say about it. He did not say, "He met me, He smote me, He destroyed me, He brought me into such awful judgment that I lost all hope." He said, *"He loved me and gave himself up for me"* (Gal. ii. 20). That meeting, terrible and devastating as it might be in one sense, was a meeting with the Lover of his soul.

I say again, we have to make over anew our conception of Divine love. It is not that sickly, sentimental thing we call love. It is something tremendous. We have so to reconstruct our conception of Divine love as to see that our highest interests for all eternity demand very faithful dealings with us by God, and the more we really know the heart of God, the more we come to be ready to say, "Thou art right, Lord; even in what I would call Thy hard handling of me, Thou art right." God in His love has the end in view, not just the pacifying of some fretful child with a sop. We are called unto His eternal glory and *"our light affliction, which is for the moment, worketh for us more and more exceedingly an eternal weight of glory"* (II Cor. iv. 17). But we do not always believe it while the affliction is on us. We do not even call it "light"; but He knows how transcendently and infinitely the glory outweighs the suffering. He has decided, with the greatness of the end in view, it is worth His while to be faithful with us and let nothing pass that would take from that glorious prize of His glory or work against it. He knows quite well that, when we are with Him afterward, were we to see something that was not taken up by Him and dealt with because of the suffering and the pain it would have caused us, and because we would have murmured and complained, that we would say to Him then, "Lord, why didst Thou not do that in spite of me?" And so, knowing the end and dealing with us in the light of it, the faithful and the true love is other than our poor sickly conception of love. Love in our thinking so often means just giving way all the time, just having everything we want or giving everything that others want. God deals with us, not as infants, but as sons (Heb. xii. 7). The presentation, you see, is all a comprehensive and detailed consummation of love.

THE CHURCHES CHALLENGED AS TO LOVE

Now you pass to the next two chapters, and you have the churches; and the Lord is here dealing with the churches on the basis of the presentation. That can be seen by noting that every one of the seven messages to the churches takes up some feature of the presentation of Christ in the first chapter. You can look at that and note it. Actual phrases in the presentation of chapter one are used in relation to the churches respectively. So He is dealing with the churches on the basis of Himself as fully presented, and therefore if the presentation is the comprehensive embodiment of love, He is dealing with all the churches on that basis.

Now you note that the messages and the churches are bounded by Ephesus and Laodicea, and not as unrelated but as embracing and covering all the seven. In Ephesus and Laodicea the trouble is defective love. Ephesus, *"thou didst leave thy first love"*; Laodicea, *"thou art neither hot nor cold."* The whole question with these churches is love. Let us hurriedly look at them separately, as far as we can.

FIRST LOVE AS COVERING ALL

Here again is the wonderful thing, that in Ephesus, which marks the beginning of everything, all turns on love. *"Thou didst leave thy first love."* What is first love? Well, first love is all-inclusive in its nature. You will not be able subsequently to find any characteristic or feature of love without finding it in first love. First love covers all the ground of love. We could not tabulate the meaning of first love. It is everything, it is all that you can say about love; utterly selfless, self-forgetting, uncalculating. It is fierce, it is fiery, it is completely hot, strong and faithful. That is where the Lord begins. First love is the basis on which the Lord takes up the whole matter, comprehensive of all love's features. So in relation to the ultimate situation, we see here, through Ephesus, that what the Lord must have in His Church is inclusive love, love in all its features. He must come at the end back to the beginning, and bring His Church likewise back to that basis. Of course, there must have been a first love; you cannot depart from what never was. That will challenge us.

To Israel the Lord said, through a prophet, with a sigh of disappointment and grief, *"I remember concerning thee the kindness of thy youth, the love of thine espousals; how thou wentest after me in the wilderness, in a land that was not sown"* (Jer. ii. 2). That is what love will do. Love will go after its lover in a wilderness where there is nothing to live on.

If necessary, it will die of starvation in order to be with its lover. *"I remember concerning thee ... the love of thine espousals."* Inclusive love is the basis upon which the Lord begins, and in effect He is saying, "I can be satisfied with nothing less." Oh, there is love in Ephesus, there is no doubt about that. *"I know thy works, and thy toil and patience"*—and this, that and the other: it is not that they are without love, but that they are without their first love, that utter, inclusive, every-sided love; that is the trouble.

Let this come to our hearts. We all love the Lord; I trust we can say that truly. We love the Lord and we will do much for Him. But is our love of this kind? Is everything in our lives prompted by love, or is much of it lived under a sense of duty, of obligation or necessity, of having to do; or are there other motives, other interests and objects that keep us in the work of God as Christians? Is it the fear that we must not drop out in case of what happens to us? That is all on a lower level of life. Inclusive love is God's starting-point, and He says, "I can be satisfied with nothing less; even you who labour and are patient and have this, that and the other thing which are very commendable, I cannot let your lampstand remain with a loss of first love." Testimony is really gone when first love is gone, however much remains.

THE NATURE OF FIRST LOVE
(a) suffering love

We look now at Smyrna, and see that a great suffering has come upon the church there, a period of intense suffering in which it will be necessary to be faithful unto death; and so the Lord, in the inclusiveness of first love, would say, and does say, as I see it here, that first love is suffering love. It is indicated by what you will go through for the Lord's sake and out of love for the Lord, what you will endure, what you will put up with. No, not just to what part of the world you will go to minister to the heathen and lay down your life for your Lord, but what you will put up with at home, what you will put up with in other Christians, what you will put up with of daily martyrdom in love for your Lord without a revengeful spirit, without wanting to see those who cause your suffering and affliction made to suffer themselves for it. Suffering love, that is first love. Are you having to suffer, and suffer wrongfully? Peter says, *"If, when ye do well, and suffer for it, ye shall take it patiently, this is acceptable* ("grace"—R.V. margin) *with God"* (I Peter ii. 20). As we have said, grace is only another name for love. Suffering love—that is first love.

I could illustrate that. You have no need that it should be done, but you know quite well that in a first whole-hearted devotion to any object you are prepared to go through anything for that object. It does not matter what people say, the love is stronger than all hindrances.

(b) DISCERNING LOVE

Next we come to Pergamum. Here we have an awful state of mixture, contamination, compromise, entanglement with evil things. If we seek for the cause, we find that the church in Pergamum has not discriminated between the things that differ, between what is of the Lord and what is not. It has compromised by reason of defective spiritual sight, and so the issue here, the matter of first love, is that first love is a discerning love. There is much about that in the Bible. Paul is rich on the matter of discerning love. *". . . having the eyes of your heart enlightened, that ye may know what is the hope of his calling, what the riches of the glory of his inheritance in the saints"* (Eph. i. 18). *"The eyes of your heart enlightened"* discerning love. Love is as far removed from blindness as heaven from earth. "Love is blind"? No—not true love. The fact is that true love sees everything, but transcends everything. The love of Christ for His disciples was not blind love that did not know His men, love that was duped, deceived, misled, but eventually found out that they were not the men He thought they were. No, *"he ... knew what was in man"* (John ii. 24). His love saw everything, could tell them beforehand exactly what they would do; but love persisted in face of it all. Love is a great seeing thing. If you are consumed with a burning love for the Lord, you will be very quick of scent as to what is doubtful and questionable. You will not need to be frequently and continuously told when a thing is not right. No, love for the Lord will bring you quickly to see and to sense there is something that needs to be adjusted. You may not know what it is at the time, but you have a sense that all is not well. Love will do it. All the instruction in the world will not bring you to it. You may have the Word of God brought to you on all such points, and you might even say, "All right, because you say so, because it is in the Bible, I will do it, I will be obedient." Do you think that is good enough? Such a thing has never come to you through the eyes of your heart. But mark you, if this love, this discerning love, has really filled your heart by all the intelligence of the Holy Spirit indwelling you, you will sense it without being told; or if it should be brought to you from the Word, that within you will say, "Yes, I know that is right, the Lord tells me that is right." Do you not think that is the kind of Christian that is needed, and what the Lord needs at the end? That is what He has had in mind from the beginning and He calls that first love that is quick of scent to see what needs to be cut off or added, what adjustments are necessary, and does accordingly. You do not have to follow round and say, "Please do this; have you never taken note that you might be helpful in this way?" You do not have to do that where there is devotion, love watchful all the time, aliveness, alertness, perception, readiness to do without being all the time told to do it. Real devotion to the Lord is something that far out-reaches legality. First love is discerning love.

I would like to spend all my time on this matter of discerning love, because there is so much about it. We do not grow by teaching and information, by being filled up with the Bible and its doctrines and its truths, however wonderful and true and great they are. We only grow by love, and we grow by love in terms of spiritual discernment. *"Love buildeth up"* (I Cor. viii. 1); but love buildeth up because love gives us spiritual insight, and the simplest child of God, who has never been brought up in profound things, in the midst of a great wealth of teaching, but who loves the Lord, will make far greater strides in spiritual growth than those who have it all mentally and intellectually and not through the eyes of the heart. It is true. If there is an adequate love there will be no compromise with error, with wrong, no permitting of questionable things, no long-drawn-out shedding of things which, while they may not be altogether wrong, would be better not there. The Holy Spirit can come along that way. Have we not seen it? Have we not seen people making all kinds of changes in their habits, in their manner, in their very adornments and fashions, as they have grown spiritually, and because of an intense love for the Lord, without anyone having said anything at all? Probably had someone pointed out

various things—I had better not mention them—
they might have said, "All right, he says we must
not do this." Is that good enough? Oh no! But without ever mentioning these things, we have seen people gripped by the love of God, some right at the
beginning of their Christian life, steadily through
following months changing themselves outwardly,
becoming different people. Love is the key. You can
see, then, why the Lord spoke to the church at
Pergamum in the terms in which He did. What was
needed there, and therefore what is needed in the
consummation, if first love as marked by discernment.

(c) UNCOMPROMISING LOVE

In Thyatira again we come to a bad state, as
well as a sad one, a state of spiritual tragedy. Look
at the language, the names, the history behind certain names there, and it is the history of the seduction of Israel. They have been seduced, and corrupted through seduction. That is summing it up.
What, then, is the requirement, in what way will
love express itself? If a state of compromise in
Pergamum requires discerning love, in Thyatira
seduction and corruption demand an uncompromising love, repudiating Balaam and all the rest of his
kind. No compromise, no seduction unto confusion,
no mixing things up, no trying to bring together
contrary things, no wearing of linen and wool, no
ploughing with ox and ass—the symbols, you know,
of two realms, of two natures—none of this trying to
bring together the life of the flesh and of the Spirit;
it cannot be done. No compromise can really be
established between the flesh and the Spirit,
between the world and Christ. No; here first love to
be recovered will mean no compromise, no mixture,
no confusing of issues.

(d) DISTINGUISHING LOVE

Sardis—what is the upshot of things in Sardis? *"Thou hast a name that thou livest, and art dead."* You look at the message to the church at Sardis and try to put it all into one word. What is the word that sums it up? Well, you have to say it is indefiniteness. So we can say again, in the light of the whole standard, that first love, ultimate love, the love of Christ, the love which He is seeking, is a distinguishing love that marks you out as clearly defined for the Lord and all that is of the Lord. Distinguished, different, outstanding, defined, unmistakable by the love that characterizes and governs. The thing that distinguishes from all else is this great love, and this great love brings about a distinctiveness of life. You cannot be indefinite if you are mastered by this kind of love. First love does not care one little bit what people think or say. Oh, everybody is saying this and that about the lover in the grip of first love. They may be using all sorts of language—He is a fool, he is mad!—it does not matter. This love is making them clear-cut—one object, one design, one thought, one intent. They are people marked by one thing and not two. There is no doubt about it. We have our humorous ways of speaking of people who are in that state. He is in love, you cannot get away from it, everything goes by the board! There is one thing and one thing only in that life. That is, of course, how it ought to be. You young people, never have any relationships in the beginning that are not like that. First love is like that, and the Lord says, "I want you where you were at the beginning." Or shall we say, "I want you where I have ever been. I am the Alpha and the Omega, the beginning and the end; I am like that from first to last. I want you back there in a distinguishing love."

(e) STEADFAST LOVE

Philadelphia is very quickly summed up. While the name itself means "brotherly love," there is one word that sums up this message, and that is patience. *"The word of my patience."* First love is patient love, or, to use the other word that is always in the margin of the New Testament when you come on patience, steadfast love. That is first love, that is the love of Christ. *"He loved them unto the end"* (unto the uttermost): *"I have loved thee with an everlasting love"*; and oh, what a triumph that kind of love was and is! It needs steadfastness to go on with all that love has to encounter and suffer and endure. It is the quality of the love of God, steadfast love.

(f) FERVENT LOVE

Finally, we have Laodicea. What is the word which sums up Laodicea? It is mediocrity, neither one thing nor the other, nothing outstanding, nothing positive. You cannot say they are not Christians, but yet again you cannot say very much that is good about them as Christians. They are very ordinary. There is no such thing as an ordinary first love. In first love you are a most extraordinary person. What then is first love? It is, as over against Laodicea, fervent love, which means red-hot love, white-hot love, fervent love.

This is the sum of first love—suffering love, discerning, uncompromising, distinguishing, steadfast, fervent. Have we the key to the messages, have we the key to the end time? There may be another, but I have not found it yet. This is the last one I have found. I think we are right this time, and it amounts to this, that the Lord is going to speak to the Church, to His people, to us at the end, and that the thing He will speak about is the matter of love. He will place more emphasis upon that than upon anything else. All other aspects of truth are important, and they will be the directions in which love will work itself out; but the foundation, the spring of all, that which is to impregnate all—whether it be the service of the Lord, the very truth of the Church's eternal calling and vocation, the greatness of the work of the Cross, whatever it may be as a matter of aspects of the one whole truth—beneath and through all must be this Divine love. Have the things in themselves—the truths, if you like to call them that—have them all without love, and they are nothing. May the Lord write this in our hearts.

CHAPTER SEVEN

The Issues of Love

In our previous meditation, we arrived at the consummation in the book of the Revelation, and we were taking note of the wonderful truth that in the first three chapters of the book of the Revelation, the whole question is the question of love, love relating to many things, but all a matter of love.

We now go on to the issues of that love. Here we do really come up against the vital point that, while the Lord is seeking in His people that love—love like His own—there are tremendous things hanging upon it. It is not just an optional matter: everything hangs upon it. That is what arises here when the Lord says, *"To him that overcometh."* You know that is said to each of the seven churches. Even where the Lord has not to point out any serious delinquency, He still says, "I see big issues bound up with this love, and everything hangs upon it." So we will spend this little time in looking at these great issues found in that final word to each, to all, to us—*"He that overcometh"*; or *"to him that overcometh."*

LIFE IN FULLNESS

Ephesus; and again we remind ourselves that the challenge there relates to the all-inclusiveness of love, the first love, and so, when we touch the matter of love in its fullness, we expect to find an all-inclusive issue. That is to say, we expect to find that the thing which is bound up with an all-inclusive love is an all-inclusive outcome, and we are not wrong in that expectation. Here it is—*"To him that overcometh, to him will I give to eat of the tree of life, which is in the Paradise of God."* Here, with love after this kind—the love of God, the love of Christ, the love of the Spirit—is bound up the whole question of life in its fulness: and what an issue that is! There is a reference to the tree of life in the Paradise of God. It is a backward look as well as a forward one. It takes us to the beginning and then to the end. We shall find that tree of life right at the end of the book of the Revelation as the ultimate thing. It was the first, it is the last; therefore it is all-comprehending, this matter of love.

But you have to look back to the beginning to see what a tremendous issue it was and is. God, having first created the heavens and the earth, and all things, then created man and set him in that garden, and in the midst of the garden placed the tree of life; and everything of the creation and everything of man and everything of the Divine heart-purpose was centered in that tree. It was the tree of life. That is more than the animal life, more than the human life, more than the natural life. That kind of life, the animal, the human, the natural, was all there, but there was a life that was not there except as represented by the tree. As constituting a test, symbolically it was there, but its real significance was spiritual and unseen. And when man failed in this matter of reciprocating the love of God, and doubted and questioned and disbelieved and disobeyed—all of which is the contrary of love— God made it impossible for that man as he was, in that state, to have that other life; and therefore the creation faded like a fading flower, was disrupted, and man came under the terrible shadow of judgment and death. Says Paul, *"Through one man sin entered into the world, and death through sin; and so death passed unto all men"* (Rom. v. 12). For the very creation, for man himself, that life was essential for God's purpose. Man never received it, and he lost it on the ground of lost love, failure in love.

Now look at the Lord Jesus. He came in the fulness of times. God sent His own Son, the Son of His love, and when the Son stepped out from His hidden years into the open, to assume definitely His great life work, the heavens were opened and God said, *"This is my beloved Son"* (Matt. iii. 17). And John said of Him, *"In him was life"* (John i. 4). Here He is, the embodiment of a new creation, in whom is that life which Adam missed. It is here in Him. *"In him was life,"* that other life, that different life, that Divine life. It is in Him, and God says of Him, as embodying a new creation, *"in whom I am well pleased."*

He is the Son of God's love, He possesses the life which no man had ever before possessed, He is the answer to all God's heart, God finds His perfect pleasure and satisfaction in Him. But look at Him. What do you see? Well, in this world amongst men, He appeared outwardly no different from any other man. There were repeatedly hints of something unusual about Him, which at times were dimly discerned by others, but these related to His nature and character and not to His outward appearance. Apart from this, men saw nothing different; even those closest to Him saw nothing. But there came a day of which it is written, *"And after six days Jesus taketh with him Peter, and James, and John his brother, and bringeth them up into a high mountain apart: and he was transfigured before them; and his face did shine as the sun, and his garments became white as the light*"; and all this was accompanied by the same voice from heaven, saying, *"This is my beloved Son"* (Matt. xvii. 1-8). Not a different Christ, not a different Son, not another, it is the same One. The life had been hidden, and now it blazed out. The life had been a secret thing, and now it was divulged. The life that was in Him was now seen to be what it was. What a transfiguring life!— His whole body transfigured, aglow, agleam with Divine glory. Everything about Him was glory, the glory of heaven, the glory of God, and it was just the nature of the life that was in Him being given an opportunity to express itself. And that is a parable and a prophecy; for does not Paul tell us that the day is coming when this body of our humiliation shall be fashioned anew that it may be conformed to the body of His glory (Phil. iii. 21), when this corruptible shall put on incorruption, this mortal put on immortality, and death shall be swallowed up in victory? (I Cor. xv. 50-55). The life which we have received in Jesus Christ is that kind of life. That is the extra life that Adam never possessed, and you see it is all on the basis of love, Christ's love for the Father. His was a love which was unto death, that would battle through the hordes of evil forces: that, in obedience to the Father's will and for our salvation would cause Him to give Himself into the hands of the evil forces and say, "I am at your mercy, do your fell work; this is your hour and the power of darkness" (Luke xxii. 53). All this He was ready to do in obedience to the Father's will.

The Cross was right in view, and when on that mount Moses and Elijah appeared, they spake with Him of the exodus that He was about to accomplish at Jerusalem. They were speaking with Him about His Cross. He was already under the shadow of the

Cross, had already accepted it in principle, already yielded by every test to the will of the Father. Love was triumphant already in Him. He was going all the way, and the Divine love and the glory broke out. This is the inclusive note from Genesis to Revelation. Love is always linked with life and life with love—that kind of life.

Is this to you merely a beautiful theme, a lovely song? Does it matter to you whether you have a body of glory? Or is it just a negative matter with you, that you will be glad when you have done with this one, and that is all there is to it? Have you no concern for the glory that is to be? Are you not interested in that great and marvellous statement that we have been called unto His eternal glory (I Pet. v. 10), to be glorified together with Christ when everything of death shall be fully and finally quenched and destroyed, and life—that Divine, uncreated life, that unique life of Christ—shall show what it is, manifest its nature, its qualities? The very glory of God is in His life. It is a big issue, the issue of life.

We know something of glory of this life even now; it is not reserved only for the end. It is not so much in our bodies, perhaps—although sometimes the Lord touches even them with a touch of the powers of the world to come and revitalizes them with His own life—but we do know the whole question of life and death in our spirits, our souls, and what a difference there is between life and death! To sense death, to know something of death inside us, in our spirits, in our souls, to be touched by, or to be in an atmosphere of spiritual death, is an awful thing. But what a glorious thing it is to be in an atmosphere of Divine life! It is glory in our spirits now. For those who have to live in a world in which there is nothing of the Lord at all, it is all spiritual death, whether it be secular or religious, and it is a horrible thing. But it is a grand thing when you can escape that and find yourself in the presence of the Lord amongst His people and taste something of life. That is glory of a spiritual kind inside. But think—that is going to be manifested in its fullness for our whole being, including our bodies! It is the prospect, the calling, of the people of God, and it is all a matter of life.

But that life is based wholly and solely upon this matter of love. If you touch anything that is other than love—if you touch hate, animosity, suspicion, prejudice, criticism, jealousy, envy or any other thing that is contrary to love—you touch death. It is horrible. When you meet somebody who is eyeing you, not sure of you, suspicious of you, oh, how helpless, how hopeless, the situation is; you cannot get on, you are glad when you have passed, but you are sad. You have met with a touch of death. You touch love in another child of God coming out to you, and oh, what a prospect fills the air, what possibilities arise! There is a way through, everything possible where there is love. That is the issue which bounds all, and that is why you begin with the tree of life.

You end with the tree of life, but it is in the garden, the garden of Divine love. That tree can only thrive in the soil of love. These are very practical matters with a challenge. Do not forget that while you need people to love you and show you love, so that your spiritual life may grow and you may be released from smallness and pettiness and limitation and be enlarged, other people need your love to the same end; and you are not going to enlarge other peoples' spiritual life by criticizing them, by eyeing

them. You are going to help their spiritual enlargement by loving them with the love of God.

This is inclusive; it includes everything else. We
are not surprised, therefore, that when at Ephesus
the matter of first love is raised, which is love inclusive of all the features of love, the all-inclusive question and issue arises, namely, that of life.

NO SECOND DEATH

You are able then to pass on to break it up with
what is said of the church in Smyrna. The issue of
love triumphant in Smyrna was to be that the over-
comer should have part in the first resurrection.
*"He that overcometh shall not be hurt of the second
death."* What is the second death? Briefly, it is that
death where there is no recovery. It is the door
finally closed, where there is then a distinct and
abiding separation between God and man. All goes
out in the second death: it is the end. There is no
hope beyond that door, no possibility of life. But
here in Smyrna, of him who is triumphant in love it
is said, *"He . . . shall not be hurt of the second
death."* Fullness of death shall be broken and
defeated and deprived of its prey. Love means that
you will never be allowed to be touched by that ultimate despair of separation from God. That is no
small thing. If the end on that dark side is to be
without hope, where God is lost and the soul has
gone out into the everlasting desolation, never able
to find God, it is a big matter that we should never
be touched of that. And love triumphant, this kind
of love in Smyrna which is suffering love (*"Be thou
faithful unto death, and I will give thee the crown of
life"*) means that, although it may cost you your
earthly life, you shall never be touched of the second
death. You may know the first death, in this sense,
that you may go into the grave, and that maybe at

the hands of murderers; you may have a martyr's grave, you may die because of the opposition and suffering that is heaped upon you; but that is only a first kind of death. There is a much deeper and more terrible death than that, and if you are faithful unto that first death, you shall not be touched of the second. You will find you will be amongst those who have completely conquered death. Now, whatever it means to you to have to exercise the love which suffers long, remember there is a big issue bound up with suffering love. You who are putting up with things for Christ's sake, who are enduring, who are suffering in any way in love for the Lord, by that suffering love you are in the way of cheating death in the end. You are undermining the power of death, you are destroying the very touch of death. Perhaps that wants explaining, but there is the fact stated, that by suffering we conquer death.

A DEEP, SECRET LIFE WITH THE LORD

We come now to the issue of love triumphant in Pergamum. It is remarkable that to this church that had come into a state of compromise from their failure to detect the inroads of evil, because of the low condition of that love for God which should normally be alert and sensitive to things injurious to God, it is remarkable that to them this word is addressed, *"To him that overcometh, to him will I give of the hidden manna, and I will give him a white stone, and upon the stone a new name written, which no one knoweth but he that receiveth it."* But I can tell you in a word what it amounts to—that there is some inner fellowship with God to be known which is not the common lot of people; some inner knowledge of God which is a secret thing to be possessed, which means a very great deal. It is something to have a personal, inner, secret knowledge of the Lord, a knowledge which other people, not having, do not understand at all; you know the Lord in your own heart and you are enjoying something of the Lord in yourself; but you have to have it to yourself, it is your own secret. Is there not something in that for believers now? *"The secret of the Lord is with them that fear him"* (Ps. xxv. 14). There is a mysterious something in the inner life of some children of God and in their walk with the Lord; they have a secret. They can never make other people understand it, it is a mystery to others, but there it is. It is their blessed possession, and oh, what it means to them! And that is what is here. Hidden manna, a white stone, a new name written thereon, His own name; *"I will set him on high, because he hath known my name"* (Ps. xci. 14); and that distinguishes people who know the Lord in some more inward and some deeper way than the majority. It is not the ordinary kind of knowledge to the Lord that is here.

And that is said to the people whose great need was discerning love, and the message, therefore, is that if you have this love, you have a secret with the Lord. If this love is in us, this first love, this complete love, this true love for God, we have a secret life with God, God means something to us in secret that He does not mean to everybody. And we are elected to that: not that we are favourites, but through suffering love we come to discerning love. That is the sequence—suffering love, then discerning love. Those who have the deepest and most inward knowledge of the Lord are those who have suffered most for and with the Lord. They have knowledge others do not possess. So you move from Smyrna to Pergamum; from suffering love to discerning love—through suffering to the hidden manna, the mystery of a love-relationship with the Lord in a knowledge which is not common knowledge.

A POSITION OF POWER AND AUTHORITY

Thyatira—seduced and corrupted, calling for uncompromising love. What is the issue of that uncompromising love? *"He that overcometh, and he that keepeth my works unto the end, to him will I give authority over the nations: and he shall rule them with a rod of iron."* Here we are touching a tremendous principle. Do not materialize that for the moment and picture yourself somewhere as a reigning monarch over the nations of this earth, and that sort of thing. That is not what I am getting at. It is the principle that matters. Here you see, when love triumphs over that state of compromise and mixture and confusion and entangling of contrary things, and comes right out into an uncompromising place of victory, you are in a position of tremendous ascendency, of power to govern. Test it the other way. You find a compromised life, a mixed-up life, a life with contraries all entangled; some of the world, some true Christianity; some flesh, some Spirit, things which ought never to be brought together. Will you tell me that such a life has any power in it, any authority, any power of ruling and reigning? Not at all! Was it not just in that connection that the devil through Balaam seduced the corrupted Israel, to bring Israel down from their high place as the ruling nation among the nations, to rob them of their spiritual government, to make them broken among the nations, when God had said, *"The Lord will make thee the head, and not the tail"* (Deut. xxviii. 13)? That is the principle here. Love, uncompromising love, brings into a position of power, of authority. You will never pray through so that God comes in and does things if your life is compromised, if there is any kind of double life going on. You may pray until you cannot pray any more, and the Lord will not come in, you will not govern in prayer if the life is mixed up. Love, which brings us out into an absolutely clear, pure, transparent place before God, means we are put into a position of great spiritual power. What that may be afterward we are not going to stop to say. I merely indicate it. The Church is going to rule in the heavenlies in the ages to come, and in the letter to the Ephesians, where the revelation of the Church and of its eternal calling and vocation is presented to us most fully, love is the triumphant note—". . . *to apprehend with all the saints what is the breadth and length and height and depth, and to know the love of Christ which passeth knowledge, that ye may be filled unto all the fulness of God"* (Eph. iii. 18-19). That is set there in relation to the Church. The Church is to come to that place. There are big issues bound up with this matter of love, both that of spiritual power and ascendency now, and afterward throughout the ages to come that of governing in the heavenlies, when the Church will take the place occupied now by the evil principalities and powers, the world rulers of this darkness. That is no small vocation. It depends on first love. Such is the lesson of Ephesus and of Thyatira. Right at the heart is love, first love, full love, and the outcome of that is authority over the nations.

OUR NAME CONFESSED IN HEAVEN

Then comes Sardis; and, because of its indefiniteness, the call for distinguishing love, the love that marks you out; not only that you are marked out by love, but love marks you out. Do you think that is a distinction without a difference? Not so. When you come here to this distinguishing love, what is the word to that church? *"He that overcometh shall thus be arrayed in white garments; and I will in no wise blot his name out of the book of life, and I will confess his name before my Father, and before his angels."* Is this not distinguishing love, love leading to distinction?—white garments, and his name confessed before the Father and the holy angels. Maybe I can help you by a very ordinary illustration. I have a brother who is an engineer, and I went to see him the other day and found him in his office behind his engineering works where some sixty men, all experts, were busy mostly on government work. I talked with him for some time, and, being an opportunist, and remembering that there was something I needed done to my car, I said, "I have a little trouble with my car; I wonder if you can do something about it?" He came downstairs to look at the car, and then said to one man, "Put that on the lift." He then sent for his chief expert on that side of things, and when he arrived said to him, "This is my brother; if ever he brings his car in here, see to it, please, and see that the job is done properly." "This is my brother"—and the whole sixty men and all the works were at my command! Everything there could be centered in my interest at that moment. *"I will confess his name before my Father, and before his angels."* "I will say, 'This is My brother' "—and all heaven will be interested. Love, honour in heaven; our names confessed and honoured in heaven, when love distinguishes us. Oh, we try to curry favour and get service and help and status by being important before men, by putting on airs, by making demands, by being something big. That is the way in which men try to get recognition. But here it says that love is the distinguishing thing in heaven. It is love that makes you a distinguished person there. It is love that will bring you before the Father and the holy angels as one to be taken account of; and that is an issue for now, not only for hereafter. Oh, if only we have this love, the Father will take account of us. "This is my beloved." The holy angels will take account and put themselves at our service as beloved of the Father. It will be because we are not only located in the Son of His love, but in heart-fellowship with what that love means, that we are marked out by heaven.

SPIRITUAL SIGNIFICANCE

Philadelphia marks the call for steadfast love, and so you expect in the issue of steadfast love to find something that would correspond. To Philadelphia the word is—*"He that overcometh, I will make him a pillar in the temple of my God, and he shall go out thence no more: and I will write upon him the name of my God, and the name of the city of my God, the new Jerusalem, which cometh down out of heaven from my God, and mine own new name." "A pillar in the temple of my God."* Again, do not materialize, for later we read, *"And I saw no temple therein: for the Lord God the Almighty, and the Lamb are the temple thereof"* (Rev. xxi. 22). A pillar in the place where God dwells, a pillar in the house of God, the place of God's abode. A pillar, a strong thing, carrying responsibility in the very house of God. Steadfast love has that issue. *"And I will write upon him . . . the name of the city of my God."* He shall have the franchise of the heavenly Jerusalem. He is a man of substance, a person that counts, he is carrying weight, he is a freeman of the new Jerusalem. *"And mine own new name";* which

—87—

means "I commit myself to that man." Are these things too big to grasp? They are not exaggerations, but that is what is implicit in this statement, and all who are of the character of Philadelphia, marked by steadfast love, become a strength in the place of God's dwelling and in His interest. They are people that count. Job said of his days before his affliction that when he went out everybody took account of him and bowed down to him and honoured him. To be not self-important, but from heaven's standpoint, with that kind of importance that is humble, meek, altogether without arrogance or pride, to be of great importance to God, in the presence of God, important in the Church which is the new Jerusalem—love is the thing that must characterize us. Do you desire in a right way to carry weight, to signify something, to be really a strength in the things of God, to stand before the Lord as one who counts for something? Do you want that? Do you know the way there? I wonder what you think it is. Do you say, "Oh well, if I study, if I get a lot of teaching and Bible knowledge, and am always busy in the Lord's work, I shall become something"? No, not at all! In the dealings of God with you, you will find you will be emptied and brought down to nothingness in yourself, until you reach the place of pure, selfless love for the Lord for His own sake. Oh, there is a difference even in loving the Lord—whether it be for what He can do for us or for His own sake. You do not want to be loved because of what you are able to do. You want to be loved for your own sake. When it is like that, and we get away from all our ambitions, all our craving for recognition and reputation, and we love the Lord for His own sake, we have attained a place of tremendous importance—pillars of strength in the things of God, in the temple of God, in the presence of God. Love is the key to all spiritual significance.

SHARING HIS THRONE

And finally, Laodicea; poor Laodicea, with its mediocre kind of testimony, neither hot nor cold, and the demand, therefore, for fervent love with no mistake about it, burning love, love at white-heat. What is the issue hanging upon love like that? *"To him that overcometh, I will give to him to sit down with me in my throne, as I also overcame, and sat down with my Father in his throne."* You have reached the highest place now—throne-union with the reigning Lord. All that that may mean we can never describe. Were we to start, we should never be able to tell it; but it must mean something that the Lord should say to people on this earth—"On certain grounds you shall sit with Me in My throne, you shall have the place that I have, you shall share with Me the position to which I have come." It must mean something tremendous. And He says that is related to victory over mediocrity in the matter of love. When you have this kind of love, fervent, full, strong love, you will come to the place of uppermost ascendency, the place in the throne.

You may not remember all I have said, the detail may go from you; but remember that in the Revelation the last times and the last things are in view. If you forget all the details, remember this one thing, that the ultimate, the supreme issue of our life and union with God is bound up with this question of love. How great, then, in importance is this question of love. How great, then, in importance is this question of His love being shed abroad in our hearts by the Holy Ghost. What a wonderful thing is His great love wherewith He loved us, when it is found in us. It is both toward us and should be in us. The Lord make it so!

—89—

CHAPTER EIGHT

"Lovest Thou Me?"

Reading: John xxi. 15-23

We are now nearing the end of our contemplation of "His great love," and we shall conclude with a word on the way of love. It is still through the Apostle John that the message is coming to us. His writings are the last of the New Testament, and the final and predominant feature is love.

The twenty-first chapter of his Gospel is a kind of appendix; almost like an afterthought. He seems to have concluded at the point marked verse thirty-one of chapter twenty, and then, as though on reflection, he seems to have said to himself, "I cannot leave it there; there is something yet to be added. I must resolve it all into a personal application, a matter of personal love for the Lord proved by *practical* devotion." So we have—in the first place—

"Lovest thou me more than these??" The challenge is made very personal and direct: not to *any* Simon, but to *"Simon, son of John."* He is penned down and is not allowed to be mixed up in a crowd of Simons. Then, it was *this* Simon who had protested that, whatever might be the failues of others, his love would be stronger and more reliable than theirs. *"Lovest thou me* MORE THAN THESE?" Doubtless many who read this, were they asked by the Lord if they loved Him, would be quite emphatic in their answer of "Yes!" But the Lord was evidently seeking an answer that was more than Simon was giving.

That is why He was so insistent. "Simon, you have protested that you do love Me; you have even gone as far as to say that you would out-love other people; but, Simon, Simon, really look into your own heart—do you? Why, under trial, when I was withdrawn from you and you were left alone, and everything seemed to have gone wrong and to have broken down and all your personal expectations and ambitions and visions had proved worthless, why did you say, 'I go a fishing'? as though you said, 'I am going to find some alternative to this kind of life, it is not sastisfactory, it is so uncertain and there are so many difficulties, I cannot see the way, therefore I am going to make a way myself.''

There was another of this group who took the course of despair, passive despair—I refer to Thomas. But Peter put his dilemma into a positive form and said, "I go a fishing." We may adopt different courses in our perplexity, in adversity, under trial. When the Lord hides Himself and we cannot see Him, or hear Him, and we do not feel that He is with us, He seems to be so far away and to have gone right out of our world, all we were expecting seems to have come to an end, and we do not know where we are, then we are prone to go some way that we choose for ourselves, and begin to take alternatives to steadfast love. It is a real challenge, it is a positive challenge, because these are experiences, these are tests, that the Lord allows. It is not a wrong thing to say that there are times when the Lord hides Himself, when the Lord lets us feel that we are left alone, when the Lord seems to close the heavens to us so that there is no to-and-fro communication, and when everything that we had looked for, expected and preached, seems to have come to an end and to have broken down, we are just left in

—91—

what seems like ruins of everything; the Lord just does do that, and peculiarly does He do that sort of things when He has people in view who are going to count. Take that, brothers, sisters! People who are going to count for Him go through deep experiences like that, and the object is to get them on to a basis which will make it possible for Him to use them. We will never be used unless we can stand on our feet in the storm. We are useless to the Lord if we go to pieces when everything around us, and in our spiritual life, seems to have come to a deadlock. If then we give it up, we are of no use to the Lord. The whole question of future usefulness to the Lord is based upon a love for the Lord which does not give up and say, "I go a fishing," "I take an alternative to following the Lord, I take an alternative to going on with the Lord because of the situation."

That is why the Lord came back, once, twice—"Follow me," "follow thou me." "You went back under trial, under testing—follow thou Me." And you have got to follow and go on following when you cannot see Him, when you do not know where He is, you have got to go on. These are the kind of people, and these alone, who will be used as Peter was. The basis of everything was that kind of personal love to the Lord Himself, not for what He was doing for Peter at the time, but for Himself. Oh, that is difficult—God only knows how difficult it is—to love Him for Himself when He does not seem to be doing anything for us at all. That is the challenge of love.

Really now, have we got very near to this? Love is something more than being a nominal Christian, bearing the name of Christian and going to meetings and taking up Christian work and all that. Love for the Lord is something very much more than that. The Lord says, "Lovest thou me?" I am not stopping with the different words that were used for "love". The Lord used one word, Peter used another. We will leave that aside. The challenge is this—"Lovest thou me?" What is the calibre, the quality, the content, of your love? "Lovest thou me?"

THE PROOF OF LOVE

Peter answered, "Yea, Lord; thou knowest that I love thee." The Lord came back upon that declaration, imperfect as it was, for He Himself had used another word, the Lord came back and said, "All right, prove it." There was the challenge of love, and then the proof of love. "Feed my lambs." "Tend my sheep." And where is the emphasis in that? The emphasis is upon "my"—*My* lambs, *My* sheep. Love is not for the ministry, love is not for the work in itself. Oh, we can love to preach, we can love to work, to be in the work. We can love the whole system of Christian organization, activity, and all that, and find a great deal of satisfaction in it and place for ourselves, but it is not that at all. It is not love for the ministry, not even for tending and feeding. There is an awful snare in that. The love lies in this, "Because they are Mine, just because they are Mine, and yours is a love for Me, anything that is Mine becomes the object of your love and your devotion and your activity." This is really a sifting out. You perhaps like to be in Christian work, you like to teach, to preach, to do things and you would say that it is for the Lord. But let us ask our own hearts, if it is because we really love that which is dear to the Lord, is that really the motive? Just because it is the Lord's, will we pour ourselves out, break our hearts over it, will we really shed tears because of genuine love for our Lord and what matters to Him? Is it like that? Why are you doing what you are doing, whatever it is, in relation to the Lord's things? Sheep and lambs can be very trying and cause us almost to despair, but love for the Lord and because they are His will keep us from giving them up.

Oh, I could break that up to apply it. I do not know what you are doing, but you may be doing various things. Where it is within the company of the Lord's people, you may be looking after the door and bringing the people in. You may be playing the instrument, you may be doing anything that people do in Christian work. Why are you doing it? Is it really out of a heart-love for the Lord, for the Lord *Himself*, because this is the Lord's, or can it be put down to anything less than that—you have been persuaded or appointed to do it. Really are you doing it from the heart as unto the Lord? This is for the Lord consciously and deliberately, He puts everything on that basis. The proof of love is our concern for what is His. It is just His, and that is all there is to it. It is something that counts for Him, that matters to Him, and I need no other persuasion, no other coercion, no other urge or invitation. It is because it is the Lord's, and that is enough.

THE MASTERY OF LOVE

And then the mastery of love. *"When thou wast young, thou girdedst thyself, and walkedst whither thou wouldest: but when thou shalt be old, thou shalt stretch forth thy hands, and another shall gird thee, and carry thee whither THOU wouldest not."* When thou was young—in other words—you did as you liked; when you get old, you are going to do what you would not have done then. And love is

going to make you do a lot of things you would not
have done before. It is something more than "like";
it is love. You are going to be mastered by another
master than yourself and your own likes and preferences. You are going to do quite a lot out of love,
because you are love-mastered, that you would
never do otherwise. When love is the master, you
are going ways you would never go otherwise.

Is not this something that discriminates
between spiritual infancy and spiritual maturity?
In effect, the Lord is saying here, "In spiritual
infancy and immaturity, people always do as they
like, as they want to do, as they choose. But when
you get to spiritual maturity it is no longer what
you want or the way you would go, it is the way the
other Master says, the Master who is love." The
day comes when you say:

"My Master, lead me to Thy door;
   Pierce this now willing ear once more:"
"At length my will is all Thine own,
   Glad vassal of a Saviour's throne."

That is a new kind of mastery. There has been service to the Lord, but this is something new, this is
maturity. You notice that Paul said the very same
thing in another way in I Cor. xiii, *A more excellent way show I unto you. If I speak with the
tongues of men and of angels, but have not love, I
am become sounding brass, or a clanging cymbal,*
and on he goes with what might be, yet without
love, and of it all being nothing, and then he goes on
to the positive unfolding of the nature of true love.
*"Love suffereth long, and is kind; love envieth not;
love vaunteth not itself, is not puffed up, doth not
behave itself unseemly, seeketh not its own..."* and
then, without a break, it is not another chapter on

another subject, he says, *"When I was a child, I spake as a child, I felt as a child, I thought as a child: now that I am become a man, I have put away childish things."* Oh, love, mature love, true love, this love is not childish in its thoughts and ideas and ways, seeking its own. But mature grown-up love, the love now of the man as against the child, is a different thing altogether from that. This is the love of the mature man that Paul is talking about, and it is his way, his lovely way, I was going to say—his clever way of just letting the Corinthians see that it was all childishness, this that was going on in Corinth. *"I am of Paul; and I of Apollos; and I of Cephas"* (I Cor. i. 12). It is childishness and it is not love, and when you come to mature love, when you grow up, all that sort of thing will go. You will not be selecting your favourites, you will not be doing any of those things the Corinthians were doing.

When thou shalt become a man, thou shalt be under another mastery, and, although you will not like it, your flesh will shrink from it, you will even go to the cross. No man chooses that for his own fleshly comfort, he would shun it; but you will go to the cross. *"Now this he spake, signifying by what manner of death he should glorify God."* He would be so mastered that he would stretch forth his hands—Peter according to tradition was crucified— he would stretch forth his hands, he would be carried not the way he would like, but another way because of another master, the mastery of love, mature love, grown-up love.

Now this brings me to this point. The Lord does really need men and women to serve *His* ends. In many ways there is a need for more young men to come on in the ministry of feeding and tending. A lot of people have interpreted that "Feed my lambs" as Sunday School work. I do not believe the Lord meant that at all. The lambs in this case are not little children, although that may be your ministry and it may be included. You know, one of the most difficult things is to tend and minister to the immature, the spiritually delayed in their growth. But whatever it is, the Lord does need those who will serve Him in ministering to His own. Young men, He does! He needs you to preach the Gospel. He needs you to teach His people, to feed His people. There is a great need. Perhaps you have thought about it and perhaps you have desired it. Perhaps that is your will or your hope. But listen—the need is very great in all phases and directions of the Lord's work, He needs you; but the fact that the Lord needs you does not mean that you can do it, or that He can come now and call you into it and open the way for you. His need may be very great, and yet He may not be able now to open the way for you to come in to serve Him in meeting it. Why? It might be that you would come in on some other ground—to be a minister, to be a teacher, to be something; to study up the Bible and then pass on the fruits of your study. All sorts of things you might begin to do, and the Lord is waiting until your heart is broken over this whole situation, and it is such a heart-matter that you come to the place where you say, "Lord, the only justification of my life is that your interests are served." It must be a matter of heart-love for the Lord and for what is His, and not for the work, the ministry; not for anything but for your Lord and what is His. When you get there, and you are found upon your face before the Lord breaking your heart because you see He is not getting what He ought to have, when this becomes the travail of your soul, you will find the Lord will begin to do something. This is the necessary basis for the Lord to bring out His servants. That is what is here. You may come in the way to the place where you find it painful and not likeable at all, but that basic grip of the master-love will keep you going when everything would make you run away. When I see young men with ambition to be ministers, I quietly say inside, "The Lord have mercy upon them." This is something to be guarded against unless the Lord puts you in and holds you in. Do not have natural ambitions in the Christian realm, but ask the Lord for this love that will hold you in when you would give anything to run away.

You say, It is terrible to talk about Christian work like that! But, in a true spiritual realm, you meet forces that you would never have imagined existed. You meet hell when you are seeking to build the heavenly kingdom. Well, here again the Lord does need you. The need is there, He wants you. There is work for you to do and plenty of it. Oh, His people are hungry, His sheep need tending and feeding; they need guiding, counselling, instructing, and to be provided for, and the Lord wants you to be His under-shepherds. I am so glad Peter wrote his letter about the great Shepherd and the under-shepherd. Yes, He wants you, He needs you. Do not be mistaken about that. And if He is keeping you waiting, do not think it is because He does not want you, because there is no need. It is all there, clamant, pressing, but He must have you on this basis, nothing else will do—your own personal heart-love for Him that will not choose your own way or go anywhere because you like it. You will go against yourself altogether under the constraint of His mighty love.

THE CONCENTRATION OF LOVE

If I were to add another word, it would be this—connected with Peter's seemingly superficial reaction to this terrific thing. Suddenly seeing John following on he turned round. The Lord has said, "Follow me," and he immediately turns round, sees John and says, "Lord, and this man, what?" What I am going to say about it is not all it contains, but it is this, that you are going to be called, appointed, to your particular ministry. Others will be called to theirs and theirs may be different from yours, theirs may be in another realm altogether from yours. The Lord's servants are often characterized by a specific ministry. They have to recognize what that is and keep to it.

Effectiveness depends upon concentration and avoidance of either distraction, diversion, or divided interest. There is something in the nature of rebuke in the Lord's rejoinder to Peter—"What is that to thee?" The whole statement seems clearly to mean that the Lord has sovereign rights to dispose of His servants as He wills, and they must not allow themselves to be diverted from what He appoints for them severally.

Love for Him must work out in giving oneself *wholly* to *the* thing to which they have been called. Superficially turning therefrom to what is not *their* calling is itself contrary to love, it is fickleness.

Well, Peter learned this lesson, did his job, and glorified his Lord. He became a true shepherd. No one can read his letters without feeling his love for his Lord above all dividedness of heart. Love works out in faithfulness to the particular function, and faithfulness thereto unto the end—the long last proves the love.

The Battle for Life.

T. A-S.

SYNOPSIS.

The Battle for Life.

CHAPTER I.

The Quest of the Eyes of Flame.

READING : Rev. i. 1-20; ii. 1.

By way of a brief introductory word let us focus your attention upon what we feel to be the Lord's concern with His people at this time.

In the second and third chapters of the book of the Revelation we have the Lord's survey of the seven churches. As those eyes that are as a flame of fire peer into the inner spiritual state and lay bare the condition—analyse, dissect, separate, place on the two sides of debit and credit, and form and pass their final verdict— we see one thing to be at issue with regard to them all. There may be particular differences in them; the aspects may vary; the elements may be very different, yet when all has been surveyed and gathered together it is to establish but one fact, namely, the presence or absence of that which, from the Lord's standpoint, constitutes justification in the continuance of anything which claims to represent Him. The issue for every one of these churches was whether, under the Lord's permission, they could remain as witnesses, whether they could continue before Him. The Lord had them before Him, shall we say, had them in His hand, and was determining whether He could keep them, or whether He would have to put them away; whether He would have to remove the lampstand out of its place, or whether it could abide in relation to Himself. So that the question was clearly one of continuing in relation to the Lord's purpose or of passing out. We have seen bodies cross the sky at night, coming from afar, gaining in brilliance it seemed as they came nearer, flashing on their way, and then disappearing altogether from view in the darkness of the sky. Here are "stars" brought in out of the eternal counsels of the Godhead, flashing in with the glory of His grace, some of them to pass right out, to fade from view, to be lost to sight.

The question concerning every instrumentality raised up by God in relation to His purpose is, What justifies His maintaining it? It is evident that there are things which do not justify Him in preserving some instrumentalities. These letters make those things clear.

In the first place, because God originally raised up an instrumentality, and it came from

Him, was His work initially, does not justify
Him in keeping it. That is made quite clear.
We should take serious account of the fact that
because God raised up a thing it does not mean
that God must of necessity keep that thing
right through, no matter what its state or
character may be eventually, or in the course
of time. Again, because God has greatly used
an instrument which He Himself raised up
does not justify Him in preserving it. Further,
because an instrument has had a wonderful
history of devotion to Him, and has at some
time been a very real and full expression of
His grace and power does not resolve itself into
a claim upon Him, and He does not regard
Himself as under any obligation to preserve it.
But we have to press the point still further.
Because at any given time many commendable
things are to be seen in an instrumentality,
which the Lord Himself may praise—there
may be not a few such things—nevertheless,
this record shows that even they do not justify
God in preserving it in its place; even their
presence does not mean that He may never
consider putting it out of its place, or that He
is bound to refrain from doing so.

That is a very thorough sifting of anything.
It might be thought that if God raised up a
thing, if it came in the first place from His own
hand; if God had used it and blessed it; if it

had shown the features and characteristics of His grace and of His love; if that instrumentality still had in it many things which God, looking with His eyes as of a flame, could commend, surely that is enough to argue for its continuance before the Lord? You understand that we are speaking about instrumentalities. We are not speaking about souls. We are not dealing with the question of salvation, but with that of service to the Lord.

What then justifies the Lord in preserving and going on with any such instrumentality? We must look to see what was behind His hand when He brought it into being, what was in His mind, and in His heart. We shall find all we need to know from the very description of the instrumentality itself. In the passage to which we have referred it is called a lampstand, "seven golden lampstands" (R.V.M.). Our knowledge of the Word gives us much light upon what that means, and the Old Testament in particular comes at once to our help; for whether it be the candlestick in the Tabernacle, or the candlestick all of gold shown to Zechariah (Zech. iv. 2), we know that in both cases there was represented the living expression of the Holy Spirit's energies. Take the candlestick all of gold. We remember the pattern of it, with its seven bowls and seven pipes; and the oil being emptied out of the living olive trees through the pipes into the bowls, to provide the resource for the light. It is a very complete, a very comprehensive illustration, and it is something that is living. At one end there is a living fountain or spring. The prophet does not say there were cisterns, tanks, some man-made receptacle, reservoir of oil, but living trees, and oil being poured continually, ever fresh, ever fresh—warm from the very arteries of that living organism, as it were—into the candlestick burning with its steady, undying light, a light which does not vary, which does not go out, which is maintained at full strength continually.

The Undying Flame.

It is the testimony of an unfailing life, an undying life, an all-sufficient life; the testimony of a life which is not an abstract, which is not something stored up, but something which is coming all the time from an inexhaustible stream; a mighty, glorious life. As the light burns, it is a constant declaration of victory, and that a victory over death, death which would seek to quench the light, quench the flame, smother it. It burns in the midst of surrounding death, a continuous declaration that death has no power to quench it.

To come back to the book of the Revelation :

What is it, and what is it that alone justifies
God in maintaining any instrumentality in
relation to Himself and His purpose? It is not
that the instrumentality has many good things.
It is not that it had its origin with Him. It is
not that it has a great history, a great past.
It is not that it has a name, a reputation, the
name of its more glorious days still carried on.
It is that there is *to-day* the same undying
flame of Divine life in its mighty testimony
against the power of death all around. That
is God's justification.

You notice, that in relation to the seven
golden lampstands, there is reference to the
seven Spirits of God, and to Jesus Christ the
Faithful Witness. He is identified with these
lamps. He is in the midst of them, closely
associated with them. They were called into
being in order that they might be an abiding
expression of the Lord Himself as the Faithful
Witness, the Living One, in the power of the
Spirit of God. When we come to analyse the
state of these churches, we find that in five of
them at least there is a variety of elements,
each of which is an expression of something
that is a contradiction to the Holy Ghost, a
contradiction to the Spirit of life. When such
a thing is found amongst the Lord's people,
within the vessel, the instrumentality, it constitutes an element of death, and provides Satan

with his foothold, his place, and all unconsciously for the most part amongst those people
the testimony is definitely contradicted and
nullified.

The point is this, that Satan will resort to
anything—his methods and his means are
numerous—to get some foothold for death into
a Divinely constituted instrumentality, so that
the thing becomes a contradiction right at its
very centre. It has a name : it has good works ;
it has many things which even the Lord Himself cannot judge because they are good, but
the vital thing by which alone the Lord can
be justified in maintaining that instrumentality
has been countered. It is not a question of
what there once was of good and whether it still
flourishes to-day, but rather, Has the Lord that
central, basic, essential, indispensable thing
for which He has ever raised up His instrumentalities, whether individuals or companies,
and brought them into relationship with Himself, that for which He apprehended them, that
which was intended to be their specific vocation ?

That applies to all of us. We have all been
apprehended of Christ Jesus, and there has
been a purpose behind that apprehending. We
have not been apprehended just to be saved.
Our salvation is but basic and introductory to
something very much more. The Lord gathers
His own together to form them into a corporate

vessel of Divine purpose. He raises up such instrumentalities from time to time; but whether it be individuals or whether it be companies, the one constant danger is that *the essential thing* in the Divine thought in raising up, in apprehending that vessel, should somehow be lost while many other things may continue.

The Lord's Standard of Judgment.

One inclusive thing arises from this survey of the churches. It is that the Lord deals with every life or vessel in the light of His specific purpose for it and not of its general usefulness. These chapters would never have been written if the Lord were simply taking this view: Well, this vessel is not wholly bad; there is much yet of value here; it has not altogether gone away from Me, therefore I must look after it and support it, preserve it and bless it, and let it stand: but He is not doing that. We may be thankful to the Lord for anything that there is in this world which is good and which is of Himself, and as we ourselves go into it, we are grateful that the Lord should have any witness in a world like this; but, oh, so far as His own people are concerned, so far as the Church is concerned, that never satisfies Him. Of that we may be quite sure.

Why are we saying this? Because so many people say, Well, you know, you are trying to get something so extreme! Why not be satisfied with what is commendable about the Church to-day! Take it as it is! Accept it and be thankful that there are so many who belong to the Lord and bear His name in a world like this! I find that this record does not allow of that. God knows we are grateful that there are believers in this world, be they but poor ones. You cannot go abroad in a world like this and see its state, its Godlessness, its sinfulness, without being thankful to find even a very poor specimen of a believer who has some love in his heart for the Lord. You are thankful for the smallest thing that speaks of Him. Oh, but when you come to see God's purpose, when you see that what He has designed for His Church is the occasion of His call, His choosing in Christ, you can never be satisfied with nominalism, or with general goodness. When you come to a word like this, you find it taking you right on—if you like to call it "extreme" you may—right on to the end. It tells you quite plainly that whether there be a great past; a great history of Divine blessing and usefulness; a great reputation for good works, and many good things still obtaining, none of these things is an adequate justification for the Lord to keep that vessel in

His hand for His purpose. He must let it go, unless the real object for which it has been raised up is being fulfilled.

The Nominal is Ultimately Rejected.

For what was the Church raised up? I do not believe that the Lord originally thought of having a general Church, and then a special one within it; a general mass of believers, and then a company called "overcomers" in the midst. That has never been the design of God. It is what we might call an emergency state of things, and is essential because of failure. It seems to me that the very word "overcomers" loudly declares that there is failure somewhere. The Lord's purpose for *all* His Church, as a vessel—which nevertheless may only be realised in a few—is that it should maintain the testimony of a life which has conquered death, and will conquer death right to the end. It is a life question.

The Lord Jesus is constituted the great Witness upon the ground of the power of God which was exercised in Him when He was raised from the dead. Remember that the testimony of Jesus is always related to His being raised from the dead; that is, that He lives by a power which has conquered death. He is the Life on that ground, on that basis, in that sense, and those whom the New Testament approves as witnesses to Jesus are not those who talk the truth about Him, but are *witnesses of His resurrection;* that, of course, in a spiritual way, witnesses to Christ as risen. The New Testament's testimony of Jesus is that God raised Him from the dead, and that He is alive for evermore. That is the essence of the testimony. Thus the whole question resolves itself into one of testimony in life, a testimony of life. It is not a testimony of truth in the first place, it is a testimony of life. Is the flame burning as at the beginning, witnessing that Jesus lives and is triumphant, even over the dark, deadly background of this world? That is the question for the Lord's people; the question for your life and for mine, and for every collective instrumentality.

If the Lord continues to lead us in this way, we shall see a great deal of what that means. We simply focus our thought upon the issue. I have no doubt in my heart as to what the issue of our time is. I trust that we may rightly claim to be of the tribe of Issachar, so to speak, in this matter, to know what the time is saying, and what Israel ought to do. I have not the slightest shadow of a doubt but that the issue of our day, of this hour in the Church's history is, more than ever, the issue of life and death in a spiritual sense. Are you not more and more experiencing that awful sapping of your very vitality, that draining of your life, that exhausting of your energy, especially in relation to prayer? Is it not true that it requires a supreme effort to pray, and to get through when you have started to pray? You need energizing from a source other than that of your own natural energies in this matter, and that increasingly so. There is a strange, deep, terrible sapping of vitality; mental vitality; physical vitality, as well as spiritual. Spiritual people, at least, know something of that. And lying back of it is the final conflict of this age. It is the spiritual issue of life and death.

The Lord would say to us something about that at this time, and we have but directed our eyes in the way of the Lord's thought to the great issue which is at stake for His people. But I trust that we shall know that He is not only making us aware of it, and not only warning us about the perils of it, but that He comes mightily to our aid, and shows us what is on our side in the battle. May that be so as we hold on definitely in prayer.

CHAPTER II.

The Controversy of Zion.

READ : Rev. xxii.   Isa. xxxiv. 8.

*" For it is the day of the Lord's vengeance,
the year of recompence in the controversy
of Zion."*

What is the controversy of Zion?   It is
nothing other than the controversy for the life
of Zion.   We are not going to allow that
historic suggestion to lead us to a survey of the
Scriptures, but we may say that Zion is often
represented in the Old Testament as Jehovah's
bride, as the one betrothed to Him, to whom
He was married.   We are familiar with such a
phrase as "the virgin daughter of Jerusalem."
The history of Zion was a chequered history.
Zion was constantly in the realm of dispute,
the object of the envy, covetousness, antagonism of the nations, and all the nations were
found at one time or another in some kind of
relationship with Zion.   The history of Zion
is a very significant and suggestive history
from a spiritual standpoint.   The controversy,
then, was God's controversy with the nations
for Zion's life.   The prophecy of Isaiah makes
that very clear.   God was taking up the cause

17

of Zion, of Zion's very life, and entering into a terrible controversy with the nations on this matter.

Let us bear that in mind as we take up the New Testament and consider the spiritual interpretation. In the book of the Revelation we find the holy city, the New Jerusalem, coming down out of heaven from God, adorned as a bride, and the angel taking the Apostle and saying to him, "Come hither, I will show thee the bride, the wife of the Lamb" (Rev. xxi. 9). The Apostle goes on to say, "And he carried me away in the Spirit to a mountain great and high, and showed me the holy city, Jerusalem, coming down out of heaven from God." The closing chapter of the Revelation brings us into the city, and the central thing therein is the tree of life, while down its centre flows the river of the water of life; and then, as this fulness is viewed, the Spirit and the bride say, "Come." Do you see the spiritual follow-through? Here the controversy for the life of the spiritual Zion is at an end, and life—full, triumphant, effulgent—is the characteristic. Throughout the book of the Revelation, God is dealing with the nations, and at its close all nations are seen as having been brought under the judgment of

His Son, the controversy of Zion has been settled once for all, and Zion is found at last triumphing in fulness of life.

We have said enough to establish the fact that the controversy is in relation to life, and it is that with which we are concerned at this time. There is a spiritual sense in which we are in God's controversy for Zion to-day. If we take the sixth chapter of the letter to the Ephesians as representing what is going on in the spiritual realm, namely, a conflict with world rulers, then the rest of that letter makes it perfectly clear that the controversy with the world rulers is concerning the Church : concerning the very life of the Church, the life of the elect. We are, then, in the controversy, and the issue is no other, and no less, than the issue of life.

In our earlier meditation, in considering the messages of the Lord to the seven churches in Asia, we were seeing that the thing which occupies the place of pre-eminent importance and value to the Lord Himself is the testimony of life; not tradition, they had that; not so much Christian work and activity, they were there; not so many good and commendable things, praiseworthy even in the sight of God, they were there; but that which is central and basic to the Divine election, choice, apprehension, is the testimony of life. In the first chapter of the book the Lord is presented as the One Who is living, Who became dead, but is alive unto the ages of the ages, and has the keys of death and Hades. Alive now from the dead, He is seen standing in the midst of the lampstands, the vessels of testimony, and judging them according to what He is as the Living One, as the One Who has conquered death. What He discovers and reveals in those churches is the measure in which that testimony to Him has been lost. This is more to Him than what is found amongst them of interest, concern, activity, for Him and for His things. He shows the things which have struck a blow at that testimony, and names them; the things, that is to say, which have interfered with the full expression of Himself as the Living One. So it is disclosed that what to Him is more precious than anything else, than all other things put together, is the spiritual life, in fulness, in power, in expression, in impact, in testimony.

The Lord's Jealousy over Life.

I want to carry that thought back into the Old Testament, to see in a fuller way how jealous the Lord is over life, and what is His relationship thereto.

I. The Tree of Life.

It is necessary to go right back to the beginning of the Book, where you will find that immediately there has been that initial disobedience by which sin has entered and man has fallen out of his position in relationship to God, and out of his state as created by God, the question of "the tree of life" arises. Following the judgment upon the serpent, and upon the man, and the earth, God takes His step of precaution in relation to "the tree of life." He proceeds to safeguard it, lest this man should put forth his hand and take of the tree of life and live for ever. God set His cherubim to keep the way to it with the flaming sword which turned in every direction, that the tree of life should not be approached.

The interpretation of that is to be found in the last chapter of the Bible. The tree of life in the midst of the city of God is something from which all sin and sinfulness is excluded. Without are seen to be all those who represent fallen Adam, sinful nature. No one can eventually be found in the presence of God, in a living relationship with God, no one can know eternal life, except the redemptive work of the Lord Jesus has been made effectual in them. The point is that right at the beginning God took a step to protect life from the touch and the appropriation of sinful man. God was not going to have a sinful state perpetuated indefinitely. The last chapter of the Bible sets its seal to the fact and shows that the sinful state is fully and finally dealt with. The state perpetuated is a state in fulness of life, by reason of what the Lamb has wrought through the shedding of His blood, even as the book of the Revelation makes clear. If at the commencement of the book we can say, "Unto him that loved us, and loosed us from our sins by his blood . . ." then at the end of the book we can be found within the city, drinking of the water of life freely, and living in the full power of that life; not now as invited to drink but living in the fulness, because I assume that the bride who says "Come" is other than those who are invited to come. Thus we see right at the beginning God's jealous attitude and action in relation to life. It is precious to note that He suspends the possession of it until the mighty work of the Cross has dealt with all that state which, if perpetuated, would be but the perpetuation of a lost world, of a world outside the Divine intention.

II. Cain and Abel.

The next step in the unveiling of God's attitude toward life is seen in His dealings with Cain. When Cain had slain his brother Abel,

God instantly appears on the scene. There is no delay; it is as though God hastens to the situation. Here is something which concerns Him pre-eminently. No sooner has Cain shed the blood of his brother, and that warm blood trickled into the sand, than God is on the scene. "Where is Abel thy brother? And he said, I know not : am I my brother's keeper? And he said, What hast thou done? the voice of thy brother's blood crieth unto me from the ground" (Gen. iv. 9-10). Then see what God has to say to Cain. He is cursed. He is marked. Everybody who shall observe him shall see him as scarred by God, branded : and he, hardened as he may have been, and insolent to God, has to humble himself and say, "My punishment is greater than I can bear." That is God's attitude toward life, His jealousy over it.

III. **Noah.**

We pass to Noah. The terms of the covenant with Noah are familiar to us, the equalizing of things in that covenant, and the terrible warning to man : "Whoso sheddeth man's blood, by man shall his blood be shed . . . " (Gen. ix. 6). God will keep things even. No man shall get an advantage in this matter. No man who touches that thing which is precious to God shall come by any gain. God will bring it to evenness. He will equalize in the realm of life. You rob man of that, then you shall be robbed ; you shall not be the gainer. That is a solemn warning. It shows to man God's attitude toward life.

IV. Enoch.

There is a great disclosure in the Old Testament of God's mind for man in this matter. God's thought is life, not death. God is against death and for life. We glance back a step and see Enoch, who breaks the long story of death : "And Enoch walked with God : and he was not; for God took him" (Gen. v. 24). That is an offset to the course of fallen man, showing what God's thought is when a man comes into real fellowship with Himself. It is life, not death. That was ever God's thought. That remains God's thought, and He is going to have it fully and gloriously expressed in a company of His own believing children who will be translated to His presence, even as Enoch was, and will not see death or the grave.

V. Abraham and Isaac.

In Abraham and Isaac it is further set forth that when God has a great purpose in mind, when He is moving out on that basis, He must have things brought on to the ground where death cannot touch His purpose. Isaac is the one in whom the purpose of God is bound up, and therefore for the sake of the purpose Isaac must be put typically beyond the power of death. He must come into death to have death destroyed, that God's purpose might be realised upon a ground where death is not future but past. That is the great illustration of Divine purpose being upon the ground of deathless life. And in the greater Isaac the purposes of God are all going to be realised, without any fear whatever of death breaking in to interrupt, because in Christ death is past and not future.

All these are vivid, strong, and, in most cases, agonised expressions of God's attitude to the matter of life. It is a very costly thing. It was infinitely costly to God. It cost those who were in fellowship with God much also. All this is the controversy of Zion in principle, God's jealousy in the matter of life.

VI. Job.

We pass on, so far as the arrangement of the record is concerned, and come to Job; and here Satan is found in the heavenlies with access to God. God challenges him : "Hast thou considered my servant Job? for there is none like him in the earth . . . " (Job ii. 3). Satan sneers back at God, "Skin for skin, yea, all that a man hath will he give for his life.

But put forth thine hand now, and touch his bone and his flesh, and he will renounce thee to thy face.'' Do you see how the question of life is bound up in that challenge, what subtlety there is in the whole movement. God gives Satan permission to touch Job; to touch his body, to touch his family, his property, everything that he has, but says, ''. . . only spare his life.'' Here again is God's jealousy for life. Satan gets to work, and the subtlety is this, that Satan presses, and presses, and presses along every line, by every means, seeking to touch his life indirectly, because he cannot touch it directly. Satan's indirect method is to move Job to break with God by cursing Him, so that his life is forfeited, his life is destroyed.* To understand the book of Job we have to recognise that it is a controversy for life. We have said it is a controversy over faith, but that is a relative factor. The real controversy is over life. We shall see the faith element at some subsequent time, but here God's jealousy for life is seen. Job is brought to great straits, but the life link is never broken, and the end is life triumphant. We see fulness, victory, everything that speaks of life at the end.

We sometimes come very near to collapse under the strain, under the trial, under the

---

* NOTE.—The suggestion of Job's wife may have been that he should break with God, and then take his own life.

tension, the testing. When the enemy is pressing to quench our spiritual life through body, through mind, through circumstance, we are often brought very low as was Job. We have our questionings, we get despondent, we may well-nigh despair. Yes, every heart knows its own story of how far it goes into gloom even about God, His wisdom, His love, His faithfulness. But because God is jealous for the life, and is the Custodian of the life (we are not talking about the natural, physical life), the issue is always more than we had before. We always emerge with increase. In a lesser way it is Revelation xx. after every conflict.

VII. **The Exodus.**

We think of the story of Israel and the emancipation from Egypt, and once again everything is centred in the issue of life and death. God heads it right up to the main, the final issue of life and death. God, moreover, takes His own way, makes His own provision, that when death is to be abroad in the land, smiting, smiting, smiting, devastating everywhere, His own people shall be immune from death, and shall be in life because of the blood. The life of His own is taken into His own custody. He takes the steps for the life of His own, and if the life of His own necessitates the smiting of a nation, grim as that necessity may be, He will follow it out. God stands at nothing when the life of His people is at stake. His jealousy over life is made very clear in all these things.

VIII. Levitical Law of Life.

I hardly need bring to your remembrance those passages of Scripture, in Leviticus for example, concerning God's attitude towards life, and the emphasis laid upon the necessity for the people to avoid drinking the blood, because the blood is the life and the life is in the blood. "Whosoever it be that eateth any blood, that soul shall be cut off from his people" (Lev. vii. 27). Here is God preserving the life. Life is sacred to *Him*. Life is *His*. Man must not appropriate it for himself. Man must not take it and make it his. Life is God's and must ever be regarded as sacred unto God. It means a good deal more than that of course, but we simply state what is apposite to our present consideration.

All these things, when summed up, bring us to this primarily, that life is sacred to God, and He is intensely jealous over it. Then, that life and not death is God's will. Again, sin and death always go together, just as righteousness and life go together. The Old Testament is an earthly type of heavenly truth, and all this is throwing its light forward and saying that what is represented there in those Old Testament Scriptures as to God's attitude toward life—there primarily represented by man's earthly, soul-life—is but figurative, typical, a foreshadowing of that dispensation to come, in which eternal life, Divine life, would be the life given to man.

A Life that is Eternal.

Thus when we come over into the new dispensation, we find that it is not merely the soul-life of man, the bodily life of man, the life of man as here on the earth which is in view, it is another life, called eternal life. "I am come that they might have life, and might have it abundantly" (John x. 10). It is over this life that God is represented as being so jealous. It is this life which is pre-eminent in God's thought. The Old Testament, we have said, is the earthly type or representation of heavenly truth. If it were only a matter of physical death, that is, if the question at issue were but that of the termination of life physically, and that were the end, that were all that mattered, I do not know that such a great deal of ado might be made about it. But the emphasis in the Old Testament upon even that takes its force from the fact that it is pointing to something else, is typical of something else, is illustrative of another life.

We are not in the New Testament very long before that which has seemed to be the controversy in the Old Testament, the life there, has been taken into another realm, and is now seen to be over man's spiritual life, over eternal life. That controversy is waged in a twofold direction; firstly, as to whether man shall become possessed of that life or not, and secondly, as to whether that life, once possessed, shall be allowed its full opportunity of final expression in man, or shall not rather be smothered and thwarted, baffled and hindered. That is the controversy. It is still over life, but now we have come into the reality as out from the shadows, out from the types.

The Persistent Assault upon Life.

So we pass for a few moments to see, in the realm of the reality, the assault of death upon that which is of God. We can take the types again in this connection, to see the conflict illustrated. We pass our eye over them.

Adam. What was in view for Adam? Undoubtedly the supreme thing for Adam was life, the tree of life. He did not possess that which the tree represented, but it was in view, it was for him. The typology clearly indicates that God's thought for man was that he should eventually become possessed of eternal life—

". . . lest he put forth his hand, and take also
of the tree of life, and eat, and live for ever"
(Gen. iii. 22). So that God had already determined eternal life for man, but man according
to His own mind. The great thing in view for
Adam was eternal life in a living fellowship
with God. Satan struck a blow at that state,
in order to thwart that life, and he succeeded
for the time being. Adam lost it through sin.
Paul tells us that ". . . in Adam all die . . ."
(1 Cor. xv. 22). It was the assault upon what
was of God, the assault of death.

Abel. The same thing is true in the case
of Abel. Abel is a spiritually minded man,
a man who recognises the great fundamentals
of true, living relationship with God, and the
blood as being basic to that relationship. Thus
Abel stands in testimony for God on the ground
of life which triumphs over death, and Satan,
through Abel's brother Cain, comes out to
murder that which is of God.

Abraham. Read chapter xv. of the book of
Genesis. There is, I think, no other explanation of that horror of great darkness than that
Abraham was at that time coming into a new
relationship with God concerning a people for
God's own name, a people who should escape
the toils of death; for at that time God was
about to speak to Abraham concerning his seed

being in captivity, and after four hundred years being delivered with a strong hand. Just prior to that assuring vision breaking upon him, there by the altar, with the sacrifice divided, the blood shed, there descended upon him a horror of great darkness.

In smaller ways many of the Lord's people know something of that experience. When God is about to do a new thing, give a further revelation, express Himself in some living way amongst His people, they go through a horror of great darkness. They approach that new thing of God feeling that all life, and all light, and all strength has gone, and anything but life seems to be their experience. Perhaps you know something of that. Some of us have experienced it in measure. As we approach a time when a word which is going to be of great consequence to His people is about to come from God, there is a going through a horror of great darkness : something deep and terrible : intangible but evil. It is death seeking to engulf that which God is about to do. It is death seeking to swallow that child immediately it is born. It is the old story.

Job. The same thing was true of Job, as we have seen. It was the assault of the spirit of death upon what was standing for God.

Esther. We pass into the book of Esther,

and are familiar with the great illustration presented therein of the plot, the device, the wicked scheme against the life of God's people, to the end that they should be engulfed in death and destroyed. That is the plot of Haman. Once more it is the assault upon the life of what is of God. You see God's jealousy coming out in that case again.

The Lord Jesus. Let us pass right on at once to the New Testament, and come to our Lord Jesus, for He gathers all up in Himself. He is the last Adam. He is the greater Abel. All these Old Testament types are gathered up in Him. But remember that at His very birth there was launched an awful design of death. The intention of the Devil was to destroy Him at His birth.

We have to pass over many years wherein we have no record of the things that touched His life, and then we find Him in the wilderness; and the explanation of those temptations in the wilderness is that they were an assault upon His life. Though from various points, by various subtleties, the issue was one; they were intended to break His union with His Father, to get Him out into a realm where He could be smitten. You have only to see that *even He,* had He cast Himself from the pinnacle of the temple contrary to the will of His Father or,

c

as the enemy would have it viewed, by way of testing God—putting God to the test instead of believing Him—would not have been safeguarded by the angels of whom the Devil spoke, quoting the Scriptures. Angels have no commission to bear in their arms any man or woman who presumptiously tries to test God when called to believe Him. The Lord Jesus in His own life has shown us this. It was a threefold assault upon His life.

From the wilderness He went to Nazareth, where He opened the Scriptures. The issue was that they led Him to the brow of the hill on which their city stood, to cast Him over. A little later the Jews take up stones to stone Him. He entered into that argument with them : "Why seek ye to kill me?" (John vii. 19). What is connected with such a question? "Ye are of your father the devil . . ." "He was a murderer from the beginning . . ." (John viii. 44). The Lord Jesus uncovers what is behind. He sees something more than man's opposition, and antagonism. He sees the Devil as the murderer, set against His life. We follow Him on to the lake, where the storm is beaten up, until those who were most familiar with those storms feared for their very lives. Being awakened by them He arose, and in words identical with those which He used in casting out demons He rebuked the wind, saying unto the sea, "Peace! be muzzled!", and the storm subsided, showing that back of the storm there were other forces trying to swallow Him up. Then we follow Him on into the garden and to the Cross. Who shall know of the death conflict in the darkness? It is all the assault of death upon what is of God.

The Church. The same thing is carried on into the Church. It is not long before Stephen is stoned, and James is killed. Peter is taken with the same object but marvellously delivered, because God had yet something to do through him. Paul was in deaths oft, despairing sometimes of life. It is a battle with the power of death. There are the sweeping persecutions, in which literally tens of thousands of Christians are called upon to lay down their lives for the testimony, and count not their lives dear unto the death. It goes on still. We are in that succession, not perhaps of outward persecution, but do we not know something of the pressing of that spirit of death? We do!

All this is very true. It is the controversy of Zion. It is the battle for the life of the Lord's people. May the Lord bring home to our hearts the nature of the conflict in which we are found. We have perhaps painted a dark picture, brought the gloomy aspect into view, have been rather strong and severe, but if you are not able at the moment through your own experience to enter into what we are saying, you will come to do so, if you are going on with the Lord. In a real way you will enter into this controversy of Zion. I am anxious that we should see this more clearly, that we should recognise it in a more definite way. We can never adequately seek the Lord in relation to it and come into line with His intention to overcome it, be to Him the instrument against it which He requires and desires that we should be, until we are fully alive to what the issue is. I wonder if the Lord's people are at times really alive to the issue, and whether their prayers are always a true index of their apprehension of this thing. I believe if you and I were adequately impressed, fully alive to the tremendous issue, we could never pray mere prayers. We could never allow words to run out of our mouths, which we call praying. We should be down on our faces in a tremendous conflict on God's side against the evil menace that is seeking to devour the life of God's people. We shall never pray like that unless we are really alive to what the issue is.

While we may know it in a spiritual way, it is necessary for us to wake up to what is happening, to what this means. The explanation of many a heaviness, and of many a difficult

experience, is not simply that we have had a
meal that does not agree with us, or that we
are none too well, and therefore not able to pray
as we would wish. No, it is not just some
physical malady from which we are suffering.
This is not something which can be explained
along any ordinary line of nature. Behind these
things there so often lies another power. We
may feel ill in body for no justifiable reason from
the natural standpoint. Our very energies and
vitalities, physical and mental, may be sapped,
and we say we are tired, but there is something
extra to that. The enemy delights in our
accounting for these things on human grounds,
when we ought to be waking up to the fact that
there is a much bigger issue at stake. Let us
ask what is its tendency, what is its effect? Is
it to destroy our prayer life? Does it work in
the direction of bringing us into a state of
weakness and uselessness to God? If so, are
we going to accept that? That is the question.
There is a good deal that seems to be perfectly
natural which should not be accepted by the
Lord's people, and we need to test everything,
try it out, see whether after all the whole thing
is natural or whether there is not something
hidden. Do not look for a Devil with horns and
a tail and a pitchfork. He hides himself. He
covers his tracks. He comes in such an
intangible way that you are often inclined to

explain the whole trouble as quite a natural thing, when it is all covering up something else, and its effect is simply to put you out of spiritual action. We have to wake up to what is the issue for the Lord's people to-day, and it is no less an issue than that of life and death.

Go out with some of our brethren and sisters into other lands, where there is not the strength of fellowship and testimony that we enjoy, to those naked realms of the Devil's activity, and you will know something of the meaning of spiritual death. Then you will know that it is a battle, and that the issue is life, your very life. I would sometimes that there could be a baptizing of us all at home into that situation for an hour, for the sake of our brethren who are out. Oh, that we might come into a living relationship with those who are fighting this battle with naked death out in the distant fields ! We could not then pray passively. We could not utter sentences and make petitions. We should be thrown into an agony before God for His testimony's sake.

Do you recognise what is actually happening ? The enemy does not mind how many so called churches there are, how much preaching there is, or how much religious worship. I do not know that he minds very much how much orthodoxy there is, how much of what we would call sound doctrine. What he is against is life.

In multitudes of places, so far as the preaching is concerned, so far as the things said are concerned, no fault can be found, but there is no sense of any vitalizing. There is no energizing, no impact, no moving of the people to register the testimony of the risen Lord against the forces of evil. The enemy is getting them all quietly, nicely, snugly into spiritual death.

Oh, may the Lord move us to a new position in relation to this tremendous issue, the issue of life and death. The Lord bring it home to our hearts.

CHAPTER III.

The Cross in Relation to the Issue of Life.

READ: Deut. xxx. 11-20; Heb. ii. 14-15; Rev. i. 18; Phil. iii. 10.

The matter we have in view is the relationship of the Cross to the manifesting of life. It is very important for us to be clear as to what that relationship is. One thing is patent, that life in this Divine sense, in this spiritual sense, this life called eternal life, is only to be had as the result of the Cross of the Lord Jesus. On the ground of His death and by His resurrection this eternal life is given to them that believe. We sometimes speak of this as simple faith in the atoning work of the Lord Jesus. In the reception of that life there may be no sense of battle, no conflict; there may be no knowledge whatever of this fuller realm where the battle for life goes on. That is because, in the matter of the gift of eternal life, the Lord Jesus Himself fought the battle in His Cross, and we receive the free gift by faith's acceptance of what He did in order that we might have the life.

That is one aspect of the Cross and the issue of life. That is to say, by the objective apprehension of the Cross we receive eternal life.

All that the Lord Jesus did for us in His Cross in order that we might pass from death unto life, appropriated, apprehended by faith, results in our having life.

But there is another side. The Cross of the Lord Jesus subjectively wrought out results in our having life more abundant. His own words are, "I am come that they might have life, and that they might have it more abundantly" (John x. 10). I believe that the first half of that statement relates to the simple faith-appropriation of the objective work of the Cross, what He did for us, but that the second part of the statement carries us further. Life more abundant requires that what He did for us shall be made good in us. May we put it in this way : In His Cross He dealt with our sins, and on the ground of His having so dealt with them, and of our believing in His atoning work for our sins, we receive the gift of eternal life. He also dealt with ourselves, but that is something which has to be made good progressively, and it is as we ourselves are dealt with in the power of the Cross that the way is made for that life to express itself in ever deepening fulness. The fact is that it is self which is in the way of the life and its full expression. It is the natural life which obstructs the course of the Divine life. Thus what has been done for us has to be done in us, and as it is done in us that life becomes more than a deposit, more than a simple though glorious possession, it becomes a deepening, growing enjoyment, a fulness of expression.

A State of Disorder in the Creation.

Let us seek to set forth the position. In the first place there is in the creation a state of disorder with which God is not united. We can all grasp that. There is nothing very profound about it, except as the fact breaks upon us, and we realise that there is this state of disorder in the creation of which we are a part, and that God is not united with that state, with the creation in that condition. It is not according to His mind. It has ceased to express His thought. It is contrary to His intention, and therefore He is not linked with it.

Death and Satan Positively Associated with that State.

Secondly, there is a positive association of death and Satan with that state. It is not just a passive mass, in confusion, in chaos, in disorder. There are active elements in it. We might say that it is a seething mass. There are forces at work in it, and those forces are not the forces of life, they are of death. Death is working, and Satan is associated with that state.

A Need Arises.

In the third place we see that a need arises, a need along various lines. Firstly, there must be *a judicial setting aside of that creation.* We mean by a judicial setting aside that a judgment must be passed upon it, and under that judgment it must be put away out of God's sight. It must come to the place where in its entirety it is under the Divine ban, where not one part of it can come into acceptance with Him; that is, it must be judicially dealt with, and judicially set aside. That becomes necessary as a preliminary step to anything which God will do after a new order. God has dealt thus with the creation in the Cross of Christ.

Secondly, an actual and a potential destroying of that power of death and Satan must take place. Let us watch our words—an actual, and a potential, destroying of that power of death and Satan. Well, God did that in actuality in the Person of the Lord Jesus. He destroyed death and him that had the power of death, that is, the Devil. In Christ it is actually done. Christ at God's right hand represents and declares that this has been accomplished. Death is swallowed up victoriously. Satan too has been destroyed. That word "destroyed," translated in the Revised Version "bring to naught," does not mean what some people take it to mean. There are times when speaking of destroying we think of going the whole length of utterly obliterating, putting out of existence. This word does not mean that. Bringing to naught means, in the intention of God, to render utterly inoperative. Do not forget that, so far as the Lord Jesus is concerned at God's right hand, Satan is inoperative. He cannot touch Him personally, and he knows it. The only way in which he can touch Him is through His members. Satan no longer has any power to touch Christ directly with death, or with any other weapon. Through death He hath destroyed him that had the power of death. It is actually done in Christ.

We have used another word—potential. That potential destroying of death and Satan was in the behalf of the saints. That is something which is secured and, though not yet fully entered into in experience, can be entered into by faith, and known in a progressive way. It cannot be said that you and I at present in the entirety of our being find that death and Satan have no power. So far as we are concerned it is not an actual fact that Satan is inoperative. But this has been secured for us potentially in Christ, that we may become those who more and more experience what Christ has wrought for us, and come progressively into the good of that work which was potentially done in our behalf. In Christ, then, we see that destruction to be accomplished in actuality; in the saints, potentially.

Thirdly, it is essential that there should be a living representation of the Divine order, which is deathless, and victorious over Satan, as the pattern to which believers are to be conformed. That is a necessity, and it is realised in Christ. He is the representation of the new creation, the Divine order, to which we are to be conformed, and which is deathless and victorious over Satan. God must work to an end, to a pattern, to a model, and Christ is that for Him. He is working in the saints to bring about conformity to Christ, which means also conformity to the Divine order represented by Christ; for we must remember that Christ is the sum total of a Divine order. So often the Lord's people fail to recognise that. We must in the first place, of course, recognise that He is a Person. Before all else He is the Divine Person, but He is in Himself the sum total of a Divine and heavenly order. If the tabernacle or the temple of old expressed a whole system of things; regulated, ordered, appointed, functioning, related, a wonderful system—do not be afraid of that word, put in the right realm it is a very good word—if the temple or the tabernacle represented that, they

are but types of Christ. Christ is the Priest;
Christ is the Altar; Christ is the Sacrifice;
Christ is the Fine Linen; Christ is the Gold;
Christ is the perfect Humanity : Christ is all,
and Christ is the order. "Let everything be
done decently and in order" says the Apostle.
It is a systematized arrangement, heavenly
planning and appointing.

When we come into Christ, while it is true
that we come into the Divine Person, we have
to come into our place in a Divine order, and
being in Christ requires that there shall be a
right relationship to one another; an appointing, a functioning, a relativity about everything. It is a wonderful Divine system. Death
and Satan have their occasion when anything
that relates to Divine order is not obeyed,
recognised, observed. It is quite easy for death
to get a chance amongst the Lord's people
when there is a disorder amongst them, when
they are not conformed to Christ in the sense
of His being an expression of an ordered,
heavenly system. Surely the New Testament
rather thunders upon that than speaks. If the
Corinthian Church is an example of weak
testimony, and indeed it is, the reason is not
far to seek. It was a matter of disorder
amongst believers.

So God must have this representation of
His Divine order, which is deathless, and

victorious over Satan, and to that believers are to be conformed. That is conformity to the image of His Son, our Lord Jesus Christ.

Fourthly, there is required *a vital union with Him as basic, and a life utterly and continuously in the Holy Spirit.* We all accept the first essential, a vital union with Him as basic, but what is just as important, if there is to be the full expression of life, is that there shall be a life which is altogether in the Holy Spirit continuously. Life in the Holy Spirit is the Divine offset of that other life in death and under the power of Satan. That other life is disordered, and God is not united with it.

That is the first state; a life in death, under the power of Satan, in disorder; tremendously active, energetic, and yet God is not in it. It may even be active in a religious way, and yet God is not in it. I sometimes wonder if religion is not God's greatest enemy in this world. It sounds a terrible thing to say, but I am quite sincere in raising that question. Religion seems to place more people in a position in which God, if we may so speak, is put to the greatest measure of difficulty to reach them by the Holy Ghost than any other thing, because it puts them into a false position. Over against that God sets this new order which is utterly under the Holy Spirit. What does it mean to be utterly under the government of the Holy Spirit? It means that everything shall be submitted to the Holy Spirit. You and I will recognise in a full way, in a complete way, in a comprehensive way, that if we move, if we act, if we reason, if we function in any way without our lives completely committed to, and wholly in, the Holy Spirit, we are most likely to function outside of God's realm : and the end is death. There may be the best of intentions. Our motives may be all right. We may even do a thing for the Lord ; but there are multitudes of things done for the Lord which are not done in the Holy Ghost. There is a whole mountain of activity proceeding from the purest motives for the Lord's interests, but they are not the Holy Ghost's activities. I believe the Lord is generous and gracious, and that because it is a matter of ignorance He is patient with us, and seeks to lead us into better ways. The mistaken course may be due to want of light, and while fuller light is not available, or until it breaks in, the Lord continues alongside and gives as much blessing as He can. But that does not mean that in the long run all that past activity is going to meet with acceptance, and prove to have been for the accomplishment of Divine ends. At some point it will break down, and those who are in it will break down, and they will have to come to a recognition of the fact that, after all, a great percentage of all that work for the Lord has not counted : and the earlier we come to that recognition the better.

The Cross the All-inclusive Answer.

All that is gathered up in the Cross. The Cross simply says that an order—though it be a religious order, a well-motived order, a good-intentioned order, but an order which is nevertheless proceeding from man in his natural state, and not necessarily in defiance of God, not necessarily in conscious rebellion against God, but just the expression of man's natural state as he is—the Cross says that this entire order is there set aside. God has judicially judged it, and put a ban upon it. In the Cross of the Lord Jesus, God has said finally : You in your natural state cannot serve Me, and cannot bear any fruit to My glory! It is possible to go out and work, labour, and die of the strain of trying to serve Me, and yet it still remains true that you cannot out from yourself, by any natural resources whatever, bear fruit unto Me. The only thing that can ever get through to God's end, and that can be in life— eternal, divine, heavenly life—is that which proceeds from the Holy Spirit.

How sweeping that is ! How that analyses and dissects everything ! Of the things we

D

say, for example, it continually presents the interrogation, Was that spoken in the Holy Spirit? It is not enough to ask ourselves, Did I mean it well? Did I intend it for the Lord, but, Was it said, was it done, in the Holy Spirit, or did I do it? It is not a question of motive, of intention, but of the power, the life in which I did it. Did I make that decision in the Holy Spirit, or did I decide according to my own judgment, after weighing the pros and cons and coming to the conclusion that it would be the best thing to do? On everything it is a matter of life in the Spirit. You may say, That is a very arduous life, a very difficult life, if we are to stop before ever we act or speak, and ask ourselves all the time, Am I going to do this, am I going to say this, in the Holy Spirit or in myself? I do not believe that it is necessary for us to take that position at the outset. But we have daily to recognise that our lives must be subject to the Holy Ghost, and when we are aware that there has been something out from ourselves, we have to be faithful before God about it. I believe that slowly and surely we shall come to the place where we live with that certain pause in our hearts which is a check on our impulsiveness, a check on rashness, a check on acting under excitement, a check on our own way of reasoning about things. That is a thing for the Holy Spirit to set up in us. Our business is to recognise that from centre to circumference our lives must be handed over to His control. The result will be that the Holy Spirit will all the time work back to the Cross. The Cross, once for all, settled that position in a comprehensive and detailed way. It stands for ever as God's judicial ban upon man by nature. The Holy Spirit will work back to that with us.

Do recognise that the Cross is the end of the risen life, not only the beginning. If you forget everything else, remember that. The Cross is the end of the risen life, as well as the beginning—"That I may know him, and the power of his resurrection, and the fellowship of his sufferings, becoming conformed unto his death." People have been to me with Philippians iii, and have said, Why did Paul put death at the end? Surely it ought to be right the other way round : That I may be conformed to His death, and know Him in the power of His resurrection, and the fellowship of His sufferings! No, there is no mistake, the order is of the Holy Ghost. The power of His resurrection pre-supposes that there has been a death, but the very resurrection-life leads to the Cross. The Holy Ghost in the power of the risen life is always leading you back to the Cross, to conformity to His death. It is the very property of life to rule out all that belongs to death. It is the very power of resurrection to bring us back to the place where death is constantly overcome. That place is none other than the Cross of our Lord Jesus Christ where the natural life is put aside. So Paul says, ". . . becoming conformed to his death . . . ," which means, to have the ground of death continuously, and progressively removed; and that, again, as we have said, is the fruit of living union with Him. It would be a poor look-out for you and for me were we to be conformed to His death in entirety apart from the power of resurrection in us, apart from our already knowing the life of the Lord. Where would be our hope? What is it that is the power of our survival when the Cross is made more real in our experience? There would be no survival were it not that His risen life is in us. So Paul prays, "That I may know him, and the power of his resurrection . . . ," and that means conformity to His death without utter destruction. The end of the risen life is the Cross. The Holy Spirit is always working in relation to the Cross, in order that the power of His resurrection may be increasingly manifested in us.

This is the background of the whole question of life. I am sure, with a greater certainty to-day than ever, that the basis in us for life triumphant is the working of the Cross

in the setting aside of all that which is natural.
There is nothing more hated by the enemy
than the Cross. Let us seek to free our minds
from all false conceptions of the Cross. So
often there has been this kind of reaction : Oh,
it is the Cross ; it is death, death, death ! This
working of the Cross in a subjective way is all
the time leading to death !   That is why we
have already mentioned that it is so important
for us to recognise that it is not that death
destroys us, but that it makes the way for a
greater fulness of life.   It is the positive side
that we have to keep in mind ; not the fact that
we are constantly being ruled out, and ruled
out, but rather that of necessity that is being
done, in order that He may come in, and come
in, and come in.   It is the life side which has
to be kept uppermost, even in the working of
the Cross with reference to what was set aside
by God at Calvary.

Is your need, then, that of life ? The Lord,
in effect, says, Well let us get this out of the
way ! And when He gets that out of the way
there is life. Do you want more life ? Well,
let us get this out of the way ; and you have
more life. You very rarely meet people who,
having really laid themselves out before God
for an increase of spiritual life, have not
promptly gone into a very bad experience and
had a difficult time. Have you ever come to

the place where you have laid yourself out for that extra thing, that new thing, which God has been revealing to you, and not gone through some dark, trying, and painful time? It is always so. It is not wrong, the Lord is only saying, Do you want that? There is always something to be got out of the way. It may be you want spiritual increase because it will make you a happier man. That motive will have to be got out of the way, so that you want it not for your own sake, but for His sake. If you go through a bad time, and the dominating element is self, you will say: Oh, well, it does not matter; I would rather not have it, if it means this! That is the selfish way of regarding it. But if you are in a dark time in relation to something, and you come to the place where you say: Well, whatever it costs, the Lord must have this thing in my life! you have come there through the course of the ruling out of self. The Holy Spirit always brings that issue. It is life that He is after, and life more abundant, and this is alone realised by His bringing back and back to the Cross. The Cross is basic to life, because it was there that the Lord Jesus conquered death, and brought life forth for the saints. The Lord lead us on into life.

CHAPTER IV.

Fellowship between Christ and His Church in Testimony.

READING : John xvii.

Keeping this chapter well before us, let us turn to two other passages :

I Tim. iii. 16 : "And without controversy great is the mystery of godliness ; He who was manifested in the flesh, justified in the spirit, seen of angels, preached among the nations, believed on in the world, received up in glory."

Before we pass to the other passage, let us notice that the word translated "godliness" in this passage is unique in the New Testament. It is not the word which is commonly used for piety, but the word which means the Divine nature, and the more correct rendering would be "Great is the mystery of the Divine nature, which was made visible in flesh." We mention that because it removes the difficulty which has surrounded this passage for so long.

Ephes. v. 30-32 : ". . . because we are members of his body. For this cause shall a man leave his father and mother, and shall cleave to his wife ; and the twain shall become one flesh. This mystery is great : I speak in regard of Christ and of the church."

In those two passages I think we have an

interpretation of chapter xvii. of the Gospel by
John. You may take this passage in Timothy
and note its clauses, and carrying everything
back into that chapter in John's Gospel you
will see that there is a twofold connection;
firstly, the connection with Christ personally;
secondly, the connection with those who constitute His Church.

"Manifested in the Flesh."

The Divine nature was manifested in flesh.
We hardly need spend time in applying that
phrase to Christ. There is no doubt that it
belongs to Him, that He is the One Who fits in
there; that He verily was God manifest in the
flesh, and that the Divine nature did become
incarnated in Him. John xvii. quite definitely
alludes to the fact : ". . . they have believed
that thou didst send me" (verse 8).

Then John xvii. carries things forward to
the Church, and while it does not give the full
unveiling of the later New Testament writings
when the Holy Spirit had come to open up the
fulness of the truth, it clearly intimates the
truth about to find fulfilment. We can even
say that it introduces that truth : "I in them
. . ." (verse 23). That clearly indicates a
company constituted as an organism, as a body,
of which they are the first members, the nucleus

to which others should be continually added through the preaching of the Gospel. Taking their place in the Body thus formed, those who believed would in turn become the vessel of the testimony, the embodiment of Him. Later the Apostle will express it in this way: "Whereby are given unto us exceeding great and precious promises : that by these ye might be partakers of the divine nature . . ." (II Peter i. 4). While there is, and ever will remain, a cleft, a division, a distinction between that and any supposition of our thereby becoming God and partaking of Deity, it is none the less true that the great and wonderful reality into which we are all called is the forming of a Body for the indwelling of that Christ of Whom it says the Divine nature was manifested in flesh. In this, one object in view was that the manifestation should not cease in this world with the return of Christ to glory, but that there should be a continuation of the earthly manifestation of the Divine nature in His Body, as there had been in Himself. That is a wonderful and glorious truth. It is a marvellous calling.

But such things are always tests as well as testimonies, always challenges as well as glorious truths. What the Lord is constantly seeking to do with His people, and seemingly more and more so toward the end, is to bring them face to face with the real nature of their calling, and to require that they should face up to it : as we say, toe the line.   The very first thing for which the Church is called in its relationship to Christ is to be the manifestation of Him, the Divine nature manifested in flesh : "I in them . . ."   The Church's calling is to maintain here on the earth a witness to the presence, the living presence, of the Lord. That may sound elementary, but it is not so elementary when you consider how things are to-day.   One would be led to think from what does exist to-day that the Church's purpose on the earth is to hold religious services and to do all sorts of good, charitable works, and to keep religion alive in the earth.   Well-meaning, well-intentioned ! but much can be brought within a compass like that, and much is brought within such a compass.   Almost anything can be put within that range.

I was reading of a church in America where a famous dancer was invited to dance the sermons, to dance the truth of the New Testament, before the congregation.   It is pathetically and tragically awful, but there by one in dancing apparel, with bare feet, dancing before a congregation, was supposed to be acted in a dance New Testament truth : and it is argued for by Scripture—"dancing before the Lord" (II Sam. vi. 16).   Brought right out of the theatrical world into what is called the Church to do that! That is an extreme case, but it can find a place within this compass of keeping religion alive, and can be argued for as good. That is a terrible and solemn departure from the truth, and in the light of such a thing we need to turn again and consider closely what it really is that the Church is for. The Church is revealed in the New Testament as constituted for the maintenance in this world of a witness to the living presence of the Lord, the Christ of God, to be the embodiment of Him. Nothing less than that, nothing other than that, justifies the continuation of a thing which goes by the name of the Church. As men and women meet the Church, whether in assembly or the individual members thereof in the common walks of life, they should register the presence of the Lord; they should be obliged to recognise the presence of "something" which is not just ordinary, natural, is not just the men or the women. The presence of the Lord in the assembly of the Lord's people should mean that strangers, the ungodly, coming in should say, God is in the midst of you! That is the witness for which the Church is called into being.

We cannot continue on any other ground. We are not now alluding to certain prevailing conditions in a general way, we are facing this matter ourselves. The only thing which will justify our being together as the Lord's people is that the one uppermost, predominant feature among us shall be that of a witness to the Lord's presence in life in our midst, and that it must needs be confessed, The Lord is in the midst of that people ! If we lose that we have lost all ; we have lost our vocation, we have lost our calling. Oh, that we should see to that ! ''I in them . . .''

Thus we have the mystery of the Divine nature, which was manifested in the flesh in Christ, continued now in His own. ''This mystery is great : I speak in regard of Christ and of the church.''

"Justified in the Spirit."

What does that mean ? When was the Lord Jesus justified in the spirit ; for undoubtedly it refers to Him in the first place ? What is the meaning of His being justified in the spirit ? I think the answer is this, His resurrection. I believe the justification of the Lord Jesus is to be found in God's raising Him from the dead. There may be a broader meaning, a wider explanation, but I believe that is the heart of the thing, that His justification was when God raised Him from the dead. Peter speaks of Him as having been crucified in the

flesh, and quickened in the spirit (I Peter iii.
18). When with regard to that death God
intervened and raised Him from the dead, God
justified Him. That was His justification. He
stood then in a place with God where all sin,
the judgment of which He had voluntarily
endured, was put away; where all and every
kind of condemnation which had been made to
light upon Him, when made sin for us, was
destroyed. All sin which was made to rest
upon Him having been put away by His Cross,
God raised Him; He is in the place where He
is justified : He is the justified One, Jesus
Christ the Righteous. That applies to something other than the righteousness, the
holiness, which was inherent in Himself; it
applies to the righteousness, the holiness,
which is His as having been made Man, and
made sin, and having borne that sin away in
judgment, so that God can be just, and the
Justifier of all them that believe. When God
raised Him from the dead it was God's great
act of justifying the Lord Jesus.

Now where do we find "resurrection" in
John xvii? "Even as thou gavest him
authority over all flesh, that whatsoever thou
hast given him, to them he should give eternal
life" (verse 2). There is no eternal life except
on the ground of Christ risen, and He here
speaks as though already in resurrection. How

often in this chapter does the Lord use this phrase : ". . . whom thou hast given me. . . ." He gives three things to those whom the Father has given him :—

He gives them eternal life (verse 2).

He gives the revelation of the Father's name (verse 6).

He gives them the words of God (verse 8). He gives eternal life.   Eternal life is the fruit of His death and resurrection.   It could not be said to be eternal life had not death been destroyed, had not all the possibility of its being corrupted been utterly abolished.   This life is ours on the ground of Christ's destruction of death, and of His having entered for us into that life which is deathless.

What is the Church's calling?   It has been raised up to maintain the testimony in this world of a life which is triumphant over death. How often that has been said.   That is the heart of the Lord's word to us at this time; the power of a deathless life, a life which cannot be conquered and quenched by death.   That is set in John xvii. against the background of a world that is hostile, inimical, hating : ". . . the world hated them . . ." (verse 14) ; "I pray not that thou shouldest take them from the world, but that thou shouldest keep them from the evil one" (verse 15).   (The word being in the masculine it is justifiable to add the word

"one.") Here is an evil one, and a hating
world, and any spiritual person will tell you
that, in effect, that is death; the spirit and
power of death encompassing the Lord's people.
Now the Lord does not ask that His Church
should be taken out from the world, but that
being in it, it should maintain a testimony
against, and contrary to, the spirit of it.   The
testimony is that of life in the midst of death.
The supreme challenge to the Church's faithfulness, to the Church's ministry, to the
Church's true vocation, is as to whether its
condition bears true witness that it is not being
overcome of spiritual death, that it really is
expressing a life which is more powerful than
the power of death which is all around it.

Do not allow the word "Church" to miss
you, and think of some entity apart from yourself.   We must make an individual application,
because if we are in living union with Christ
we are members of His, we are a part of the
Church which is His Body, and what we are
saying applies to us individually as well as
collectively.   It is not possible for us all to have
the advantage of a collective fellowship of the
Lord's people.   Some of us have to live in
places where we are desperately alone.   It may
be that there is not very much spiritual life
where we are, not much help along the line of
spiritual fellowship; nevertheless this word is

for such. We have to do not only with the responsibility and the challenge, but with the glorious fact that this into which we are called, and which is provided for by the Lord, and ordained, is that His people here, whether they be able to gather together with all the advantages of so doing, or whether they be scattered and isolated, shall have in them the power of His life to transcend the power of death around them.

If that is revealed as the Lord's will, let us first of all readily admit the possibility of its realisation, and then, accepting the fact that since it is the Lord's will, it must be possible, stand for it. As for you and me, let us stand in our spirit for that life expression from the risen Lord which shall transcend the death that is all around us, and which presses upon us—the evil one and the hatred of men. The Lord said, "I pray not that thou shouldest take them from the world, but that thou shouldest keep them . . ." The power in them is the power of His risen life.

What we have been saying is so very much in accord with the fuller revelation of the Ephesian letter : "The exceeding greatness of his power to usward who believe, according to that working of the strength of his might which he wrought in Christ, when he raised him from the dead, and made him to sit at his right hand

in the heavenly places, far above all. . . ."
(Ephes. i. 19-21) : ". . . to usward who believe.
. . ." We must stand for that strongly and
definitely, because that is the testimony of the
Lord Jesus.

"Justified in the spirit"! What is the
Church's justification? It is that it stands on
resurrection ground, manifesting resurrection
life. Blessed be God, so far as our salvation is
concerned, we are justified on the ground of
being risen together with Christ. We take it
that if we have been raised together with Him,
we have been justified. God would never have
brought us into resurrection union with Christ
apart from justification. But so far as our
calling, our vocation, is concerned, we are
justified by the maintaining of the witness of
His resurrection. That is the justification that
applies to service, to instrumentalities.

"Seen of Angels."

After His resurrection He was seen of
angels. We hardly need go back to the Gospels
to indicate the record of the angelic attendants
after His resurrection. There was the angel
who rolled away the stone. There were two
who sat on the tomb. There were the angels
who spoke of the risen Lord and told certain
women exactly where they would find Him.
Yes, angels saw Him after His resurrection.

E

Now where in that connection does the Church
come in? Oh, the Church is related in a
wonderful way. Come again to the letter to
the Ephesians and read : "To the intent that
now unto the principalities and the powers in
heavenly places might be made known through
the church the manifold wisdom of God"
(Ephes. iii. 10). I think there is little doubt
that this reference to principalities and powers
includes the unfallen celestial bodies, not only
the diabolical ones. I do not know that angels
of Satan need instructing about the manifold
wisdom of God, but God is revealing Himself
in a wonderful way to His own angel ministers
by what He is doing through the Church. I
cannot understand that : I cannot comprehend
that : it is far beyond me. But there is the
statement. It is a clear declaration that God is
teaching principalities and powers concerning
Himself by His activities in the Church;
which means that there is a realm of spiritual
intelligence, very high spiritual intelligence,
angelic intelligence, receiving instruction
through the Church. For what I do not know,
but it represents some tremendous values. It
evidently represents something of great
meaning.

Very often it may seem but poor comfort to
us in times of suffering, times of trial, times of
adversity, times when Satan is pressing hard,

to be told that, while we can see nothing of the meaning of all this, God is instructing angels, and that principalities and powers are deriving the benefit of it all. We do not draw a great deal of comfort from that, but if we understood I think we should realise that, while we may not at such times be fulfilling a very big ministry on the earth, there is a big ministry going on towards principalities and powers through our instrumentality. Do not think that running about taking meetings, and doing work for the Lord, is the only kind of ministry that members of the Church can fulfil. Ministry may be equally being fulfilled when these things have been brought to a standstill, and all earthly activities for the Lord are stopped, and we are in one of these painful periods of inaction. Do not conclude that because of such inaction no ministry is being rendered, or that everything of that kind is cut off at such a time. Here is the word : ". . . that NOW unto the principalities and the powers in heavenly places might be made known through the Church the manifold wisdom of God"—not in the coming age, but now. They are learning from the Lord, by reason of those very difficult and trying experiences through which the Lord is taking us, what the Lord is doing in the Church.

Supposing the principalities and powers,

these angelic ministers that wait upon Him,
should one day come to us and thank us very
much for going through that dark time, and
say : I came to know a lot through that ; I came
to understand the wisdom of God in a wonderful
way through that bad time which you had!
You would be surprised, would you not? You
would say : Well, I never imagined that anything could come out of that; I thought
everything was dried up, and that nothing was
happening at all! Oh, that angel minister
would say, You were very mistaken; I was
getting a great deal of benefit out of your bad
time! That is not a flight of imagination.
Surely that is the logical outworking of a statement like this. There is a ministry that the
Church fulfils which is altogether apart from
platforms and meetings and the numerous
kinds of activity as here amongst men. There
is a mighty ministry which reaches out and
touches the fringes of the universe. God is
doing something out there through His dealings
with the Church here. That is a ministry in
which we do well to desire to be.

"Preached among the Nations."

I think we need not tarry with that. The
Church's ministry is to be in all the nations,
and its ministry is Christ in all the nations. Its
testimony to Him is to be in all the nations.

"Believed on in the World."

That certainly was true of the Lord Jesus. John xvii. says : ". . . the words which thou gavest me I have given unto them; and they received them, and knew of a truth that I came forth from thee, and they believed that thou didst send me" (verse 8). He was believed on in the world.

In verse 21 we have the words, "That they may all be one . . . that the world may believe . . ." There is a believing on the part of the world as a result of His being in the Church, and of His making the Church thereby a spiritual unity. Perhaps it might be wrong to speak of the Church being believed on, but in a sense we might even say that. I am quite certain that the Church will not be believed on, or believed in, until, and unless, there is a manifestation of the spirit of Christ in mutual love. The world is put back from Christ so much by failure in that direction. While we may view the situation as hopeless in general, that does not excuse us from standing for a true testimony, and realising that faith in the Lord Jesus will be begotten by the expression of His love amongst ourselves.

"Received up in Glory."

That was true of Him, and, blessed be God, that is going to be true of His Church, His Body. I Cor. xv. gives us a grand revelation :

"We shall not all sleep, but we shall all be changed, in a moment, in the twinkling of an eye, at the last trump . . ." We shall be caught up to meet the Lord in the air. That may not be so far ahead as many people think. It may be very soon : the sooner the better so far as His people are concerned. Our hearts really do say from their depths, "Even so, come, Lord Jesus." There is no hypocrisy about that. There was a time when we used to be scared of the thought, but we have come to see that His coming is the way of all hope. This world will never see a better state, but an increasingly worse condition, until the events subsequent to, and consequent upon, His coming have taken place. There is coming an age when every evil thing will be blotted out from this cosmos. Wars shall be no more. Strife shall be no more. Hatred shall be no more. Sin shall be no more. Pain shall be no more. Sorrow and tears shall be no more. Death shall be no more. Oh, what a day! What an age! We can hardly imagine it, but our hearts surely leap at the thought of it.

Do you say you are afraid of that? Do you dread to think of that? The Lord must come for His Church first, and then things will rapidly hasten to that day. It may be a very terrible passage. Things may become very awful in the earth for a while after the Church has gone, but things will happen very rapidly, and very vividly, and move on toward that great day when He makes a new heaven and a new earth. But the day of the Church's being received up into glory is imminent. No one who knows his Bible and has spiritual perception, or even good common-sense with the Bible before him, can fail to see that day hastens. The counsels of men are being blown to pieces by God. They cannot hold their decisions together for a week or two. Their most solid decisions, and intentions, and agreements, fall to pieces within a few days. God is bringing the counsels of men to naught, but the counsels of God, says His Word, stand for ever. In the eternal counsels of God this is one of the things determined : ". . . we . . . shall . . . be caught up in the clouds, to meet the Lord in the air . . ." (I Thess. iv. 17). "Received up in glory"! His end is going to be our end. The Church is going to know the counterpart of her Lord as her Head in His experience of being received up in glory.

Now, it may be that some unsaved ones have been looking in the window and becoming envious? Are you going to stand outside? Do you want to be apart from all this? Why, here is a revelation of Divine calling. Here is a presentation of the Word of God as to what it is that has been made possible for you by the

Cross of the Lord Jesus, if you will believe. Are you going to let it all go? Surely you are wanting to draw near. Surely you are wanting to come in. Surely those on the fringe of things will want to be more in. Surely all of us will want to be more faithful, more devoted, in the light of that day which at longest cannot now be far off. God's Word has always been fulfilled, and proved true, and this will not break down; this will be equally true.

The Lord draw us right into the purpose of our calling. There is very much more which could be said on this matter, but we have said enough to see that the mystery of Christ is carried over into the Church which is His Body in all these respects, and that a part of the mystery—such a mystery to the men of the world, such a mystery to the unbeliever, such a mystery to the one who does not know spiritual secrets—a part of the mystery is the translation of His waiting Church to meet Him ere He comes again to the earth. By the world translation to glory is ridiculed, jeered at, discounted, ruled out as a mere fantastic idea. But those who, so to speak, know the mystery of being born again; who know the mystery of being preserved and kept by Christ through the intensity of well-nigh universal opposition and antagonism, of being preserved and sustained therein; who know also that it is not in themselves at all to keep on, but that it is the Lord alone Who so enables, He Himself as their very life—those of us who know these mysteries find no difficulty in accepting that extra part of the mystery related to the consummation of our lives, namely, to be caught up, received up in glory. It is a strange thing that men of the world can accept as commonplace to-day things which at one time they would have laughed at—radio, flight, television, all these things. Had you spoken of such a century or two ago men would have mocked. Jules Verne was regarded as a sort of wonder man at one time, but all that he forecast has come true. Things he spoke of are commonplace to-day. Yet men will believe these things, but they cannot credit the translation from this earth to the presence of God of a company whom He has redeemed. But we see it : in our hearts we see it. We are looking for it, and we are hastening unto it, and we shall hail it with joy. The cry is in our hearts, "Even so, come, Lord Jesus."

CHAPTER V.

The Continuation of the Conflict in Relation to the Individual Believer.

We are seeking to take a further step in the apprehension of what is related to this great and pressing matter. We are going to deal with the continuation of the conflict, with reference to its nature and its sphere.

The Nature of the Conflict.

The work of the Lord Jesus in His Cross has now been set forth in two respects. On the one hand, we have noted there was that which was actually complete and final in His work, the fact that the Lord did destroy him that had the power of death, and also death itself. With regard to Himself, that is a finished work. His presence at the right hand of God declares that death, the grave, and Satan, have been brought to naught, and no longer have any power over Him. On the other hand, there is what we have called the potential work of His Cross; that is, that Christ did something which in Himself is full and final, but which has yet to become full and final in the saints; something which was for the saints, but which has still to become complete in their experience. It is potential, so far as the Church is concerned, although in

Him, its Head, they have it in finality. As the result of the work of His Cross, and as the grand issue of His resurrection, eternal life is received already by those who believe. But while that life is in itself victorious, incorruptible, indestructible, the believer has to come by faith to prove it, to live by it, to learn its laws, to be conformed to it. There is a deposit in the believer which in itself needs no addition, so far as its quality is concerned. So far as its victory, its power, its glory, its potentialities are concerned nothing can be added to it. But the course of spiritual experience, of spiritual life, is to discover, to appropriate, and to live by all that the life represents and means. That is to say, the course of spiritual life and experience is the course of discovering and living by the values of that life which is within, and which is succoured from above.

It is important to recognise that as a discriminating word. We are very often inclined to think that the life of the Lord in us needs in some way to be improved, to be added to, when really what is required is that we should discover what we have, and, discovering it by experience, live according to it. This life is not something apart from the Lord Jesus, and we can never think of His standing in need of some improvement, nor of the possibility of something being added to Him to make Him complete, or more complete. We would never think like that. And this life is one with Himself. As the Apostle says, it is Christ Who is our life, and our need is to discover what Christ is in us, and to live accordingly. So in a very real sense it is a matter of the life getting more of us, rather than of our getting more of the life. That at any rate is the way of its working.

This, in the ordering of God, has to be done in a world where death still rules and works; for in this world the destruction of death has not yet been made manifest. Death, like the Devil, goes on, although Calvary still remains full victory. We are left in this world, and it is in this world where death reigns and works as a great energy that we, by this sovereign ordering of God, have to come to prove the values of the life which has been deposited in us, to discover its potentialities. This is an experimental discovery. It therefore resolves itself into a battle between that which is in this world and the life which is in the believer. It is the battle for life; not as to the forfeiture of that life—not as to whether death can take eternal life away from us, that is not the question at issue—but as to the triumphant expression and the full manifestation of the power of that life, that is the issue. We may have eternal life, and yet that life may be pressed away in our very being without expression, without manifestation, without any triumphant issue. It may be there, but cramped, smothered.

That which is true in the case of the individual believer can be equally true in the case of the Church, the collective company, that it may have life, eternal life, and yet there be no expressed testimony of its presence, or but a very limited manifestation. With this expression, this manifestation—not only with the possession of life but with the testimony to that possession—there are bound up no lesser issues than the resurrection and lordship of Jesus Christ. The testimony to the fact that Jesus Christ has been raised from the dead, and is at the right hand of the Majesty on High in absolute lordship is bound up with an expression here, let us repeat, of that life which is His risen life. That is no small matter. The last Adam was made a "life-giving spirit"— life-giving, that is, life manifesting itself, life being transmitted, life expressed—and if that is not exemplified in and through the believer, and through the Church as a whole, there is something taken away from the testimony of the Lord Jesus. How is there to be the proof, the demonstration, the evidence, the final establishment of the fact that Jesus is alive from the dead, and is Lord? It is by the triumphant expression of His life in His own.

It is not by a doctrinal statement. Christ is never proved to be alive from the dead, or to be Lord, by doctrinal statements. Your statement of faith may include the fact that you believe Jesus died and rose again, ascended to heaven, and is at the right hand of the Majesty on High, but how are you going to prove your statement? What has God given as the evidence of that? You may believe it; you may be willing to lay down your life for that faith; you may state it with tremendous emphasis, and yet you are not thereby proving it. You will never prove anything by saying, I believe with all my might that this is the case! You will never prove a thing by standing up and declaring it as something which you believe. You will never prove a thing by saying, I believe in all the fundamentals of the Christian faith! and calling yourself by some name which indicates that you believe in the inspiration of the Bible. Nothing is ever proved in that way. Reducing the whole matter to these two points, that Jesus Christ has been raised from the dead, and is Lord of all, you have still to prove your statement after you have made it. If you have appealed to the fact that the Word of God says so, even then you have proved nothing. Your proof can never be by argument, because what argument can build up argument can pull down, what logic can construct logic can destroy.

How then are you going to prove that this is so? By the expression and manifestation of His risen life, that is all—but it is a mighty "all." That signifies that you are the embodiment of the thing which you declare, that besides the doctrinal statement there is the living expression. Thus the resurrection and the lordship of Jesus are bound up with this expression which is called "the testimony." The testimony is not a system of truth. The testimony is that extra factor to the statement and presentation of truth which is the power thereof, and that power is the power of a life which conquers death. How, then, will you prove that Jesus has conquered death? The proof of it will be a death-conquering life that expresses itself in you.

This being the case, it means that the whole issue is one of a life-power by which Christ is attested. We do not put the life in the place of Christ, but we say that the attestation of Christ is by the life. We do not mean the manner of life, but the life-power, the impact of a spiritual force which emanates from Him as in the throne, the registration upon a spiritual realm of a greater spiritual power. That is the attestation of the Lord Jesus. Therefore the major weapon of the enemy will be death.

Death is also a spiritual power. Thus it becomes a battle between two spiritual powers, the power of life and the power of death. That battle goes on, and will go on, until the Church becomes so vitalized by this Divine power that, in a moment, those who are in the grave, and those who are alive and remain, are in a mighty resurrection-ascension caught up to the Lord in glory. The battle between these two great spiritual powers will go on till then.

That is the battle in which we find ourselves. It is an intensifying battle, and we had better recognise it once for all. It is difficult to accept that sometimes, even though we assent to it mentally. When things become difficult we are surprised and wonder, and perhaps think it strange that it should be so. But it must be recognised and accepted that this spiritual warfare between life and death will intensify toward the end, and it will reach its highest point of tension right at the point where the Church is about to be translated. That is undoubtedly made clear by the Word of the Lord.

The Sphere of the Conflict.

We speak in the first place about the individual believer. We must remember that this life of the risen Lord, as linked with the

Holy Spirit, Who is the Spirit of life, resides in the very deepest part of our being, in our spirit, in what the New Testament calls "the inner man." Therefore the most spiritual people will find that the conflict for life rages around and upon their spirit. There is a direct assault upon their spirit to get their spirit weakened, to get their spirit shut in and pressed down, so that somewhere in the depths of their being they feel they are unable to breathe. They cannot actually locate it, but they are conscious that right within there is a locking up, a pressing, a hemming in, a suffocating of spirit. One of two things will result. Either their spirit will be pressed out under this weight of spiritual death, and they will go under; or else they will have to call earnestly upon the Lord, that they may be strengthened with might by His Spirit into the inward man, and then exercise faith on the ground of their prayer and seek to assert their spirit against this thing.

The trouble with a great many of the Lord's people is that they do not, so to speak, stand straight up on the feet of their spirit; that is, they do not rise up in spirit and in the name of the Lord meet and resist that thing which is threatening to crush the very life out of their spirit. There is an accepting of things; there is a consenting; there is a passive attitude; or

F

else there is a getting into an awful swirl of questionings, doubtings, arguments, discussions with the Devil, going round in an eternal circle of introspection and analysis, when really in such circumstances believers ought in their spirits to rise up in faith in the name of the Lord to resist this thing, and to refuse to have it, calling in His name upon the energies of the Holy Ghost. We shall never get through until we learn how to do that. If the enemy finds that he can hold the situation by keeping us in that circle, that awful going round of debate, argument, discussion, of analysing, of questioning, of doubting, he will keep us going round; he will whip us up like a circus horse to keep us running round all the time, while we never get beyond the point where we started. If you keep going back there all the time, not making one fragment or fraction of real spiritual progress toward victory, you can go on so for fifty years.

Another favourite method of the enemy is to try to get us to explain this thing along lines which are less than the real explanation, to draw in other things which he would like us to believe may account for it. The things may be numerous and various. If we settle down to accept such an explanation it will prove our undoing. While there may be much that he can use and play upon in natural conditions,

while it may be true that he is making the most
of all that is available of our own human weakness, and perhaps our physical condition, and
our constitution, our make-up, and our sur-
roundings, nevertheless ultimately it is not a
question of anything in nature, but a matter of
being strong in spirit. You may take it as one
of the settled things that there is no hope for
anybody in the direction of those natural
conditions. If you start working from the
circumference to the centre, you are working
the wrong way, and you will not get through;
you will be held on the circumference until you
are dead. The enemy will not let you reach
the centre from the circumference. You must
start at the centre and work outward. The key
to victory is our spirit-union with our risen and
reigning Lord.

There are other realms, of course, in which
this death battle goes on, and where this assault
of death is made upon the believer. Sometimes
it is upon the mind. There is a darkening, a
numbing, or something like a paralysing of the
mind, when you turn to consider the things of
the Lord. At other times you may be quite
clear and free, and your mind have little trouble
in working in ordinary things, but immediately
you come to spiritual things, immediately you
come to the things of the Lord, you discover
that your mind is becoming overclouded; you

find that your mind is not functioning, it is being paralysed; there is a darkness and a death creeping over it. The enemy does make assaults upon our minds, there is no doubt about that. He attacks our soul : not only the intellectual side, but every side. The enemy makes an assault upon the emotional side, to dry up and freeze our feelings, so that we are totally incapable of giving any response, of exercising any kind of heart function in relation to the Lord. The same is true in the realm of the will. There are times when it seems we cannot make a decision, *cannot* will in the way of the Lord. The will comes under assault like that.

Death breaks upon us in each of these spheres, and the experience is more or less common to us all. It is the battle. As is the case with the spirit directly, and also with the soul, so it is with the body. There is no doubt at all that the enemy makes assaults upon the bodies of the Lord's people. I do not say that every malady, every sickness, every physical weakness, every bit of natural tiredness is the direct work of the Devil. Of course, historically it is the outcome of his work, but immediately it need not be the direct work of the Devil. We are not saying that it is. We should find ourselves in great difficulties were we to teach that. But there are direct attacks of the enemy in the spirit of death upon the bodies of the Lord's people, that where there is a weakness he fastens upon it, and adds to it, and would seek to cripple us altogether through our weakness, when, although that basic weakness might remain, we need not be crippled by it.   That has been the history of the Lord's people.   It becomes a question as to whether the enemy is going to use that thing to undo us altogether, or whether, in spite of it, we are to be found proving the power of a life which triumphs over it, and carries us on.

Paul's Thorn in the Flesh.

The Apostle Paul always comes to our help in these matters.   Paul has placed it on record that because of the greatness of the revelation which came to him, lest he should become exalted above measure, there was given unto him a thorn in the flesh, a messenger of Satan to buffet him, to smite him in the face.   For this thing he besought the Lord thrice, but the Lord said, "My grace is sufficient for thee, for my strength is made perfect in weakness."   We have good reason to believe that the weakness was physical weakness.   I find it difficult not to believe that it was malaria.   There is every reason, I think, to believe that to have been the malady.   Paul's journeys were oft times in places which were infested with the malarial elements, while he was without any of the modern helps to overcome them. And when you remember that the complaint affected his eyes—anybody who knows anything about malaria knows of those sharp pangs through the eyes which in the long run do interfere with the organs of sight—it all points strongly to malaria. We are not arguing that it was so, but we find difficulty in believing that such was not the case. But, whatever it was, here is something which from time to time laid hold of Paul, and he despaired of life; and it seemed that he never knew when this thing was going to overtake him. His "thorn" was undoubtedly physical weakness, and it is called "a messenger of Satan." The whole direction of it, from the enemy's side, was a working of death. In relation to that, Paul speaks of death working in this mortal flesh. It was all in the direction of death, death, death; he was facing and fighting death all the time. But the point is that while the Devil most clearly had to do with this physical state, as the statement shows, and the Lord Himself permitted it, it did not work out in death; but on the contrary the course of that man's life is the course of a continual triumph over that death and Satan. That the power of death does assail, and that the Lord does not all the time prevent the Devil from attacking these bodies is manifest. But that does not mean that the Lord intends us to die! You might think the logic to be that if the Lord sends a messenger of Satan, whose effect is death, surely the Lord means us to die. There is no justification for such an argument. Quite the opposite is the case. The Lord had a very salutary purpose for everything in the case of the Apostle, and this working of death was expressly used to keep the man spiritually alive; for had he not had the thorn, his spiritual life would have been smitten with a blight. Hear his own words : "Lest I should be exalted above measure . . ." (II Cor. xii. 7). Find the man exalted above measure, and you find the man of poor spiritual life; his spiritual life has been blighted. Find the man who is kept humble in this way, and yet triumphant in a way which is not explained on a natural ground, and you will find the man who is a giant in spirit.

Yes, the enemy does attack the body. He impinges upon what is already there and seeks to intensify it. He seeks to cripple the saints. But the whole of this word, especially in relation to the life of the Apostle Paul, is one great declaration that even in the presence of a natural handicap, a natural weakness, or something with which the Devil himself has come in

at a given point, in the permission of God, there
is a life which can carry us on to the fulfilment
of a great Divine purpose which need not be
curtailed because of natural conditions.   Get
hold of that !   Do not sink under your condition
and say, Because such and such is the case with
me, then the Divine purpose in its greater
dimensions is impossible !   That is despair,
not faith.   The Apostle's declaration was this :
". . . that life which I now live in the flesh I
live in faith, the faith which is in the Son of
God, who loved me, and gave himself up for
me" (Gal. ii. 20).   It was life by faith in the
Son of God.   And what a living it was !   What
a life it was !   Indeed, in his case it was a life
triumphant over ever present death.

But it was a battle.   Read the second letter
to the Corinthians, and you will see the traces
of the battle.   Paul has just emerged from that
desperate situation where he despaired of life.
He had been laid so low with this thing, whatever it was, that he never expected to recover.
But he came out.   He bore the marks of the
battle with death, but he continued on his course
long after he wrote the second letter to the
Corinthians.   Some of the most glorious things
found expression after that.   Let us believe in
the possibilities of the Lord's life within us, and
disclaim all the arguments in our own state,

or which the enemy would impose upon us by reason of how we feel and how things appear. We must all take this to heart.

Life is Deeper than our Consciousness.

We close by referring to this one point. We must seek always to believe in the fact that this Divine life, with all its tremendous potencies, is far deeper down than surrounding conditions and circumstances, and far deeper down than our own physical life, and far deeper down than our own soul-life. Unless we grasp that, unless we hold that firmly, we have not the ground of victory. When we feel that death is working with such tremendous force in the realm of our bodies, and when we feel it working in the realm of our souls, and everything in this sentient life of ours speaks of death, we are too often in danger of surrendering the whole position. I believe that this thing which is of God is deeper than our mortal being. I believe that it is possible even for children of God, being truly born again, possessing eternal life, to lose their reason, to go into an asylum, and yet to have no change made in the deepest fact and reality of the being in relation to the Lord. We touch that point to indicate what we mean, that if our rational life is the sum total of our life, then it is a poor look-out for us. If our sanity, our natural mental balance, is the ground of our being children of God, then some of us from time to time would have real reason to doubt whether we were born again. And if that is true in the mental, it is true in the physical. This life of the Lord is far deeper than this mortal life, than this mortal being.

I am going to say a thing which may sound to you to be very terrible. It may help some; it may perplex others. I am going to risk it! I believe that it is possible for children of God, living in full fellowship with the Lord, walking truly with the Lord in the light as far as they have it, to enter into an experience of feeling that they are devil possessed. I mean that they lose all sense of being in touch with the Lord, and of the Lord being in touch with them, and there are fighting and striving forces of evil which seem to be in their own being. It is not only that this is felt in the atmosphere, they find themselves so stirred up in their own being, so moved with evil, that they can verily believe that there are a thousand and one devils inside of them. Does it sound terrible to say that of a child of God? I am not saying that such are devil possessed, but I say that it is possible to enter into an experience from time to time where it seems like that, as though the evil were not outside but inside. At those times all gracious forbearance seems to desert you; all quiet, calm grip seems to go; all spirit of life seems to fade away, and you find that you are in the vortex of a terrible conflict, which is hell itself : it seems that hell is in you. Forgive me, if you think I am altogether wrong, but I believe that to be a possible experience of a true child of God. And I believe with all my heart that the explanation of it is that God has a special purpose in such a life, and the Devil has aroused every force of hell in an evil antagonism to swamp that life.

We need to remember that these are spiritual forces, and spiritual forces stand at no physical barriers. We have a soul, a great nervous system. Children of God for many reasons, and very often after a time of pouring out spiritually, will find their nerves are all a jangle, and they feel anything but good and holy. But are you going to say that means that after all they are not children of God, that it is all a myth? Do you mean to say that Elijah was no longer the prophet of the Most High when he cast himself under the juniper tree and asked the Lord to take away his life? He was still the servant of God, still as true to God as ever. We are not trying to excuse our weaknesses, but trying to get to the heart of a situation. It is possible for true saints to pass for special reasons into a realm which seems naked hell, and that within themselves, not as only around them, because the conflict is registering itself upon their nervous system, registering itself upon their soul life. In that moment they could believe that, rather than the Lord being resident within, the Devil himself has taken up his seat there. That does not argue that the Lord has forsaken, that the Lord is not there, and that such are not the Lord's children or the Lord's servants. It indicates that the enemy has made them marked men or women because of something he is trying to destroy in the life. If you get into that realm, do not accept the suggestions of the enemy or seek to interpret things in the light of circumstances.

If you do not understand this that we are saying, do not strive after an explanation, and please do not put your own construction upon it. There are some who know what it is to have such an assault upon their being, their physical and nervous life, as to make them feel that they are lost. I do not believe that it means that they are lost, and it is because some people accept that suggestion from the Tempter that they sink into darkness. Oh, that many of these people who feel this thing upon them could know what we are trying to say, that it is for the spirit in faith to rise up and refuse the argument of the seeming. The seeming is sometimes so terribly real. People say to us :

It only seems to be so, it is not really so! And we reply: You do not know what you are talking about; it is more real than anything else! But the Lord will teach us as we go on not to accept that as the final thing. There is something deeper than that. The Lord is deeper than our physical feelings. The Lord is deeper than our soul. If we hold on we shall come out. That will pass, and there will be another expression of His life, and we shall learn by this battle for life what victory there is for us in Christ by His Cross.

CHAPTER VI.

The Continuation of the Conflict in relation to the Church as the Corporate Company.

We will now deal more specifically with the continuation of the conflict in relation to the Church as the corporate company, the Body of Christ.

We have said enough to make it abundantly clear that there is an age-long battle for spiritual life, and that if that life can be arrested in its manifestation, its expression, it will be so arrested. There is a great power and force working by the instrument of spiritual death to quench the testimony of the risen and ascended Lord within the individual believer, and within the Church as the Body of Christ. The individual believer and the Church are together in that battle for the manifestation of that life of the Lord. The issue is not as to the forfeiture of Divine life, eternal life; as to whether Satan can take that away from us, but as to the keeping of it from its full expression in believers individually and in the Church as a whole. That is the battle in which we are more or less engaged and concerned, according to the measure of our spirituality and our utterness for the Lord. What is true of the individual, then, is true of the whole Body.

The Higher Realms of the Battle and the Testimony.

I think we can best get to the inside of this matter by noting the contrast between the first letter to the Corinthians and the letter to the Ephesians. By this means we shall be greatly helped in understanding the nature and realm of the battle for spiritual life. There are many practical suggestions and presentations in these two letters by which we can be governed in this matter. To begin with let us note the realms in which these letters stand ; for undoubtedly there is a great difference between them in this respect.

We are familiar with the governing clauses of the letter to the Ephesians. The phrase "in the heavenlies" is one of its dominating notes. We know quite well as soon as we take up the letter to the Ephesians that we are in the realm of the heavenlies. A great emancipation has taken place, a great lifting out, a great extrication, a great separation. One whole world has been left behind and another has been entered, entered in a spiritual way, where things partake of the utterness of the Lord, where the Lord is seen in a full way as Sovereign Head over all things to the Church. Here there is nothing fragmentary, nothing partial, nothing imperfect, but everything is viewed as complete, full and final, and as linked in a perfect way with the Lord in heaven. Here all the expressions are heavenly expressions. It is a realm, and even as that is the realm which is presented by the letter to the Ephesians, the testimony also is there seen in true heavenly character and vigour. We mean that the testimony is operating in a heavenly realm. It is operating back of all that is mundane, earthly, of flesh and blood, the things of this sentient world. It is in those ultimate relationships which are spiritual, with forces and intelligencies which are supernatural, and which are more than human, and more than the forces and intelligencies of this earth, that the testimony is seen to be operating. The testimony is reaching the ultimate ranges of this universe, touching principalities and powers, world rulers of this darkness, spiritual hosts of wickedness. It is there that something is being registered, being made to tell, being made effective. It is back there that the testimony is being established, fulfilled, expressed. It is a heavenly realm.

We cannot get further back than that. It goes behind everything seen, everything handled, everything known here, and it touches that realm which is responsible for all that is going on here. That realm is perfectly clear in the letter to the Ephesians.

Turn to the first letter to the Corinthians, and see into what a different realm you enter. You find very little that is heavenly there. You find that immediately you begin to move into this letter you are touching the earthlies, mundane things, natural things : and what a mass of such things there is.   There is none of the atmosphere of the heavenlies here.   You find yourself down in somewhat sordid things even amongst the Lord's people.   Sordid is not too strong a word in some connections.   You are having to deal with all the unpleasantness, all the wretched aspects of mixture and spiritual weakness and immaturity, occupied with things which you would fain sweep aside and have done with. • You feel as you move here : Oh that we could get out of this realm of things, divisions and schisms and quarrellings, lawsuits, and what not !   How earthly it is !   It is another realm altogether, and because it is so earthly, so mundane, because there is such an absence of the heavenly, you are not surprised that the testimony is so poor.   You can find here no trace of registration upon spiritual forces.   If you read this first letter to the Corinthians from an entirely spiritual standpoint, you have to say that the situation is rather one where the evil forces have gained an advantage than of their having been overthrown.   You have to admit that the enemy is running rough-shod

G

here amongst these saints. He seems in some things to be having his way altogether, carrying things into a realm which even in the world it is a shame to speak of. Yes, it is true that the enemy is no defeated foe, so far as these believers are concerned, or so far as the situation in this letter is concerned. He is having too much of his own way, simply because they are so much on the earthly level of things.

That speaks for itself, does it not? The testimony, for its real value and effectiveness, demands that the Lord's people, the Church, be a heavenly Body. It demands that! It is clear that these believers at Corinth—of course we speak now of those referred to in the letter who stood in a better way—had come into a very small measure of the power of His resurrection, simply because they had not entered into the meaning of His death, His Cross. It is a sad and a painful reflection that the Apostle should have had to remind them of the opportunity that had been theirs by what he says in the opening section of this letter: "And I, brethren, when I came unto you, came not with excellency of speech or of wisdom . . . I was with you in weakness, and in fear, and in much trembling. I determined not to know anything among you, save Jesus Christ, and him crucified." That had been Paul's attitude, Paul's message, and Paul's aim when he went to Corinth some considerable time before he wrote the letter. Now, his having been amongst them, stressing, emphasizing Jesus Christ and Him crucified, and nothing else, and then much later writing such a letter, exhibits the fact that they had not learned what he had been there for, had not entered into that which he had stressed among them, and all this is a consideration of that fact.

If there is a living apprehension of Jesus Christ, and Him crucified, you will not have divisions like this, and schisms, and fornication, and all these things. They had missed the meaning of the Cross. They had failed to apprehend the message upon which the Apostle had laid such undivided and such exclusive stress in his presence amongst them. And if they do not know the meaning of the Cross, how can they know the meaning of the resurrection, how can they know the power of the resurrection? And if they do not know that, then how can they know the power of that resurrection-life registering the impact of the risen, living Lord upon spiritual forces? You can never undo divisions among the saints by bringing saints together to discuss their differences, and to ask them to make them up. The only way in which such things can be dealt with amongst the Lord's people is to get down on your knees and deal with the forces behind.

The power of the enemy behind that thing has to be broken. You can never patch up a situation like that, because it is devilish.

What is true in the matter of divisions is true in every other matter in this letter. It is the enemy behind who is ultimately the occasion of all this disorder, and there is nothing but the impact of a risen, ascended, sovereign Lord against the enemy behind which will make for a better state of things. All this is made very evident in Corinth. They could not register that impact upon spiritual forces because they were not in the right realm. That is a heavenly realm of activity, and they were on the earth, amongst the earthlies. The realm makes a lot of difference to the testimony.

If you are trying to operate in the power of the testimony of the ascended and reigning Lord, and living an earthly life, you are going to be absolutely worsted and proved completely insufficient for the situation. If we are really going to have the coming through of the power of His throne, then we must be severed in a spiritual way from this world, from this earth. We must be in a spiritual sense a heavenly people, seated together with Him in the heavenlies, blessed with every spiritual blessing in the heavenlies, and so on. The realm is an important one for the testimony's functioning.

It is to this testimony that we are called. This is not some ideal impossible of realisation. This is not something presented as a high level of truth. This is the thing for which the Church is constituted. I do not believe, as some people seem to believe, that the Church in Corinth and the Church in Ephesus are two different Churches. There is a teaching which says that the Body in Corinth is not the same Body as that of Ephesus. I do not believe that for a moment, and I do not believe that the Corinthians were called for anything less than the Ephesians. It is the same calling. The Corinthians were as much called to a heavenly life and heavenly testimony as were the Ephesians or any others. It is a matter of whether we accept the meaning of the Cross to bring us through into the power of His resurrection, and that will determine how far we shall be the expression of that ultimate power of the enthroned Lord.

That "realm" question touches any number of contingencies. It raises the whole question of whether we are living on an earthly level; whether we are officially bound up with something which, after all, is only earthly in its constitution, even though it be of a religious kind. All such questions as these are raised, and with them the issue as to whether we are out with the Lord in an emancipated, free, clear

way as His heavenly people. We are content
to leave it there for the time, and you can ask
the Lord to show you what it means in a fuller
explanation to your own heart.

The Range of the Battle and the Testimony.

Running parallel with the realm is what we
may call the range of things; not so much the
dimensions as the values, the qualities. Turn
again to the Ephesian letter, and note some of
the great words that are found in it. There are
some wonderful statements, and phrases, and
terms. "The *exceeding greatness* of his
power," "*Strengthened with all might* by his
Spirit in the inward man," "Able to do
exceedingly abundantly above all that we ask
or think, *according to the power that worketh
in us*"—the power that worketh in us is
capable of enabling us exceeding abundantly
above all that we ask or think—"Raised him
. . . and made him to sit at his own right hand
in the heavenly places far above all rule, and
authority, and power, and dominion . . . and
gave him to be head over all things to the
church . . . the fulness of him that filleth all
in all." Pick out all these transcendent, superlative things in the letter. Do not regard them
just as words, just as oratory, but mark the
tremendous range of value and calibre represented by these things. You have nothing to

compare with them in the first letter to the Corinthians. If you turn to the chapter in that letter which perhaps carries you farthest in thought and revelation, the fifteenth chapter, you will find you are, after all, only dealing with resurrection, and that the resurrection of the body; great things it is true, and glorious things, as to the nature of the resurrection body. But when you have your resurrection body you are only then entering upon the great realm of the eternities. It may be a marvellous thing for this corruptible to put on incorruption, and I am quite sure we shall think it is a marvellous thing when it happens. It will be a glorious thing when the final touch of death with regard to our bodies is swallowed up victoriously. But we are only then started on the career which is presented to us in the letter to the Ephesians for the ages to come. There are very vital things in the first letter to the Corinthians, but in the range, in the depth and the height, the length and the breadth, so far as spiritual value is concerned, there is no comparison. Even when you deal with the Church, the Body, in 1 Cor. xii. you are largely dealing with it from the side of its expression here. When you deal with it in the Ephesian letter you are carrying it higher, away from conditions where it is necessary to say such a thing as this : One member cannot say to another, I

have no need of you! How that reveals what
the spirit of things had been at Corinth, what
an earthly level it was that had obtained there.
The Apostle, it is true, is giving an unfolding
of spiritual relationships, but it is of such a
kind as is largely occasioned, if not wholly, by
spiritual disorder among the saints. But when
you come into Ephesians iv. and touch the truth
of the Body there, you are breathing an
altogether different atmosphere.

Pass on to Ephesians v. 32 : "This mystery
is great : I speak in regard of Christ and of the
Church." You are carried away into the great
mystery of the Body. That is something
deeper. What is the explanation of this difference? It is not that they are two different
Churches, nor that they represent two different
callings. It is that there are two different levels
upon which they live. If all these wonderful
things presented in Ephesians, these mighty
things, these weighty things, are elements of
the true testimony of Jesus, then these things
belong to a place where the earthlies are left
behind. To put that in another way, you have
to leave the earthlies, if you are coming into the
realm where those mighty forces are operating.

Would you know the exceeding greatness
of His power which is to usward who believe?
You cannot if you live on a Corinthian level, if
you live on a natural, earthly basis, even as a

Christian. Do you want to know the fulness of Christ? Do you want to become in a related way the fulness of Him that filleth all in all? You can never be that if you live spiritually at Corinth. The testimony is a mighty thing. It is a thing fraught with these massive elements and features of the risen and ascended Lord. There will be a universal expression of that fulness in the ages to come, but even now we are to partake of it. It is to be known and set forth now in a spiritual way in the life of the Church, but the Church has to come out on to the ground which is presented in this letter to the Ephesians. I am not saying that the Ephesian Church was on this level. It may have been or it may not have been. But it seems perfectly clear that the Ephesian saints were in a position to have such a revelation given to them and the Corinthians were not. The Corinthians were not ready for it. But if Paul's visit to Ephesus and the results are indicative of anything, they do speak of thoroughness there. They brought their books of magic and made a great bonfire of them, and the price of them was two thousand pounds. They sacrificed everything to the fire because they had found a new mystery, a heavenly force which was more than the force of the magicians, the occultists, the spiritists, something far above all that. They had discovered Christ, and at great cost they let all else go, and that prepared the way for a wonderful revelation to them.   Paul was able to say to those Ephesian elders : "I shrank not from declaring unto you the whole counsel of God" (Acts xx. 27).   You can never declare the whole counsel of God to any company of people unless they are ready for it.   He had a clear way at Ephesus, and on their part it represented a spiritual position of abandonment of earthly connections, relationships, interests, and religious systems.

We focus our attention for a few minutes upon some of the more specific reasons and causes.   These have been included in our general survey.   We now mention them particularly.

The Comparison of the Corinthian and Ephesian Assemblies.

I.   The place of Man.

Look at these two, and focus your attention upon one word, or one title, one designation, namely, that of "man."   What was the place of man in these two different assemblies?   In Corinth man, as such, had a very large place. The Apostle says : "I could not speak unto you as unto spiritual, but as unto carnal, as unto babes in Christ . . . for whereas there is among you jealousy and strife, are ye not carnal, and walk after the manner of men? For when one saith, I am of Paul; and another, I am of Apollos; are ye not men?'' (1 Cor. iii. 1, 3-4). Is it not man, as such, that is very much in view? Man was coming into the view to the obscuring of Christ. All the way through that letter natural elements in man are being dealt with. Whatever it is, at whatever point you touch this terrible trouble that engaged the Apostle, you are touching some expression of man in himself; some dispute, for example, though over what we do not exactly know. But two believers, members of the same assembly, have perhaps been in some business transaction, and there has been something not straight, something upon which they have come to a serious difference, and one says, All right, I will take it to court, and will fight you in legal quarters! It is man doing things as man does them. All the time it is a case of man occupying a strong place of possessiveness and forcefulness.

Turn to the letter to the Ephesians, and see where man comes in there. You cannot find him; but we find ''one new man,'' that new man which we are exhorted to put on (Ephes. iv. 24). The old man has given place to the new man. It is not the individual standing for himself that we see now, but rather the individual rightly functioning in the corporate new man. It is no longer a case of so many

separated individuals all thinking of their own
interests, but here all that individualism is lost
in the one collectivity and relativity of the new
man.   You can almost see them growing up
into Him—"Till we all attain unto the unity
of the faith, and of the knowledge of the Son of
God, unto a full grown man, unto the measure
of the stature of the fulness of Christ" (Ephes.
iv. 13).

That word "man" is a key to the situation
in both letters.   How?   If he is allowed to
come in, there will be a state such as you have
at Corinth.   If he goes out, the prospects are
of an Ephesian position.   That is the work of
the Cross.   You are not surprised, then, that
in the Ephesian letter fairly early you come
upon the words ". . . quickened us together
with Christ . . . and raised us up in him, and
made us to sit with him in the heavenlies in
Christ Jesus. . . ."   All that quickening and
raising pre-supposes a death, and that is the
death of the old man, the man by nature.

II.   The place of the World.

The word "world" occurs a number of times
in the letter to the Corinthians—"the wisdom
of this world," "the princes of this world."
Read down those first two chapters, and see
what a large place the world takes.   The world

and its wisdom, the world with its spirit, the
world with its way, had a large place amongst
Corinthian believers. If you follow through
the letter you cannot get away from it. It is
the way of the world, the way the world does
things, or conditions ruling there, that is continually before us—the spirit of the world.
The world has a large place in their reasoning.
They are even handling heavenly and Divine
things with worldly wisdom.

Turn to the letter to the Ephesians and see
where the world is. It is left behind, and
believers are spiritually seen as out of the
world : not literally so; they were here on the
earth as much as ever Corinthians were, in the
world as a sphere; they were here, and yet not
here. Recall those strange and seemingly con-
tradictory phrases in John xvii : ". . . the men
whom thou gavest me out of the world. . . ."
"They are not of the world." "I pray not that
thou shouldest take them from the world. . . ."
We know what is meant in a spiritual sense,
and that there is no contradiction; in it and out
of it at the same time. In Ephesians vi. those
things which belong to ordered life here are
mentioned. There are families; husbands and
wives; parents and children; masters and
servants. You say, Merely earthly! No!
they are the relationships proper to life here,
and yet in them is the possibility of a heavenly

life. All are lifted on to a heavenly level where spiritual interests govern those relationships with a view to heavenly purposes and not just earthly interests. The world, in the sense in which it is found in 1 Corinthians, is not found in Ephesians.

That explains the testimony; that shows what is necessary for this impact upon spiritual forces. That can never be unless we come to the same position, with the world left behind in this sense. "Our wrestling is not against flesh and blood—that is the world's way of doing things—but against the principalities, against the powers. . . ." It is a case of getting behind flesh and blood, and what a much more effective wrestling that is. What mighty issues there are in the spiritual realm. How things count when we know the secret of functioning there in the power of the risen Lord. But that requires that we shall know here in mind, in spirit, absolute separation from this world.

III. The Difference in the Order at Corinth and Ephesus.

At Corinth two things, or two sides of the one thing are presented. In what the Apostle has to say you have brought before you a heavenly order. He is indicating what that heavenly order is as in the Church. He is seeking to recover it, or to establish it. But over against at least the intimation of heavenly order—for the Apostle does not develop it in fulness—there is a terrible disorder in the assembly. Read through the letter again, and see how everything is out of order. Their procedure, their government, their relationships, all are in disorder. In dealing with the causes the Apostle has raised questions and issues which have become the battle ground of the Church ever since, with regard to relationships and orders, positions and administrations in the Church. All this was out of order at Corinth.

We are not going to deal with the specific points. It would take too long, and might not be altogether profitable. At any rate, it might swing us away from our specific intention at this time. Sufficient to say that the question at Corinth is largely a question of order or disorder. We must recognise that. There is nothing arbitrary about the Apostle in that letter. A false explanation and interpretation has been put upon a great deal that Paul said in that letter as, for instance, upon his reference to the place of the sisters in the assembly. The interpretation or construction placed upon his words have been that Paul was a woman hater, that he was caught up in the Rabbinical idea of women, which held they were subject and had to be kept in a place of subjection, and therefore that what he wrote in that letter was out from that mentality, that conception. Nothing is further from the truth. Nothing is a greater libel against the Apostle. The Apostle was not dealing for one moment with the question of status, of honour, he was dealing purely with a matter of order. He will not rule sisters right out of the assembly in the matter of functioning, but he will show that their functioning is relative, and that it is both right and profitable when in its place. It is a matter of order. Let that be established, and be quite clear. We fasten upon this one point to indicate what we mean.

Turn to the letter to the Ephesians, and you can discover nothing about disorder in the assembly. Chapter iv. presents the Body and its relationships established; or that part of the letter brings it mainly into view. It is a beautiful heavenly order. There is no reference to an upsetting of that order, it is simply presented as though it obtained there. There is no quarrel over it, no fighting for it; it is a statement of a heavenly order. You are in a different atmosphere altogether. The point is that the Church's testimony to the risen Lord in the power of His risen life, is bound up with order in the House of God. If the Divine order is upset, the testimony is weakened, the testimony is nullified in that measure. There is a tremendous amount bound up with order. Let no one think that the appeal for order is simply with a view to having a domination, a control, a power over others, a desire to subject people. The word "subjection" has become anathema to a good many because they have missed its significance. It is the value of Divine order, heavenly order, expressed amongst the Lord's people that is in point; for this is so vital a factor in the meeting of the enemy. A Corinthian disorder cannot destroy the power of the principle, and world rulers cannot stand before spiritual forces when a Divine order is established and adhered to, and sacredly guarded. Then there is a wonderfully clear way for the Lord to come through and meet the enemies of the Church. Very often a church is divided and broken, and crying out for victory, for deliverance, for power, for effectiveness, and if the Lord could only be heard speaking He would be heard to say : Set your house in order; that is the way to power ! Put things right in your midst, and your prayers will be answered. You are crying to Me to give you something which you call "power," effectiveness, and the way to it is through the clearing up of the disorders that are among you. So the expression of His life demands a heavenly realm; separation from the world by the death of the old man in his natural strength and life; the constituting of things according to the heavenly pattern.

This is all practical. There are no flights of thought to carry you away into ecstasies, but there is a coming down on to the practical basis of every-day things. I am persuaded that nothing touches the heart of the whole issue more than this. I am certain that the Church's defeat, and weakness, and failure in testimony to-day, in the first place, is because it has become such an earthly thing; because of the worldly elements that have gained entrance; because man, as man, has such a large place in it; because the heavenly order does not obtain, but a man-made order in what is called the Church. These things are as closely related to the effectiveness of testimony as anything can be.

Do you know heavenly union with the Lord? Have you from your heart abandoned this world? Have you accepted the meaning of His Cross for the putting aside of all that belongs to man as such? Are you quite sure that you are fitting in your place in the House of God, that you are not out of your place? So far as your devotion to the Lord is concerned, are you really bent upon being in your place, and remaining in your place, and there functioning for the Lord? Are you a party to something which is not an expression of the heavenly pattern? Are you an official of an official connection, supporting and upholding an order which is not the Lord's order? Well, you will be beaten in the general defeat of such a thing. It is bound to be defeat so far as the main testimony is concerned. These are practical, direct questions. The Lord give grace, and understanding, and response to what this means. I have no doubt that as you go on from now the meaning of all this will come to you in a growing way. You may not grasp it all now, but it is something laid in store. Remember it does matter tremendously whether you are in a Corinthian condition or in an Ephesian condition, and these are the features, these are the differences.

The Lord make us, if we may say it in a spiritual sense, good Ephesians.

CHAPTER VII.

The Divine Purpose in the Continuation of the Conflict.

READ : Judges i. 1-26 ; Col. ii. 15 ; Ephes. vi. 12 ; Exodus xxiii. 29-30.

We come to a closing word on this matter, the nature of which is indicated by what is contained in the passages we have read.

The first thing which we have to grasp fully is the fact that is brought before us in the Colossian passage, that in the case of the Lord Jesus the battle is a finished thing. So far as He is concerned the victory is secured in absoluteness, in fulness and finality. He did strip off from Himself principalities and powers and made a show of them, exhibiting them, triumphing over them in His Cross. That brings us to the ground represented by Israel when the Lord said, "I will drive them out . . ." That means that the Lord is in the place of complete possession already. So far as He is concerned the victory is secure. Now from that point there is this other side of the progressive realisation of that victory by the Lord's people. We have the victory in absoluteness in Him, but we are to enter into it progressively ourselves. It is the progressive aspect of this conflict, and the great need in relation to it, that is to concern us for a little while at this time.

The Progressive Nature of the Conflict.

I. The Fact.

The progressive character is clearly seen; that is, we see it to be a fact. From the Old Testament type, as well as from the New Testament statement, that is perfectly clear. The words in Exodus xxiii. are true to what we find later in the latter : "I will not drive them out from before thee in one year . . . by little and little I will drive them out . . ." (verses 29-30). We may cite Ephesians vi. as a chapter in the New Testament that indicates this progressive nature of the conflict : ". . . our wrestling is not against flesh and blood, but against the principalities, against the powers . . ." (verse 12). In spite of the Lord Jesus having Himself stripped them off, overcome them, displayed them as defeated, we are still in conflict with them. We are not represented as having sat down with the battle over; we are still in it. Of course, that hardly needs to be said to those who have spiritual experience, but here is the fact of the progressiveness of this battle for spiritual life, spiritual ascendency, over the forces, the powers of spiritual death. We need not dwell more upon the fact.

II. **The Divine Reason.**

Seeing that the Lord Himself has gained an absolute victory, and that so far as He is concerned there is nothing more to be done—all the enemies have been met and vanquished in His Cross—why could He not just give that victory over to us in its completeness, and we go happily on through life without any spiritual conflict at all? That may sound rather a foolish question. But we have to bring that question to the Lord and ask Him to explain why it must be that in His will, in His ordaining, conflict should go on and victory be progressive, instead of absolute all at once. Why must the fight go on to the end? Why must it continue? This passage in Exodus explains the matter for us : "I will not drive them out in one year; lest the land become desolate, and the beast of the field multiply against thee. By little and little I will drive them out from before thee, *until thou be increased. . . ."* The Divine reason then is that there must be development in order to possess the ground which the enemy still usurps. Our full possession of the victory tarries because of inability to occupy; because of lack of capacity; because of spiritual limitation, spiritual immaturity.

Now let us pass from the Old Testament literalism into the New Testament spirituality, and, if we can, think in terms of spiritual territory, see territory occupied by spiritual forces. No material forces can dispossess them, can occupy that territory. Spiritual forces alone can occupy spiritual territory. If such are found in possession, and the only thing that can supplant them is what is spiritual, then there has to be that which is at least equal to them in capacity, in dimensions, in order to occupy the place which they as yet occupy. Therefore it becomes a matter of spiritual measure, spiritual capacity. What the Lord says here in principle is that He will make spiritual ascendency contingent upon spiritual growth. So often in the battle we go to the Lord, and pray, and plead, and appeal for victory, for ascendency, for mastery over the forces of evil and death, and our thought is that in some way the Lord is going to come in with a mighty exercise of power and put us into a place of spiritual ascendency as in an act. We must have that mentality corrected. What the Lord does is to enlarge us to possess. He puts us through some exercise, through some experience, takes us by some way which means our spiritual expansion, an increase of spirituality, of spiritual capacity, and as we increase spiritually so we occupy the larger places spontaneously. The statement in Exodus makes that so clear.

The figure is interesting. Here are people who are called to victory, called to conquest, progressive and ever developing, and the Lord is doing the dispossessing, the Lord is going before: "Behold, I send an angel before thee ..." Now supposing the Lord goes in advance of His people and drives out all the enemies and leaves the territory unoccupied, while His people are so small that they can only dwell in a part of it, what is going to happen? Neither God nor the Devil believes in vacuums. Leave yourself in a state of passivity and lack of definite occupation, and you will soon find yourself in trouble. The Devil does not believe in having vacuums so far as the Lord's people are concerned, he fills them. The principle of this is seen in the story told by the Lord Himself about the man in whom there was a demon : the demon was cast out, the house left without an occupant, and the demon went wandering in waterless places seeking rest. Finding none the demon at length returned to the man out of whom he had been cast and found the house swept and garnished, but unguarded, and promptly took possession. But this time the evil spirit entered with seven others. It is quite clear from the Lord's illustration that the enemy does not believe in vacuums.

The Lord likewise does not believe in vacuums. He believes in things being filled.

He believes in full possession, full occupation.
In a spiritual matter, that demands that there
shall be spiritual enlargement, before the Lord
can give greater space. I am afraid that
Christendom has twisted things round the other
way, and made large space and hoped to grow
to it. So great buildings are put up, and then
an immense amount of work and labour is set
in motion to try to fill them. The Lord does
not do things in that way. First of all He
enlarges, and then He gives accordingly. Let
us not, however, bring the matter down on to so
low a level, but keep it in the realm of spiritual
conflict and warfare. The law which the Lord
sets forth here in this passage is that spiritual
ascendency over the forces of darkness and
death corresponds to spiritual growth, and
spiritual growth is essential to spiritual ascendency, to enlarged territory. The challenge
with which the Lord meets us is this : Can you
fill it ? Can you occupy it ? Can you possess
it ? Are you able, if I give it to you ? The
disaster would be all the greater, if the Lord
gave large territory and we could not occupy it
and fill it. How important is spiritual growth,
spiritual maturity, spiritual increase.

The whole question of progressive victory
rests upon progressive spiritual development.
It does not rest upon our having from the Lord
the gift of ascendency. Ascendency is, in effect,

developed in us by spiritual growth and enlargement; it is a matter of capacity. Hence those
who know most of victory are not always those
who talk most about it, but those who have
been through those experiences and processes
by which they have been mightily extended in
Christ spiritually. Turning that round the
other way, it should be a comfort to know that
everything the Lord does with us which is in
the nature of a stretching, a painful stretching;
that cutting of deeper channels, deeper furrows;
that leading into depths; that breaking up
and breaking open; all that which is in the
direction of making for a deeper, wider, higher
energy of the Lord through suffering, is
intended to bring into a place of spiritual power,
spiritual ascendency. Thus the power of the
enemy becomes weaker, because the power of
the saints is becoming greater through their
growth in grace and in the knowledge of our
Lord and Saviour, Jesus Christ. The power of
the saints only becomes greater on that ground.
We have to be built up unto power, built up
unto ascendency, built up unto conquest. It is
quite evident that if there is not an adequate
spiritual background to the life of those who
make assaults upon the enemy they will be
knocked to pieces, they will not be able to stand
up to him. It requires that there should be
spiritual competence, spiritual wealth, spiritual

background, spiritual fulness in order to stand up to the enemy and force him to quit the position. It is important that we should recognise that.

We must be enlarged to occupy. The Lord will not give otherwise. He is governed by infinite wisdom in the way in which He deals with us. "I will not drive them out from before thee in one year . . . by little and little I will drive them out from before thee, until thou be increased. . . ." The measure of spiritual ascendency is the measure of spiritual increase.

III. A Deterrent if Regarded in a Wrong Way.

We hurry on to note another thing. That progressive character can become a deterrent, if it is regarded in a wrong way. It seems clear that many of Israel were deterred, discouraged from going on in the fight and utterly driving out the enemy, because it was a progressive or a slow business. Somehow or other this human nature of our likes to get things done with one bound, to have it all cleared up with one stroke, and the long-drawn-out process of spiritual growth is often a very discouraging thing to the flesh. So they did not utterly drive out those nations, simply because it required persistence. It required, as we say, pegging away at it. It required a steady devotion. It demanded a continuous prosecution, ever something more yet to be done.

It is like that with us. We are so often discouraged and deterred from going on because we seem to make so little progress; because there always seems to be more before us than behind; because we seem, after all, to have gained so little; because we see so much still to be gained. Mark you, that is a part of the Divine, sovereign ordering. So long as we are here the Lord will not give us any occasion whatever for saying, Now we can settle down! Oh, but how we are expecting that almost any day. Our thought is that it will not be long before we come to a place where we have got the upper hand, where we are in ascendency, and the fight will then be over, at any rate in the main, and we can come to rest. I want to tell you in all faithfulness that right up to the last stroke in this battle you will feel that practically nothing has been done in comparison with what there is to be done. You will have a sense that the forces before are still well-nigh overwhelming. No matter how far you progress spiritually, you will often come to the place where you feel that you are being almost overwhelmed, that the real back of this thing has not been broken. The pathway to the glory is the pathway of increasing conflict, and the most bitter part of the conflict will take place just before entering the glory. The Lord will never give us reason for settling down.

That is another phase of Israel's failure. On the one hand, while many were discouraged because of the progressive and long-drawn-out character of the conflict, it is quite clear that many others entered into a state of unholy content. They said, We have fought, and we have got so far, that will do. Discontent can be both holy and unholy. There is such a thing as holy discontent. While there remain spiritual forces to be driven out, to be dispossessed; while the whole range and realm of what is spiritual still has in it that which is opposed to the Lord, you and I have no right to be content. We must not settle down and say, Oh, that is the ideal, but it is impossible! It is all very well to see what ought to be, but it is no use setting up a counsel of perfection, and expecting and aiming at what is not possible amongst the Lord's people or in our spiritual experience! If we begin to reason like that, we shall find ourselves in a very sorry state. During the four hundred years occupied by the Judges, an attitude of that kind produced misery, continuous defeat and weakness, a terrible state of up and down experience throughout that long period. Look at the account in this book of the Judges, and mark the periods under which

Israel laboured in bondage and defeat. Why? The explanation is found in the first chapter. Read through the chapter again, and note how repeatedly it is said of certain of Israel that they drave not out their enemies. The result was that they had this long time of defeat, and failure, and misery. What had happened? They had entered into a state of unholy content. They had said, Well, the ideal, of course, would be to possess the whole land, but the present measure of occupation seems to be all that is possible, and we must accept things as they are!

That comes to us as a very serious challenge in relation to the Lord's Testimony. We look out on the world to-day, on what we call the Christian world, and we see its state, a state which is indeed very like to that in the days of the Judges. We see divisions, we see failures in what is called the Church. The question arises, Is it possible to have a whole testimony, a full testimony? Is it possible to have a complete expression of the Lord's mind? The answer so often returned may be stated thus: Well, that is the ideal, but you are setting yourself an impossible task if you attempt it. You had better accept the situation, regard it as all in ruins, and make the best of it! Are you content with that? I am not, and I have decided that even if I die in the attempt I will give myself to the obtaining of a fuller expression of the Lord's mind. In so far as my own life is concerned, it is going to be poured out to the last to get His people to the fulness of His will, and I am not going to accept this situation which is so far short of it. It is an unholy thing to enter into a contentment of that kind. It is that failure to go on in spite of the seemingly impossible which has produced the terrible paralysis and spiritual ineffectiveness of the Lord's people which is almost worldwide to-day.

The Necessity for Fellowship.

We come to the final word which we feel to be the note which must stand above every other note. We see the reality of the battle, we see many laws which govern the battle, but what is it that we need if we are to win? You might answer in different ways, but what I see as being a dominant need, if not the predominant one, is that which is at least suggested in the first part of the first chapter of the book of Judges. There the question is asked, "Who shall go up for us first against the Canaanites, to fight against them? And the Lord said, Judah shall go up. . . . And Judah said unto Simeon his brother, Come up with me into my lot, that we may fight against the Canaanites;

and I likewise will go with thee into thy lot. So Simeon went with him. And Judah went up; and the Lord delivered the Canaanites and the Perizzites into their hand : and they smote of them in Bezek ten thousand men.'' Here you have real business, real effectiveness. What was behind it? It was fellowship. It was co-operation. Here you have the spirit of brotherhood manifesting itself in mutual helpfulness, mutual support in the battle. The enemy has held the possession and withstood the people of God because of the lack of that. One of the strategies by which he has gained his end has been to keep the Lord's people from a downright spiritual co-operation in the battle; to get them scattered, get them divided, get them disintegrated, get them on individual lines instead of coming right in as a corporate and collective instrument for God and dealing with the issues in a mighty way together. We cannot lay too much stress upon that.

This is the burden of my heart, that the Lord's great need is of a prayer instrument that comes together with one object, the driving of the enemy off the ground; not just offering petitions, not just pouring out words which are intended to be prayers, for however good they might be, however right they might be, such prayers fall short of this mighty laying hold of the Lord's own victory and bringing it into

operation where the enemy is. The victory is in
the Lord's hands. He did strip off principalities
and powers. He has said, "I will drive out."
What has to follow? There has to be a coming
together, and in faith a laying hold, as it were,
of that victory; an appropriating of it, and a
bringing of it to bear upon the spiritual situation. Until we get something like that we are
not going to see the spiritual counterpart of this
mighty sweep of triumph in Judah and Simeon.
Here is real progress. Here we see the enemy
having to quit.

Oh, for the coming together of God's people
for business in prayer, real business; coming in
business-like spirit, with a business-like mind,
with full purpose of heart and as one man in a
spirit of fellowship, because of the testimony of
the Lord which is at stake, which is involved,
which is bound up with it; this coming together
and squaring right down upon Satanically
ridden situations to clear the ground of the
enemy. That is the Lord's need to-day. I feel
that to be the Lord's pre-eminent need. We do
not take the thing to heart enough. We have
not got the Lord's testimony sufficiently at
heart. If we really were concerned for the
Lord's testimony in this earth we should only
need to hear of the impact and prevailing of
death in any one situation against the Lord's
people, and we would get down on that situation

I

with such purpose that we would not give the enemy any rest until he withdrew from it. But we can hear of such situations, hear of need, hear of our brethren in the fight pressed out of measure, and can be content with a mere momentary petition : Oh, Lord, help them ; oh, Lord, bless them ; oh, Lord, come to their rescue ! when the Lord is saying quite definitely, if only we had ears to hear, "Wherefore criest thou unto me ? . . . lift up thy rod . . ." (Exodus xiv. 15-16). We have the rod of the Lord's victory in our hands, or we ought to have. We have the rod of the mighty name of Jesus, and we come with cries to the Lord, when the Lord says, in effect, Bring to bear upon that situation this victory which is in Me for you ! It is the coming together in fellowship, in co-operation, to bring to bear upon the situation the great victory which is in the Lord's possession for us.

Oh, may the Lord stir you in this matter unto this mighty prayer in the name of Jesus, and get an instrument, a vessel, in which and through which there will be this registration of the power of His throne upon those situations which are under the domination of the enemy. That is the Lord's great need. There are many of the Lord's people and many places in this world where the Lord's testimony is defeated, arrested, locked up, smothered, unable to break through; everything is at a standstill; the enemy is holding the ground. It is as much as the Lord's people can do to hold their own, to stay there. There needs to be some power coming through to clear that ground of the enemy, and that power will come through only when the Lord's people take up that matter in such a mighty fellowship of prayer that through that prayer the throne will operate.

There are many who know they are not getting through in their prayer life on their own, that they cannot deal with the situation themselves. Many are deeply and terribly conscious that what they need is a mighty reinforcing by prayer co-operation to get through, but the trouble is as to where such reinforcement is to come from? There are not to be found those who are sufficiently concerned. There are not those who know how to pray like this in the power of the name. Forgive me for being so emphatic, but the prevailing conditions demand strong words. The need is to recover a prayer instrument by which the power that is in the hand of the Lord Jesus shall be released upon situations which are locked up in the power of the enemy. The Lord rouse us, stir us deeply in this matter, and make us at least a part of such a prayer instrument.

Let us purpose to come together for prayer. Let us not wait until we are called. If it is possible to get together, if there are those around us whom we can call together for prayer, let us do it. Do not wait for the appointed meeting of prayer. If you can get prayer fellowship with anybody, get down on the Lord's interests with them, and lay yourselves out in this matter for the deliverance of situations from the domination of the power of the enemy.

SeedSowers
P.O. Box 3317
Jacksonville, FL 32206
800-228-2665

904-598-3456 (fax)   www.seedsowers.com

THE CHRONICLES OF THE DOOR *(Edwards)*

The Beginning 8.99
The Escape 8.99
The Birth 8.99
The Triumph 8.99
The Return 8.99

THE WORKS OF T. AUSTIN-SPARKS

The Centrality of Jesus Christ 19.95
The House of God 29.95
Ministry 29.95
Service 19.95

COMFORT AND HEALING

A Tale of Three Kings *(Edwards)* 8.99
The Prisoner in the Third Cell *(Edwards)* 5.99
Letters to a Devastated Christian *(Edwards)* 5.95
Healing for those who have been Crucified by Christians *(Edwards)* 8.95
Dear Lillian *(Edwards)* 5.95

OTHER BOOKS ON CHURCH LIFE

Climb the Highest Mountain *(Edwards)* 9.95
The Torch of the Testimony *(Kennedy)* 14.95
The Passing of the Torch *(Chen)* 9.95
Going to Church in the First Century *(Banks)* 5.95
When the Church was Young *(Loosley)* 14.95
Church Unity *(Litzman, Nee, Edwards)* 14.95
Let's Return to Christian Unity *(Kurosaki)* 14.95

CHRISTIAN LIVING

Final Steps in Christian Maturity *(Guyon)* 12.95
Turkeys and Eagles *(Lord)* 8.95
Beholding and Becoming *(Coulter)* 8.95
Life's Ultimate Privilege *(Fromke)* 7.00
Unto Full Stature *(Fromke)* 7.00
All and Only *(Kilpatrick)* 7.95
Adoration *(Kilpatrick)* 8.95
Release of the Spirit *(Nee)* 5.00
Bone of His Bone *(Huegel)* 8.95
Christ as All in All *(Haller)* 9.95

* call for a free catalog 800-228-2665